THE BHAGAVADGITA

The *Bhagavadgītā* is one of the most renowned texts of Hinduism because it contains discussions of important issues such as liberation and the nature of action as well as the revelation of the Kṛṣṇa as the highest god and creator of the universe. It is included in the ancient Indian *Mahābhārata* epic at one of its most dramatic moments, that is, when the final battle is about to begin. In contrast to many other studies, this book deals with the relationship between the *Bhagavadgītā* and its epic contexts. Angelika Malinar argues that the theology of the text not only delineates new philosophical concepts and religious practices but also addresses the problem of righteous kingship and appropriate use of power. The book concludes by considering the *Bhagavadgītā*'s historical and cultural contexts and those features of the text that became paradigmatic in later Hindu religious traditions.

ANGELIKA MALINAR is Senior Lecturer in the Department of Study of Religions at the School of Oriental and African Studies, University of London.

THE BHAGAVADGĪTĀ

Doctrines and contexts

ANGELIKA MALINAR

CAMBRIDGE
UNIVERSITY PRESS

CAMBRIDGE UNIVERSITY PRESS
Cambridge, New York, Melbourne, Madrid, Cape Town, Singapore,
São Paulo, Delhi, Dubai, Tokyo

Cambridge University Press
The Edinburgh Building, Cambridge CB2 8RU, UK

Published in the United States of America by Cambridge University Press, New York

www.cambridge.org
Information on this title: www.cambridge.org/9780521122115

First published 2007
This digitally printed version 2009

A catalogue record for this publication is available from the British Library

ISBN 978-0-521-88364-1 Hardback
ISBN 978-0-521-12211-5 Paperback

In memory of my grandmother

Contents

Acknowledgements

Many colleagues and friends contributed to this book by sharing their views, ideas and criticism, by offering their help and support and by welcoming the idea of revisiting the *Bhagavadgītā*. I am especially grateful to Heinrich von Stietencron for his inspiring insistence that this book simply had to be written. Gregory M. Bailey offered his encouragement, suggestions and support all along. My warm thanks go to him and to James L. Fitzgerald for the many discussions on the epic. I should also like to express my gratitude to John and Mary Brockington, Johannes Bronkhorst, Heidrun Brückner, Harry Falk, Ulrich Pagel, Alexandra Leduc-Pagel, Theodore Proferes, Peter Schreiner, Ingo Strauch and Michael Willis for discussions, conversations and sharing manuscripts and other valuable material and information.

Almost against all odds Robert Parkin meticulously and with astonishing efficiency went through the final version of the manuscript. I am indebted to him and to Kate Brett, Gillian Dadd and Rosina di Marzo of Cambridge University Press for giving shape to the book, and to Jo Bramwell for copy-editing it so patiently. Many thanks also to the School of Oriental and African Studies, University of London, for the generous grant in support of the finalisation of the manuscript. Lastly, there is Helene Basu, who is beyond thanks.

Angelika Malinar

Abbreviations

TEXTS

AG	*Anugītā*
AN	*Aṅguttara Nikāya*
ArthaŚ	*Arthaśāstra*
AV	*Atharvaveda*
BĀU	*Bṛhadāraṇyaka-Upaniṣad*
BhG	*Bhagavadgītā*
BhīṣP	*Bhīṣmaparvan*
BhāgP	*Bhāgavatapurāṇa*
ChU	*Chāndogya-Upaniṣad*
DhP	*Dhammapada*
DN	*Dīgha Nikāya*
HV	*Harivaṃśa*
ĪśaU	*Īśa-Upaniṣad*
KaṭhU	*Kaṭha-Upaniṣad*
KauU	*Kauṣitaki Upaniṣad*
MaitU	*Maitrāyaṇīya Upaniṣad*
MB	*Mahābhāṣya*
ManuS	*Manusmṛti*
MBh	*Mahābhārata*
MDh	*Mokṣadharmaparvan*
MuṇḍU	*Muṇḍaka-Upaniṣad*
PrU	*Praśna-Upaniṣad*
Rm	*Rāmāyaṇa*
ṚV	*Ṛgveda*
ŚāntiP	*Śāntiparvan of Mahābhārata*
ŚBr	*Śatapathabrāhmaṇa*
SK	*Sāṃkhyakārikā*
SN	*Saṃyutta Nikāya*

ŚvetU	*Śvetāśvatāra-Upaniṣad*
TaitĀr	*Taittirīya Āranyaka*
TaitBr	*Taittirīya Brāhmaṇa*
TaitU	*Taittirīya-Upaniṣad*
UdP	*Udyogaparvan*
ViP	*Viṣṇupurāṇa*
ViS	*Viṣṇusmṛti*
YājñaS	*Yājñavalkyadharmasūtra*
YS	*Yogasūtra*

JOURNALS

ABORI	*Annals of the Bhandarkar Oriental Research Institute*
AJP	*American Journal of Philology*
ALB	*Adyar Library Bulletin*
AS	*Asiatische Studien*
ASIAR	*Archaeological Survey of India Annual Report*
BEFEO	*Bulletin de l'Ecole Française d'Extrême-Orient*
BSOS	*Bulletin of the School of Oriental Studies*
CIS	*Contributions to Indian Sociology*
DLZ	*Deutsche Literaturzeitung für Kritik der internationalen Wissenschaft*
EI	*Epigraphica India*
EW	*East and West*
GSAI	*Giornale della Società Asiatica Italiana*
HR	*History of Religion*
IA	*Indian Antiquary*
IHQ	*Indian Historical Quarterly*
IIJ	*Indo-Iranian Journal*
IPhQ	*International Philosophical Quarterly*
IPQ	*Indian Philosophical Quarterly*
IT	*Indologica Taurinensia*
JA	*Journal Asiatique*
JAAR	*Journal of the American Academy of Religion*
JAIH	*Journal of Ancient Indian History*
JAOS	*Journal of the American Oriental Society*
JASBeng	*Journal of the Asiatic Society of Bengal*
JASB	*Journal of the Asiatic Society of Bombay*
JASt	*Journal of Asian Studies*
JBBRAS	*Journal of the Bombay Branch of the Asiatic Society*

JBRS	*Journal of the Bihar Research Society*
JGJRI	*Journal of the Ganganath Jha Research Institute*
JIP	*Journal of Indian Philosophy*
JISOA	*Journal of the Indian Society of Oriental Art*
JOIB	*Journal of the Oriental Institute,* Baroda
JORM	*Journal of Oriental Research,* Madras
JRAS	*Journal of the Royal Asiatic Society of Great Britain and Ireland*, London
JUB	*Journal of the University of Bombay*
NAWG	*Nachrichten der Akademie der Wissenschaften zu Göttingen*
NIA	*The New Indian Antiquary,* Bombay
OH	*Oriental Heritage*
OLZ	*Orientalische Literaturzeitung*
PEW	*Philosophy East and West*
PIHC	*Proceedings of the Indian History Congress*
PTAIOC	*Proceedings and Transactions of the All-India Oriental Conference*
RS	*Religious Studies*
VIJ	*Vishveshvarananda Indological Journal*
WZKM	*Wiener Zeitschrift für die Kunde des Morgenländes*
WZKS	*Wiener Zeitschrift für die Kunde Südasiens*
WZKSO	*Wiener Zeitschrift für die Kunde Süd- und Ostasiens*
ZDMG	*Zeitschrift der Deutschen Morgenländischen Gesellschaft*
ZII	*Zeitschrift für Indologie und Iranistik*

Introduction

The *Bhagavadgītā* (*BhG*) is perhaps one of the most renowned and often quoted texts in Hindu religious traditions. Commentaries, interpretations and translations abound. Yet some aspects and questions still need to be addressed. How are we to understand the text having been handed down as part of the *Mahābhārata* (*MBh*) epic? What are the threads which connect the different ideas and levels of arguments that build up the text, and how were they twisted and woven in order to put forward philosophical and theological frameworks of meaning? What are the characteristic features of the theology of the *BhG* that explain its influence and paradigmatic role in subsequent Hindu traditions? Can we adduce evidence to connect the *BhG* to specific cultural-historical contexts? The present study attempts to address these and other issues through a chapter-by-chapter analysis of the text and by relating some of its doctrines to the epic, literary context in which it is embedded. Although exegetical commentaries by academics such as Zaehner (1969) are available, no such analysis has been undertaken.[1] In this respect, the aim of the study is to fill a gap in *BhG* scholarship too. This also concerns the inclusion of the relevant secondary literature and a discussion of the problems involved in translating and interpreting the text. While this might seem not worth mentioning in an academic publication, the consideration of previous research is not the strongest aspect of *BhG* studies. Often scholars seem to start anew, which explains the proliferation, as well as the redundancy, of publications on it (cf. Minor 1987: 150, note 13). Therefore, the present study will depart from a survey of research and instead establish a referential framework for further discussion. It is against this background that the relevance of the epic context for understanding the *BhG* will be explored as well as the way in which different concepts and traditions are used in order to establish the theological framework

[1] The present study is based on my earlier book on the *BhG*, published in German (Malinar 1996). Although the approach and principle results are maintained, it includes new materials and perspectives.

for declaring Vāsudeva-Kṛṣṇa the 'highest'. This is followed by an analysis of the individual chapters of the *BhG*, in which the major steps of the argument will be identified and their consistency examined. In a final move, the possible historical and cultural contexts for the theology of the *BhG* will be considered. The interplay of texts and contexts and the most important doctrines and features of the *BhG* will be outlined in the following sections of the Introduction.

EPIC CONTEXTS: GODS, KINGS, DIALOGUES

One of distinct features of the *BhG*, the dialogue between the epic hero Arjuna and his charioteer, the epic hero Kṛṣṇa, transmitted in the *MBh* epic, is that it is situated at a dramatic moment in the latter. The dialogue takes place right in the middle of the battlefield between the two armies, which are ready to fight. It unfolds when Arjuna refuses to fight against his relatives. He declares that he sees no use in gaining a kingdom by shedding the blood of his kin and feels that it is better to refrain from doing so and live a mendicant's life. This crisis of the hero brings the epic plot to a halt and delays the beginning of the battle. The inevitable course of events narrated by the epic bards is temporarily suspended and thereby reflected upon. This point of departure became so characteristic of the text that it even became an object of iconographic depiction. However, it also became one of the major points of critique in academic studies of the texts. Seen as an intolerable interruption of a narrative that would be much better off without it, some scholars regarded the *BhG* as having originally been composed without any concern for the epic. Other scholars, however, took a different view and argued that the text is part of the well-attested 'didactic' dimension of the *MBh*, or even that it is intimately connected to the themes and issues of epic narrative and thus expresses an important dimension of its meaning. This debate raises important questions with regard to the possible relationship between the religious teachings of the *BhG* and the epic context, which consists not only of stories, but also of debates on ways of living, legitimate forms of kingship and power relations in the world.

The importance not only of the *BhG*, but also of the oldest extant epics, the *Rāmāyaṇa* and the *Mahābhārata*, for the formation of Hinduism and potentially for the reconstruction of its cultural-historical context has long been recognised. Both epics relate a painful crisis in a royal family and include in their narrative, in different degrees, not only a plot, but also discourses on kingship, the socio-cosmic order (*dharma*), kinship and gender relations, personal loyalty and individual duty, as well as teachings on paths to liberation and philosophical ideas. The *MBh* especially was turned in the course of the history of its composition into a confluence of different narratives, myths, legends, didactic intentions and religious orientations revolving around some of the central issues of the epic plot. These include the distribution of power in a world structured not only by moral boundaries (*maryādā*) and socio-juridical laws (*dharma*) defining social status, but also by desire, fate, fatalities, suffering, doubt and individuals' quest for liberation and spiritual empowerment. The conflict between these different referential frameworks and orientations is enacted in the epic on different levels: we see some characters transgressing the boundaries of their social position, while others are torn between social duty and the quest for liberation; a family-clan is split up and wages war over the distribution of land and power; gods and other powerful beings (sages, *yogin*s and epic bards) are involved in this encounter and interfere in the course of events; and notions of fate are introduced as explanations for the unpredictable and uncontrollable features of existence. The relationship of the gods to the story that unfolds in the epic is by no means less complex and is addressed in various aspects. There are speculations concerning divine scheming in some passages of the epic, but the latter are not made the overarching framework, as is the case, for instance, in Homer's *Iliad*. The redactors of the extant version of the epic, its 'final redaction', did not weave a coherent theistic 'red thread' into the manuscripts they produced, nor is there just one major god presiding over or pervading all the epic events. Not only are Viṣṇu, Nārāyaṇa and Kṛṣṇa praised, but Śiva and other gods are also encountered in 'visions' or other places. Although important studies of some of these issues are available, their relationship still needs to be explored in greater detail.[2] Nevertheless, the interplay and sometimes the clash between divine and human power constitute a major epic topic, addressed and dealt with by drawing on various concepts and offering different conclusions.

In dealing with these topics, the epic composers did not only use the literary device of a 'friendly conversation' (*saṃvāda*) entertained by senior family members, renowned teachers and gods and goddesses – reflections on this issue are also included in the epic narrative itself and prove to be important for the portrayal of the characters and the dynamics of the story. These discourses highlight certain aspects of the place of human activity within the cosmic order. On the one hand, human beings are able

[2] See, for instance, Biardeau 1976, 1978, 1997, Hiltebeitel 1977, Scheuer 1982, Laine 1989, essays in Schreiner 1997.

to acquire exceptional positions of power by using either ritual (kings) or ascetic (*yogins*) techniques of empowerment. On the other hand, there are factors that place a limit on human aspirations, such as fate, individual *karman* and, last but not least, god(s) and demon(s). Vedic sacrifice is one of the important arenas of divine and non-divine beings. Its elements and actors, its tropes and semantics, are dispersed throughout the epic to such an extent that sacrifice can be regarded as an idiom or paradigm that serves to connect different levels of discourse and meaning. In spite of its criticism of certain groups of sacrificers, the *BhG* draws on sacrifice in order to explore the nature of action and the chances to control its workings. It is made one of the arenas and purposes of 'detached action' and is used for explaining why karmic bondage can be avoided by people who remain active and perform their ritual and social duties. Yoga practices and knowledge of salvation are equated with ritual performances in which all defilements and desires are offered up in the 'sacrificial fire' (*agni*) of knowledge. In addition, Kṛṣṇa's supremacy is in various ways related to sacrifice: he is made the protector of all sacrifices and asks his followers to dedicate their lives to him as a continuous sacrifice.

However, the religious and philosophical doctrines of the *BhG* are connected not only to other religious doctrines and practices, but also to various political and social issues raised in the epic, many of them connected to royal power. The monotheistic theology presented in this text also offers an interpretation of kingship and royal power. In revealing Kṛṣṇa as the highest god, a new position of power is propagated that serves to reshuffle existing power relations that previously revolved around the ambiguous or double-sided position of the king. He is a figure that combines, on the one hand, aspects of a divine being when he emerges from the ritual coronation and consecration performed by the Brahmin priests as an aggregation of cosmic powers, but he remains, on the other hand, a human being and resembles other householders in that he functions as a patron of sacrifice and thus remains dependent on ritual reciprocity established by his relationship with the Brahmin priests. Since the royal power is brought about by the ritual empowerment of kings, it needs to be re-confirmed through repeated rituals and is not absolute. The structure and place of the king are shifted by introducing the position of a highest god, who is at the same time the overlord and protector of all living beings, as well as the 'highest self', who guarantees liberation for all embodied selves. With regard to the conceptualisation of kingship, this means that a king is now regarded as subordinate to Vāsudeva-Kṛṣṇa, the highest god. The king is now defined in relation to the highest god, who unites the ascetic power of the detached and liberated *yogin* with the creative and protective dimensions of his being the overlord of all beings, including kings. This limits the chances of kings to depict and present themselves as divine. This re-mapping of power relations also concerns other groups of people, such as Vedic gods, Brahmans and successful ascetics, but also the 'common' and 'lower' people, including women and Śūdras. The new conceptual framework, which came into being along with the monotheistic doctrines of the *BhG*, became the model for later texts and traditions of subsequent religious traditions within Hinduism. With regard to the relationship between the *BhG* and the *MBh*, my analysis will show that studying the former in the context of the latter enriches our understanding of both. This will be shown in some detail in the analysis of the debates on war and peace in the *Udyogaparvan* of the *MBh*, the book preceding the battle books of which the *BhG* is part. The analysis will deal with the extant texts of both the *BhG* and the *MBh* in their final redactions. This does not exclude the use of a text-historical perspective in the course of the analysis. While agreeing with most scholars that an epic without a *BhG* is certainly conceivable, I argue that the *BhG* was not composed independently of the epic tradition, but in relation to the epic and even for it. The *BhG*, or more precisely the different parts of the *BhG*, were incorporated in the epic in the course of its composition.

DOCTRINES

The analysis of the *Udyogaparvan* of the *MBh* as one important epic context of the *BhG* will be followed by a study and interpretation of the various religious and philosophical doctrines presented in the *BhG*. The text established a conceptual framework that became paradigmatic for the development of later Hindu religious traditions such as those expressed in the Purāṇas. It will be argued in detail that the impact of the *BhG* lies in its attempt to mediate between two opposing referential frameworks of human aspirations: on the one hand, the realm of socio-cosmic relationships encompassed by *dharma* and based on ritual performances as transmitted in Vedic texts; and on the other, the quest for liberation from this very realm through ascetic practices and the employment of new forms of knowledge. This mediation is achieved on two levels:

(A) Ascetic practices are interpreted in terms of sacrificial activity as a detached performance of duties (*karmayoga*) for the sake of 'holding the world together' (*lokasaṃgraha*). In explaining why this activity (*karman*) is exempt from karmic retribution and thus conducive to a quest for liberation, it is argued that ascetic action means equating one's actions with those of the cosmic cause of all activity (called *brahman* or *prakṛti*). Anyone who manages to substitute his own agency with 'cosmic' agency for the sake of 'the welfare of all beings' can be liberated, whether he is a king or an ascetic (cf. *BhG* 3). This principle is also applied when Kṛṣṇa is made the cause of all existence in that one is now asked to renounce all desires and cast all actions on him – in brief, to turn detachment from personal interests into attachment to the god.

(B) The concept of a single highest god called Vāsudeva-Kṛṣṇa is developed. This god represents the possible mediation between ascetic detachment and royal engagement. He combines the two dimensions of (human) aspirations that were previously ascribed to different discursive realms implying different life-styles: he is both the mighty ruler and creator of the world and its dharmic order, as well as the ever-liberated and transcendent 'highest self' (*paramātman*; *puruṣottama*). Both aspects are brought together in the depiction of Kṛṣṇa as the most powerful Lord and *yogin*. This means that he is in control of the workings of *karman*, since he has power over nature (*prakṛti*), the cosmic cause of activity, but remains at the same time detached from the created world, being forever 'unborn' and transcendent. The paradox implied in the doctrine that the god is both absent and yet present is explained by Kṛṣṇa's capacity to appear in various forms and disguises that are apparitional and can disappear at any moment because they result from *māyā*, the god's power to create forms, and are *māyā*, appearances that serve specific, well-defined purposes.

In the theological elaboration of these different levels, the *BhG* establishes a monotheistic framework that displays the following characteristic features:

1. There is a single highest god who is responsible for the creation, protection and destruction of the world. This world is based on a socio-cosmic order (*dharma*) created by the highest god, but threatened by transgressions and transgressors of all kind. According to the different tasks, the highest god has the following characteristics:
   a) He creates the world by the activation of a creative, often (his) creative powers (*brahman*, *prakṛti*).
   b) He is present in the world in different embodiments (*tanu*) or appearances (*māyā*) in order to protect *dharma* and destroy *adharma*.
2. The creation of the world, the different species of being and the common basic elements that form a body are explained by using concepts drawn from Sāṃkhya philosophy.

3. The highest god is the liberated 'highest self' who guarantees the chance of liberation for all selves when they realise that they are part of it. This can be achieved by ascetic practices and devotional attachment (*bhakti*).
4. The double-sided relationship of the god to the world and to individual embodied selves is indicated by making him a supreme *yogin* ('mighty lord of yoga') with regard to his power over nature and his supremacy over all cosmic regions and other gods (the 'mighty lord of all worlds'), as well as in relation to the individual self striving for liberation, the 'highest self' and 'supreme *puruṣa*'. He is the one and only, the unique god who combines supreme royal and cosmic power with ultimate detachment.
5. Sacrifice is acknowledged as the major arena of enacting and acknowledging the mutual dependence of all living beings in the world, thus securing their prosperity. Ritual reciprocity is necessary to maintain the socio-cosmic order, to 'keep the world together'.
6. The Vedic gods are subordinated to the highest god and regarded as dependent on ritual transactions.
7. New forms of ritual communication with the highest god are endorsed (offerings of flowers etc., so-called *pūjā*, recitation of mantras at the moment of death, complete ritualisation of one's life) and are declared to be available to all, irrespective of their social status, gender or rules of ritual purity.
8. A new interpretation of *bhakti*, loyalty and affection, is proposed that calls for one's exclusive devotion to the god as the means of salvation and is considered accessible to everyone, irrespective of social status, ritual purity, gender or karmic baggage.
9. Kings are subordinated to the highest god by emulating his altruistic concern for 'the welfare of all beings', which occasionally implies using violence against the enemies of socio-cosmic order.

Scholars were often hesitant to categorise or give these doctrines a name. This theology was rather loosely called 'theistic', or a 'concept of god', and some spoke of 'monotheism'. However, most scholars seem reluctant to apply the term 'monotheism' to Hindu religious traditions, since they differ in certain respects from the somehow normative 'monotheism' taught in Judaism, Christianity and Islam. While these differences indeed have to be acknowledged, this need not mean that there is only one form of monotheism. Other cultures, such as ancient Egypt and ancient India, developed a different type of 'monotheism', which can be called, with J. Assmann (1993: 10), 'cosmological monotheism'. Its characteristic feature is the acceptance of other gods either as partial manifestations of the one and only, transcendent god, or as 'lower' divine powers responsible for certain tasks or domains in the world. It is a theology that proclaims the 'one' in relation to the 'many' and establishes its sovereign and transcendent character in relation to other gods or powerful, cosmic beings. This does not necessitate the abolition of all other gods, since they are subordinated to the highest god and turned into domains of his being. This is signified in the *BhG* by the appearance of Kṛṣṇa in his cosmic 'All-Form' (*viśvarūpa*). The important point here is that these appearances are not regarded as contradicting the god's ultimate, transcendent state of being. Paradoxically, his cosmic presence and power are based on his distance and absence as the ever-liberated 'highest self'. This distinguishes him from older concepts of cosmic power and sovereignty as the unification, coagulation and embodiment of cosmic powers and regions in one being, called *brahman* or *mahān ātman* in the Upaniṣads (see van Buitenen 1964). Yet the depiction of Kṛṣṇa as 'cosmic' draws on these older notions, showing that the new theology not only mediates between the ascetic aspiration for liberation and empowerment on the one hand and social duties and a quest for happiness in the world on the other, but also includes the polytheism of the Vedic pantheon and older notions of kingship in its cosmological re-mapping. Seen from a historical perspective, this form of monotheism can be understood as emerging from the exploration and use of earlier interpretations and speculations about the 'one' and the 'many' in the Vedic and Upaniṣadic traditions (and perhaps also other traditions such as the Iranian). On the one hand, this concerns models of relationship established between the different gods of the Vedic religion, such as reciprocity, mutual dependence, the formation of alliances and distinct domains of power. On the other hand, it relates to reflections and models of a 'one' as, for instance, a 'source' of the many, as already formulated in cosmological speculations in late Vedic texts, such as the *Atharvaveda*, or as a power that lends them unity and cohesion as expressed in Vedic discourse on sovereignty and kingship. Although some of these historical and discursive connections still need to be studied in detail, the *BhG* provides enough evidence for its 'working' on and with older ideas of polytheism, which means exploring unions and alliances between them as well as their possible relations to the 'one' or 'highest' being often articulated in discourses on sovereignty.[3] However, one must also include the other dimension of its theology, which represents an already extant critique of these Vedic notions: discourses on renunciation, asceticism, teachings of empowerment and liberation in yoga and concepts of 'nature' (*prakṛti*) and consciousness developed in early Sāṃkhya teachings, as well as the presence

[3] Cf. Assmann 1986, Hornung 1971 on ancient Egypt.

of the Buddhist and Jaina traditions. They also contributed to the depiction of Vāsudeva-Kṛṣṇa as the transcendent being and to the delineation of the paths that lead to him. The yogic and ascetic road-maps make the quest for liberation an upward movement through the different levels of the adept's 'manifest self' and connect it to the cosmic planes that represent the general version, the 'matrix' of the individualised levels. They play an important role in the *BhG* and are integrated into the monotheistic framework. However, the *BhG* also offers a new way of establishing connection to the 'highest' by proclaiming the accessibility of the god in the world in his appearances. While these appearances are given the definite purpose of removing disorder (*adharma*), they mark the god's presence in the world and become legitimate targets of worship. It comes as no surprise to realise that this theology needs no special reconciliation with the emergence of image worship and temple cults. Indeed, for some forms of the god described in the *BhG* we have pictorial representations, some of them dating back to the second century BCE. This points to another feature of 'cosmological' monotheism which distinguishes it from Christian or other forms of monotheism: it is not iconoclastic, but allows images of the god. However, as is repeatedly pointed out in the *BhG*, this does not mean 'idolatry', since the image must not be confused with the 'true' god, who is forever 'unborn', the liberated 'self'. Yet the god's temporal appearance is fundamental for establishing a direct relationship, not only between the god and the cosmos, but also between himself and individual beings, the 'embodied selves'. This is one important feature of the concept of *bhakti*, the reciprocal, loving relationship between the god and his followers, presented in the *BhG*. The god is thus not only 'the all' in terms of his relatedness to the cosmos, but he is also 'for all' in that he is connected to all individual beings. Neither kinship nor gender nor other possible or desirable alliances determine this relationship, since it can be established, or rather activated, by all beings, irrespective of the rules and boundaries that usually structure social relationships. Therefore everyone can be his follower, his *bhakta*, which means to become 'dear' (*priya*) to the god to the same extent as the god is 'dear' to him. This means realising that one actually and solely belongs to the god, that one is his 'own' (drawing on the older connotation of *priya* as 'one's own'; cf. Scheller 1950). While these features will be studied in detail in the course of the analysis of the *BhG*, this general outline may explain what is meant in what follows by the term 'monotheism'. I propose to use this notion of 'cosmological monotheism' for the theology of the *BhG* because it accounts for many of its features and may invite further comparative and historical studies within and beyond the Indian traditions.

EPIC CONTEXTS: KINGSHIP AND *BHAKTI*

This 'cosmological monotheism' results in a re-mapping of power relations, not only with regard to the traditional Vedic gods who possess power over distinct realms of the cosmos and can be approached through rituals, or to well-known causes of creation and realms of liberation, such as the Upaniṣadic *brahman*, but also in respect of kings. This aspect seems no less important for the depiction of Kṛṣṇa as the 'mighty lord of all beings', which gains additional dimensions of meaning when seen in the context of the debates on kingship. The concept of a supreme god results in a reinterpretation of the socio-cosmic position of the kings by subordinating them to the higher power of the god while at the same time making the king the representative and protector of the god's cause on earth. This affects the older, Vedic interpretation of royal sovereignty. While the king is regarded as occupying a very high, if not the highest, position on earth, since he unites in his consecrated body the powers of the gods and the cosmos, his power depends on repeated ritual consecrations and is thus intimately connected to continual priestly endorsement. This concept, like much of the epic and the *BhG*, confirms a characteristic feature of kingship pointed out by Quigley (2005: 1f.): 'Kingship is an institution that develops its full reality in a world where the political has not emerged as an autonomous sphere from the ritual.' According to the Vedic ritual idiom and practice of empowerment, the king emerges from his consecration as an aggregation of the different powers that have been conferred on him. His body consists of the qualities of different gods, his virtues belong to him through his association with those who are in charge of them, etc. Yet he does not retain this divine position, but returns to the world and needs to prove himself a king by promoting and protecting the prosperity of the people and by retaining his 'virtues' (see Heesterman 1957, Gonda 1959). The epic not only describes 'royal rituals', but generally testifies to the idea that the powers and qualities of a king are conferred on him (see Hopkins 1931, Gonda 1966, Hiltebeitel 1976). This paradigm is also confirmed by means of negative examples, as time and again the epic deals with kings who fail to keep their power or to live up to the standards of royal virtue and in consequence lose everything. Deserted by Śrī, the goddess embodying royal fortune, they roam around in disgrace or exile. On the other hand, for example, in Duryodhana, the epic highlights kings' claims to absolute power and sovereignty that extends even to the gods, which causes destruction and ruin. This claim, put forward in the *Udyogaparvan* of the epic, expresses a notion of kingship that is not endorsed in the *BhG*.

While neither all the aspects the epic's treatment of kingship nor their relationship to Vedic and other concepts of sovereignty have been thoroughly studied, it may not be overstating the case to suggest that these debates point to a situation of transition in which different concepts and social formations not only co-exist, but also compete, a situation that incited debates and new conceptual frameworks. One of these, but not the only one, is the *BhG*'s concept of the highest god who rules over the singular source of all creation (*prakṛti*), so that the different gods, their rituals and the effects that are ascribed to them are subordinated under him. In contrast to human kings, the god appears in corporeal forms that are not subject to the human or natural condition, and he is not dependent on ritual consecration or nourishment. This reintroduces the ascetic, liberated dimension of this god as the other fundament of his supremacy. While Kṛṣṇa is the 'overlord' of the world, he also protects it for the sake of liberation, that is, to permit each individual, embodied self to reach the 'highest self'. In making the transcendent state of being the 'highest', the hierarchical relationship between ascetic liberation and cosmic empowerment is clearly demarcated: the ultimate goal is to turn away from the world, not to strive for cosmic or worldly power.

These two dimensions of Kṛṣṇa's divinity converge in the concept of *bhakti*, which demands from a follower of the god the development of an unconditional 'loyalty' and 'affection' based on a knowledge and sense of belongingness. To be a *bhakta*, a loving follower of a god, means to know that one belongs to the god by virtue of sharing his immortal nature as being an 'individual self' (*jīva*) and by acting for the sake of the cosmos created by him and thus sharing the god's mode of detached activity. In using the notion of *bhakti* the *BhG* draws on older concepts of relationships that imply loyalty and reverence based on authority (of kings, teachers), seniority (father, mother), or a recognition of belongingness rooted in kinship. However, the mutuality implied in *bhakti* also makes it important for relationships that are established apart from kinship ties, but that may not be any less important or affectionate than these, such as alliances like comradeship or friendship. *Bhakti* is the very affection and loyalty one shows towards another because one finds oneself in a relationship that is as close and indissoluble as kinship. This implies a confidence that not only is emotional, but also includes intellectual and aesthetic aspects and is based on positive evidence and experience of its validity. Sharing oneself in a relationship of *bhakti* also implies that each receives a share of the other. When seen in the context of the epic, it is by no means surprising that the relationship between the highest god and a potential king is made the model of the new theological interpretation of *bhakti* which implies exclusiveness and subordination. This model clarifies, first, that the legitimacy of a righteous, *dharma*-protecting king depends on his affirmative subordination to the highest god by accepting the ultimate supremacy of that god rather than deeming himself to be the overlord. As the epic bards show with regard to Duryodhana, a king who regards himself as the absolute is doomed and must be treated as an enemy. Secondly, entertaining a *bhakti* relationship with the highest god has repercussions for the position of the king and the representation of royal values, since the king's conduct can now be judged with regard not only to his dharmic and ritual performances, but also to his ability to serve god and the world for their own sakes. Devotional detachment – that is, the combination of an ascetic relinquishment of personal interests and attachment to the highest god – can now be expected as an appropriate form of royal conduct. However, this subordination not only delimits royal power, but is regarded as the source of empowerment too. *Bhakti* implies that the god will protect the king as one of his kin and kind, but mutuality also works the other way round.

In yet another respect, the new hierarchy between god and king implies a similarity in that both are characterised by distance from the ordinary people, in the case of the king due to his consecration, in the case of the god because of his ultimate detachment and absence. However, this distance allows that both are connected to 'all people' or the 'whole universe' in a unique way, because they are both in principle accessible to all because their position in the world is not defined by relations of kinship. The king resembles the god in that he is made as responsible for his kingdom and his subjects as the god is for the embodied selves and the orderliness of the world he has created. What Quigley (2005: 4) notes as a characteristic feature of kingship in different societies can be applied, although on a different level, to the 'highest god' too: 'the king is that individual who is uniquely connected to everyone in the society', while all the others are usually connected only to some other members of the society. While the *BhG* advocates this view, it simultaneously regulates this connection. Moreover, this view is not representative of the whole epic, since the *MBh* includes different views on kingship, some of them laying a strong emphasis on the interdependence between royal and priestly power and the special responsibility of the kings with regard to the Brahmins and vice versa (see e.g. van Buitenen 1973, Fitzgerald 2006). Yet the many levels on which the divinity of Kṛṣṇa is connected to themes of sovereignty and kingship may explain why this specific knowledge revealed by the god Kṛṣṇa is called *rājavidyā*, 'the knowledge of kings' or royal knowledge. This indicates that kings should not only be the model for this new relationship with a highest god, but should also use it themselves. In this regard, the relationship between Kṛṣṇa and Arjuna as staged and transformed in the text establishes a paradigm. Arjuna is depicted, at least temporarily, as the ideal king because he is made the ideal *bhakta*, the loyal follower who can expect to receive his share of Kṛṣṇa's power and, ultimately, his transcendent state of being (cf. Biardeau 1997).

Describing *bhakti* with regard to the king sets the example for other social groups who can be expected to follow suit. The text claims that the ideal of *bhakti* needs to be represented as a religious, liberating path that is open to all strata of society, not only kings, priests or sages. Therefore, the idea of *bhakti* is not presented as a practice of lower-status, illiterate people or as a 'folk' religion that priests and aristocrats had to concede in order to remain in power, as some interpreters would have it, but as 'secret' knowledge and a rather demanding practice of transforming attachment to oneself into detachment, which is in turn based on attachment to god. In its highest form, it amounts to asceticism in terms of turning one's life into a sacrificial activity to god. This does not support the view that *bhakti* is an easy path or indicative of a 'folk' religion, as has been assumed with regard not only to the *BhG* but to other traditions too, such as Buddhism and Jainism. Recent studies now point to a more intimate relationship between reverence of a superior (teacher, family member, etc.) and ascetic traditions. Similarly, image worship is no longer seen as a bottom-up process, but as a practice supported and even introduced by the well-off, such as kings and merchants, or religious experts, such as resident monks or teachers.[4]

HISTORICAL CONTEXTS

The analysis of the epic context of the *BhG*, and especially the connection with debates on kingship and power, shows that its religious doctrines are also connected with social and political dynamics, and conversely, that the political sphere is not separated from the religious. The *BhG* mirrors this situation because its theology touches on the relationship between different dimensions and representatives of power, be they ascetic, divine, cosmic, royal or ritual. The epic contextualisation of themes and doctrines invites one to deal with cultural-historical contexts and doctrinal traditions

4 See, for instance, Schopen 1997, Harrison 1995, and Bailey and Mabett 2003, for Buddhism; Folkert 1989 and Cort 2002 for Jainism.

not only handed down in other literary sources, but also preserved in inscriptions, coins and images. Therefore, the analysis of the *BhG* will be followed by a discussion of these other contexts and of possible historical dates for the text.

With regard to the position of the *BhG* in the larger epic framework and its supposed historical context, which is characterised by major cultural and political transformations, the concepts of divinity and kingship propagated in the *BhG* may be connected to the presence of different powers in Greater Northern India in the period to which the *BhG* can most plausibly be dated, that is, between the third and first centuries CE. The *BhG* delineates a new constellation in which gods, kings and devotees play a dominant role, a role, however, which can be properly delineated only when it is considered against the idiom of sacrifice and ritual, seen as being intimately connected to the presence and power of brahmanic priests and teachers.

In dealing with such constellations in historical perspective, much depends on the historical framework and dates which are assumed for the textual history and the final redaction. Here we can note a silent agreement in that most scholars assume that the extant epic was composed between 400 BCE and 400 CE, a time of major transformations in the cultural region of Greater Northern India. Most of the studies move within this framework and often attempt to refine it in analysing and dating individual texts, recensions, layers and doctrines. Refinement is also intended in discussing the possible connection between the *BhG* and the major signposts that demarcate this historical field, such as the emergence of ascetic communities (*śramaṇa*), Buddhism and Jainism, and other new religious movements, the establishment of a great kingdom under the Nandas, the reign of the Emperor Aśoka and the quick succession of dynasties following the usurpation of power by the so-called Śuṅgas, and the presence of foreign powers such as the Indo-Greek kings, the Scythians and finally the Kuṣāṇas, who were again able to hold power over large parts of Northern India. They mirrored the syncretistic, multicultural constellation of this period, which takes a new course with the rise of the Gupta dynasty and the flourishing of Sanskrit culture. Many generations of scholars have attempted to date the extant text and its different layers by drawing on parallel passages in related texts and using archaeological, iconographical, epigraphic and numismatic sources, as well as by considering the relationship to doctrines that may or may not have been known to the authors of the *BhG*. With regard to the historical argument that is put forward in this study, the 'hermeneutic circle' has to be kept in mind from the very start: the text is taken as reflecting a stage in the history of Hinduism and is regarded as being itself one of the major contributors to this very history. The history of ideas is thus the context of the text, which may very well have been the context for other features of this process too, such as temple worship, other gods being propagated as the highest gods, etc.

By drawing on epigraphic, numismatic and iconographical sources, it is suggested that the monotheistic framework belongs to a time when image worship, a cult of Vāsudeva-Kṛṣṇa and different concepts of kingship and liberation were to become important features of the cultural context (that is, from the second century BCE onwards). Against the background of the available evidence and a consideration of scholarly opinions, I will argue that the extant text (that is, the final redaction, including all chapters) can probably be dated to the early Kuṣāṇa period (first century CE), at which time intensive competition and debate between different religious communities can be noted, all striving for representation and royal patronage. After the retreat of the Indo-Greek kings from the region of Madhyadeśa, Mathurā underwent an upsurge and seems to have regained its position as a centre for the worship of Vāsudeva-Kṛṣṇa. The plurality of 'highest' beings, new practices of image worship and the concept of the king as representing and serving a highest god for the sake of 'the welfare of all beings', which were characteristic of the teachings of the *BhG* too, are well documented. Taking all these aspects together as 'cumulative evidence', it is highly plausible to place the final redaction of the text in this historical setting, which can then be taken as the starting point for the continuous reception of the text in the centuries to come. This history of reception begins already in the later parts of the epics with the inclusion of texts like the *Anugītā*, the dialogue between a female mendicant and king Janaka, and the Nārāyaṇīya section. This points to a future task to be undertaken, the comparative study of these texts and of those features which became paradigmatic for subsequent Hindu religious traditions. In doing this, another text must be considered which equally proclaims a single highest god: the *Śvetāśvatara-Upaniṣad.* This situation is indicative of the pluralistic, multiform structure of the emerging Hindu religious traditions. The co-existence, interaction and competition of different religious communities and traditions have been characteristic features of Hinduism since its very beginning. Different gods are declared to be the one and only, though at the moment it is very difficult to prove who was first. Rather, we are dealing with a plurality of theistic doctrines that share certain characteristic features, but are yet distinct. We find different monotheistic doctrines as well as other theistic cults. It seems that each monotheistic school is aware of the existence and doctrine of another monotheistic school. The god of the competing school is regarded as belonging to the lower sphere. In the further history of Hinduism, this initial structure allowed for a continuous branching out of schools and the addition of new ones. A clearer picture of the co-existence of the different highest gods, and later also goddesses, already at the very beginning of the formation of classical Hinduism, may help us understand and trace later developments.

CHAPTER 1

The Bhagavadgītā *in the history of research*

The *BhG* has incited an apparently endless stream of publications. However, only a few have been influential, and much of the literature seems redundant, since it is rarely based on previous research. It seems that scholars start each time anew when they turn to this text, as pointed out by Minor (1987: 150, note 13): 'It is extremely unfortunate that most of what is being written on the Gītā has been written before. There is a noticeable lack of citation of secondary literature in studies of the Gītā.' Nevertheless, major publications and developments in the field can be discerned, which can be classified according to two dominant approaches. Whereas one group of scholars, the 'analysts', follows methods of textual criticism that are aimed at reconstructing the Gītā's textual history, others, the 'unitarians', follow a holistic approach and take the extant text as a meaningful whole and interpret it according to different theoretical perspectives.[1] Since both methods were regarded as mutually exclusive, they were only rarely employed together as is done in the present work.[2] The following critical survey of major and original publications will not only present a survey of research on the text, but is also intended to establish a referential framework for the subsequent analysis of the text. It is not an account of the *BhG*'s 'history of reception', therefore neither the later Sanskrit tradition of commentaries nor modern Hindu interpretations of the text will be included, since each author establishes his own hermeneutics on the basis of the religious or philosophical tradition he adheres to. These deserve a separate study.[3] Apart from tracing the development of different interpretations, this survey will also point to

1 The terms for both approaches are suggested by Latacz (1979) in his summary of the history of research on Homer's epics.

2 See, however, von Humboldt 1826a, Mangels 1995, Malinar 1996.

3 For the same reason, studies of the commentaries on the *BhG* are not included. Many explanations of words given by commentators are included in Zaehner's translation (1969). For modern contexts and commentators, see Sharpe 1985, Minor 1988 and Robinson 2005. As perhaps no study of the *BhG* can claim to notice, let alone cover, all publications, the interested reader may consult the following bibliographies: Kapoor 1982, Callewaert and Hemraj 1983, von Stietencron et al. 1992.

the historical and political contexts of the academic discourse, as they help us in understanding certain evaluations. Roughly speaking, three phases in the history of research can be distinguished. First, the nineteenth century sees the beginning of *BhG* research as part of British colonial and German Romantic and philosophical endeavours. However, although the *BhG* was a topic for Christian and theosophical authors, in this period it remained on the periphery of Indological research, since at that time the Veda and Indian grammar were more important. This changed at the beginning of the twentieth century, which marks the start of a second, perhaps more intense phase, which lasted some forty years and corresponds to the surge in new interpretations of the text by some of the most important Hindu reformists, such as Tilak and Gandhi. As we will see, this did not go unnoticed by scholars. After the Second World War, thirdly, some Indologists adopted a Marxist perspective or employed structural methods, and the debate between textual critics and scholars following a 'holistic' approach entered another phase.

THE BEGINNINGS

The *BhG* became an object of academic study in the course of the British expansion in India, which included the study and appropriation of important religious texts through editions and translations. The *BhG* was among the first Sanskrit texts to be translated into a European language, thus becoming well known and entering new public arenas. Contrary to what one may expect of the analysis of 'Orientalist' strategies, there is no unified European attitude to the text, and discussions therefore varied within different academic circles.[4] Seminal to all these debates were the editions and translations prepared by the early scholars, a task often accompanied by producing the basic instruments of textual scholarship such as dictionaries.

Charles Wilkins was the first to translate the *BhG* into a European language in 1785. Governor General Warren Hastings supported the publication and recommended the text to a Western readership, arguing that the *BhG* demonstrates the 'wisdom' of the ancient Indian sages, which, in spite of its ultimately 'perverted morality', shows certain similarities to Christian doctrines. Moreover, he claimed that British support for the publication would also positively influence the perception of colonial rule among the Indians: 'Every accumulation of knowledge, and especially such

4 Recent research has argued for a more differentiated approach to the so-called Orientalist discourse, although I cannot go into further details here. See, for example, the studies in Brückner et al. 2003.

as is obtained by social communication with people over whom we exercise a dominion founded on the right of conquest, is useful to the state: it is the gain of humanity . . . it lessens the weight of the chain by which the natives are held in subjection' (Hastings, in Wilkins 1785: 13). Wilkins's translation was itself soon translated into other European languages (French in 1787, German in 1801) and thus became influential, although it was 'full of distorting misunderstandings', as A. W. Schlegel (1826a: 17) noted. More credit was given to the *editio princeps* published in 1806 under Wilkins's direction. Schlegel's Latin translation of this edition was published in 1823, and this resulted in a renewed European interest in the text. In Germany it incited a debate between the philosophers W. von Humboldt and Hegel that is representative of two different attitudes towards Indian culture and became paradigmatic for many decades to come: Romantic enthusiasm on the one hand, and criticism and even rejection on the other. This bifurcation of the German imagination of India developed with the publication and philological study of the original sources and runs somewhat parallel to the debate between 'Orientalists' and 'Anglicists' in Britain.[5] The German debate remains interesting not only because it illustrates the historical context, but also because the *BhG* is interpreted by means of a specific philosophical terminology, which influenced, more or less explicitly, later interpretations.

The debate starts with W. von Humboldt's review of Schlegel's translation, which was severely criticised by Langlois (1824–25). Von Humboldt took sides with Schlegel, and in 1826 he published his sympathetic analysis of what he regarded as the 'philosophical system' of the text. Being aware of the possibility that the text had been composed by more than one author over a considerable period of time, he nevertheless proposed to reconstruct a philosophical doctrine by systematically arranging the different teachings dispersed through it. This method was also later employed by Indologists such as Edgerton and Lamotte, who tried to lend meaning to a text which to others seemed rather incoherent. However, Humboldt employs a text-historical perspective too, in that he regards the first eleven chapters as the 'original' ones. In these chapters he detects an artistic principle of composition, similar to painting, which is lacking in the final six chapters (cf. Leitzmann 1908: 179). According to Humboldt, the philosophy of the text consists of two doctrines: (1) the separation of body and mind ('*Geist*'); and (2) that indifference towards the results of one's actions

[5] On India and the German Romantic movement, see Behler 1968 and Willson 1964. On the 'bifurcation', see Malinar 2003.

is the precondition for salvation. He thinks that terms like 'theism' or 'pantheism' as designations of the teachings of the *BhG* are best avoided, since they have (Christian) implications which are not appropriate in the Indian context. In contrast to later studies, the acknowledgement of the text's history does not preclude a reconstruction of its meaning, and the application of certain philosophical terms is critically reflected.

In 1827 Hegel published two articles in which he rejects von Humboldt's views and criticises some of the terms Schlegel has chosen in his translation as suggesting a false similarity with Western ideas. This criticism, which is often appropriate, is also part of Hegel's agenda of denying the value of Indian culture, which has been overestimated by the Romantics. In contrast to von Humboldt, Hegel takes one passage, *BhG* 12.8–11 (from a chapter not belonging to von Humboldt's 'original text'), as the key to the whole. In consequence he turns the text into a treatise on yoga. For him, yoga is the essence ('*das Allgemeinste*') of Indian culture, which he generally places on the lower ranks of his taxonomy of human history and culture. Another reason why India did not develop the idea of freedom and individuality is that the system of yoga is aimed at achieving a complete depletion of individual consciousness, which will then vanish in the abstract (and therefore equally empty) absolute (*brahman*). Nothing valuable can be based on such a teaching, and therefore the *BhG* has no morality or ethics to offer. It is remarkable that none of the philosophers who debated these issues saw any similarity between the *BhG*'s doctrine of 'detached activity' and Kant's 'categorical imperative'. While the comparison with Kant has become a favourite exercise in later scholarship (see Gauchhwal 1958), it seems that, for the philosophers of the early nineteenth century, such a connection was rather far-fetched, as indeed it is when the respective philosophical frameworks are taken seriously. After this early discussion, the *BhG* moved to the periphery of Indological and Indian-related research. Only several decades later, at the turn of century, did the *BhG* again stand in the limelight in connection with an increasing interest in the ancient epics.

RESEARCH IN THE LATE NINETEENTH AND EARLY TWENTIETH CENTURIES

By the end of the nineteenth century, the *BhG* was included in Max Müller's *Sacred Books of the East* in a new translation by Telang (1882), who regarded it as a philosophical text. The *BhG* became, on the one hand, part of the academic canon as one of the authoritative Hindu or brahmanical scriptures, and interpretations of the text as a whole now show a greater concern with classifying its philosophical and religious doctrines. On the other hand, we also witness the emergence of a new framework for the study of the text, the *Mahābhārata* epic. The composition and originality of the *BhG* were now considered in relation to the textual history of the epic. Two main views emerged in dealing with this issue. Either the *BhG* was regarded as a text that was composed independently and then interpolated into the epic at a rather late stage of its composition, together with other 'didactic' or 'sectarian' texts, or else it was seen as consisting of different layers that mirror stages of the composition of the epic and thus form part of its textual history.

In his four-volume study of the *MBh* (1893), A. Holtzmann argues for the latter view by isolating different textual layers in the *BhG*, which he then connects to the different stages in the evolution of the epic. Thus he regards the author of the oldest layer of the *BhG* (chs. 1 and 2) as being identical with author of the 'Ur-Epos', who seems to have believed in an immortal 'world-soul'. In contrast to subsequent scholars, he does not consider Arjuna's breakdown and Kṛṣṇa's subsequent didactics as something 'un-epic' or a literary 'monstrosity', but as demonstrating the author's freedom (1892–95: II: 154). From chapter 4 onwards, the text is characterised by a tension between 'pantheistic' and 'theistic' teachings. There is no real solution to the contradiction between paths of salvation ending respectively in an abstract, impersonal absolute (*brahman*) and the god Kṛṣṇa. For Holtzmann the theistic parts belong to a more recent layer, which he describes as the 'Viṣṇuitic revision' of an original 'pantheistic' text that teaches *brahman* as the goal of salvation. This revision is motivated by a specific historical context and took place at 'a time when the Brahmins were interested in reconciling their polytheism with folk belief, in order to take up the fight against Buddhism' (Holtzmann 1892–95: II: 163f.). Although it has been questioned and debated, this reconstruction remained influential in subsequent discussion, especially with regard to the view that the theism of the *BhG* is part of an epic redaction aimed at fighting Buddhism and giving theological support to 'folk' religion as expressed in devotional or *bhakti* practices. This view is based on certain assumptions about the development of Indian religions or of religion in general, such as the rise of 'folk' religion, which had to be accommodated by brahmanical or ascetic elites. These assumptions were applied to Buddhism and Jainism too, and have only recently been questioned and qualified (see Schopen 2005, Cort 2002). We will see that this thesis that much of the epic is the product of an anti-Buddhist agenda has been repeated and refined over the last hundred years and that it remains an issue for current debates too.

In course of his metrical analysis[6] of the epic, E. W. Hopkins (1895: 389) distinguishes three phases in the textual history of the *BhG*: 'This Divine Song . . . is at present a Krishnaite version of an older Vishnuite poem, and this in turn was at first an unsectarian work, perhaps a late Upanishad.' According to Hopkins, the *BhG* is one of the oldest poems to have found their way into the epic. In its extant form, the text is a 'medley of beliefs' (1895: 390), quite similar to the Upaniṣads, but held together only by the theistic strand that pervades the whole text. The poetic quality suffers from unsystematic presentation, which has unwelcome effects on the reader: 'The same thing is said over and over again, and the contradictions in phraseology and in meaning are as numerous as the repetitions, so that one is not surprised to find it described as "the wonderful song which causes the hair to stand on end"' (1895: 400).

The publication of R. Garbe's translation and interpretation in 1905 marks the beginning of what is perhaps the most productive period of research on the *BhG*. Garbe rejects Holtzmann's reconstruction of the textual history and argues that the theistic doctrines are not only the 'essence' of the text, but also older than the 'pantheistic' teachings that indicate a later revision. He regards the Sāṃkhya and yoga teachings of the *BhG* as belonging to the same type of philosophical reasoning characteristic of the other philosophical texts that were incorporated into the epic, which he describes as a *Mischphilosophie*, a free combination of different elements of otherwise separate philosophical schools. The *BhG* is not a poem, as von Humboldt had claimed, but a 'didactic text' (*Lehrgedicht*) propagating Kṛṣṇaism (Garbe 1921: 16). According to Garbe, the original, theistic text did indeed belong to the older epic. Both the epic and the *BhG* were changed and their poetics distorted when later redactors superimposed on theism an impersonal *brahman* as the highest realm. This mirrors a later stage in the history of Indian thought, marked by the rise of Vedānta philosophy (1921: 19), and can be dated to the second century BCE.[7] According to Garbe, the god Kṛṣṇa is not an incarnation of or identical with Viṣṇu, but a god in his own right: the equation is a product of the later development. Rather, Kṛṣṇa is a clan deity, whose origins have to be sought in the deification of a hero. His followers called themselves Bhāgavatas, thus

[6] This assessment is based on the study of *Vipulā* frequency, which shows that *BhG* 1–14 may be the older core text of the *BhG*. For further metrical studies resulting in different reconstructions, see M. R. Smith 1968, Yardi 1978, von Simson 1974.

[7] While Winternitz shared Garbe's view of the character of epic philosophy (Winternitz 1907: 197), he deemed chapter 11 a 'distasteful' product of later Purāṇic redactors. Like Hopkins, he feels that the text is a 'hotch-potch' and the reconciliation of asceticism and devotion is not convincing (cf. Winternitz 1909: 1: 373).

professing an 'ethical Kṣatriya religion' (1921: 32), which rejects brahmanic ritualism.[8] One important feature of their doctrine is that the Bhāgavatas reinterpret the older teachings of yoga according to the theistic framework as 'worship of God' (1921: 53).

H. Jacobi took issue with Garbe's views, his criticisms resulting in a sequence of exchanges published in the *Deutsche Literaturzeitung.* While Jacobi agreed that the *BhG* is a 'textbook of the Bhāgavatas', he rejected the view that the oldest layers of the *BhG* are genuine parts of the older epic. He was the first in a line of scholars to follow Schrader's (1910) suggestion of an epic 'Ur-text' of the *BhG*, that is, a text that would not have interrupted the epic narrative. He argues that the insertion of a longer treatise would have destroyed the dramatic situation described in the epic, since the text stops a fight which is about to begin: no 'true' epic bard would have allowed this to happen (Jacobi 1918: 323). Jacobi accepts only a brief admonition and suggests that the Ur-text consisted of 2.1–12, 18, 25–27, 30–37 and 18.73 only. Jacobi is also sceptical of Garbe's theory of the development of theistic yoga in the context of the Bhāgavata religion, because yoga has always been 'theistic' (Jacobi 1921: 718). However, Garbe (1922b: 603), in his turn, was not impressed because none of these positions can be proved. But neither was H. Oldenberg (1920) convinced by Garbe's reconstruction, since like Jacobi he felt that Garbe had not succeeded in establishing a more meaningful text. Following Schleiermacher's interpretation of religion as based on an 'experience' (*Erlebnis*), Oldenberg regards the text as expressing a 'sudden vision' of the poet. In contrast to Winternitz and Garbe, who rejected Arjuna's vision in *BhG* 11 as superfluous, Oldenberg sees it as a document of true experience not needing patronising scholars eager to use their philological scalpels (Oldenberg 1920: 325, 332, note 1).

It was not only scholars who followed the text-critical method who were critical of Garbe's views, but also those who adopted a 'holistic' approach and considered the text to be a meaningful whole. The first to adopt this approach is P. Deussen (1911), who criticises Garbe without mentioning him and suggests that the *BhG* superimposes a theistic doctrine on the older monistic teachings. However, Deussen does not offer a text-historical reconstruction, but divides the text into the following three thematic and coherent units, each covered by six chapters: (1) ethics (chs. 1–6), the doctrine of an altruistic fulfilment of one's duty; (2) metaphysics (chs. 7–12), the transition from the 'idealistic' doctrine of absolute *brahman* to theism by subordinating the immortal self (*ātman*) under the god Kṛṣṇa; and

[8] For further details on the opposition between 'brahmanic' and 'Kṣatriya' religion, see Malinar 2003.

(3) psychology (chs. 13–18), or the discourse on the obstacles on the path to liberation based on Sāṃkhya and yoga. This is, according to Deussen, the most 'tiresome' part of the *BhG*. Deussen interprets the *BhG* as a unified text by applying the categories of Western philosophy; as a result, the theistic doctrines are pushed into the background.

Also following the unitarian approach, F. Edgerton (1925: 2) deliberately ignores the epic context of the *BhG*, which he considers 'a dramatic absurdity' (1925: 1), and interprets it as an independent text: 'We must think of the Gītā primarily as a unit, complete in itself, without reference to its surroundings.' It is a mystical, devotional text that 'seeks to inspire and exalt, not to instruct or train the intellect' (Edgerton 1940: 447f.). Therefore it does not offer a rational solution to the tension between salvation and social life and is a compromise 'between the speculations of the intellectuals and the emotionalism of popular religion' (1946: 71) that appeals not to logic but to experience. Although Edgerton concedes that the text is not coherent and may contain interpolations, he refuses any reconstruction of its layers because of a lack of proof. Although sharing Edgerton's view that the *BhG* is a unified text, Douglas P. Hill (1928) and E. Lamotte (1929) offer a new and influential perspective on the nature of this unity, which, according to them, consists of a synthesis of different religious and philosophical ideas, which became the foundation of Kṛṣṇaism. While Hill accepts von Garbe's basic premise, his interpretation of the historical development is different, since in his view the theism of the *BhG* shows a strongly monistic tendency in that Kṛṣṇa is identified with *brahman* rather than vice versa (Hill 1928: 35). Lamotte establishes the unity of the *BhG* by arranging the text according to certain themes. Like Edgerton, he refuses to enter the uncertain terrain of text-historical reconstruction because 'the conclusions of each author depend less on scientific evidence than on subjective impressions' (1929: 8, my trans.). He proposes instead to analyse the text's intellectual milieu, which is constituted by the Kṣatriya ethics (which includes *bhakti*) of the Bhāgavata sect on the one hand, and the monism of the Upaniṣads on the other, the latter being more important than Sāṃkhya and yoga. The only original contribution of the text, composed around the second century BCE, is the doctrine of 'divine descents' (*avatāra*).

These 'holistic' interpretations of the *BhG* were regularly rejected by text-historical scholarship.[9] J. Charpentier started off by rejecting Edgerton's and Lamotte's critiques of Garbe's approach and finds the thesis of the unity of the *BhG* 'unacceptable'. Following Schrader's and Jacobi's reconstructions

[9] In the 1930s there was also a debate on the number of verses of the extant Vulgate text of the *BhG* and the relevance of the 'Kashmirian Recension'. While Schrader (1930) thought it an older version of the *BhG*, Edgerton (1932) and Belvalkar (1939) rejected this view.

of the 'epic Ur-Text', he argues that what follows in *BhG* 2.38 'can in no wise have belonged to the original epic text' (1930: 77). In contrast to his predecessors, Charpentier also removes 2.12–30 from the 'epic original', because this passage contains many quotations from other texts, especially the *Viṣṇusmṛti*. Bhāgavata authors then added their own texts, whose core consisted of the hymn to Kṛṣṇa in ch. 11, because it contains many old *triṣṭubh* verses (1930: 101).

In 1934 R. Otto offered yet another reconstruction of the textual history. Adhering, like Oldenberg and Edgerton, to the idea of religion as 'experience', Otto finds the Ur-text in a 'genuine epic' expression of such an experience, which makes the oldest passages those in which Arjuna's problem is directly addressed. The purpose of the Ur-text was to make Arjuna understand that he is merely an instrument of God's will (Otto 1934: 17). As a consequence, his original text, which is quite similar to Charpentier's theistic layer, includes the following parts: 1.1–2.13, 20, 22, 29–37; 10.1–8; 11.1–51 and 18.58–61. However, through the later addition of eight different 'treatises', the *BhG* became the extant, rather incoherent '*Traktatkranz*' ('a wreath of treatises'; Otto 1935a). Otto was heavily criticised by Schrader (1936), Strauss (1936), Belvalkar (1937) and Edgerton (1940). S. K. Belvalkar attacks Otto's emphasis on subordination to God's will as the *BhG*'s core doctrine as a 'miracle-mongering mysticism'. Alluding to Nazi rule in Germany, he comments (1937: 81): 'Arjuna of all persons in the world cannot be expected to meekly submit to such Hitlerism from Olympic Heights.'[10] What may seem mere polemic today is, however, indicative of the political contexts of certain academic debates. This becomes most explicit in W. Hauer's interpretation of the *BhG*, where he openly intends to use the text's 'Indo-Aryan metaphysics of battle' in support of the Nazis' 'movement of national awakening'. He interprets the text according to his ideas of 'true Germanic religiosity' that was originally free from any 'Semitic' influence. The characteristic feature of their world-view is the 'tragic' tension between a life dedicated to contemplation and the necessity to fight for one's survival (Hauer 1934: 3). Accordingly yoga is interpreted as a technique that prepares one for unquestioned obedience to the 'higher powers' when it comes to accepting 'destiny's requirement' (*das Muß des Schicksals*). Important elements of the National Socialist ideology are discernable in Hauer's interpretation, such as the 'leader-principle' (*Führerprinzip*), 'survival of the fittest', etc. The *BhG* is turned into timeless Indo-Aryan metaphysics (cf. Hufnagel 2003).

10 In 1929 Belvalkar published his own synthetic interpretation.

Aspects of this phase of research are summarised by S. C. Roy in his book *The Bhagavadgītā and Modern Scholarship* (1941) in his discussion of the different attempts to reconstruct its textual history. He sets out to demonstrate the meaningfulness of the text and argues that it was composed as an Upaniṣad and only later incorporated into the epic. Therefore, all passages that refer to the epic situation should be removed as interpolations.

AFTER THE SECOND WORLD WAR

In the decades following the Second World War, new approaches, Marxist, structuralist and comparative studies of literature, as well as computerised and statistical methods of textual analysis,[11] were employed on the *BhG*, though the divide between textual criticism and holistic interpretations nonetheless remained a characteristic feature of such studies.

In examining the literary devices used by the author of the *BhG*, M. Marcovich (1958) shows that the doctrine of devotion to Kṛṣṇa is established by an 'operation of substitution'. In an analysis of the attributes and adjectives used for the two goals of liberation taught in the text – impersonal *brahman* and the god Kṛṣṇa – he concludes that in most cases the god is made to replace and supersede *brahman* by the ascription of the attributes of *brahman* to him (1958: 28). He regards the *BhG* as a text that was composed independently of the epic and interpolated into the *MBh* between the fifth and third centuries BCE. Adopting a Marxist perspective, W. Ruben (1951: 176) regards the doctrine of 'disinterested action' as a document of 'healthy materialism' and as the highest expression of Hindu moral thinking. However, he concedes that one detects in the text the voice of the despot, 'who wants that his people work'. In a similar vein, D. D. Kosambi (1962) considers the economic and social environment of the *BhG*, viewing the text as a 'review synthesis' of contradictory positions that was incorporated into the epic shortly before the Gupta era (1962: 15). The syncretistic features of the god Kṛṣṇa mirror the antagonism between two different modes of production, the pastoralism of the Aryans and the agriculture of the pre-Aryans. Only one aspect of the *BhG* points to the next stage of historical development: the doctrine of *bhakti*,[12] which perfectly suits the structure of a feudal society based on loyalty and hierarchical subordination.

[11] See, for example, M. R. Smith 1968, Yardi 1978, von Simson 1974.

[12] In principle Thakur (1982) agrees with Kosambi, but he offers a different assessment of *bhakti* as primarily an ideology of exploitation. In a review essay, G. Bailey (1984) points out that the antagonism negotiated in the *BhG* is primarily religious, not economic.

In his introduction to his translation and exegetical commentary,[13] R. C. Zaehner (1969) employs categories developed in the comparative study of religion and interprets the text according to his typology of 'mystic experience'. This is based on the distinction between a path of salvation aimed at the liberation of the soul on the one hand, and devotion to god on the other. The *BhG* combines both in aiming 'to demonstrate that love of a personal God, so far from being *only* a convenient preparation for the grand unitary experience of spiritual liberation (the *mokṣa* or *mukti* of the Upanishads and the *vimutti* of the Buddhist), was also the crown of this experience itself which, without it, must remain imperfect' (Zaehner 1969: 3). Although the *BhG* is, according to Zaehner, a genuine part of the epic, this context does not play a vital role in understanding its teaching. The Gītā's familiarity with Buddhism is repeatedly pointed out in Zaehner's commentary.[14] It is dealt with in terms of different religious orientations, not as indicating a religious or political conflict, as suggested by other scholars. The text is dated by Zaehner to between the fifth and second centuries BCE.

Meanwhile studies of the text's history continued with G. von Simson's (1968–69) essay on the interpolation of the *BhG* into the epic. Following Jacobi (1914), von Simson argues that the *BhG* displays many 'un-epic' features and was incorporated in the epic for apologetic reasons, that is, to justify the 'mean tricks' that brought about the victory of the Pāṇḍavas. Apart from this judgement, von Simson suggests that alternative readings in manuscripts of the chapters following the *BhG* indicate that they were originally connected to the chapters preceding the *BhG*. He concludes that nobody would miss anything if the *BhG*, which he regards as the latest interpolation in this part of the *parvan*, was omitted (von Simson 1968–69: 168).

In his text-historical reconstruction, G. S. Khair (1969) divides the text into three different layers, each consisting of six chapters. He analyses the use of personal pronouns and argues that the passages in which Kṛṣṇa uses the first-person pronoun are more recent than those using the third person. While the author of the very first and oldest six chapters teaches yoga, the second author added another six chapters presenting various doctrines. The third author, in turn, was a 'prophet of a new faith', the Bhāgavata religion, who moved the interpolations of the second author

13 Exegetical commentaries have also been presented by Minor (1982), who discusses the differences between the individual verses. He tends to reject the synthetic view of the text.

14 See Upadhyaya 1968, 1971.

to the end and inserted his own contribution in the middle of the text (chs. 7–12).[15]

Offering a fresh approach to the study of the textual history, M. Ježic (1979a) focusses on repetition, not on contradictions and inconsistencies, in order to detect interpolations. He distinguishes between two types of repetition: first, 'continuity repetitions' indicating coherent text passages; and secondly, 'duplication repetitions' marking unconnected passages. However, he points out that this scheme permits different layers to be detected, though they may not be precise with regard to individual verses (1979a: 629). He applies this scheme in an analysis of the 'yoga layer' (Ježic 1979b). On a more general level, he suggests that the composition of the extant *BhG* is characterised by the combination of a 'hymnic layer' with an older 'epic layer', which was later supplemented by didactic passages. The hymnic layer was composed independently of the *MBh* and included in the epic when the *bhakti* doctrine was added to the text (1979: 633).

The publication of L. Dumont's essay on *World Renunciation in Indian Religion* (1960) marks the beginning of a new, structuralist line of research. Dumont argues that one of the characteristic features of Hinduism is its opposition between the values of the householder and those of the renouncer. This perspective was adopted by M. Biardeau in her in-depth studies of the *MBh* and the Purāṇas. As a consequence, she interprets the *BhG* as belonging to the epic's general discourse on the mediation of these values. Accordingly, the *BhG* occupies a central place in the epic, in that it reconciles ascetic doctrines with the householder's *dharma* of the king by allowing his liberation in spite of the violence implied in the duties of his class. In this regard the doctrine of 'disinterested action' plays a central role, in that all activity is transformed into a sacrifice for the sake of maintaining the world. Arjuna is forced to realise that he should act like the patron of the sacrifice 'who never stops sacrificing' (Biardeau 1981: 93). In addition, the *BhG* suggests that ascetic renunciation is not necessary to practise yoga. Instead an attitude of detachment must be developed that allows complete devotion to Kṛṣṇa (Biardeau 1976: 127). In making Kṛṣṇa the highest god, the *BhG* expresses the basic structure of the 'universe of *bhakti*' based on what Biardeau calls the '*avatāra* model' (1997). Kṛṣṇa is the '*avatāra* god' who 'has to combine in himself the values of the renouncer that he is and the values of the world of *dharma*' (1976: 170), while Arjuna is the 'impersonation of the ideal king'. Their alliance is paradigmatic for epic and later purāṇic Hinduism (1976: 78–80). However, this intriguing interpretation

[15] A detailed critique of this reconstruction is given by Minor 1982.

is not discussed in a detailed analysis of the *BhG* that would demonstrate how this reconciliation is brought about.

Parallel to Biardeau's interpretation of the 'structural unity' of the *MBh* and the *BhG*, the importance of the critical edition of the epic was made even more prominent by the publication of the first three volumes of J. A. B. van Buitenen's translation. He combines a historical view of the epic and its evolution with a discussion of its meaning, an approach he also applies to the *BhG*. According to van Buitenen, the conflict the text intends to resolve is not primarily structural, but was caused by changing historical and social circumstances. This can be seen in the changing attitude towards violence, in that war and heroism were no longer praised, but regarded with scepticism and ambivalence. Since the extant epic signals the end of the 'heroic age', the *BhG* can be fully understood only by studying it in relation to the epic: 'The *Bhagavadgītā* was conceived and created in the context of the *Mahābhārata*. It was not an independent text that somehow wandered into the epic. On the contrary, it was conceived and developed to bring to a climax and solution the dharmic dilemma of a war which was both just and pernicious' (van Buitenen 1981: 5).[16] While van Buitenen agrees with Biardeau here, his interpretation moves in a different direction. For him the importance of the *BhG* lies not in its mirroring the overall structure of meaning implied in the epic, but in its establishing a new conceptual framework for dealing with the 'dilemma of war': 'the Gītā provides a unique religious and philosophical context in which it can be faced, recognized, and dealt with. Whatever the further thrust of Kṛṣṇa's teaching and its elaborations, the Gītā addresses itself in the first place to a specific issue that the Bhārata war posed to a more reflective age, whose attitude toward violence was changing' (1981: 5). In addition the *BhG* also addresses the presence of new religious and philosophical ideas by offering the possibility of choosing with the doctrine of *bhakti*: 'as all loyalty, *bhakti* presupposes the possibility of other choices . . . In this abounding polytheism a person needed *bhakti* to find for himself his *iṣṭadevatā*, "the god of his choice", to whom he could demonstrate his loyalty' (1981: 24). Yet the god of the *BhG* is 'suprasectarian' (1981: 28).

TEXTUAL HISTORY AND TEXTUAL UNITY

The discussion of this history of research has demonstrated not only how changing historical contexts influenced the various interpretations of the

[16] For a similar view, see Lévy 1917 and Pisani 1939.

BhG, but also the continuous divide between the methods of textual criticism on the one hand, and on the other the application of various interpretive perspectives to a text that was considered to be a meaningful whole. In their various reconstructions of the textual history, most scholars have relied on 'internal' criteria for detecting inconsistencies in the text, such as changes in terminology, contradictory doctrines or the inconsistent use of personal pronouns. The application of these criteria was, however, often determined by some general assumptions about the history of ideas (such as whether theistic doctrines belong to the older or more recent layers). Other scholars used formal criteria such as repetitions or statistics. Discussions centred around the following layers (as mentioned above, in each layer others could be traced): (1) an 'epic layer' that originally ended with *MBh* 6.23.38 (= *BhG* 2.38) and was later expanded; (2) a 'theistic' layer promoting Kṛṣṇaite doctrines (Holtzmann, Jacobi, Schrader, Oldenberg, Charpentier, Hauer); and (3) a 'non-theistic' layer, which was given different names such as 'monistic', 'pantheistic', or Sāṃkhya-yoga. While those who accept the 'epic layer' agree that it is the oldest, scholars are not unanimous with regard to the text-historical relationship between the other two. While some regard the 'theistic layer' as older (e.g. von Garbe, Otto, Ježic), others give priority to the non-theistic doctrines based on Upaniṣadic and Sāṃkhya notions (e.g. Holtzmann, Jacobi, Khair). While I will follow this latter view in my analysis of the text and argue that the theistic framework is in many respects based on concepts explained in the non-theistic sections, this heuristic assumption and the acceptance of a text-historical perspective are not unconditional in the sense of excluding a synchronic perspective. This approach will be clarified with reference to some general considerations with regard to the place of a 'didactic' text like the *BhG* within the *MBh* epic.

As has been seen, text-historical reconstructions are often intimately connected with the question of whether the *BhG* was originally an independent text or composed in the context of the epic tradition. The answer to this question depends on the different views of the nature of the epic literature in general and the *MBh* in particular. For some scholars, the epic belongs to the 'heroic age' and can be compared to Indo-European epics, which are primarily intended to tell a 'heroic tale', not to offer didactic instructions or theological insights. The tale served to praise the values of heroism and manliness that were ingrained in a hero's social identity: by fighting for his cause, the hero would increase his fame and the prosperity of his clan. Firmly rooted in the belief of the meaningfulness of his endeavour, a hero would confidently take his weapons and meet his enemy in battle. The extant *MBh*, however, presents a more ambiguous picture with a mixed set of heroes. While some are depicted as being eager to fight, others are shown as reflecting on the implications of war, and sometimes even questioning their social obligations. We hear of warriors who are depressed when they have to fight and of heroes who are criticised as warmongers. In addition, the epic relates the efforts that are made to prevent a violent conflict, as ambassadors are sent not just to declare war, but also to negotiate peace. Some modern interpreters of the *MBh* feel that these ambiguities testify to ideologies of a later age that were inserted into the older text: the conflict of values is said to reflect the impact of changing cultural-historical contexts on the textual history of the epic. In consequence, for most scholars, the original epic, the Ur-text, was mostly an example of epic lore narrating a sequence of actions, while the 'didactic' passages were often treated as later additions.[17]

By taking the 'hero in crisis' as a point of departure for a religious-philosophical discourse, for many scholars the *BhG* belonged to the later age of reflection and didactics, or even to a period when the epic's final redactors included important contemporary texts in order to realise the claim that the *MBh* covers whatever there is to be known. Thus, for example, according to Hopkins and Roy, the *BhG* was originally an Upaniṣad, and had nothing to do with the epic. This is based on assumptions about the epic as a distinct literary genre that are not made explicit, nor is their applicability to the *MBh* examined. However, recent studies of the literary devices used in the epics have opened up new approaches, which deal with the epic's composition as a more complex and opaque process that is sometimes difficult to disentangle into clearly defined layers.[18] A increased awareness of the differences between oral transmission and scriptural codification has influenced text-historical studies and questioned the point of searching for an 'Ur-text' at all beyond the manuscripts, at least when this means searching for a narrative or compositional 'logic' in a literary tradition that followed other parameters.

This situation, and the transformation brought about by turning the bardic tradition into scripture, have perhaps never been better described than by Nietzsche. In his comments on the debate on the textual history of Homer's *Iliad*, he points out that what the 'original' scholars looked for was not thought of in terms of presenting a 'whole' because the context-bound

17 See Hopkins 1901, who distinguishes between 'epic' and 'pseudo-epic', which consists mainly of book 12, the *ŚāntiP*. In contrast, Dahlmann (1895) and Pisani (1939) argue that the didactic sections are intrinsically connected with the epic plot. For a fresh approach see Fitzgerald 2004, 2006.

18 See, for instance, Minkowski 1989, Pollock 1984, Mangels 1994, Malinar 2005a.

performative structure of oral epic composition and recitation focussed on particular episodes or themes:

> The blueprint of an epic such as the Iliad is not a whole, nor an organism, but a stringing together (*Auffädelung*), a product of a reflection that follows aesthetic criteria . . . The Iliad is not a wreath [garland], but a bouquet of flowers. As many pictures as possible are put into the frame, but their arranger was not concerned whether the grouping of the assembled picture was always pleasant and rhythmically beautiful. He indeed knew that the whole is not relevant for anyone, but only the particular . . . Thus, those who search for the 'original and perfect blueprint' tilt at windmills because the dangerous course of oral tradition had just been completed when methodicalness was added; the distortions that this course brought about could not possibly have affected a blueprint that was not included in the material that was handed down.[19]

When it comes to studying the textual history of the *BhG*, this means not only thinking about the evolution and development of texts and ideas, but also allowing for the co-existence of different types of texts, themes, stories and doctrines included in an epic plot as being differently arranged, 'strung together' and used in different bardic traditions. While the production of a written form certainly changed the way the material was arranged, it did not result in any textual canonisation or purification resulting in unification or coherence of the text in terms of (linear) plotting, a reduction of 'digressions' or 'un-epic' didactics, a streamlining of religious and philosophical doctrines, a wiping out of the character's ambivalence and ambiguities or, to turn to the *BhG*, a coherent presentation of Kṛṣṇa as either god or hero. Yet this does not cease to trace the history and contexts of the composition, but allowing for co-operation between the two perspectives. In the case of the *BhG* in terms of the present study, this means analysing the extant text on its own terms and coping with the co-existence of different doctrines and modes of speaking in tracing the threads that hold them together. Yet in the text itself this co-existence is turned into a development when it is declared that the revelation of Kṛṣṇa as the 'highest god' is something never seen before. While the transformation of Arjuna's comrade and epic hero Kṛṣṇa into a god could be regarded as showing just another aspect of an already multi-form epic or even its Indo-European character (as has been suggested from a structural perspective), it can equally be argued that the text expresses and theologically explains a process of the deification of the hero Kṛṣṇa, which can be traced in other sources too. The acceptance of this new theology can be observed in different 'theistic' interludes

[19] Nietzsche 1980: V: 171; my trans.

or revelations elsewhere in the epic. However, so far no straightforward redaction of the epic along these lines has been attempted: the epic has not been turned into a Vaiṣṇava or Kṛṣṇaitic text, as is the case with the Purāṇas. This points to the diversity and plurality of views, as well as of the 'highest gods', at the time of the final redaction. Yet not even in the final redaction has such a unification along the lines of a *bhakti* theology been undertaken. The doctrine of 'disinterested action' can be presented without reference to Kṛṣṇa, as it can be used with reference to the god. This situation can be considered in two ways: while it can be regarded as a contradiction that may have to be dissolved by assuming there has been a historical development, it can also be seen as mirroring the referential framework of meaning of the final redactors, who obviously expected the juxtaposition and co-existence of these different historical levels to be accepted by their audience. The present study will therefore suggest that this 'simultaneity of the non-simultaneous' be examined against the background of a historical development of the text. While agreeing with most scholars that the *BhG* was not an integral part of the oldest version of the epic, I nonetheless argue that it was not composed independently of the epic tradition, but in relation to and even for the epic. The *BhG* became part of the epic in the course of its own textual history.

Turning now to the other side of the coin, we have seen that the different interpretations of the *BhG* as a unity in itself are also based on certain hermeneutic perspectives. Generally we can distinguish between the following interpretations: (1) the *BhG* is the 'bible' of the Bhāgavata religion and was inserted into the epic to promote Kṛṣṇaism (R. G. Bhandarkar, Dandekar, Hill, Lamotte, Charpentier, Senart, Marcovich); (2) the *BhG* is a philosophical text aimed at producing a synthesis of different schools (Kosambi, Dandekar, Hill, Lamotte, Marcovich); (3) the unity of the *BhG* lies in its mystical and therefore irrational character (Edgerton, Otto, Hauer, Zaehner); (4) the *BhG* expresses the ideology and interests of the ruling classes (Kosambi, Ruben, Thakur); (5) the *BhG* is a genuine part of the epic and cannot be fully understood without considering its epic context, since it offers solutions to important issues brought up the epic narrative (Biardeau, van Buitenen) or provides an apologetic justification for the moral tricks used by the Pāṇḍavas and Kṛṣṇa to win victory (Holtzmann, Lévi, von Simson).

The present analysis of the *BhG* attempts to place the text in the epic context and thus takes up some of Biardeau's and van Buitenen's general views, which have not been substantiated by a thorough analysis of the whole text. The following analysis will show that the *BhG* is embedded in the epic by: (1) presenting a mediation of the conflicting values of liberation and social duty; (2) balancing the contradictory claims of different levels of *dharma*; (3) introducing a monotheistic framework, which provides a theological explanation for divine revelation and the worship of a 'highest god', and also serves to re-map existing power relations between gods, kings, successful *yogins*, powerful ascetics and priestly power connected to ritual; and (4) addressing the issue of legitimate kingship by subordinating the king to the 'highest god', who regards himself as responsible for the welfare of all beings. As pointed out before, in dealing with the structure and development of these doctrines and arguments, I shall not neglect the text-critical perspective but will point out the tensions and contradictions implied in the text, and I propose to regard the introduction of the theology of Kṛṣṇa in chapters 7–11 as later than the doctrine of 'disinterested action' presented in the earlier chapters. The text-critical, historical perspective is not regarded as an alternative to a 'holistic' view of the extant text, but as a helpful complement, provided it is allowed not only that individual layers make sense, but also that they co-exist in the final redaction. Conversely, the holistic approach will be exposed to history and to diverse traditions and groups, and the theological message that is so prominent in the text is seen as participation in a manifold and multi-layered epic tradition. Therefore, the present study of the *BhG* does not begin with the *BhG* itself, but with an analysis of some of the debates on war and peace in the *Udyogaparvan*, the fifth book of the epic, which precedes the BhīṣP into which the *BhG* was incorporated.

CHAPTER 2

Debates over war and peace in the Udyogaparvan *of the* Mahābhārata

The *BhG* is related to other parts and texts of the epic in different ways. It is connected to the religious and philosophical discourses on asceticism, *karman* and right knowledge, as well as Sāṃkhya and yoga, to teachings on fate and the ages of the world, to the appearances of other gods, the role of the hero and god Kṛṣṇa, and to discourses on *dharma* in the third and twelfth books of the epic. While parallel passages and similarities in the terminology that connect the *BhG* to the so-called didactic parts of the epic have attracted a few studies, the relationship to discourses on fate and *dharma* have been dealt with only rarely. This is also true when it comes to studying the immediate literary context of the *BhG*, the fifth book of the *MBh*, the *Udyogaparvan* (*UdP*).[1] Seen from the perspective of the debates on war and peace that pervade the *UdP*, the *BhG* can be regarded as a continuation or even commentary on some of the issues raised in this book. This connection of the *BhG* to the *UdP* may have been one reason for including the *BhG* in this part of the epic, since, for the last time, it addresses the question of why this war has to be waged. The following analysis is based on the extant, critically constituted text of the *UdP* and thus deals with those dimensions of meaning that were established by the time of the final redaction of the epic. At this stage, the text of the *UdP* testifies to a cultural-historical situation in which different notions of asceticism and heroism have already been developed. Therefore the *UdP* also includes texts in which Kṛṣṇa is presented as the highest god, one who should be approached with devotion, thus pointing to the influence of the theology of the *BhG* in some parts of the *UdP* that are then regarded as being later than the *BhG*.[2] However, these theistic interpolations did not

[1] With the exception of Deshpande (1991), who discusses some thematic parallels between the *BhG* and the *UdP*. Brockington (1998: 271, note 92) adduces a list of parallel passages between the *BhG* and the *MBh*.

[2] Such passages are, for instance 5.129; 5.65–69; see also Deshpande 1991. A reconstruction of the textual history of the *UdP* is outside the scope of this study.

result in a general revision of the *UdP* and therefore we meet with different perspectives on Kṛṣṇa as a neutral party, an ally and ambassador of the Pāṇḍavas, a teacher of fate and a god, a situation that resembles the *BhG*.

In what follows, it will be shown that Arjuna's crisis and some of the arguments put forward to call him to action are connected to the debates on war and peace in the *UdP*. These revolve around issues such as the conflict between the law of the family (*kuladharma*) and the law of the warrior (*kṣatriyadharma*); indifference (*samatva*) towards the outcome of an activity as a value and an attitude that one needs to develop; the legitimacy of territorial claims; the definition of kingship and the qualifications of a king; and the influence of human actions on a course of events that is regarded by some as caused by fate (*daivam*) or time (*kāla*). In the context of the *UdP* these are familiar sets of ideas and reflections; however, the *BhG* offers some new perspectives and thus changes the structure of the contradictions that remain unresolved in the *UdP*. The extant *UdP* suggests that this dilemma arises because Duryodhana, in contrast to other members of the family, no longer defines his role as a king and warrior in terms of the interests of the family-clan alone. When faced with a choice between his responsibility towards his family-clan and his duties as a king responsible for the territorial integrity of his kingdom, he chooses the latter. By stepping out of the framework of familial obligations, he forces the other members of the family to do the same, even those who would prefer to maintain peace. It comes as no surprise that this no-win situation is regarded by some as a matter of fate which makes the course of events irreversible and inevitable. While the refrain that runs through the *UdP* and many other passages in the epic is that one must put up with fate and surrender one's personal interests to the power of destiny, the *BhG* offers an alternative view of fate by disclosing the identity of the god who is in charge of it and propagating the view that accepting and enacting the fatal course of events is an act of devotion to this god and his cause.

This cause is a struggle against Duryodhana and his idea of a god-king who wields absolute power even over the gods. While this interpretation of kingship, which is put into Duryodhana's mouth in a speech in *MBh* 5.60, is not explicitly discussed in the *UdP*, the *BhG* provides a different definition of royal power, which explains why Duryodhana must be defeated. The *BhG* demands the king's subordination to the power of the 'highest god'. The depiction of Duryodhana in the *UdP* is one of the epic contexts of the *BhG*. The transgressive or perhaps also innovative character of both Duryodhana's position and that of the *BhG* are best understood in relation to the arguments for war or peace put forward by the members of both parties. For the sake of orientation, the conflict that triggers the diplomatic activities depicted in the *UdP* will be briefly recalled.

THE CONFLICT

The two parties that are made to collide in the *MBh* are in fact kin, as they both belong to the clan that traces its pedigree back to King Bharata. The epic tells the story of King Bharata's descendants, who are divided into two dynastic lineages. One lineage and the first party to the conflict is the Pāṇḍavas, five brothers married to one lady, Princess Draupadī. After the early loss of their father, King Paṇḍu, the brothers and their mother Kuntī take refuge in Hastināpura, the residence of their paternal uncle, the blind king Dhṛtarāṣṭra. He is the patriarch of the Kauravas, the second lineage and the other party in the developing conflict. He is also the father of Duryodhana, who is depicted as having already been the principal enemy of the Pāṇḍava brothers in their youth. The conflict between the cousins is temporarily resolved by giving Yudhiṣṭhira, the eldest Pāṇḍava, his own residence in Indraprastha and by consecrating him as a king. However, when Yudhiṣṭhira is invited by Duryodhana to a game of dice, he loses his kingdom and everything he possesses to his cousin. Thanks to the intervention of Draupadī, this complete ruin is changed by the patriarchs of the family into a temporary exile of thirteen years. After that, it is declared, the kingdom will be returned to the Pāṇḍavas. The *UdP* begins when the period of exile is over and the story can now foresee a happy end, if only Duryodhana would return the Pāṇḍavas' share of the kingdom. However, this does not happen, since Duryodhana denies their claim and wants to keep what he feels is now rightfully his. Yudhiṣṭhira does not react to this rejection immediately; although called to war by his ally Kṛṣṇa and some of his relatives, he hesitates. In order to prevent a violent confrontation, ambassadors are sent from one place to the other, different stages of diplomacy are depicted,[3] and arguments on the pros and cons of war and peace are exchanged. Finally, only one ambassador is left, Kṛṣṇa, who is sent by the Pāṇḍavas to find a compromise, but each time he returns with a negative reply. In the course of this exchange of messages, it becomes evident that diplomacy is bound to fail. Thanks to the diplomatic mission, however, it has also become clear why war has become inevitable. The *UdP* ends by depicting both parties preparing for battle.

[3] On the diplomatic techniques employed in the *UdP*, see Kalyanov 1979.

THE ARGUMENTS

What arguments are exchanged, and why can the conflict not be avoided? The structure of the debate is rather complex, since we are not dealing with a situation in which we find the aggressors on one side and the defenders on the other. Rather, each side regards the other as the aggressor. Therefore, on both sides we find supporters of both war and peace. A central point of the dispute is the question of how to define the law of heroism: what law must a warrior follow, on what authority, and how does the definition of *kṣatriyadharma* affect the position of the king, who is supposed to protect and represent it? The Sanskrit word rendered here as 'law' is *dharma*, a term that covers law, prescriptions, right moral behaviour, and normativity, as well as socio-cosmic order. The debates in the *UdP* are intriguing because the definition of 'warrior law' is discussed on two different levels which are opposed to each other. On one level, the law of heroism is defined as absolute, as a value in itself. On another level, a relative definition is suggested that allows the absolute definition of heroism to be overruled by other considerations, such as laws of kinship (*kuladharma*). There is yet another element that complicates the debates: the demand for an attitude of indifference towards one's personal gains, which is held in high esteem in ascetic as well as in heroic circles. Both heroes and ascetics should be indifferent (*sama*) towards their emotions (such as love and hatred) or the consequences of their actions (success or failure; fame or blame; life or death). Concerns about the outcome of an action should not influence judgements about its legitimacy. This claim makes indifference a rather ambiguous value, and this ambiguity worsens the dilemma dealt with in the debates. I will put this dilemma into more concrete terms and start with texts that deal with the law of the warrior (*kṣatriyadharma*) as that very social duty that each family member should accept as *svadharma*, one's personal set of rules and social obligations acquired by birth. This view is not unquestioned, as we see heroes doubting its glory and dreading the violence and death it entails. Yudhiṣṭhira, for example, proposes ascetic values as the choice of the moment and thus also thinks about appeasement and relinquishment out of adherence to family obligations, the *kuladharma* that demands that one should not kill one's relatives.

THE 'ESSENCE' OF THE HEROISM

The series of diplomatic missions begins in 5.29, when Yudhiṣṭhira sends his house-priest to Duryodhana's court to convey his claim for a share in the kingdom. In response, Duryodhana sends his ambassador with the message that he is not willing to give away anything. The ambassador reminds Yudhiṣṭhira that, as a noble-minded person, he should not engage in a violent conflict that would result in the destruction of the family. The ambassador seems to have touched a sensitive point, since Yudhiṣṭhira is shown to be quite open to this reasoning and starts to blame himself for losing his kingdom in the game of dice. Also, he questions his motives by asking whether it is just greed that is driving him into the conflict. He muses whether it would not be better to live on alms like an ascetic and peacefully accept one's fate. Although admonished by Kṛṣṇa, who regards the war against Duryodhana as a warrior's duty, Yudhiṣṭhira hesitates and shows signs of weakness when he thinks of not obeying the essential law of a warrior, which means being strong and taking one's stand at all costs. This meets criticism, perhaps most strongly, in a message that Yudhiṣṭhira's mother Kuntī conveys to her son in order to remind him of his duty as a Kṣatriya.

This duty consists first of all in standing one's ground and fighting for status. The main duty of a warrior is never to submit to anybody. A warrior must resist any impulse towards self-preservation that would make him avoid a fight. In brief, he ought to be a man (*puruṣo bhava*; cf. 5.157.6; 13; 15). Some of the most vigorous formulations of what is called the 'heart' or 'essence' of heroism (*kṣatrahṛdaya*) come from the ladies of the family. They are shown most unforgiving with regard to the humiliations they have gone through, the loss of their status and honour, not to speak of the shame of having a weak man in the house, whether husband, son, or brother. Time and again in the epic, it is not only the older men, but also the women who formulate the rules of manliness.[4] Just such a message is sent to the hesitating Yudhiṣṭhira by his mother. In accusing him of behaving like a Brahman and thus not performing his duty, she touches a sensitive point by indicating that he may become an object of ridicule and lose his social reputation.[5] She admonishes him to follow his *dharma* (cf. 5.130.6–10) and makes him listen to what is called a 'fierce speech of encouragement that incites the fighting spirit' (*uddharṣaṇaṃ bhīmaṃ tejovardhanam*; 5.134.16) that belongs to the ancient tradition (*itihāsa purātana*) and probably to the older parts of the epic (see van Buitenen 1973–78: III: introduction). This speech is delivered by Vidurā, a Kṣatriya lady and queen (*īśvarī*; 5.132.14f.),

4 For an analysis of Draupadī's criticism of her husband Yudhiṣṭhira's inactivity during the latter's time in exile, see Malinar 2007.

5 On the embarrassment caused by this accusation and the threat of being laughed at, see Tschannerl 1992. See also below, on Yudhiṣṭhira's imagining he is being laughed at.

who is depicted as a passionate champion of the warrior code. Infused with wrath (*manyuvatī*; cf. 5.131.2–3),[6] she addresses her son, who has lost a battle and is unwilling to retaliate. Enraged by her son's lamentations about the cruelties of war (which echo Yudhiṣṭhira's worries, see below), she declares (5.131.5–7, cf. 11): 'You are neither the son of your father nor are you mine. Where do you come from? Without wrath, of petty status, you are a man who is as efficient as a eunuch (*klība*)[7]. . . Get up, you weakling, you are not supposed to hang around defeated.' In her view, neither regrets nor self-pity, but only indifference towards the outcome of an action, makes the hero (5.131.15): 'The wise men do not care about winning or losing (*alabdhvā yadi vā labdhvā nānuśocanti paṇḍitāḥ*); they immediately take action and never run for their lives.' This is one of a number of passages to come in which indifference indicates not an ascetic ideal, but the stout determination to fight for one's social position. In his reply, the son wonders whether his mother does not feel pity for him and continues to question the point of winning a kingdom. Like Arjuna at the beginning of the *BhG*, the purpose and value (*artha*) of a warrior's *svadharma* is doubted. The refusal to fulfil one's duty is justified by denying its purpose.

In her reply, Vidurā points out that it is indeed a warrior's duty to regain the kingdom and restore the status of his family. If he fails to do so, he is guilty of 'theft' because he is not reciprocating the tribute he takes from his subjects. This reproach is based on the traditional notion that kings and warriors are consumers rather than producers when it comes to defining their economic position. Therefore, a king's 'income' consists of what is given to him as tribute, tax revenue, etc.; in return, he pays his people by protecting them and their economic resources from their enemies. If a king takes but does not return, he is guilty of theft (5.132.2): 'He who does not forcefully display his fighting spirit is a warrior who is clinging to his life. He is regarded as a thief (*stena*).'[8] Then Vidurā explains the 'essence of heroism' (5.132.36–38): 'I know the essence of heroism (*kṣatrahṛdaya*). It is eternal and has been handed down by the ancestors and their ancestors . . . He is born a warrior and knows the law of heroism who neither out of fear nor for his livelihood ever bows to anyone. He must stand erect. He must never submit. Manliness means steadfastness (*udyacched eva*

[6] As Malamoud (1968) has shown in his study of Vedic texts, *manyu* is regarded as an essential quality of (royal) gods like Indra or Varuṇa.

[7] A warrior who is unable or reluctant to fulfil this duty is usually accused of being a 'eunuch' (*klība*), a figure representing impotence and cowardice. At the beginning of the *BhG*, Arjuna meets the same reproach (see 6.41.37, 52, 67, 78). Cf. also 2.34.21; 2.38.24; and 5.73.17.

[8] To live from alms (*bhaikṣa*) is not desirable for a king. Also, Kṛṣṇa reminds Yudhiṣṭhira that the life of a Kṣatriya is not that of an ascetic (5.71.3). The rule he must follow is 'victory or death in battle' (5.71.4; *jayo vadho vā saṃgrame*).

na named udyamo hy eva pauruṣam)! Even if he feels like (inwardly) falling apart he should never bow to anyone here on earth.'

It demonstrates the skill of the epic poets that Duryodhana is made to express the very same attitude that Kuntī demands from her son Yudhiṣṭhira. In one of his replies (5.125) to those who ask him to settle the conflict peacefully, he refuses to take responsibility for the conflict and argues that he is just following the warrior's law when he wages war in search of victory or death: 'If we, who fulfil our duty, may in due time meet death by sword in battle, O Mādhava, (then) this will be heaven indeed . . . Who, once born in a family and following the law of the warrior, would here on earth bow down to anyone, only because he worries fearfully for his life?' Duryodhana uses the very same words that Vidurā used in her speech to her son (5.12515–19): 'He must stand erect; never must he submit. Manliness means steadfastness! Even if he feels like (inwardly) falling apart, he should never here on earth bow to anybody! – this is Mataṅga's saying.'[9] This definition of heroism does not leave much room for negotiation; it is a clear-cut rule that can be applied to any situation, because the consequences of violence and war are no criteria for its validity. Strength and manliness (*balapauruṣa*) are the values that count and have to be displayed; otherwise one runs the risk of being laughed at. This is also the gist of a message that Duryodhana sends to the Pāṇḍavas just before the war is about to break out (5.157.6–7): 'Remember the molestation of Draupadī and be a man (*puruṣo bhava*)! The purpose for which a Kṣatriya lady gives birth to a son has now been achieved. Appease your rage by displaying your strength (*bala*), bravery (*vīrya*), valour, your superb handling of weapons and your manliness (*pauruṣa*) in battle.' Duryodhana reminds the Pāṇḍavas that they should know that shameful treatment, contempt, loss of status and the molestation of their wives are situations that call for heroic action. In referring twice to Draupadī's public humiliation at the court of Dhṛtarāṣṭra, Duryodhana touches on the most painful point,[10] that the Paṇḍavas were not able to protect their wife following the dice game. In combining this reference with the demand to be a man, Duryodhana uses the code of honour and social norms against the Pāṇḍavas. According to Duryodhana, this does not allow afterthoughts or doubts; moreover, they are unnecessary, since a fighting warrior will always win. Both victory and defeat will bring a fighting hero into Indra's heaven, the warrior's paradise. Again Duryodhana (5.158.11–12) and Vidurā express the same opinion (5.133.11; cf. *BhG* 2.37):

9 Note that 5.125.19 = 5.132.38. In the *ŚāntiP* Bhīṣma gives Yudhiṣṭhira the same advice; cf. 12.131.9. A similar message is conveyed to Arjuna in *BhG* 2.31–37.

10 Cf. 5.157.6cd; 5.157.13cd; the line 'be a man' occurs a third time in 5.157.15. Draupadī, in turn, reminds her husbands of her humiliation in order to stimulate their fighting spirit. See Bailey 1983b.

'The warrior has been created for fighting (*yuddhāya kṣatriyaḥ sṛṣṭaḥ*) . . . for victory here on earth, for the cruel duty of protecting the people. Whether he win or whether he die, he will reach the heaven of Indra.' Indifference is a basic requirement of a hero, since disregard for the consequences of his actions makes the rule 'Never submit' a value in itself. This definition of heroism is, however, criticised in the extant text by other family members and by counsellors on both sides.

CRITICISM OF WARRIOR LAW

The praise of indifference as a heroic value is questioned by epic characters on both sides, for example by Yudhiṣṭhira on the side of the Pāṇḍavas, and by Dhṛtarāṣṭra on the side of the Kauravas. In contrast to his opponent Duryodhana, Yudhiṣṭhira considers heroism as just another version of the rather crude law of the strong defeating the weak (5.70.45–48, 71–73):

> Is there any beauty in war? Evil is this law of the warrior (*pāpaḥ kṣatriyadharmo*), and we all belong to the warrior class. Our law is like lawlessness; another way of life is forbidden. A warrior kills a warrior, fish lives on fish, a dog kills a dog – just see what kind of law this is! . . . First they wave their tails, then they growl and faintly bark, next they run around each other, baring their teeth and then barking loudly; after that they start fighting. He is strong and the winner who in the end devours the flesh. It is the same with men: there is not the slightest difference. It is well known how the strong treat the weak: with contempt and violence. Whoever submits is weak.

It comes as no surprise to find that Yudhiṣṭhira's naturalistic comparison of warriors with dogs results in a realisation of his own situation of weakness. Although there is nothing attractive in war, he cannot draw the conclusions of his own analysis and give up his claim to the kingdom. At the end of his speech, he imagines that this relinquishment will not be understood by his opponents. They will not regard it as an act of respect towards his paternal uncle or as a gesture of forgiving or nobility, but only as a sign of weakness. Stepping back would bring Yudhiṣṭhira into the situation he seems to fear most, that of being laughed at (5.70.75). As a result, his reflection about the nature of war results in a dilemma. Although war is not desirable and being a warrior is nothing to be too proud of, yet it is extremely risky to refrain from it. Searching for peace and reconciliation will be taken as a sign of weakness that will invite one's opponents to indulge even more in disrespect and violence. A solution to this aporetic situation seems difficult, if not impossible.

Apart from these considerations, Yudhiṣṭhira also thinks about the aftermath of war: 'War always has a miserable end. Is he who has killed in the end not also killed? To those who are killed, victory or defeat is just the same' (*sarvathā vṛjinaṃ yuddhaṃ ko ghnan na pratihanyate / hatasya ca hṛṣīkeśa samau jayaparājayau*; 5.70.53). Here, the logic of indifference is inverted: in the face of death, neither victory nor defeat matters. However, according to the heroic logic, it is because of the prospect of victory that life and death become the same. Nonetheless, Yudhiṣṭhira wonders, will war ever result in peace? Killing will never be perfect, because there are always those who have survived defeat and think of retaliation: 'Victory produces enmity. Grievingly the defeated goes to rest. The peaceful man sleeps happily as he has given up both victory and defeat' (*jayo vairaṃ prasṛjati duḥkham āste parājitaḥ / sukhaṃ praśāntaḥ svapiti hitvā jayaparājayau;* 5.70.59).

How can peace be brought about? Yudhiṣṭhira considers two possibilities. First, peace is achieved when one side has been totally exterminated and none of one's enemies survives; this is called *mūlaghāta* (5.70.76), 'extinction down to the root' or 'extinction of the root'. This method of 'peace-keeping' is, however, dismissed as too cruel and not practicable. A second possibility is to stop thinking and acting in categories of 'strength' (*bala*) and 'manliness' (*pauruṣeya*; 5.70.65). This implies allowing the law of heroism to be overruled by other values, although this may result in subjugation (*praṇipāta*; 5.70.68), social disrespect or even poverty. This alternative matches the ascetic morality taught in many passages of the epic, in which property, power and social status are regarded as obstacles, not means, to happiness. According to this view, real strength and final peace result from renunciation, which implies enduring disrespect and violence, at least to a certain degree. In order to be successful on this path of renunciation, one should develop an attitude of indifference towards success and failure, happiness and suffering, social status and social disgrace – in brief, towards social life as such. As pointed out above, a hero should also be indifferent towards his personal happiness and concentrate on his duty. However, heroic indifference is an attitude that belongs to the arena of social relationships, whereas ascetic indifference means leaving this arena for good. Thus, asceticism resolves the conflict not in terms of the conflict itself, but by refusing to deal with it at all – one should simply not fight. Obviously this alternative was not chosen, although it is repeatedly considered and proposed in the epic. Asceticism is regarded as an alternative to violence, but not as its solution, because it has nothing to do with social life and therefore is not practicable for those who want to come to terms with it. Ascetics are of no use in this conflict, because ideally they have taken a one-way ticket and will never enter the social arena again. While an ascetic attitude may provide peace for the individual, it may not do so for the society that he has left behind. However, though the applicability of ascetic values to social contexts is restricted, they still had some influence in shaping the image of the ideal king as, for example, a man who has self-control and has 'conquered' himself before he conquers others (see below). In this connection, the *BhG* can be regarded as a final discourse on the necessity of war just at the moment it is about to begin, in that it delineates a concept of a king who should act like a devoted ascetic. In the *UdP*, however, no such mediation of values is offered, which is why appeals to asceticism seem unconvincing.[11] Having thus shown that a discourse on indifference is well established in the *UdP*, I shall deal with the other argument put forward by the 'peace party': the respect for kinship. The 'law of kinship' (*kuladharma*) is advocated on both sides, stressing that the killing of relatives is prohibited. Like ascetic values, the kinship law could theoretically serve to overrule the absolute definition of *kṣatriyadharma*, as Arjuna does at the beginning of the *BhG*.

FAMILY LAW AS AN ARGUMENT FOR PEACE

Most of the characters in the epic view themselves and their lives in the context of patrilineal kinship. However, this context not only defines their status and their duties within the clan, but is also connected to the law of the warrior. As we have seen, ideally, the duties of a warrior should not be in conflict with family law; yet it is precisely such a conflict that is at the centre of the *MBh*. In fulfilling his social duty, a warrior usually serves his family too. This also applies the other way round in that the fulfilment of one's duty serves one's kin, the *kula*, as well. The pragmatic and paradigmatic harmony between *kuladharma* and *kṣatriyadharma* is disturbed in the epic. Waging war against other family members is regarded by some epic characters as a breach of family law that burdens them with guilt and evil consequences (*pāpa*) that do not seem to be automatically wiped out by their adherence to *kṣatriyadharma*. For most characters, violent action, heroism and war make sense only when they enhance the family's fame, prosperity and status. This seems impossible in the given situation because it requires one to fight against one's relatives. Therefore, those who argue for peace claim that family law should be respected, since a war between

[11] Even with the *BhG*, such mediation was considered dubious; cf. the dialogue between the female mendicant and King Janaka in *MBh* 12.308 (see Fitzgerald 2002).

relatives will ruin them all. A battle that results in the destruction of the family makes no sense. Thus, for example, Saṃjaya, Duryodhana's ambassador, reminds Yudhiṣṭhira of the consequences of killing relatives (5.25.7–9; cf. *BhG* 1.34–45): 'Those are righteous who fulfil their duties towards their relatives. Your sons, friends and kin shall regrettably sacrifice their lives (and) thereby assure the existence of the Kurus. When you have punished the Kurus and have subjected and humiliated all your enemies, your life may be like death. After killing your relatives you will not live well.' Also, Yudhiṣṭhira states (5.70.45) that he has to fight against 'relatives, friends and teachers. Killing them is extremely sinful' (*jñātayaś ca hi bhūyiṣṭhāḥ sahāyā guravaś ca naḥ / teṣāṃ vadho 'tipāpīyān*). Yudhiṣṭhira at one point seems ready to draw the consequences and think of subjugation for the sake of peace (*śānti*; 5.70.68). This argument, however, loses weight not only when the consequences of subordination are imagined (one is laughed at; 5.70.75), but also because some family members simply do not obey it, as is the case with Duryodhana. Therefore, the analysis will now switch over to the other side of the conflict, to Duryodhana, who stands for this breach of this rule. A different and, historically speaking, probably new understanding of the conflict is articulated in the figure of Duryodhana.

DURYODHANA

In contrast to other members of the family, Duryodhana is not motivated by his being the perfect son and thinking about his family. Rather, he is driven by some other dynamic for which different explanations are offered in the course of the epic. None of them, however, succeeds in stopping him, and therefore the others are dragged into war too. As a consequence, he is depicted as uncompromising, self-confident, and determined not to show any weakness by submitting to his cousins' claims. He is shown to bask in his successful revenge for the humiliation he has previously experienced from the Pāṇḍavas, for instance during his visit of the *sabhā* of Yudhiṣṭhira (cf. *MBh* 2.43). This attitude provokes opposition from those around him, especially from his father Dhṛtarāṣṭra. Duryodhana is heavily criticised for ignoring family relations and is accused of being the 'killer of the family' (*kulaghna*) out of selfishness and greed. Others, especially his mother Gāndhārī, accuse him of lacking the one quality that would make him a righteous king, that is, the capacity to control himself and his greed for power. She appears in the *UdP* as a *dharmadarśinī*, the teacher of a (royal) *dharma* that includes certain ascetic qualities resulting from the 'conquest of the senses' (*indriyajaya*). Gāndhārī (5.127.21–29) declares that a king must first of all be able to control himself before he can claim to control others. He must conquer himself like a country:

> A kingdom, you intelligent man, cannot be obtained, protected, nor enjoyed as the whim takes you, bull of the Bhāratas. For one who is not in control of his senses does not keep his kingdom for long. By controlling his senses, the wise man guards his kingdom (*vijitātmā tu medhāvī sa rājyam abhipālayet*). Greed and anger drag a man away from his profits; by defeating these two enemies, a king masters the earth . . . However, he who at first masters himself as if he were a country shall not strive to master his counsellors and enemies in vain. Fortune smiles on him who rules himself.[12]

These statements correspond to similar views voiced in the *BhG* and elsewhere in the epic, often in connection with yoga and Sāṃkhya teachings. In the passage quoted above, self-control is intrinsically connected with a king's capacity to rule permanently over his kingdom. This connection is also established in a passage in the *Arthaśāstra* (*ArthaŚ*), in which the 'conquest of the senses' (*indriyajaya*) is regarded as one of the qualifications a king has to acquire and maintain through continuous practice.[13] This aspect connects the power of the king with ascetic values and the powers of yoga; it is prominent in the *BhG* too.

By contrast with Duryodhana's self-portrayal, his intransigence towards his cousins is generally regarded not as a sign of his fulfilling his duty as a king, but as a sign of sheer greed. For instance, when Kṛṣṇa tries to call Yudhiṣṭhira to action, he points out that Duryodhana is driven by greed (5.29.27–28): 'When an evil man desires another's land and gathers troops because he does not respect the law, then there will be war between kings. For this reason, armour, sword and arrow were created . . . He who thinks in his greed that law is what he desires, is in the grip of wrath' (*yo 'yaṃ lobhān manyate dharmaṃ etaṃ yam icchate manyuvaśānugāmī*; 5.29.28ef). Therefore, negotiations are bound to fail and Duryodhana must be removed from power. For some, Duryodhana is even guilty of theft, since he has taken property that does not really belong to him. In addition, his indifference towards the possible destruction of his family is criticised. These traits make him the perfect villain, the dark force that causes ruin. Accordingly, in some passages of the epic he is declared to be the incarnation of the demon Kali. In the *ArthaŚ* too, he is cited as an example of a bad or even evil king (cf. 1.6.8).

[12] Cf. 5.34.55–56. *Kāma* and *krodha* are both regarded as enemies (*paripanthin*) in *BhG* 3.37 too.
[13] Cf. *ArthaŚ* 1.6.; in 1.6.8 Duryodhana is listed as one of the 'evil kings'.

However, the epic's redactors do not just play off the 'good guys' against the bad ones; rather, on each side one finds dark stains and ambiguities,[14] although, in the end, the Pāṇḍavas and especially Yudhiṣṭhira shine more brightly. This ambiguity contributes to the narrative depth of the epic, which does not emerge as a byproduct of the contradictions that result from the many additions in the course of the epic's textual history just by coincidence. Rather, different perspectives, voices and even epic traditions seem to have co-existed. The many different versions of the epic, including those in which the Kauravas, especially Duryodhana and Karṇa, are made heroes, as well as its dramatic adaptations, testify to the complexity of both the plot and its characters. Thus, in the extant *UdP* too, the epic narrators make Duryodhana a figure not only to condemn or to make fun of, but also to reflect upon. This is the case when a speech (5.60) is put into his mouth that gives reasons for his disregard of the ancient law of the family. The speech is one of the many conversations between Duryodhana and his father Dhṛtarāṣṭra in the *UdP*. Once again the blind king had tried to prevent his son from waging war against his cousins (5.56–59). Dhṛtarāṣṭra had argued that the Pāṇḍavas are invincible because the gods are on their side and therefore Duryodhana's position is weak (cf. 5.59.8ff.). In his reply, a furious Duryodhana rejects this view and the theory of 'divine support' by pointing to its logical flaws, also giving us his ideas about kingship. However, first of all he rejects the alleged superiority of the gods by considering the sources of divine power and status (*devatvam*). The following two interpretations of divinity are rejected: (1) gods are gods because they represent the values of renunciation and are detached from human emotions; (2) divinity is connected to the power of sacrifice. The first view is rejected by pointing out that ascetic-like gods cannot become a third party in a human conflict because their power is based on their detachment from all social obligations and personal inclinations; they have this power as long as they do not use it for worldly purposes. On the other hand, the power of the gods is restricted by their ritual dependence because they can be called to the sacrifice of any patron or priest who knows the right invocations. This reasoning ends with Duryodhana's self-proclamation as the overlord of all beings, who is capable of dealing with matters human as well as divine. At this point his speech turns into a praise of his own mightiness (*māhātmya*; 5.60.23).

Duryodhana's argument starts by reflecting on ascetic qualities as a source of divinity (5.60.2–8):

14 This holds especially true for the trickery and disregard for the codex of fighting that Kṛṣṇa and the Pāṇḍavas display in the course of the epic. For other views on Duryodhana and the Kauravas, see, for instance, Holtzmann 1892–5: II, von Simson 1984 and Gitomer 1992.

Lose your fear, best of kings, when you think that the sons of Pṛthā were invincible because the gods are their friends! "The gods obtain their status as gods because they are not subject to love and hatred, malice and greed, and due to their indifference towards living creatures" (*akāmadveṣasaṃyogād drohāl lobhāc ca bhārata / upekṣayā ca bhāvānāṃ devā devatvam āpnuvan*) – this is what Dvaipāyana Vyāsa and Nārada once told us, as well as Rāma Jāmadagnya. Gods never act like men, out of love, greed, compassion or hatred, Bull of Bhāratas. So if Agni, Vāyu, Dharma, Indra or the two Aśvins were to act according to their sympathies, the sons of Pṛthā should not come to grief. Therefore, never ever must you harbour this worry, since they always have an eye for divine affairs only.

Here Duryodhana puts forward a concept of divine power based on ascetic values. According to this notion, gods are gods because they are perfect ascetics since they are not subject to all the emotions characteristic of human beings. Gods are gods because they are not involved in worldly affairs. Since they are indifferent towards living beings, they cannot take sides. If they were to become a third party in the present conflict, they would be just as weak as men. For Duryodhana the suffering of the Pāṇḍavas proves that the gods do not interfere. Were interference a sign of the gods' power, the fate of the Pāṇḍavas would certainly be a chance to make this known. Involvement, taking sides, is part of social life, but not a proof of divinity (*devaprāmāṇya*). Detachment and partiality in a violent conflict do not go together. In the very moment when ascetic gods interfere, they lose their special position of divine power and become useless for the Pāṇḍavas. Given this sophisticated reasoning, Duryodhana rules out the possibility that ascetic gods and the values they represent could serve as a model for judging social actions. On still another level, we are confronted with the paradox of ascetic values, and especially of indifference. Once one has realised ascetic ideals, it is not possible to return to the world without losing one's achievements.

Duryodhana then turns to another argument and considers the case that the gods' involvement proves their divinity. In this case their power is limited, because it is based on ritual exchange and interdependence:

Even if the proof of being a god were in the case of gods to be established on the basis of their sympathies or by criteria of hatred, greed, or love, this will not prevail (*atha cet kāmasaṃyogād dveṣāl lobhāc ca lakṣyate / deveṣu devaprāmāṇyaṃ naiva tad vikramiṣyati*). Even if Agni Jātavedas were to have enclosed the worlds from all sides, wishing to burn them down, he will have to sing hymns of praise when he has been invoked by me (through ritual formulas; *mayābhimantritaḥ*).

Here Duryodhana uses the well-known characteristic of Vedic gods, that they are related to men through the ritual transactions of the Vedic fire sacrifice in a relationship of mutual dependence (*paraspara*). Men are generally dependent on the gods, who guarantee their subsistence by maintaining the socio-cosmic order. However, in order to fulfil this task, the gods expend their energy and therefore need food in the form of sacrificial offerings. Thus, when men call gods to their sacrificial fire through ritual invocations, the gods are not just accepting an invitation, they are also attending for their own sakes. In addition, they are bound to the correctness and truth of the ritual language: when invoked correctly, they respond. According to Duryodhana, this dependence makes it highly improbable that the gods can ever become the permanent allies of the Pāṇḍavas. Since the gods cannot reject Duryodhana's sacrifice for moral reasons, they have to respond to his ritual invocations too. Agni in particular, the god of the sacrificial fire, cannot help transporting the sacrificial offering to its addressee. It is the correctness of the invocation that matters, not the respectability of the invoking priest or sacrificer. In consequence, Duryodhana declares that, even if one of these gods would like to take sides with the Pāṇḍavas, he would bind them to his sacrifice by ritual invocations (*abhimantraṇa*) and make them his servants. It seems that Duryodhana's reasoning mirrors a cultural milieu in which participation in ritual exchange implies the subjection of the gods to the patron's goals and priestly invocations. Ritual is primarily considered to be an instrument for achieving the goals of patrons and priests.

The comparison of the conflict with a sacrifice, in which Duryodhana acts as the patron-priest, is presented in greater detail in another speech (5.57), which starts with another assertion of his entitlement to the whole kingdom: 'The whole earth has been created for me' (*sarvā ca pṛthivī sṛṣṭā madarthe*; 5.56.39). In reply to his father's suggestion that he could happily live on his share of the kingdom and thereby prevent war, Duryodhana answers that he and Karṇa are already consecrated for the 'sacrifice of battle' (*raṇayajña*[15]):

> Karṇa and I, O father, have laid out the sacrifice of battle, and here we stand consecrated with Yudhiṣṭhira as the victim (*paśuṃ kṛtvā*), Bull of Bhāratas. The chariot is the altar, the sword the sacrificial spoon, the club the ladle, the armour the sacrificial assembly, the four horses are the four priests, the arrows the *darbha* grass, fame the oblation. Having offered up ourselves to Manu Vaivastava in this battle, O king, we will win and return, covered with glory, the enemies slain. (5.57.12–18)

His intention is to perform a sacrifice in which he functions as the patron and the priest, and at the same time offers himself up as a potential victim as his *tyāga*, that is, what he is willing to give up as an offering. The sacrifice

[15] This interpretation of the battle as a sacrifice is repeated by Karṇa in a conversation with Kṛṣṇa (5.138). Cf. also *MBh* 6.16.36–38 and the interpretation of duty as sacrifice in *BhG* 3 (see below).

is addressed to Manu Vaivasvata, the protector of creation and *dharma*. However, the actual sacrificial activity of offering, the killing of the victim, takes place in the battle, thus leaving it an open question who in the end will be the victim.[16] The survivor is the winner in that he reaps the fruits of sacrifice by making his opponent the sacrificial victim. He does not offer anything but himself, that is, his readiness to become the victim himself. This willingness for 'self-sacrifice' stands in contrast to the interpretation of social duty for the sake of sacrifice and the ritualisation of all activity as an act of devotion to the highest god in the *BhG*. Although expressed in the idiom of ritual, it is not the actual performance but the attitude of detachment towards its fruits that is emphasised in the Gītā. This prevents the sacrifice from becoming a means to the ends of the sacrifice's patron as is the case with Duryodhana. His willingness to give up his life is based on his attachment to the fruits – he desires sovereignty. The instrumentalisation of sacrifice is even more explicit in Duryodhana's analysis of the ritual dependence of the gods quoted earlier, and it is not by chance that this use of ritual power is criticised in the *BhG* (cf. 2.42–44; 16.12–17).[17]

Taking Duryodhana's arguments together, the conclusion is that those who are usually deemed powerful 'gods', be they the gods of ritual or ascetic-like gods, are in fact rather powerless. What does he propose instead? Duryodhana declares that, as the king, he is supreme because he is neither dependent on sacrificial food nor indifferent towards his kingdom. As a true hero, he is indifferent only towards his life, which he is ready to sacrifice. In this way, Duryodhana is made to present a particular blend of ascetic and ritual aspects of divinity. He is presented as a god-king whose duty is to defend the territory and to conquer and protect the earth. For this purpose he is ready to use all his ritualistic skill and energy, his *tejas*, his 'fiery might' (van Buitenen). He declares himself to be the overlord of the gods:

> Supreme indeed is the fiery might the celestials possess, but my own surpasses that of the gods, know it, Bhārata. I will steady the earth, when it cleaves asunder, and the peaks of [its] mountains with my ritual invocations while the world is watching . . . I am the one and only promoter of gods, demons and living creatures . . . All my subjects are most law-abiding and there is nothing that plagues them. (5.60.10–17)

[16] Heesterman (1985) assumes an intimate connection between war and the original Vedic sacrifice, and the depiction of the 'sacrifice of battle' resembles Heesterman's scenario in some respects. However, according to Biardeau and Malamoud (1976), this parallelism between battle and sacrifice serves to legitimate the violent duty of a warrior in a way that resembles the legitimacy of violence in a sacrificial context – that is, ritual violence is to be regarded as non-violence. See also Biardeau 1997: 83. For later views in the *Dharmaśāstras* that the king is to be regarded as pure, although his role is rather an impure one, see von Stietencron 1998.

[17] For a detailed analysis of the epic contexts of Duryodhana's speech, see Malinar forthcoming.

In declaring himself the superior power,[18] it is obvious that Duryodhana's authority and responsibility are based only on himself, proof of the righteousness of his rule lying in success and the prosperity of his kingdom. He regards himself as being in the position of a god-king who does not reckon with anyone above or beyond him. On this basis, he declares that he cannot be defeated and again points out that the Pāṇḍavas would not have suffered if the gods had been able to prevent it (5.60.18–19). Drawing on his reputation as a 'speaker of truth' (*satyavāg*), he promises his father that there is no rescue for those he hates:

Neither gods nor *gāndharvas*, neither demons nor *rākṣasas* are able to save the ones I hate – this is the truth I am telling you . . . So, when I say, "This will happen", it has never turned out to be otherwise. Therefore I am known as the "speaker of truth". This greatness of mine (*māhātmya*), witnessed by the world, heard of in every quarter, I declare to you to cheer you up, not in order to boast, king; since I have never praised myself before, to praise oneself is the act of the mean . . . In me are superior insight, the greatest splendour, the greatest prowess, superior knowledge, superior yoga. I surpass them [the Pāṇḍavas and their allies] all (*parā buddhiḥ paraṃ tejo vīryaṃ ca paramaṃ mayi / parā vidyā paro yogo mama tebhyo viśiṣyate*). (5.60.20–7)

In this speech, Duryodhana's reluctance to give up parts of his kingdom in the name of family bonds has been given a reason. He has left the discourse of family law and has instead depicted himself as the overlord of all beings, expanding the power of a king by appropriating ritual and ascetic powers. He justifies his intransigence by drawing on his specific understanding of a kingship focussed on the persona of the king and the power of his truth-speech. For Duryodhana, defending the territorial integrity of his kingdom and keeping his riches at all costs are part of his duties as a god-king – there is nothing to negotiate over. The epic will narrate his defeat, in which regard the *BhG* functions as a text that proves his logic wrong. A sign of the presence of a 'higher power', which is fully revealed in the *BhG*, is already inserted in the final part of the *UdP*, when Kṛṣṇa shows himself as a powerful, divine being. Duryodhana's claim to overlordship in the *UdP* is not denied by rejecting his arguments; instead, either he is morally discredited, or else the superiority, both physical (*bala*) and moral (*dharma*), of the Pāṇḍavas and Kṛṣṇa is pointed out. Two reasons are given for their superiority: (1) it is assumed that they have a god-like status and

[18] Consequently, the colophons call this speech Duryodhana's *māhātmya*. A *māhātmya* displays certain characteristics of 'self-praise' and boasting that may serve to read Duryodhana's claims as signs of vanity. Boasting is normally rejected for a warrior since it is inappropriate for a 'noble' (*ārya*; cf. 7.166.34; *āryeṇa tu na vaktavyā kadācit stutir ātmanaḥ*).

have the other gods as their allies; (2) Kṛṣṇa is depicted as the higher power. As already indicated, the few texts that present Kṛṣṇa in this way most probably mirror the monotheistic doctrines of the *BhG*. Like the extant *BhG*, the extant *UdP* depicts Kṛṣṇa as both the epic hero and the highest god. In this way, Duryodhana and Kṛṣṇa are juxtaposed by pointing to the latter's hidden identity as the highest god (cf. 5.65–67, 83; see Malinar 1996: 87–93) and even by revealing it near the end of the *UdP* (5.129). These encounters, however, do not change the situation, since Duryodhana does not care for any higher power and insists on performing his duty as a warrior and king. The Pāṇḍavas, in their turn, end up doing the same for similar reasons, though claiming that they only want to retrieve their share of the kingdom. The inevitability implied in the conflict is regarded by some epic characters as indicative of the workings of fate or destiny (*daiva*) and time (*kāla*). This discourse on fate and the deadly power of time has also entered the *BhG* in its depiction of Kṛṣṇa as the time in *BhG* 11.

SUMMARY

As has been demonstrated, the referential framework for the arguments that are exchanged in the *UdP* is the definition of the law of the warrior. This law calls on one to fight one's cause at all costs. Indifference to the consequences is demanded. However, this position is questioned by the 'peace party', who point out the consequences of war. It is argued that the mere fact that one is able to stick to one's position does not prove its validity. Moreover, once there is war, peace is hard to win because those who survive but are defeated will not find peace. Added to these principal considerations are reflections that draw on other values. One of these values is asceticism, which calls for renouncing the motives and emotions that nourish the conflict. Asceticism implies that one always keeps the desirable attitude of indifference. The other value that is put forward in favour of a peaceful solution is the law of family and kinship, which demands that family members and elders must not be killed. Therefore, peace should be kept for the sake of the family. However, Duryodhana is depicted as the one who has left this level of discourse because he defines himself as a god-king who is responsible for his kingdom above all, not his family. Seen from this perspective, the epic also deals with the historical transition from a clan-based definition of kingship to a concept of kingship based on territorial rights.[19] Here, one is confronted with a conflict that arises

[19] As has been argued, for instance, by Thapar (1977–78, 1979).

because Duryodhana disregards ancient laws and traditions and proposes a different and probably new notion of power. Therefore, the conflict cannot be solved in the traditional, well-established ways. In this situation, new concepts and institutions of power are sought and developed, and the implications of a definition of kingship as an absolute power are already critically reflected upon. Historically speaking, such a self-perception of kings is represented by the Nanda dynasty (fourth century BCE), which is recorded as the first to centralise power and establish themselves as overlords (*samrāṭ*). In later accounts of dynasties they were depicted as cruel rulers who abused their power. A rejection of such a definition of royal power is offered with the *BhG*'s concept of divinity, which can serve to prevent a king from claiming for himself a god-like status. This concept supersedes Arjuna's idea of loyalty to his family (*kuladharma*), as well as Duryodhana's concept of overlordship. In the *BhG*, another concept is developed that makes the king again dependent on a divine realm, or, to be more precise, on the one and only god he ought to serve. Seen from the perspective of the *UdP*, the *BhG* can be interpreted as a reply to the concept of kingship that the authors of the epic make Duryodhana represent. The *BhG* provides arguments for rejecting Duryodhana's concept, but not for securing peace. Rather, it is a call to expel kings who claim a god-like status and instead to establish the legitimate rule of a god-obeying king. According to the *BhG*, the ideal king fights neither in order to keep his family and himself in power, nor as a god-king to prove his glory – rather, he has to fight for the cause of the one and only god and for the preservation of the world that that very god has created. This new theological concept allows concepts of kingship to be rejected that make the king an absolute monarch. Rather, god is the only ruler, since he is eternally, not just temporarily, in power. The king in the *BhG* is regarded as dependent on and responsible to a single god. This god differs from the Vedic gods and their limited powers in that he is not dependent on sacrificial food, while he differs from ascetics in showing an interest in the world he has created while keeping his yogic detachment. In addition, the highest god is depicted as himself being the mover of time and destiny by revealing that time is just another manifestation of god. Against the background of the analysis of important issues discussed in the *UdP*, I shall now turn to the *BhG*.

CHAPTER 3

The doctrines of the Bhagavadgītā

The following chapter-by-chapter analysis of the *BhG* is based on the heuristic assumption that the epic is regarded as a literary and discursive framework that opens up new perspectives for the interpretation of the text. In order to do this, it is not necessary to take sides with either the text-critical or the 'unitarian' approach, as has been the case in much of the history of research on the *BhG*. In what follows I will explore the connections between the *BhG* and the epic in detail without denying its textual history. On the contrary, the historical perspective helps to interpret the extant text, the *BhG*'s final redaction. Therefore, text-historical considerations will be included in the analysis of the text. As has been pointed out before, scholars are divided about whether the theistic layers or the non-theistic Sāṃkhya and yoga layers blended with notions of sacrifice form the original core of the *BhG*. In what follows, it will be suggested that the monotheistic framework in which Kṛṣṇa is proclaimed the highest god draws on concepts developed in the non-theistic chapters. These chapters are also characterised by theistic interpolations that in their turn are based on the later chapters and have been inserted into the earlier texts. However, this did not result in a consequent reworking of the whole argument along Kṛṣṇaitic lines. A similar handling of later additions can be observed elsewhere in the epic, as is the case, for example, in the *UdP*, when Kṛṣṇa is depicted on the one hand as an epic hero and ambassador with limited means to prevent war, and on the other hand as a god who is the most powerful party in the conflict. While the text-historical perspective allows what may appear as a contradiction or at least a tension between two different views to be explained in terms of a sequence of layers, this should not lead us to the conclusion that the extant text does not make sense or is less meaningful. On the contrary, the analysis of layers must be complemented by addressing the question of what these different perspectives and layers result in. With regard to the *BhG*, for instance, the question is whether and how the theistic layer manages to reorganise and reinterpret the previous concepts and arguments. While text-historical reconstructions were often based on or resulted in privileging the older layers as more important and meaningful, any analysis of the final redaction must take into account the relevance of the whole text, which means understanding the relevance of the later additions. Studying these interplays can also result in rethinking 'our own sense of what constitutes contradiction and propriety in a text that at times can be very foreign to us', as Pollock (1984: 508) puts it. The following analysis will from time to time invite such rethinking, for instance with regard to the blending of notions of Sāṃkhya and Vedic sacrifice in *BhG* 3.

In the case of the *BhG*, the monotheistic framework is certainly the most important aspect of the text, at least when measured by the history of reception and by the fact that it has been transmitted in the epic at one of its most dramatic moments. This interpolation found the support of the epic's transmitters since the text was not transferred into the 'didactic' book *par excellence*, the *ŚāntiP*, as was the case with many other texts. This indicates that the *BhG* might not have been a very late text within the epic, although some chapters may be quite recent. When analysing the text with regard to different layers and arguments, it seems that chapters introducing the divinity of Kṛṣṇa (roughly the first part of *BhG* 4, 7–11) are conceptually based on the earlier chapters that deal with the doctrine of 'disinterested action' by drawing on notions from yoga, Sāṃkhya and Vedic sacrifice. We also witness 'theistic interpolations' in these chapters that do not affect the basically non-theistic doctrines. Therefore I regard the theology of Kṛṣṇa as the second step in the composition of the text, while chapters 12–18 seem to have been added afterwards. While I will take notice of these operations, the analysis of the concepts, arguments and imagery of the extant *BhG* is at the centre of this chapter.[1]

BHAGAVADGĪTĀ 1: THE DILEMMA

In the extant *MBh*, the *BhG* forms chapters 23–40 of the *Bhīṣmaparvan* (*BhīṣP*) and is placed at the beginning of the so-called 'battle-books', which, according to some scholars, should be regarded as the oldest core of the epic. As noted in my survey of the history of research, this placing of the *BhG* was regarded as an unwelcome interruption of a tale that was about to reach a climax, namely the beginning of the final battle. It was argued that no 'real' epic poet could have deliberately delayed this by composing

[1] For a detailed reconstruction of these different layers, see Malinar 1996: 394–415.

a discourse of over 700 verses, and therefore one either tried to cut down the *BhG* to an epic text (see above, ch. 1), comprising only a few verses, or to regard it as a text that was composed separately from the epic and then interpolated at some point in the epic's composition. The latter view was argued by von Simson in an analysis of different manuscript readings, which was accompanied by judgements about the *BhG* as an 'epigonic' text that was distorting a better, more original text. This resulted in rather negative assessments of its opening chapter as 'unrealistic' and as thus testifying to the meagre poetic skills of its author. While I would agree, although for different reasons, with von Simson that its seems highly probable that the extant *BhG* was not part of an original or even the oldest 'bouquet' of the epic, I see no reason to pass negative judgements on the text, especially its first chapter. However, this chapter, especially the first half of it, has been widely neglected in studies of the text.[2]

The *BhG* begins when both armies have already been deployed on the battlefield and the blind king Dhṛtarāṣṭra asks his bard, Saṃjaya, what happened next. The marching up to battle is described in the first chapters of the *BhīṣP*, in which the chances for preventing the war are once again discussed and ultimately denied. In one of these chapters we find an explanation for an important change in the narrative framework at this point in the narrative: the battle will be reported by Dhṛtarāṣṭra's bard Saṃjaya. In order to understand the impact of this change, it is necessary to recall that the *MBh* is narrated by using several narrative frames represented by different interlocutors. Many of the preceding books of the epic are related using the dominant narrative frame of the epic, the dialogue between the bard Vaiśampāyana and King Janamejaya. While this frame is basically an account of a tale which the bard had been told by his teacher, the present frame is established by two interlocutors who appear elsewhere in the epic as narrated characters. In this way, the epic events and their narration are brought closer together. Both Saṃjaya, the bard-narrator, and Dhṛtarāṣṭra, the blind king-audience, are at the same time 'insiders', characters involved in the events, and 'outsiders', distant narrators and observer-listeners producing an epic story. This allows their reactions to the events to be shown, which, especially in the case of Dhṛtarāṣṭra, are often highly emotional. More often they offer comments, which are usually voiced by Saṃjaya, as is the case in the *BhG* too. Another effect of this narrative device is that the narrated time and the narrative time seem to converge by creating the fiction

[2] For instance, Zaehner's otherwise comprehensive exegetical commentary is completely silent on ch 1.

of a 'live report'.[3] In this connection Saṃjaya is turned into an 'authorial first-person narrator' (Malinar 2005a), which means that he is made an eyewitness producing an 'I-narration', but at the same time is placed in the position of an overall narrator who has access to the 'whole story' and is therefore not subject to the restricted perspective of a first-person narrator. An explanation of Saṃjaya's exceptional position is given in *MBh* 6.2, when the overall narrator of the epic, Kṛṣṇa Dvaipāyana Vyāsa, appears in the story and confers on the bard the 'divine eye' (see Mangels 1995). This allows, for instance, Saṃjaya to witness Arjuna's otherwise exclusive vision of Kṛṣṇa in *BhG* 11, and his comments in *BhG* 1, 2, 11 and 18. However, the *BhG* is connected to epic narrative techniques not only by being embedded in this dialogue frame, but also by using devices that are typical of the epic's depiction of a confrontation on the battlefield. Yet another connection to the epic context is Arjuna's dilemma itself, since it is not just a 'psychic breakdown', but a final summary of the arguments against war previously discussed in the *UdP*.

The *BhG* starts with Dhṛtarāṣṭra's question about what happened 'in Kurukṣetra, the field of righteousness (*dharmakṣetra*)', when the armies were arrayed in battle formation. This not only serves to trigger the next step in the narrative, but, as is the case in other opening chapters, it permits a fresh description of the situation. Calling Kurukṣetra a field of *dharma* indicates that the battle is not just about victory or defeat, but that it is also the arena in which one fulfils one's *dharma* and proves oneself a warrior.[4] With regard to the larger debate on *dharma* in the *UdP* and other parts of the epic, it is also the field in which it will be decided whose interpretation of *dharma* will prevail. In his reply, Saṃjaya turns at first to what is happening on the side of the Kauravas and reports that Duryodhana looks at the army of the Pāṇḍavas and approaches Droṇa, the teacher of both the Pāṇḍavas and the Kauravas. Duryodhana honours his teacher by enumerating the eminent heroes of both sides. This is extended to Dṛṣṭadyumna, the son of Drupada fighting for the Pāṇḍavas, once Droṇa's pupil, and to other heroes who equal the great archers Bhīma and Arjuna, who were also taught by Droṇa. However, there is also another aspect in play in that Duryodhana's address serves to rouse Droṇa's fighting spirit by drawing attention to the fact that his pupils Arjuna and Dṛṣṭadyumna have now turned into enemies.

3 The closeness to the epic events is also corroborated in that both Saṃjaya and Dhṛtarāṣṭra die, that is, vanish from the story, soon after they have ceased being frame interlocutors. On the technique of 'framing' in the epic, see Bailey 1987, Minkowski 1989, Mangels 1994 and Malinar 2005b.

4 See 6.1.1, where *kurukṣetra* is called *tapaḥkṣetra*, 'the field of ascetic heat or suffering'. For these two meanings of *tapas*, see Hara 1977–78.

Moreover, his former friend Drupada, with whom he fell out bitterly, is also ready to fight against him. Duryodhana then praises the heroes on his side and asks for Droṇa's approval or for 'code names' (*saṃjñā*)[5] for the army (1.7–8). He then praises the determination of his warriors, and declares that 'they have given up their lives for my sake' (*madarthe tyaktajīvitāḥ*; 1.9). This formulation refers to the sacrificial structure of the battle, explained in detail in Duryodhana's speech in *MBh* 5.57 (see above, pp. 49ff.), in which the warrior gives his life as the offering (*tyāga*) in the sacrifice of battle in order to reap the fruit in the form of Duryodhana's victory.[6] Duryodhana then turns to Bhīṣma (1.10–11),[7] the patriarch of the whole clan, who is the leader of Duryodhana's army and therefore needs special protection, since the victory of Duryodhana depends to a great extend on Bhīṣma's invincibility. Immediately, Bhīṣma displays his fighting spirit by 'voicing the lion's roar' (*siṃhanāda*), indicating determination, strength and victory. This, in turn, enthuses Duryodhana (*tasya saṃjanayan harṣam*; 1.12). Bhīṣma blows his conch, obviously the sign to begin the battle (1.12), and to make use of all the other instruments so that enthusiasm abounds in a tumultuous noise. In these first twelve verses of the *BhG*, many of the standard rhetorical devices used to describe the beginning of a battle are employed, such as looking at the enemy, praising one's own strength, reconfirming the agreement on the battle formation and the leaders, inciting the fighting spirit (*harṣa*), using instruments and the outbreak of sounds.[8] In the present context, this standard description of the beginning of a battle serves a double purpose: on the one hand, it meets audience expectations, while on the other, it lays the ground for Arjuna's departing from the expected course. A familiar scene has been created which sets the stage for a skilful description of the crisis, which starts when Saṃjaya shifts the focus of his narration to similar activities on the side of the Pāṇḍavas (1.14–19).

[5] The word *saṃjñā* seems to have a more technical connotation. It is used elsewhere in the sense of 'code name', for example in the description of the battle preparations in *MBh* 6.1.11–12. Yudhiṣṭhira is said to have distributed *saṃjñā*, the special code names of the warriors: "Yudhiṣṭhira arranged many different code names (*saṃjñā*) for them. The one who uses them appropriately can be identified as belonging to the Pāṇḍavas. Duryodhana too, when the time for battle had come, laid down signs of identification for all, both code names and code signs (*saṃjñāś cābharāṇi*).' With regard to *BhG* 1.7, another connotation of the word can be considered: approval or agreement on the leaders and the battle formation. On *saṃjñeṣṭi* as agreement on a leader in the Vedic literature, see Heesterman 1985.

[6] The sacrificial character is also expressed by the warriors wearing the antelope skin and *muñja* grass, signs indicative of their being 'consecrated (*dīkṣitā*) for the world of *brahman*, firmly resolved upon Duryodhana's purpose' (*MBh* 6.17.36–38; cf. 5.57.16–17; 6.41).

[7] Verse 1.10 has caused much discussion, since here Duryodhana seems to proclaim the superiority of the Pāṇḍavas' army, but it is most probably a scribal error, and some manuscripts reverse the order. For further details, see van Buitenen 1965.

[8] For a study of these elements in the battle books, see von Simson 1974: 167ff.

However, Saṃjaya does not concentrate on Duryodhana's direct opponent on the 'field of *dharma*', Yudhiṣṭhira, but on the two epic characters who will be centre stage in what is about to happen: Kṛṣṇa and Arjuna standing on their great chariot yoked to white horses, harmoniously blowing their 'divine conches'. The unity and alliance of the two are stressed by using the Sanskrit dual in 1.14. The names of their conches indicate claims to sovereignty and victory. Kṛṣṇa's conch Pāñcajanya probably refers to the mythic five Vedic tribes, which are united and represented by his conch; Arjuna's 'Devadatta', given by the gods, points to Arjuna's gaining of divine weapons and perhaps to his being specially protected by the gods. The next to be named is Bhīma, and only then Yudhiṣṭhira. This sequence indicates a hierarchy of powers among the Pāṇḍavas, since those who are to become most important in securing the Pāṇḍavas' victory are named first.

Saṃjaya summarises the heat of the moment by pointing to the tumultuous din that 'made heaven and earth resound' (1.19). The usual course of events begins to change when the bard turns to Arjuna. Again, what is first said about his doings is that he is 'looking' at the Kauravas (*dṛṣṭvā*; 1.20) and raises his bow. It seems, however, that he has not seen enough, and indeed, what he asks for next represents a different viewpoint: 'Then, lord of the earth, he said to Hṛṣīkeśa (Kṛṣṇa): "Halt the chariot in the middle of the two armies, O imperishable one, so that I may look for myself at those who have marched up eager to fight, with whom I have to fight in this battle about to begin! I may look at them as they are here assembled, ready to fight, wishing the best (success) in this battle for Dhṛtarāṣṭra's stupid son"' (1.21–22). The change in Arjuna's attitude is further expressed by paying attention to the act of seeing. Having complied with Arjuna's request, Kṛṣṇa turns to his friend: 'Son of Pṛthā, behold the Kurus as they are assembled here!' The following verses deal only with Arjuna's seeing and its consequences. As elsewhere in the epic, 'seeing' is a powerful activity and a highly sensitive form of social communication, as well as a form and process of knowledge.[9] Therefore it plays an important role in the narrative.[10] A change of perspective, behaviour or attitude is often expressed in the epic in the idiom of 'seeing', as a close or more distant look, as gazing, staring or looking away. Conversely, not seeing is often equated

9 Cf. similar emphasis in 6.1.33; 6.19.3; 6.21.1; 6.41.6. Most telling with regard to the effects of seeing is perhaps the description of the reaction on both sides, after the troops have marched on to Kurukṣetra: 'When the Kurus, Pāṇḍavas and Somakas had completed their preparations for battle, they saw each other and were very astonished' (*eva te samaya kṛtvā kurupāṇḍavasomakāḥ / vismayaṃ paramaṃ jagmuḥ prekṣamāṇāḥ parasparam* //6.1.33).

10 This aspect is overlooked when von Simson (1968–69: 171) regards the description of Arjuna's seeing at the beginning of his crisis as indicative of a lack of literary skill on the part of the interpolators.

with a lack of understanding or insight. The different ways of seeing are accompanied by various reactions that range from laughter, anger, desire and astonishment, to doubts, questioning and reflection. How does the new viewpoint, in the middle of the armies, change Arjuna's perspective? He no longer sees enemies on the other side, who want to please Duryodhana or the Kurus, as Kṛṣṇa has called them, but '*bandhus*', relatives: fathers, grandfathers, teachers, mother's and father's brothers, sons and grandsons, companions and in-laws (1.26–27). The term *bandhu* (1.27) summarises this network of social relationships, structured precisely by seniority and mutual dependence. Through these relations, Arjuna is related to the social world he knows, belongs to and feels obliged to. He realises this relatedness through the very act of seeing and is, according to Saṃjaya, immediately 'grasped', 'infused' by 'deep compassion' (*kṛpayā parayāviṣṭo*). In his analysis of the semantic values attached to 'being grasped' (from verbal compound '*ā* + *viś*'), Hara (1979: 270) concludes that this condition is 'characterized by overpowering impulses, psychological and physiological as well, which originate either from outside or inside the human being'. Seeing his 'own folks' (*dṛṣṭvaimān svajanān*) causes a chain reaction, which he describes by listing its symptoms (1.28): physical weakness, drying up of the mouth, trembling, goose-bumps, the bow slipping from his hand, a burning skin rash and dizziness (1.29–30). In contrast to Saṃjaya, who interprets the situation as a reaction and overwhelming emotion,[11] Arjuna says that he sees 'inauspicious signs' (*nimitta*). The notion of omens is related to concepts of time and destiny that play an important role elsewhere in the epic and in the vision of Kṛṣṇa in *BhG* 11 too, since the quality of time is indicated through *nimitta*.[12] Arjuna interprets the omens as both a warning and an opportunity to prevent a catastrophe, since he sees nothing good in killing his kin (1.31).[13] He then puts forward his views which recall the arguments for peace discussed in the *UdP*. Arjuna declares he desires neither victory (*vijaya*) nor the kingdom (*rājya*), although this is exactly what he should

[11] This catalogue of symptoms (see also *BhG* 2.1) can be compared with the instructions for staging (*abhinaya*) *karuṇa-rasa*, the sentiment of compassion in the prose passage in the *Nāṭyaśāstra* (6.62–63). According to *Nāṭyaśāstra* 6.62, one of the reasons for this *rasa* is to view the killing of the beloved ones (*iṣṭavadhadarśana*). Most of the symptoms listed are called in the *Nāṭyaśāstra* '*sāttvika-bhāvas*', which occur when the body is under the influence of an insight or an extreme condition.

[12] In *BhG* 11, Kṛṣṇa reveals himself as 'time' (*kāla*) and asks Arjuna to become a *nimitta*. See below, pp. 175ff.

[13] Such adverse omens were also pointed out by others after the armies had marched up to one another in Kurukṣetra. Cf. Vyāsa's appeal to stop the battle after the enumeration of adverse omens (*MBh* 6.2.16ff.; 6.4.43), which Dhṛtarāṣṭra declares to be futile, since what happens is a matter of fate (6.4.44–46). Vyāsa is called in 6.5.2 a '*kālavādin*', an interpreter of star constellations and of omens.

desire as a warrior.[14] He claims that the purpose of fulfilling one's duty as a warrior by re-conquering the kingdom lies in increasing the prosperity of the family-clan. In the present situation, however, the family members for whose sake he should fight are his enemies and will meet destruction: 'Those for whose sake we desire the kingdom, enjoyments and pleasures are the ones assembled here, having given up their life and wealth in battle' (1.33). In contrast to Duryodhana, Arjuna regards ruling a kingdom or the earth as less desirable than the prosperity of the family. For him, the purpose and meaning of his actions are based on loyalty to his family: therefore, fighting against them is ruled out. In consequence, he reflects on the sinfulness of killing relatives and its negative consequences.

Arjuna denies the pragmatics of *Realpolitik* and argues that the fact that his cousin Duryodhana does not care for the welfare of the family-clan does not justify doing the same. In claiming superior insight, he argues that destroying the family is a crime (*kulakṣayakṛtam doṣam*) that must be prevented, even if the others do not see it, because they are possessed by greed (1.38–39; cf. Yudhiṣṭhira at 5.70). The result of this offence is the breakdown of the whole family system, the 'family laws and practices' (*kuladharmāḥ*; 1.40):

> Once the family is destroyed, the ever-present family laws collapse; once law is destroyed, lawlessness (*adharma*) will overwhelm the family as a whole. Because lawlessness prevails, O Kṛṣṇa, the women of the family are defiled. When the women are defiled, there will be a mixing of caste. For those who kill the family and for the family itself, the mixing of castes leads only to hell, since their ancestors lose [their status] because the ancestral rite of offering rice is no longer carried out. (1.40–42)

What is described here is the destruction not only of family members, but of the larger network of social relationships as defined by appropriate marriage alliances on the basis of the agnatic and affinal relationships that create a reliable ancestral genealogy. This genealogy can be maintained only when the agnatic system is protected and the women of the family marry appropriately. When most of the men of the family are killed, the protection of the women and the family laws is no longer guaranteed. The downfall of the ancestors destroys the purity and continuity of the genealogy of the family, which ensures its status and esteem, because it excludes them from the older marriage alliances. By drawing on his traditional education

[14] This is at issue in the dialogue between Vidurā and her son discussed above, pp. 38ff. The son expresses views similar to Arjuna's in *MBh* 5.131.36; 133.3. Both verses conclude, as does *BhG* 1.32, with the formulaic refrain, 'What is the use of enjoyments or life?' (*kiṃ bhogair jivitena vā*).

('thus we have learned'; *ity anuśuśruma*; 1.44) Arjuna conjures up a social nightmare as the consequence of offending against family rules. This 'great sin' is certainly the highway to hell, and he who commits it must indeed be greedy for the 'sweets of sovereignty', as Zaehner renders *rājyasukha* (1.45). Arjuna wants to have nothing to do with this and declares that he will indeed do nothing; he is prepared to be slain in battle, which he will enter unarmed, offering no defence (1.47). He deems this suicidal surrender to death more beneficial (*kṣemataram*) than being actively involved in the family slaughter. Saṃjaya concludes the chapter by depicting Arjuna sitting on the chariot; he loosens his grip on his bow and arrows and lets them slip, 'his heart immersed in grief' (*śokasaṃvignamānasaḥ*; 1.47).

Seen from the perspective of the *UdP*, the authors put forward familiar arguments for peace. However, Arjuna's speech highlights certain aspects that delineate even more sharply the conflict between loyalty to the family and his duty as a warrior. First, he points out that the purpose of fighting is the welfare of the family. Secondly, he imagines the consequences of extinction with regard to the larger network of social relationships. Thirdly, he is affected by what he sees in a way that is otherwise reserved only for Dhṛtarāṣṭra (see Malinar 2005). Seen in the context of Kṛṣṇa's reply in the next chapter, Arjuna's speech can be regarded as an anticipation of mourning for the dead and as a desperate attempt to avoid this. On the other hand, his speech represents a skilfully crafted dramatisation and escalation of the conflict between *kuladharma* and *kṣatriyadharma* that dominated the *UdP*. While Duryodhana represents a breach with the older tradition, Arjuna is shown clinging to it. He does not see any higher cause that might provide a solution.

BHAGAVADGĪTĀ 2: THE FRUITS OF DETACHMENT

At the beginning of this chapter, Saṃjaya says again that Arjuna is 'overcome by compassion' (2.1a = 1.28a) and introduces Kṛṣṇa's first and brief reply. As Jacobi (1918: 325) has pointed out, this reply consists of a catalogue of topics that are also used elsewhere in the epic when a warrior refuses to fight. In addition to the example cited by Jacobi (Arjuna's reply to Uttara's fear of the Kurus in *MBh* 4.36.17–23), Kṛṣṇa's reply to Bhīma joining the peace party (5.73) and Vidurā's 'speech of encouragement' (5.131–134) to her son also corroborate this point. Kṛṣṇa declares that only the lowly will praise Arjuna's demeanour, since it is disgraceful and will exclude him from the heavenly world of heroes. He must stop being a eunuch (*klība*) and overcome his weakness. Although the reproach of being like a eunuch is familiar in speeches to weak heroes (see above, pp. 40ff.), it has a special twist here because Arjuna spent the last year of exile disguised as a eunuch at the court of the Matsya King Virāṭa (*MBh* 4). The effect of these words cannot be overestimated in a social context in which 'keeping face' is the first commandment, and shame and disgrace must be avoided in order to maintain social status (see Tschannerl 1992). However, in the present context this threat is only one step in a longer discourse which addresses a complicated issue, not just a moment of weakness.

Arjuna basically repeats his main argument: How can he kill his teachers Bhīṣma and Droṇa, to whom he owes respect and worship (*pūjārhāv*; 2.4)? This point is emphasised even more by changing the metre from *śloka* to *triṣṭubh*: 'For better it is to live even from alms (*bhaikṣyam*) here on earth than to kill one's generous teachers. Were I to kill my teachers, though they would be desirous of wealth, then I would eat food covered with blood' (2.5). In this verse Arjuna no longer thinks about getting killed, but argues that it is better to 'live from alms' than to gain victory at the expense of relatives and teachers. Again a peace argument is put forward. In this connection, 'living from alms' indicates the relinquishing of territorial claims and social status and agreeing to live in the realm of another king, which may amount to ascetic renunciation.[15] He reconfirms that neither a kingdom nor the earth is worth fighting for and refuses to follow *kṣatriyadharma*, which demands exactly this.[16] Arjuna closes as follows: 'my whole being (*svabhāva*) is attacked by the vice of despair; my mind is confused over what is the law' (2.8). In turning to Kṛṣṇa he makes himself his disciple and asks him what he should do. He does not see what could possibly dispel his grief (*śoka*), which dries up his senses (2.9). This final reference to the breakdown, described at the end of *BhG* 1, makes it clear that Arjuna's problem exists on two levels. On the one hand, he is faced with a conflict of *dharma*. While he may fulfil his duty as a warrior, he will not gain merit, but will be commiting a crime against his own family. On the other hand, he anticipates the pain and grief that the death of his relatives and friends will cause and wants to avoid this. The two levels reinforce each other and, finding himself in this aporetic situation, Arjuna declares, 'I will not fight' (2.10).

15 In the *UdP* we see Saṃjaya, Duryodhana's ambassador, recommending this solution to Yudhiṣṭhira: 'I think it is better to live on alms in the kingdom of the Andhaka-Vṛṣṇis' (*bhaikṣācaryam andhakavṛṣṇirājye śreyo manye* //5.27.2). In a speech to Yudhiṣṭhira, Kṛṣṇa points out that victory or death is the alms a Kṣatriya lives on; cf. 5.71.3–4.

16 Cf. the description of the earth as the purpose of war in *MBh* 6.4.

While some scholars have raised text-critical objections to the compositional unity of the beginning of the *BhG*,[17] others have seen in Arjuna's arguments the key to understanding the text.[18] For Holtzmann (1971: 154), Arjuna's crisis results from a fear of death which is dispelled through the doctrine of the immortality of the soul. A more psychological interpretation is proposed by Hejib and Young (1980), who regard Arjuna as experiencing a 'crisis of identity', since he does not know whether he is a warrior or still the eunuch he was at the court of Virāṭa. Kṛṣṇa's reply functions as 'shock therapy'. While these scholars focus on the emotional impact of Arjuna's words, others regard the conflict of *dharma* to be most important. According to Biardeau (1981), the purpose of the *BhG* is to reconcile the violence implied in the *kṣatriyadharma* with teachings of salvation and thereby allow not only ascetics and Brahmans but also warriors to gain liberation. In van Buitenen's view, the conflict is caused by the fact that legitimate claims have to be enforced by illegitimate means (1981: 3). Therefore, the tension is not between two different goals (social duty and liberation), but between two dharmic injunctions, which can be removed only by teaching a different 'level of values'. However, both dimensions of Arjuna's dilemma, the emotional (grief, confusion) and the conceptual (conflict over *dharma*), are presented as being interrelated. This is corroborated by Kṛṣṇa's reply, which also addresses both aspects. This reply is introduced by Saṃjaya as follows: 'To him who sat desperate between the two armies, Hṛṣīkeśa (Kṛṣṇa) spoke almost bursting out in laughter' (2.10). Poignantly, this verse contrasts Arjuna's sad situation with Kṛṣṇa's laughter. Again the author is familiar with epic conventions in that he has Kṛṣṇa showing a typical reaction of a warrior when someone else fails to fulfil his duty (*svadharma*) – it causes a slight outburst of laughter (*prahasann iva*) because such a misdemeanour is shameful and laughable (see Tschannerl 1992: 101–112). Desperation and last-minute appeals for peace are not deemed respectable in the social world created in the epic, but result in social disgrace. Consequently, Kṛṣṇa not only rejects Arjuna's fear of death, but also describes how he will lose his social esteem (2.32–38). However, this is only one part of the answer, as a survey of the topics dealt with in the rest of the chapter shows. The following four levels of argument can be distinguished:

[17] Seen from this perspective, Arjuna's arguments do not seem redundant and contradictory as suggested by Ježic (1979a).

[18] For Otto (1934: 8), the original *BhG* consisted only of the reply to Arjuna, which was primarily a lesson on the necessity of surrendering oneself to God's will. Others would accept Kṛṣṇa's teachings only up to *BhG* 2.39 (e.g. Jacobi 1918).

2.11–30	Consolation of Arjuna's grief by emphasising the immortality of the self
2.31–37	Endorsing *kṣatriyadharma*
2.38–53	Right knowledge is the precondition for right action. An action must not be judged by its results; rather, one must relinquish all desires attached to it.
2.54–72	Discourse on the qualities of a man 'whose insight is firm' (*sthitaprajña*)

The immortality of the self and the mortality of the body

First of all Arjuna's grief is addressed, it being pointed out that his sorrow does not demonstrate a superior insight, although it may appear as such. Kṛṣṇa declares that the truly educated, the *paṇḍita*, do not grieve when there is nothing to grieve for. They never mourn for either the living or the dead because they distinguish between the mortal body and the immortal 'owner of the body' (*dehin*, *śarīrin*). Rather than propagating a certain interpretation of this immortal entity, this distinction is explored from different perspectives, which all amount to just one conclusion: there is nothing to worry about. Real knowledge is when one realises this immortality and is therefore capable of enduring the changing conditions of the body. Both this knowledge and the power of endurance are represented by the wise man (*dhīra*), 'for whom happiness and suffering are the same' (*samaduḥkhasukham*; 2.15). As in the *UdP*, indifference is called for, this time towards one's personal experiences, which include birth and death. This indifference mirrors the indifference of the one 'true', indestructible being (*sat*), which is exempt from all states of being and becoming that the body undergoes (*bhāva*; 2.18). Therefore, it is only possible to kill the body, not the embodied self: 'He who thinks of it as a killer and he who deems that it is killed – they both do not know that it does not kill, nor is it killed' (2.19). This message is emphatically repeated in the following *triṣṭubh* verse (2.20) and turned into a rhetorical question that makes the whole business of killing an illusion (2.21). Death is only an occasion for 'changing old clothes', for transmigrating into a new body (2.22).[19] Thus, whether one thinks of the self as eternal or as being constantly born or dead, the conclusion is the same: there is nothing to grieve for. This message is conveyed in the refrain-like formula, 'You must not grieve' (*na socitum arhasi*; 2.25, 26, 27, 30), which is a perfect conclusion of this speech of consolation,

[19] This comparison is also used in *MBh* 11.3.6; both passages are probably based on *BĀU* 4.4.5.

drawing on the style of funeral oration. That consolation is the main purpose of these verses is corroborated by their inclusion of the *Viṣṇusmṛti* (*ViS*), one of the later manuals on *dharma*. In this text, the verses are cited as an example of words of consolation that should be addressed to mourners (cf. *ViS* 19.24). Almost all the verses in the *BhG* are cited, with slight variations and certain omissions, as a repertoire of aphorisms to be used on such occasions. It is probable that the authors of the *BhG* are drawing on an extant stock of teachings as is the case in other passages from the *MBh*,[20] but this does not mean that the text is not original, or that the *BhG* is quoting the *ViS*.[21]

The author is obviously drawing on teachings that were current in certain contemporary philosophical schools that make the ontological distinction between a mortal body and an immortal entity functioning as the temporary 'owner' of a mortal body. 'Ownership' is based on the idea of transmigration, or rather re-embodiment, characteristic of the older Upaniṣads and early Sāṃkhya philosophy. Upaniṣadic ideas are recalled when death is described as a chance to acquire a new body and compared with 'weaving a new cloth' (*BĀU* 4.4.5; cf. *BhG* 2.22). Sāṃkhya notions seem to be behind the emphasis of the transformational character of physical existence, such as the change between appearance (birth), disappearance (death) and various modifications in between (*vikāra*). This terminology is used in *BhG* 2.25, when the immortal being is described as being the opposite of the products of nature (*prakṛti*): it is 'unmanifest' (*avyakta*), 'unthinkable' (*acintya*), 'not modifiable' (*avikārya*). Another connection with Sāṃkhya is established by emphasising that death is not 'non-being' (*asat*), but only a change in appearance, because nothing that (truly) is (*sat*) can vanish into non-being (*asat*).

The connection with Upaniṣadic texts extends not only to doctrinal but also to verbal parallels, as is the case with *BhG* 2.19–20 and *Kaṭha-Upaniṣad* (*KaṭhU*) 2.18–19 on the illusionary nature of killing.[22] There was some discussion of the question whether the *BhG* quotes the *KaṭhU* or vice versa, since this would help determine the chronological relationship between the *BhG* and the so-called 'middle-verse' Upaniṣads, like the *KaṭhU*

[20] See, for example, Vidura's speech of consolation (*MBh* 11.2.3ff.). Here, the refrain *tatra paridevanā* ('Why should one complain?') is frequently used, as is the case in the *BhG* 2.

[21] Charpentier (1930: 80) has argued that this whole paragraph is a late interpolation based on the *ViS* (see also Otto 1935a: 20). For a detailed discussion of the parallel passages in the *BhG* and the *ViS*, which demonstrates the priority of the *BhG*, see Malinar 1996: 131–133. With regard to the parallels between *BhG* 13 and the *ViS*, Oberlies (1988: 58) comes to a similar conclusion.

[22] For a survey of all the parallel passages between the *BhG* and the Upaniṣads, see Haas 1922.

and the *ŚvetU.*[23] A close analysis shows that the often assumed priority of the Upaniṣadic texts is based on the view that the genre as such is older than the *BhG*, but this does not necessarily apply to its individual representatives. More recent research has indicated that the *BhG*, or certain layers of the text, may be older than or at least contemporary with these Upaniṣads (see Oberlies 1988).

However, the whole passage is interesting not only for what is said, but also for what is not. It is significant that the otherwise prominent connection between re-embodiment and the doctrine of *karman* is passed over in silence. Instead, these passages recall older ideas that do not postulate any connection between the self and *karman*, but rather stress that the self is not touched by what is good or bad. *BĀU* 4.4.22, for instance, declares: 'This one (*ātman*) does not increase by good deeds, nor does it decrease by bad. It is the ruler of all, the overlord over the elements.'[24] This idea could easily have been used in order to dispel Arjuna's fear of guilt, which he inflicts on himself by killing his relatives. If one argues from the perspective of the immortal being, then there is no crime and no guilt, because the immortal being cannot be the victim of a crime. However, in the present context, this argument is rather problematic, since it might be concluded that it does not matter whether one fights or not. In addition, this reasoning might be taken and misunderstood as a blanket legitimation of violence. Such difficulties are avoided in this passage, and the problem of the consequences of one's actions is discussed later. That the *karman* doctrine is not an issue here corroborates the idea that we are dealing with a speech of consolation. This is supplemented by an exposition of the dreadful consequences of failing to fulfil a warrior's duty.

Kṣatriyadharma

BhG 2.31–38 suggest that, not only from a metaphysical perspective, but also with regard to his duty as a warrior, his *svadharma*, Arjuna has nothing to worry about, since, for a warrior, death is always welcome as a chance to gain entry into the heavenly world (2.31). Instead of grieving and complaining, he should deem himself lucky that this battle offers him this chance (2.32).

23 Devasthali (1954) regards the *BhG* as the borrower, while Hillebrandt (1921: 12) and I (Malinar 1996: 129–131) argue that it is probably the other way round. Weller (1953: 100ff.) thinks that both texts have used the same, unknown source. For an analysis of the different interpretations of *BhG* 2.20, see Rocher 1963.

24 *Sa na sādhunā karmaṇā bhūyān na evāsādhunā kanīyān eṣa sarveśvaraḥ eṣa bhūtādhipatiḥ*. Cf. *ChU* 8.7.2: *ātmā 'pahatapāpmā vijaro vimṛtyur viśoko* ('The self is free from sin, fever, death and sorrow').

There is nothing more beneficial (*śreyas*) than a 'righteous' (*dharmya*; 2.31, 33) battle. According to Kṛṣṇa, *svadharma*, the general social obligations of a warrior, clearly overrules *kuladharma*, Arjuna's concern for the family. Seen against the background of the debates in the *UdP* and elsewhere, Kṛṣṇa's position is in accordance with those of many other epic characters, including his opponent, Duryodhana. Not killing his relatives and refusing to fight constitute a sinful deed (*pāpam*, 2.33). Again, it is interesting to consider what is not used as an argument to exculpate Arjuna from any potential offence. In contrast to other parts of the epic, fighting against relatives is not treated as an emergency situation, a calamity that allows *āpaddharma*, the 'rules in times of distress', to be applied.[25]

The next three verses confront Arjuna with the consequences of his refusal. Disgrace (*akīrti*), not honour, will be his legacy, as common lore will have it. This is worse than death (2.34). Since nobody will understand his motives, his combatants will think he did not fight out of fear, and he will be despised. It is this that is pitiful, not the killing of relatives (2.36). The paragraph ends by encouraging Arjuna to fight, since he has nothing to lose, and he can only win, whether it be a kingdom on earth or the warrior-heaven (2.37). Again the hero is depicted as the all-time winner. This is followed by a reminder to fight with due indifference towards happiness and unhappiness, gain or loss (2.38): 'Holding happiness and suffering, gain and loss, victory and defeat to be the same, then harness yourself for battle. In this way you will not bring anything bad on yourself.' Thus, attachment to the outcome of the battle is unworthy of a warrior. Indifference is therefore instrumental in avoiding any negative consequences of one's doings and can therefore be regarded as a direct answer to Arjuna's concerns about the consequences of war.[26] The demand for indifference recalls similar statements in the *UdP* discussed in ch. 2. However, does this solve the problem of guilt and destruction? This question arises especially because mere indifference is not a sufficient criterion for claiming moral superiority over Duryodhana. Indifference is not a value as such, since it can indicate quite different motives and conditions, which range from insight, heroism and the relinquishing of all personal desires to recklessness, egoism and pride. In the case of the warrior, indifference towards one's life is the wager in an otherwise safe bet. As we have seen, the hero can only win. However, such indifference extends only to the actual performance of the warrior's duty – a general ascetic indifference is not required. Otherwise, the very

[25] This is explained in the Rājadharma section of the *ŚāntiP*; see Fitzgerald 2004: introduction.
[26] This function of the verse is neglected by Ježic (1979a: 546), who separates 2.37 from 2.38.

same problem implied in the argument about the immortality of the soul would arise: why not be indifferent towards fighting or social disgrace too? Seen against the background of these difficulties, the argument of indifference adduced in 2.38 does not carry us very far and therefore cannot be regarded as a solution to Arjuna's problem. As seen in my survey of the history of research, for quite a few scholars the 'original', 'epic' *BhG* ends in 2.38, the rest being regarded as a later interpolation. Along with many other scholars, I think that such a text does not offer a satisfying answer to Arjuna's dilemma and is certainly too short to be called *BhG*.[27] While a version of the epic which included only Arjuna's crisis and Kṛṣṇa's reply up to 2.38 is certainly imaginable, it does not make much sense to call it the 'original *BhG*', since there is nothing exceptional about what is perhaps then better called the 'epic text' that would distinguish it from other instances of 'heroic crisis' in the epic. It rather seems that what turned Kṛṣṇa's instructions into a text accepted as the *BhG* are new ideas and concepts, or at least a specific treatment of the issues that had not been offered before. The *BhG* became so important, not only because it uses older, well-known ideas, but also because it reinterprets them and teaches something original and new. This starts in the next section.

Buddhiyoga

Seen against the background of the problems implied in the attitude of 'indifference', this section can be regarded, first, as an explanation of how this attitude should be understood, and secondly, as applying the law of karmic retribution to the problem. The introduction of the hitherto unmentioned *karman* doctrine highlights the conceptual framework of the previous arguments. Obviously fighting has no karmic consequences for the warrior: whatever happens, he wins, provided he does not violate the rules and regulations implied in his *svadharma*. This interpretation is challenged when fulfilling one's social duties is primarily thought of in terms of *karman*, or to be more precise, as a way of living that is not conducive to final liberation, since this usually demands the reduction and annihilation of violent *karman*. Such a view and thus a new level of argument are introduced. This is clearly marked in *BhG* 2.39, in which four new terms are used to announce the changing context of the discourse. As already indicated, the first reply did indeed avoid certain aspects of Arjuna's problem,

[27] Oldenberg (1920: 334) wondered whether 'one still wants to call this little piece Gītā'. See also Belvalkar 1937: 80.

and it did not explain why the Pāṇḍavas could claim any moral superiority over Duryodhana, since ultimately both sides fulfil only their own *kṣatriyadharma*. Such an explanation requires new arguments and ideas, especially in comparison with the debates in the *UdP*.

The argument turns from consolation and encouragement to a more philosophical level, which 2.39 announces clearly: 'Hear now about the faculty of discrimination (*buddhi*), which is known to you in regard to Sāṃkhya, in regard to yoga. When yoked with the faculty of discrimination, Partha, you will get rid of the bond of *karman*.'[28] Sāṃkhya, yoga, *buddhi* and *karman*; these are four terms not used before and whose explanation is a major task in the following chapters. The ideas and practices implied in the first three terms are used in order to teach Arjuna how to rid himself of *karman*. For the first time in the *BhG*, the problem of evil and sinful deeds (*pāpam*) is related to the notion of *karman* or retributive action. In doing this, it is possible to turn Arjuna's worries about a future in hell, or at least in misery, into a general discussion about techniques of liberation. It seems that a basic knowledge of these terms is taken for granted: it is assumed that Arjuna, and with him the listeners and readers of the text, share a common educational background and that Sāṃkhya and yoga are familiar. However, each of these terms allows different interpretations, especially in the context of the epic, which presents different accounts of these schools. These are marked by a certain terminological and systematic fluidity which is characteristic of the epic philosophy because it does not deal with these schools in the form of a philosophical and argumentative exposition of the doctrines as we find it in texts such as the *Sāṃkhyakārikā* (*SK*) and the *Yogasūtra* (*YS*). It seems, however, that the word 'Sāṃkhya' is used quite consistently in the *BhG* as the name of a tradition of knowledge, which in *BhG* 5.4–5 is equated with yoga with regard to the goal. In contrast, *yoga* is used with more than one meaning and rarely in the sense of a philosophical school.[29] It can be translated, for instance, as 'yoking', 'harnessing', 'restraint', 'control', 'practice', 'connecting', 'applying' or 'uniting', depending on the context and on the interpretive perspective of

[28] *Eṣā te 'bhihitā sāṃkhye buddhir yoge tv imāṃ śṛṇu / buddhyā yukto yayā pārtha karmabandhaṃ prahāsyasi* //2.39/.

[29] Edgerton (1924) has proposed to interpret Sāṃkhya and yoga, especially when they are juxtaposed or occur as a dual compound, as 'theory' and 'practice' respectively. Thereby the technical character of both terms is perhaps underestimated. As a consequence, Zaehner (1969: 139) translates: 'This wisdom has [now] been revealed to you in theory; listen now to how it should be practised.' Without further discussion, van Buitenen renders *buddhi* as 'spirit'. Schreiner (1999: 763), analysing the occurrence of both terms in the *MBh*, argues that Sāṃkhya presupposes yoga and can be regarded as a 'special type of yoga' in many passages in the *MDh*.

the translators. Since the authors seem to be fully aware of the semantic polyvalence of the word, it is not possible to stick to just one translation, which makes it necessary to discuss the different options repeatedly. The word *buddhi* allows at least two different translations as well, first as a faculty of knowledge, and secondly as a content of consciousness. This latter meaning is in play when *buddhi* is translated as 'knowledge' or 'wisdom'.[30] However, given the explicit breach with the previous line of argument, it seems advisable to look for Sāṃkhya teachings in what follows. As a consequence, a more technical understanding of *buddhi* seems to be called for, as has been proposed by Schreiner (1991: 62), who renders *buddhi* '*Bewußtheit*' (awareness) as understood in the context of Sāṃkhya terminology. I follow Schreiner's view, but give a slightly different emphasis and translate *buddhi* as 'faculty of discrimination', as not only elsewhere in the *BhG*, but also in the Upaniṣads and in other epic Sāṃkhya texts, it being considered one of the constituent elements of creation (*tattva*) taught in these texts. Within the scheme of these elements, *buddhi* has two aspects: (1) it is the first product that arises from the contact between an immortal self about to be embodied and the creative powers of nature (*prakṛti*); (2) as the first product, it is also the highest cognitive faculty whose general function is to assess the data provided by the other faculties (mind, senses) and to decide on the proper reaction; its purpose is discrimination between right and wrong, truth and error, and even between the immortal self and the physical realm of nature. This is referred to in *BhG* 2.41, where *buddhi* is defined as *vyavasāyātmikā*, 'of the nature of discrimination'.[31]

Why is Arjuna reminded here of this faculty of discrimination, and why does it help him rid himself of *karman*? First of all, it is declared that it helps: 'even a little of its practice saves from great danger!'[32] This is explained by distinguishing between two ways of employing *buddhi*, the faculty of discrimination: 'A *buddhi* that is fully determined is united,[33] O Kuru hero, while the *buddhis* of those who lack discrimination are countless and

[30] Oldenberg (1920: 33) regards the verse as a commentary on the previous section and looks for Sāṃkhya teachings in *BhG* 2.11–38, which, however, he finds only in 2.11–30.

[31] In *SK* 23 *buddhi* is defined as *adhyavasāya*, 'decision-making', 'discrimination' (German, *Urteilskraft*).

[32] *Svalpam apy asya dharmasya trāyate mahato bhayāt.* In contrast to most translators, I propose to translate *dharma* as 'practice' and take *asya* as its object, referring to the yogic application of *buddhi* mentioned in the previous verse, and not as a pronoun. Although van Buitenen translates it as 'law', he stresses the practical aspect in his comment: 'term borrowed from Mīmāṃsā, where *dharma* is tantamount to the (ritual) act'.

[33] *Eka* stresses the singularity and unity, in contrast to the 'branching out' of those who lack determination. The 'many branches' (*bahuśākhā*) is an allusion to the Vedic doctrine (*vedavāda*), transmitted in branches of families (*śākhā*), addressed in the next verse. Van Buitenen (1981: 162) notes that Vedic rituals require a determination of the specific purpose (*saṃkalpa*) for every single ritual.

many-branched' (2.42). The followers of the Veda serve as an example of a 'lack of discrimination': they are without real knowledge, but indulge in flowery language (*puṣpitāṃ vācam*) and in the Vedic doctrine (*vedavādarata*) that teaches 'There is no alternative.'[34] What follows is a critical summary of the ritualistic world-view (2.43–44):

For them, who consist of desire, heaven is the highest (goal), they are keen on gaining pleasure and power, which are found in many different rituals and brought about in the (next) birth by the fruits of ritual acts. The faculty of discrimination, which is of the nature of determination, of those who are addicted to pleasure and power, whose mind is robbed by this (goal), is not ready for concentration.

The dogmatism of the followers of the Veda stands in sharp contrast to their lack of discrimination. Another aspect of this description of the followers of the Veda is to identify Arjuna as one of them, since he wants to act only when he can enjoy the fruits happily and reach heaven, which is also secured ritually through ancestral rites. In this conceptual framework, (ordained) ritual action is regarded as an instrument for pursuing one's interests. This instrumentalising view of action is rejected because it assesses activities on the basis of their benefits only. This lays the foundation for the following reformulation of Arjuna's problem, which consists not in the painful fruits of action, but in the fact that Arjuna measures the legitimacy of action according to what it means to him, that is, whether it makes him happy or unhappy. This view is rejected, and a different perspective has to be developed that allows him to see the purpose of action appropriately. In order to be able to do that, the faculty of discrimination (*buddhi*) has to be purged of all personal interests in order to bring all activities under its control.

Such a purification of the *buddhi* means leaving the realm of 'acquisition and conservation' (*yogakṣema*) behind one. *BhG* 2.45 lists the qualifications that Arjuna must acquire on the basis of Sāṃkhya ideas in order to transcend the Vedic world-view. While the Veda has its objects in the realm of the three powers of nature, the 'three *guṇas*' (*traiguṇyaviṣayā vedā*), Arjuna must be free of them (*nistraiguṇyo bhava*) and always abide in the clarity of the *buddhi* (*nityasattvastha*).[35] This argument on the limited use of the

[34] A similar depiction of Vedic ritualism is given in *MuṇḍU* 1.2.10: 'They think that the desired fruits of rituals are best. Deluded, they declare: "There no greater good".' (*iṣṭāpūrtaṃ manyamānā variṣṭhaṃ na anyac chreyo vedanyante pramūḍhāḥ*). In both texts, their dogmatic position is summarised in the formula *na anyad* ('nothing else'). While the *BhG* is critical of desire only, the *MuṇḍU* rejects sacrifice in general.

[35] This compound causes difficulties because of the semantic polyvalence of the word *sattva* (see van Buitenen 1957a: 88). Since the *BhG* passage deals primarily with the *buddhi*, I suggest understanding *sattva* here as synonymous with the ideal, purified *buddhi*.

Veda is summarised in the following image: 'As much use as there is in a well when water overflows on all sides, so much use is there in all Vedas for the enlightened Brahman.'[36] The ritualistic concept of *karman*, that is, the performance of ordained rituals for the sake of the fruits in heaven and here on earth, is then contrasted with the following definition of 'true knowledge' and 'correct practice', which amounts to the famous doctrine of 'disinterested action' (*niṣkāma karman*): 'Your entitlement (*adhikāra*) is only to the ordained act, never to its fruits. Be not motivated by the fruits of [ordained] acts, nor be attached to inactivity'[37] (2.46). In this redefinition of *karman*, one of the key concepts of ritualistic thinking, *adhikāra*, entitlement, ritual right and duty, is used. This term is employed in the Dharmaśāstras and in the Mīmāṃsā school of philosophy, which is focussed on the interpretation of the Veda: 'It covers the sum total of those properties such as birth, initiation, and stage of life as well as specific purpose, that qualify and thereby entitle a person to perform a certain act and reap the reward of his performance.'[38] This concept is reinterpreted in the *BhG* by being regarded as an obligation, a duty, whose performance must not yield any merit. *Adhikāra* now means the right and duty to perform a ritual, but with no entitlement to its fruits or merits (van Buitenen 1981: 163). Instead, the merit lies in the very relinquishing of rewards as the only way to leave the realm of *karman*. The connection between *adhikāra* and *karman* must be severed by erasing any personal attachment, which is the 'glue' connecting the fruits of an act to the actor. Therefore, one has to establish oneself in the highest cognitive faculty taught in Sāṃkhya, the *buddhi*, since this allows desire to be controlled. According to *BhG* 2.48–53, this can be achieved through yoga; as 2.48 declares: 'Perform the (ordained) acts as one who abides in yoga (*yogastha*), abandon (your) attachment (*saṅgam*), Dhanaṃjaya, and be indifferent towards success and failure. Yoga is called indifference.'[39] Again, the attitude of indifference is claimed as the solution to the problem, though this time indifference is to be combined with self-control and knowledge with a practice called *buddhiyoga* (2.49). The interpretation of this term varies:[40] van Buitenen, for instance, renders *yoga*

36 Van Buitenen (1981: 163) comments: 'a metaphor for the plenitude of spiritual experience transcending the ephemeral consequences of a strict Vedic ritualism'. The older debate on this verse seems to be settled (see Malinar 1996: 141–142).

37 *Karmaṇy evādhikāras te mā phaleṣu kadācana / mā karmaphalahetur bhūr mā te saṅgo 'stv akarmaṇi* //2.46/.

38 Van Buitenen 1981: 19; cf. Kunhan Raja (1946: 18ff.) on the relationship between Mīmāṃsā and the *BhG*.

39 *Yogasthaḥ kuru karmāṇi saṅgaṃ tyaktvā dhanaṃjaya / siddhyasiddhyoḥ samo bhūtvā samatvaṃ yoga ucyate* //2.48/.

40 See Zaehner's (1969: 146) list of possible translations.

as 'application' and translates 'application of the singleness of purpose', which does not indicate that *yoga* may refer here to an ascetic path to liberation and power, as it is presented elsewhere in the epic. In these contexts, *yoga* is a regimen of practices of self-control, self-harnessing and meditation often based on Sāṃkhyistic cosmology and somatology. Given the use of more technical terms at the beginning of this section (2.39) and the reference to liberation as the fruit of yoga (which surpasses the heavenly realms of the Veda) in 2.51, it seems more appropriate to indicate this connection too in the translation. In addition, it is only on the basis of the philosophical doctrines that *buddhiyoga* can be regarded as a means of liberation from *karman*.

In suggesting a more technical translation of *yoga*, one has to bear in mind that yoga may refer either to a state of 'self-control' and 'yoking' or to the practices that serve to achieve this goal. It is either a state or a process, although the two often converge, since success in yoga implies a mastery of the technique and results in a state of 'being in control'. This ambiguity needs to be kept in mind. In the case of *buddhiyoga* in 2.49–53, it seems that the state of a successful practice is being referred to, that is, 'being yoked to' or 'armed with the *buddhi*'. The *buddhi* is the faculty that permits such control, and therefore Kṛṣṇa exclaims: 'Take refuge in the *buddhi*!' However, in order to achieve this state, one has to practise self-restraint: 'Yoke yourself to yoga (self-control)! Yoga is skill in the ordained acts' (*yogāya yujyasva yogaḥ karmasu kauśalam*; 2.50ab). Conversely, the process aspect of yoga is also indicated in 2.53, when it is declared that yoga, the state of self-control, will be achieved when the *buddhi* has gained control and remains 'unmoved in concentration' (*samādhāv acalā*). It is claimed that all attachment is thereby removed and indifference will prevail. This requires an explanation which is not given here, obviously because it is taken for granted that the audience knows of the function of *buddhi* in Sāṃkhya (as announced in 2.39). The explanation is given later in *BhG* 3.5–6, but it should be given here too in order to understand the argument.

According to early Sāṃkhya, the *buddhi* is the highest principle within the hierarchy of the elements of the body which are produced by the powers of nature, the three *guṇas*. Therefore, the *buddhi* can influence and control all the other, lower faculties, such as 'ego-consciousness' (*ahaṃkāra*), which is responsible for creating the bond between the mind (*manas*), the senses and the sense-objects. In order to reach the stage of '*buddhi* in control', the other faculties must be restrained, and the many desires that incite the ego and its receptivity for pleasure and pain must be destroyed by cutting attachments and thereby stopping the production of karmic retributions and entitlements. This is a precondition for reaching the 'place that is free from harm' (*padam anāmayam*; 2.51). A corollary effect of this state is described in 2.50, which recalls the critique of Vedic teachings. Kṛṣṇa promises Arjuna that once his 'faculty of discrimination' has crossed the 'quagmire of delusion', he will experience disgust (*nirveda*) for what he has learned or ought to have learned in the traditional context of Vedic injunctions. This announcement is further discussed at the beginning of *BhG* 3. In the extant form of *BhG* 2, Arjuna now raises a question about the characteristics of one who has achieved this position, which Kṛṣṇa answers in what has been called by scholars the '*sthitaprajña* section' of the *BhG* (*BhG* 2.54–72), probably a later interpolation (see Ježic 1979a: 549; Malinar 1996: 309f.).

The man whose insight is firm (sthitaprajña)

Arjuna wants to know more about the actual practice and condition of that person who 'abides in concentration' (*samādhistha*) while his 'insight is firm' (*sthitaprajña*). While the word *samādhi* refers back to 2.53, the word *prajñā* is now used instead of *buddhi* – a word that will not be used again in the *BhG*. Kṛṣṇa's answer is a treatise on yogic meditation that culminates in liberation, not in a life dedicated to desireless action, as promoted in the previous section. It begins with the following definition (2.55): 'When a man gives up all the desires that occupy his heart and is satisfied with himself in himself, he is called "a man whose insight is firm".'[41] The word *prajñā* is used in Buddhist texts[42] and the *Yogasūtra* for the insight and knowledge that arise when the cognitive faculty (called *citta* or *buddhi* in these texts) has become stable as a result of meditative practices. In the present context, a similar distinction is drawn between the condition of the cognitive faculty and the insight gained by its yogic application. In order to be of 'firm insight', an ascetic attitude of indifference and freedom from emotion needs to be developed, as described in 2.56–57. While this qualifies the detachment in the performance of ordained actions recommended to Arjuna earlier as being similar to that of a *yogin*, it also shows that complete detachment results in a meditative withdrawal from the world, as expressed

[41] *Prajahāti yadā kāmān sarvān pārtha manogatān / ātmany evātmanā tuṣṭaḥ sthitaprajñas tadocyate //2.55/*. The compound *sthitaprajña* does not occur in the *MDh*. We find *sthirabuddhi* (12.223.22; 12.294.3; 12.313.47; *BhG* 5.20), *kṛtaprajña* (12.187.46; 12.215.30; 12.216.27; 12.223.20; etc.), *parimitaprajña* (12.213.15) and *akṛtaprajña* (*MBh* 12.246.6). Only rarely are *prajñā* and *buddhi* used as synonyms (e.g. 12.215.17; 12.222.5), while they are distinguished in 12.168.32.

[42] See *YS* 1.20; 1.48–49; 2.27; 3.5. On *prajñā* in the Upaniṣads see Bakker 1982: 134; on *paññā* in the Buddhist *Nikāyas* see Underwood 1973; Vetter 1988: 35ff.

in the following comparison with the tortoise (2.58): 'When he entirely withdraws his senses from their objects as a tortoise withdraws its limbs, his insight is firmly established.' If this withdrawal is continued, it results in a vision of 'the highest' (*param*; 2.59): 'The sense-objects vanish for the embodied self, who no longer takes them, with the exception of drink; but also drink disappears for him who has seen the highest.'[43] Remarkable is the change of subject, which is no longer the practising ascetic, but the 'self' who resides in the body and is about to gain liberation. While liberation is explicitly addressed only at the end of *BhG* 2, this is done in a parallel passage in *MBh* 12.197.16–18, in the context of a dialogue between the sages Bṛhaspati and Manu. Manu declares that one reaches the 'highest' at the hour of death, when one manages to keep the *buddhi* clear of all attachment. Using exactly the same words as in *BhG* 2.59, the departure of the 'embodied self' is described as a process in which all the senses vanish:

> The sense-objects vanish for the embodied self, who no longer takes them, with the exception of drink; but also drink vanishes for him who has seen the highest. When the faculty of discrimination functions in the heart free from the qualities of *karman*, *brahman* is reached. There the [process of] dissolution comes to an end. Feeling nothing, hearing nothing, tasting nothing, seeing nothing, smelling nothing, thinking nothing, this [liberated] being (*sattva*) enters the highest.[44]

We have thus in *BhG* 2.59 an abbreviated description of salvation as a process of a gradual dissolution of the senses and other faculties, which results in liberating knowledge and the death of the body.[45] This process is again referred to at the end of this chapter (2.69–72).

Having indicated the goal, its practice is dealt with in more detail (2.60, 61–68). In this connection, the struggle implied in the practice of 'yoking' is highlighted and illustrated by a chain of causal reactions that need to be

[43] *Viṣayā vinivartante nirāhārasya dehinaḥ / rasavarjaṃ raso 'py asya paraṃ dṛṣṭvā nivartate //2.59/.* Edgerton (1944: 27) interpretes *nirāhāra* as referring to practices of fasting and translates 'abstains from food' (cf. Garbe 1921: 90; van Buitenen 1981: 79). However, Zaehner (1969: 152) argues that it should be understood not only as 'fasting', but as avoiding any sensual intake. While the latter is probably to be preferred because it is the more comprehensive with regard to all the different sense-objects, fasting seems to be part of the practice and is perhaps the more important when the self is about to leave the body. This situation is also indicated by making *rasa* an exception. While *rasa* can be understood as 'taste' for the sense-objects in general, Edgerton points out that it is also the last remaining realm of the senses. In even more concrete terms *rasa* is the essential attribute of water and all other liquids and therefore may refer to their intake as the only nourishment an ascetic about to be liberated may accept. This is indicated in my translation.

[44] *Viṣayā vinivartante nirāhārasya dehinaḥ / rasavarjaṃ raso 'py asya paraṃ dṛṣṭvā vinivartate //12.197.16/. Buddhiḥ karmaguṇair hīnā yadā manasi vartate / tadā saṃpadyate brahma tatraiva pralayaṃ gatam //12.197.17/. Asparśanam aśṛṇvānam anāsvādam adarśanam / aghrānam avitarkaṃ ca sattvaṃ praviśate param //12.197.18* = *BhG* 2.59.

[45] However, I no longer propose that 2.59–60 is an interpolation (cf. Malinar 1996: 150–151).

stopped so that the cognitive faculty (called *buddhi* in this passage) gains control. However, this description is interrupted in 2.61, which declares Kṛṣṇa to be that highest goal (*matpara*). The verse is out of context, since nowhere else in this chapter is Kṛṣṇa treated as the 'highest'. This is one of several verses in which Kṛṣṇa's divinity is asserted in the chapters dealing with meditation without further explanation. When these verses are inserted, his divinity is regarded as established, and therefore it is probably based on the theistic framework presented in the following chapters. However, given the dramatic structure of Kṛṣṇa's self-revelation in these later chapters of the *BhG*, such verses seem to be interpolations that were inserted when the theistic layers were added. The description of ascetic practice begins in 2.60 by pointing to the difficulties in keeping the senses under control. *BhG* 2.62–66 juxtapose the situation of the senses being in control with that of the senses being under control. The first (2.62–63) describes how the *buddhi* is destroyed (*buddhināśa*, 2.64) in a chain reaction (→ indicates causation): sense objects → attachment → desire → anger → delusion → destruction of memory (*smṛti*) → destruction of *buddhi*. This is contrasted in 2.64–65 with the successful taming of the senses that brings about clarity (*prasāda*). The result of the successful practice is summarised in two images: 'The controlled man is awake in what is night for all creatures; likewise it is night for the envisioning ascetic when the other creatures are awake' (2.69) What is sleep and unconsciousness for 'common folk', the darkness that is caused by the withdrawal of the senses and is close to death, is welcomed by the ascetic, since this very darkness allows him to see the 'highest'. Conversely, what is 'daylight', sense-contact for the others, is darkness for the ascetic, since the highest is overshadowed. The other image also occurs elsewhere[46] and deals with the end of desire (2.70): 'As the rivers flow into the ocean, which remains unmoved, even when it is filled, so do all desires enter him who has gained pacification, and not the one who desires desire (*kāmakāmin*).' This image also indicates an inversion of the 'regular flow' of life. Whereas *kāma*, desire, is usually directed towards its objects, it flows back into the ascetic, where it gets lost, like rivers once they have entered the ocean. In the present context, both images serve to describe the state before liberation which in what follows is dealt with in more philosophical terms (2.71–72). The man who has given up all his desires and moves around free from longing, who is without possessiveness (*nirmama*) and egotism (*nirahaṃkāra*), achieves peace. This

[46] In the Upaniṣads, it serves to describe the dissolution of the particular beings into a greater one; see *ChU* 6.10.2; *MuṇḍU* 3.2.8; *Pru* 6.5. In the Nārāyaṇīya section of the epic, it illustrates how individual selves enter the god Nārāyaṇa (see also *MBh* 12.243.9).

is the condition characteristic of *brahman*: having obtained it he is not deluded. When he remains in this condition even in the hour of death, he attains that vanishing away that is *brahman* (*brahmanirvāṇa*).

In this passage, a term that is also met with in Sāṃkhya is used, namely *ahaṃkāra*, the cognitive faculty of ego-consciousness. Its function is attachment to the sense objects and appropriation of the world by relating to it through the word 'I'. Karmic bondage occurs only when an ego claims agency and responsibility for what happens. As a consequence, it is held that renouncing all desires means to rid oneself of 'egotism' (*nirahaṃkāra*) and possessiveness (*nirmama*). This results in a '*brahman*-like' condition, which means that all attachment is gone and an impersonal state of being has been obtained. When this condition is maintained, one reaches '*brahmanirvāṇa*', the *nirvāṇa*, the fading away that is *brahman*.[47] However, this happens only when this *brahman*-like stability is also retained at the hour of death (*antakāle*).[48] The designation of the final goal as *brahmanirvāṇa* can be regarded as another piece of evidence for the use of Buddhist terminology in this section of *BhG* 2. Although, as Dasgupta (1952: 450, note 1) points out, *nirvāṇa* is not an exclusively Buddhist term, it is characteristic of Buddhist meditative practices and also suits the use of other terms that establish a connection with Buddhist practices.[49] The question is, why would the author of this section want to do this? A possible answer is to assert that the *buddhiyoga* promoted earlier is connected to already well-established traditions teaching liberation from *karma* through ascetic and meditative practices. In doing do, Upaniṣadic and Sāṃkhya terminology is confounded with, or at least brought close to, Buddhist terminology. In contrast to similar strategies used in chapters 5 and 6, which serve to establish a hierarchy among the different paths of liberation, such a classification of goals is not suggested here. Neither is *nirvaṇa* regarded as lower, nor *brahman* explicitly as higher; nor would Kṛṣṇa be considered superior to both. Therefore, I see the function of this passage as turning *buddhiyoga* into a step on the way to liberation and bringing it closer to competing ascetic traditions. However, the price for this is that the 'outward' orientation of *buddhiyoga* as a technique enabling one to perform one's duties in

47 An alternative translation might be 'fading away in *brahman*'. For a discussion, see below, pp. 118ff.

48 Zaehner doubts whether *BhG* 2.71 and 72 belong together: 'The philosophical transition in this stanza and the next is abrupt.' This impression is based on his general, questionable assumption that there is a fundamental difference between meditation in the theistic and Upaniṣadic texts, which aims at 'sublimation' or 'integration', and the one taught in the Buddhist-nihilist traditions, which results in 'suppression'. I do not think that such a distinction is being drawn here.

49 For instance, *smṛti*, 'memory' or 'awareness'; cf. Mahā-Satipaṭṭhāna Sutta (*DN* 22); *bhāvanā*, meditative realisation; cf. *AN* 2.2.1 and Vetter 1988. Zaehner (1969: 157ff.) lists many other references to Buddhist texts.

the light of day in the world is qualified in the extant text in this rhetorically skilful section on final liberation. On the other hand, in the extant text, this interpolation places an additional emphasis on the possible contradiction between the indifference obtained by *buddhiyoga* and the demand not to be indifferent to the performance of ordained action. This contradiction also emerges if this chapter is seen as ending with 2.53, as it probably did before the *sthitaprajña* section was included. With or without interpolation, though, the *BhG* makes even more urgent the question: why should one not strive for liberation by total withdrawal instead of living a social life while being totally indifferent towards it? – a question that is promptly raised by Arjuna at the beginning of *BhG* 3.

BHAGAVADGĪTĀ 3: TURNING THE WHEEL OF SACRIFICE

At the beginning of this chapter, Arjuna raises the very question one would expect after Kṛṣṇa's discourse on *buddhiyoga* (3.1): 'If you hold that insight is better than (ordained) action, why then do you yoke me to this terrible deed?' Rather than seeing a solution to his problem, Arjuna feels even more confused. Kṛṣṇa's reply begins with a distinction between two points of view (*niṣṭhā*): the followers of Sāṃkhya practise *jñānayoga* (discipline of knowledge), while the followers of yoga are engaged in *karmayoga* (discipline of action). Kṛṣṇa claims authority as a teacher when he declares that he taught these doctrines long ago (*purā*).[50] However, in what follows, this distinction is not explored further and is only again taken up in *BhG* 5.4–5 by stating that both viewpoints yield the same fruit. Although the verses may have been inserted at a later stage (perhaps in order to subsume both doctrines under the common umbrella of yoga), in the extant text, the reference to the two schools serves to equate them as two possible ways of dealing with the problem of karmic bondage. Such an equation seems especially called for in the new teaching of *karmayoga*, which is now declared to be a path to liberation as efficient as the practice of Sāṃkhya. This echoes the way the topic of yoga was introduced in *BhG* 2.39, where it was the place of *buddhi* in yoga, not in Sāṃkhya, that required explanation.

Action as 'nature'

Thus, the chapter focusses on *karmayoga*, self-control through action that allows one to act without experiencing any consequences. The exposition of this teaching begins by rejecting two other possible ways to achieve

[50] This is similar to *BhG* 4.3, where Kṛṣṇa proclaims himself the original teacher of yoga; see below.

freedom from *karman* (3.4): first, the idea that by merely doing nothing one would rid oneself of the fruits of action (*naiṣkarmya*); and secondly, that renunciation (*saṃnyāsād*) brings about this goal. The first view may refer not only to Arjuna's attitude of refraining from violent action, but also to Jaina teachings of inactivity and the suppression of all physical activities.[51] The second is the idea of *saṃnyāsa* or the renunciation of social duties and ritual obligations as an alternative way of life for those who seek liberation. This alternative is the subtext in other debates in the *MBh*, and is, in fact, present in the many ascetics who feature in the epic. It is a tradition whose historical and social impact is mirrored in the epic in philosophical debates as well as in stories. Indeed, as Biardeau (1981) suggests, parts of the *BhG* can be read as an attempt to qualify renunciation and allow for the pursuit of liberation while remaining within the social arena. We find in the *BhG* different ways in which such a mediation between ascetic values and interest in preserving the socio-ritual order is attempted. In *BhG* 3, the *prakṛti* concept of Sāṃkhya philosophy is used to explain why 'doing nothing' is an illusion. Since *prakṛti* is the cause of the visible world and activity is one of its ontological characteristics, every individual being is driven by activity, since it is a product of *prakṛti*, the ever-active nature (3.5, van Buitenen's translation): 'For no one lives even for one moment without *some* act, for the three forces of nature cause everyone to act, willy-nilly.' By adopting the Sāṃkhya view that every being is active by nature, even if it decides not to act, a critique is launched of those who think they do nothing. In addition, the Sāṃkhya doctrine allows criticism of a concept of action that is based on intentionality, as is the case, for instance, in the ritualistic interpretation of action. Here it is argued that only purposeful and intended action that yields fruits is *karman*. From a Sāṃkhya point of view this is an illusion, because thinking, feeling, eating etc. also count as *karman* and have consequences, and it is not easy to rid oneself of this aspect of *karman*, since the ever-active senses and cognitive faculties are difficult to control. Practising yoga therefore aims at exercising control over the automatic and usually uncontrolled (*avaśah*) activity of one's physical, emotional and mental apparatus. As a consequence, an ascetic practice is criticised in which outward inactivity covers intense, mental activity: 'He who, while checking the faculties of action, yet in his mind imagines the sense objects, is full of delusion; he is called a hypocrite. But he who checks the senses with his mind and then practises self-control in action using his faculties of action without any attachment, he stands out' (3.6–7). This

[51] This view is also quoted in *BhG* 18.3, which Bronkhorst (1993) identifies as the Jaina one.

depiction of false asceticism addresses the problem of how to assess the achievements of an ascetic. Outward inactivity is obviously rejected as the sole criterion, detachment in action being regarded as the yardstick of true relinquishment. Therefore, Kṛṣṇa demands, 'Carry out the ordained acts, since action is better than non-action', and he adds that 'the journey in the body' (*śarīrayātrā*) does not succeed without action. This extended, Sāṃkhyistic meaning of *karman* remains the basis of much of the *BhG*[52] and the following reinterpretation of the Vedic sacrifice.

Sacrifice as the purpose of disinterested action

A remarkable feature of the use of the Sāṃkhya concept of *prakṛti* is that it results in an almost 'anti-sāṃkhyistic' interpretation. The conclusion advocated here is not to stop acting and concentrate on gaining that knowledge which liberates one from the ever-active realm of *prakṛti*, but to continue acting while ending attachment. As a consequence, the purpose of such acting cannot be found within Sāṃkhya because neither activity nor the manifest world is purposeful as such – they exist only for the sake of the immortal self, to bring about its purpose, which is liberation. This leads to the question: why should one prove self-control in the realm of social duties? This brings us back to Arjuna's doubt at the beginning of the chapter: why not be indifferent toward duties and activity too? What is the use of disinterested action? These queries can be answered by propagating a purpose (*artha*) for acting, and this is exactly what is done in 3.10, where sacrificial activity is declared to be the purpose of *karmayoga*, of acting without attachment. At first sight, it seems odd that now the very notion of sacrifice, which had been condemned earlier, should be the solution, and scholars have time and again rejected 3.9–16 as an interpolation.[53] However, a different definition of sacrifice is given here that is meant to restore the original idea of sacrifice. Kṛṣṇa argues that only actions for the sake of sacrifice do not produce karmic results (3.9): 'This world is bound by acts, except the act for the sake of sacrifice (*yajñārtham*). For this purpose, you must perform action, son of Kuntī, as one who is free from attachment (*muktasaṅga*).'

[52] Van Buitenen's (1981: 14) remarks that in Hindu tradition action was 'never centrally regarded as an indifferent or spontaneous form of behaviour' needs qualification. W. von Humboldt had earlier pointed to the difference between Western, intentional concepts of action and the extended notion in Sāṃkhya which includes all effects of matter in beings and not only what is meant in the West by 'the morality of action' (1826b: 368).

[53] For instance, Garbe 1921: 21; Otto 1935a: 40; Ježic 1979a: 550. Often the only reason for regarding the passage with suspicion is that it deals with sacrifice.

For the followers of the Vedic tradition (*vedavādin*) criticised in *BhG* 2.42f., this must sound rather absurd, since the very purpose of sacrifice is to fulfil desires and to bind the sacrificer to the fruits of his ritual *karman*. However, Kṛṣṇa declares that it is wrong to regard sacrifice as an instrument serving an individual's purpose. Rather, it should be the other way round: the ritual is the very purpose of action. This means that the fruits of the ritual are in the ritual and for the ritual. Therefore, one must become a ritual actor by participating in ritual retribution without attachment. This idea is explained by referring to the origin of sacrifice (*BhG* 3.10–13):

> At that time when Prajāpati created the creatures together with the sacrifice (*sahayajña*), he declared: 'Through it you shall prosper, it shall be the cow that yields your desires (*iṣṭakāmadhuk*). Through it you shall nourish the gods and the gods shall nourish you. By mutually (*parasparam*) nourishing each other, you shall attain the highest good. For the gods, being refreshed by the sacrifice, will give you the desired enjoyments.'

After reporting this speech, Kṛṣṇa declares: 'Who enjoys what is given by them without returning (anything) is but a thief (*stena*). The good ones who eat what is left over from the sacrifice are free from all taints, but the evil ones who cook (only) for themselves eat sin (*agham*).'

In contrast to the interpretation of sacrifice current among the followers of the Veda (see *BhG* 2.42–44), this passage stresses the cosmogonic function of sacrifice as being an integral part of creation. This function extends to the present, since sacrifice is regarded as mandatory for maintaining the created world as the hub of all the reciprocal relationships that creatures entertain. Sacrifice guarantees the prosperity of those who participate in it through its retributive, reciprocal structure (*parasparam*). It is the arena where the separated spheres of gods and men meet, but are also kept apart, otherwise no mutual profit would be possible. This means that each sphere is maintained through what it is not – the gods through the human beings, men through the gods. Both eat and thus continue living because of what is sacrificed. This point is stressed in 3.12–13. Eating is justified only when it is based on ritual and when the gods have eaten first. This is to acknowledge that the very existence of eatable substances (plants, animals) is based on the activity of the gods, who sustain the order and orderliness of creation as a realm of mutual dependence and reciprocal relationships (*parasparaṃ bhāvayanataḥ*). Reciprocity (*paraspara*) is the basis of ritual and the cosmic order that is based on it (Bailey 1983a: 26–32). Strictly speaking, one always eats the remnants of sacrificed substances; one eats what has once lived. Therefore those who eat the leftovers of sacrifice (*yajñaśiṣṭāśin*) are justified in doing so: they do not commit any offence or produce karmic bondage, because they have given before they take and thus acknowledge retribution as the basis of living. They are free from any negative consequences of the violence that is implied not only in sacrifice, but also in sustaining one's life. This 'paradoxical pretense of destroying life in order to gain life', as Heesterman puts it (1993: 34), is at the centre of this old interpretation of sacrifice quoted here in the *BhG*.

Conversely, it is characteristic of an evil person (*pāpa*) that he cooks for himself (*ātmakāraṇāt*) alone and thus eats without acknowledging the sacrificial character of life. He is a thief because he lives from the sacrifices performed by the others, which he takes without paying the price by entering the structure of ritual retribution.[54] According to *BhG* 3.13, he eats not food but 'sin', because he has taken another's life outside the ritual context, which amounts to murder. This interpretation is also corroborated by the following parallel passage in ṚV 10.117.6 (*TaitBr.* 2.8.8.3): 'A man without understanding obtains food in vain; I speak the truth: it will be his death (*vadha*). He nourishes neither friend nor ally. The man who eats alone is guilty alone.' This seems to be the basis for both the *BhG* verse and the following statement in *ManuS* 3.118: 'A man who cooks only for his own sake eats nothing but sin; for the food prescribed for good men is this – eating the leftovers of a sacrifice.'[55]

In contrast to these parallels, the *BhG* stresses the purifying character of eating the 'leftovers of the sacrifice', which corresponds to the interpretation of violence as 'non-violence' in the context of ritual given in *ManuS* 5.39: 'the sacrifice is for the prosperity of this whole world. Within sacrifice, therefore, killing is not killing' (*yajñasya bhūtyai sarvasya tasmād yajñe vadho 'vadha*; trans. Olivelle; cf. the discussion in Biardeau and Malamoud 1976: 53–54). This reinterpretation of sacrificial action as exempt from negative karmic consequences opens the door to interpreting the battle against one's relatives as a 'sacrificial action' equally exempt from negative consequences. All this serves to explain why only actions for the sake of sacrifice do not produce karmic bondage (*karmabandhana*; *BhG* 3.9). It is not a specific, for instance expiatory, ritual (*prāyaścitta*) that is offered here as the solution to the problem of violence, but rather the structure of ritual itself. However,

54 Cf. *MBh* 5.132.2: a king who does not fight is declared a thief because he lives off his subjects without performing his duty in return (see above, pp. 40ff.).

55 *Aghaṃ sa kevalaṃ bhuṅkte yaḥ pacaty ātmakāraṇāt / yajñaśiṣṭāśanaṃ hy etat satām annaṃ vidhīyate* (trans. Olivelle). Cf. *ManuS* 3.285, where the 'leftovers of sacrifice' are called the 'nectar of immortality' (*yajñaśeṣaṃ tathāmṛtam*). However, nothing is said about its purifying character, as is the case in *BhG* 3.13–14 and 4.31. On sacrificial food, see also Weber-Brosamer (1988); for 'leftovers', see Malamoud 1972, Wezler 1978.

in the present context this ritual structure is further reinterpreted, since the performance of ritual is not primarily regarded as a way to fulfil one's desires, but is turned into an occasion for proving one's yogic detachment. The reference to sacrifice is thus an attempt to deal with the intrinsic problem of advocating disinterested action: it needs a purpose. Otherwise the argument regarding reasons for renouncing all activity cannot be refuted. The reinterpretation of sacrifice as the purpose of ascetic activity has great impact on subsequent arguments, since the model and idiom of sacrifice will be used in other passages on yoga and in the theistic chapters to come. It amounts to what Biardeau (1976: 129) calls a 'generalisation of the notion of sacrifice', which means not only that *karmayoga* is defined as a ritual act, but that each and every act can now be defined as a sacrifice. This interpretation results in upgrading *svadharma*, one's social duty, in two regards. First, social duties can be equated with sacrificial action. Secondly, they can be removed from the realm of (negative) karmic retribution. However, this solution contradicts the philosophical basis of many ascetic traditions, which postulate that liberation is possible only if one stops any karmic activity (including that which results in merit). Thus, the question remains: how is it explained that *karman*, as ritual action, does not produce *karman* in the sense of karmic bondage as claimed in *BhG* 3.9? Does the following description of the 'wheel of sacrifice' (3.14–16) offer any explanation?

The 'wheel of sacrifice'

The discourse on sacrifice continues with more details on the cyclical structure of sacrificial causation and reciprocity. It ends with the warning that those who do not contribute to the maintenance of this structure live in vain. *BhG* 3.14–15 is discussed by scholars as presenting the 'wheel of sacrifice', although only *cakra*, the Sanskrit word for 'wheel', is used in 3.16, not *yajñacakra*. Nevertheless, it confirms the idea that we are dealing here with some 'original' notion of sacrifice in which the sacrificed food is described as moving in a circle of cosmic regions and substances, with each living from other beings, while also contributing to their subsistence. Such 'wheels' or sacrificial cycles are indeed described in Vedic texts (see Wilden 2000), while the *BhG* offers its own version:

> Creatures arise from food, food arises from rain, rain arises from sacrifice, sacrifice arises from (ordained) action (*karman*). You must know that (ordained) action arises from *brahman* [the ritual knowledge and formulations contained in Veda], and *brahman* arises from the 'indestructible' (*akṣara* [the syllable *Oṃ*]). Therefore the ubiquitous *brahman* is forever founded in the sacrifice (*yajña*).

This wheel and the relationship between the different elements were much discussed, especially with regard to the interpretation of the terms *brahman* and *akṣara*. Here I follow van Buitenen, who stresses that both terms are best understood as referring to *brahman* in the sense of the 'true formulations and knowledge' contained in the Vedic texts and *akṣara* as the syllable *Oṃ*, the essence of Vedic language and truth, *brahman*.[56] While there are parallels for some elements of the wheel in other texts, the description as a whole seems original to the *BhG*; in particular, the elements *brahman* and *akṣara* are not mentioned in other texts. *YājñaS* 3.121–124 describes in great detail how the sacrificial substance, the food offered in the sacrificial fire, moves through different cosmic realms and returns as food after it has nourished the gods and rewarded the sacrificers. It concludes with: 'From food arises sacrifice, then again food, and again sacrificial performance (*kratu*). In this way this beginningless and endless wheel (*anādyantaṃ cakram*) moves on and on.' This passage uses the word 'wheel', as does the *BhG*, and stresses the mutual dependence of food and sacrifice.

Causal connections between other elements of the wheel are highlighted in the Upaniṣads too.[57] Another parallel to the *BhG* is *ManuS* 3.76: 'An oblation duly consigned to the fire reaches the sun; from the sun comes the rain; from rain, food; and from food, offspring.' Here the sacrificial cycle is used to place the householder (*gṛhasthin*) on top of the different 'ways of life' (*āśrama*). The *ManuS* account starts, as is the case in *Chāndogya-Upaniṣad* (*ChU*), with the performance of sacrifice. This sequence is inverted in the *BhG*, where sacrificial action is mentioned only at the very end. This shows how purposefully the author of the *BhG* passage uses the well-known elements of the 'sacrificial wheel' in order to demonstrate that everything is based on sacrifice. In addition, the wheel shows some characteristic features that qualify its circular character and may help one to understand why acting for the sake of sacrifice has no karmic consequences.

The wheel describes not only stages in the transformation of sacrificial food, but also a cycle of production in which the preceding element brings about the one that follows. The description of this process ends with the

56 Cf. van Buitenen (1959: 186): 'The whole passage (3.9–15) is devoted to ritual, and brahman in this context can scarcely be anything but old brahman "Vedas and Vedāṅgas".' With regard to the word *akṣara*, he notes: 'Akṣara is . . . no longer the syllable as such . . . but a certain syllable, or rather sound, which hypostasized brahman and from which the Veda and hence the world originate' (1959: 181). In rendering *brahman* as 'true formulation', I follow Thieme (1952: 117).

57 Some of the causal connections appear in the so-called 'science of the five sacrificial fires' (*pañcāgnividyā*; see *ChU* 5.4–10; *BĀU* 6.2.9–13). For the connection between food and creatures, see *TaitU* 2.2; *TaitĀr* 8.2, *MaitU* 6.11; 6.12; 6.37. For rain and food see *ChU* 5.5.2; *BĀU* 6.2.10; *ChU* 5.6.2; *BĀU* 6.2.11; *MaitU* 6.37; *ManuS* 3.76.

statement that '*brahman* is forever founded in sacrifice' (*brahma nityaṃ yajñe pratiṣṭhitam*). Sacrifice as the foundation of *brahman* is not only a location, it also has a creative quality, which is indicated by the perfect participle of the verbal compound *prati* + *sthā* (to establish, ground). In his study of *pratiṣṭhā*, Gonda (1954: 338) considers the following two meanings the most important: 'a firm and ultimate ground to rest upon', and 'the "hold" one has on the object on which one is standing'. However, to give something 'support' also implies a causal connection. In this connection, causality applies not only to cause-and-effect relationships, but also to location (Gren-Eklund 1984: 107), of taking and holding ground. A *pratiṣṭhā* is such a 'ground' on which something established there can unfold and function. This is why *brahman*, although qualified as 'ubiquitous', still needs to be 'grounded' in order to becomes manifest and effective. The process of 'gaining ground' implies this mutual dependence between the place of production and its activation by that being which is 'established' there. This corresponds to the reciprocal character of sacrifice, which was mentioned as its main characteristic in *BhG* 3.10 (*parasparam*). These considerations also help to explain why sacrifice is the only element that is mentioned three times in the wheel: twice as a cause for other elements of the wheel (sacrifice → rain, *brahman*), and once when its own place of production is given (*karman*, ritual action → sacrifice). Within the wheel, sacrifice is bi-directional and recursive because it is caused by the very elements it itself brings about. While *karman* brings about sacrifice, sacrifice is the cause of *brahman*, ritual knowledge that unfolds only in ritual performance. *Brahman*, containing injunctions for sacrifice, in turn causes *karman*. A similar structure applies to *brahman*, which is mentioned twice in the wheel, both times connected with *karman* and sacrifice. *Brahman* is said to have its foundation in sacrifice, but is also the cause of *karman* (*brahman* → *karman*), from where, in turn, sacrifice comes. We see that *karman* is mentioned twice as well. The cyclical movement of the wheel thus implies the following recursive structure:

sacrifice → *brahman* → *karman* → sacrifice
brahman → *karman* → sacrifice → *brahman*
karman → sacrifice → *brahman* → *karman*

We meet here with a rather strong connection between the three most important factors that are used in the *BhG* to describe the structure of mutual dependence and causal interdependence as the characteristic feature of the ritually created world. It demonstrates that within this world there is no absolute position, and that there exists nothing which is not based on another, or conversely, that does not contribute to producing something else. In addition, due to the recursive structure of the three elements, the process is self-contained, which means that the cause produces itself as the effect, and the end of the process rewinds back to its beginning. The recursive and somehow paradoxical character of sacrifice is also expressed elsewhere, when it is said that 'they sacrificed the sacrifice with the sacrifice' (*yajñena yajñam ayajanta*; *ṚV* 10.90.16). Anyone entering this wheel enters a structure of production which does not leave much surplus, but produces only 'leftovers'. Each product of the activation of an element is itself turned into the cause of the subsequent one; it is consumed or used by the next. Creatures arise from food, which means they consume food, which in turn has consumed the rain, etc. The cycle of production is thus also a cycle of consumption. The texts mention only one surplus arising out of it for those who keep up this wheel, the 'leftovers' of sacrifice, food which is the 'nectar of immortality'. There is no mention of other fruits or merits or other notions linked to karmic bondage. The wheel of sacrifice thus demonstrates that actions for the sake of sacrifice do not cause karmic bondage because *karman* is itself part of the cycle of production and consumption. *Karman* that produces sacrifice is caused by ritual injunctions (*brahman*) based on sacrifice. There is no productivity claimed for *karman* outside the scope of ritual, which has only 'leftovers' as surplus. The 'wheel of sacrifice' thus implies a ritual economy producing a residual surplus which allows the food-cycle to be maintained and thus the well-being of all who participate in it. Nothing is done that produces a surplus or fruit apart from enabling its continuation – in the case of the sacrificer, 'the journey in the body' (3.8). Therefore, it is not harmful to act within this framework – and not only this; it is necessary to do so in order to maintain life as such. This is pointed out in 3.16: 'He who does not keep this moving wheel rolling accordingly lives in vain, Pārtha, since he indulges in his senses, living a life that is sin.' One must become a 'turner of the wheel' in order to avoid sin, and this can only be done by performing *karman*, ordained action for the sake of sacrifice, and thus maintaining the cosmos. As a consequence, Kṛṣṇa asks Arjuna to perform the ordained actions (*kāryam karman*; 3.19) and says he should follow the ideal of King Janaka and others: 'You too must act while looking only to what holds together the world (*lokasaṃgraha*)' (3.20). The important word is here *lokasaṃgraha*, which summarises the ultimate purpose of ritual action, which does not serve primarily to achieve a goal or fulfil desires, but to contribute to the maintenance of cosmic order. This is made the purpose of detached, sacrificial activity, of *karman*, since it is the ordained contribution for sustaining the reciprocal relationships that are regarded as the basis of life. When confined to this purpose, *karman* is consumed in the sacrificial wheel it helps to roll on. This task is especially connected to the king, since he is vested with the task of protecting the world and striving for the prosperity of his kingdom. The king in particular is called on to take care of *lokasaṃgraha*, since his achievements are the yardstick (*pramāṇa*) for the people.[58]

This is a reinterpretation of the Vedic, ritualistic understanding of *karman* in that it is not desires but ascetic detachment that is required for the beneficial performance of one's social duties. In this way, renunciation is placed not outside the socio-ritual context, but at its very centre.[59] Kṛṣṇa proposes that Arjuna can be true to his *dharma* and still be purified from any sin that he might commit in the meantime. One can rid oneself of karmic consequences only when the link that ties actions to the actor, consisting in the egoistic appropriation of the mechanism of action, is severed. Although this passage is a critique of the Vedic doctrine of a pursuit of desires and marks a shift in the ritual paradigm, at the same time it confirms one of its basic assumptions: that action needs a purpose or is done for a purpose. *Karman* must be regarded not as an instrument, but as a factor in the wheel of sacrifice, a wheel that 'keeps the world together'. Drawing the arguments of *BhG* 3 together, we see a blending of the Sāṃkhya concept of nature (*prakṛti*) and reciprocal, circular structure of sacrifice: just as action is regarded as ingrained in the 'nature' of beings because they have been created by 'nature' (*prakṛti*), and produces karmic bondage only when appropriated by an agent, so *karman* is an element in ritual that brings about the sacrifice and thus the 'grounding' and manifestation of *brahman*. It is claimed that *karman* is best regarded as one's contribution to the reciprocal structure of the cosmic order: since its only purpose is maintaining this order, no karmic bondage can arise. Eating the 'leftovers' of the sacrifice as the only surplus one should accept as the outcome of the sacrificial process does not cause any bondage, as is the case when one sustains the natural activity necessary for continuing the 'journey in the body'.

Kṛṣṇa concludes the exposition of the *lokasaṃgraha* idea by presenting himself as its model: although there is nothing left for him to achieve, he still 'moves in (ordained) action' because otherwise the people would follow his

58 The compound *lokasaṃgraha* occurs in seven other instances in the epic, mostly in connection with kingship (12.58.19; 12.122.14; 12.150.16) and *dharma* (12.251.25; 14.46.37). Parallel passages confirm that *saṃgraha* is connected to the duties of a king. According to *ManuS* 7.113, 'maintenance' of the kingdom (*rāṣṭrasya saṃgrahe*) is one of the main duties of kings. See also *MBh* 12.88.1–2. See Dhadphale 1978 for a similar usage of *saṃgraha* in Pāli texts.

59 De Smet (1977) calls this a 'Copernican reversal' of the traditional view of *karman*.

example and stop performing their duties too (3.22–23). This in turn would result in a breakdown of the social order, as indicated by 'mixture of caste' (*varṇasaṃkara*) and the destruction of the people that will follow. Here, Arjuna's fear of ruining the family (1.41ff.) is rejected by pointing out that he will cause even greater destruction if he refrains from action. What counts is whether an action helps to 'keep the world together' or not. This argument is summarised as follows (3.25): 'As ignorant men do their acts being attached to them, Bhārata, the wise shall act without attachment as one who wants to keep the world together.'[60] This juxtaposition of those who do not know and still contribute to the maintenance of order while suffering the fruits of their actions, and the one who is detached yet wishes (desiderative form!) to keep the world together, highlight some important implications of the doctrine. First, seen from the perspective of worldly order, it does not matter how one acts, whether with or without attachment, since performing one's duty is all that counts. It is only with regard to the prospect of individual liberation that detachment is important. This is also emphasised in the next verse (3.26), which warns one not to 'sow doubts' (*buddhibheda*) among the ignorant. It is deemed better to be secretive about one's insights than to cause turmoil in the minds of ordinary people.[61] Apart from considering this an 'elitist' statement concerned to maintain restricted access to education, the verse could be read as a rejection of those who promote renunciation and asceticism as the alternative to the performance of one's social and ritual duties as it is known from the so-called *śramaṇa* movements. Secondly, the verse confirms that detached action can be considered a positive value only when it is done for a purpose. Even when detached, one has to be attached to something (as indicated by the desiderative form 'wish to act' in 3.25). The purpose makes it possible to welcome an act (cf. 3.26: 'he should take kindly to all actions'; *joṣayet sarvakarmaṇi*). Thirdly, there are purposes (and thus forms of attachment) which have no repercussions for the actors, since they do not produce any fruit apart from allowing them to live. Sacrifice and the concern for 'holding the world together' are two such purposes. Actions performed for these purposes are regarded as part of a natural and socio-cosmic process in which they are circulated but not appropriated by an agent. When karmic bondage is caused by a subject's appropriation of

60 *Saktāḥ karmaṇy avidvāṃso yathā kurvanti bhārata/ kuryād vidvāṃs tathāsaktaś cikīrṣur lokasaṃgraham* //3.25/.

61 Seen from a modern perspective, this appears as a rather elitist statement, but it is not untypical of structures of education that are based on restricted access to knowledge. It also confirms that knowledge was regarded as a practice and thus as something that has repercussions on one's way of life.

activity, then activity and what accrues from it must be redirected, that is, cast upon something and someone else in order to remain untouched by it. When it is given up in sacrifice or regarded as a natural process, *karman* is diverted away from the agent. We will meet a similar interpretation in the subsequent chapters, which explain the activity of a successful *yogin* and of a loyal follower of the god Kṛṣṇa. In the present context, this idea is pursued by again drawing on Sāṃkhya concepts.

Social duty as enacting one's 'way of being'

This section explains, from the perspective of Sāṃkhya, how to sever the connection between the actor and the act, and how to turn the performance of social duty (*svadharma*) into an enactment of one's nature (*svāprakṛti*). First of all, the mechanism of karmic appropriation is explained as being brought about by the cognitive faculty of 'ego-consciousness' (*ahaṃkāra*). In the Sāṃkhya hierarchy of faculties, it is placed beneath the *buddhi*, and in 3.27–28 it is identified as the place where karmic bondage is produced: 'While actions are everywhere performed by the three powers of nature, one who is deluded by ego-consciousness thinks, "I am the actor." However, he who knows the constituents of being (*tattva*; taught in Sāṃkhya) knows that (only) powers of nature (*guṇa*) operate on powers of nature according to the distribution of activities among these powers, and he is not attached to them.' Thus, while people usually appropriate the activities of nature through the syllable 'I', the followers of Sāṃkhya know that in fact only *prakṛti* acts and all activity is ultimately caused by it. If one manages to let nature act and dissociates oneself from these activities, karmic repercussion does not apply, because the activity of *ahaṃkāra* has been stopped by superior knowledge, which is gained when the higher faculty of discrimination (*buddhi*) is in control. We have here the Sāṃkhya explanation why *buddhiyoga* (taught in *BhG* 2.39–41, 49–52) and consequently *karmayoga* work. Natural activity has to be controlled at all times, since there is no escape from it, even when one thinks oneself inactive. Even a successful practitioner continues to live and behave according to his nature (*svā prakṛti*; 3.33). There is no escape from being active, only from being trapped in love and hatred and other forms of attachment (3.34). In this situation it is better to perform one's own duties (*svadharma*) than another's (*paradharma*; 3.35).[62] This reference to the problem of *dharma* signals an explicit expansion of

[62] A similar opinion is expressed in *ManuS* 10.97. On the parallels with *ManuS*, see also Raghavan 1962; Steinmann 1989: 170–3.

the *prakṛti* doctrine to the realm of ritual and *dharma* that remained rather implicit in the previous sections. It offers a perhaps unexpected mediation of Sāṃkhya philosophy and ritual by drawing a clear distinction between the basic, ontological structure of the world and an individual's participation in it: since the visible world is a product of *prakṛti*, whose powers operate in mutual dependence, the socio-ritual order belongs to the realm of *prakṛti* too, and this is mirrored in the reciprocal structure of sacrifice and society. The performance of individual acts in the context of ritual is equated with 'natural activity': what is taught as one's duty (*svadharma*) is in fact one's nature (*svāprakṛti*). Conversely, what appears as nature follows a certain order of activities (cf. *guṇakarmavibhāga*; 3.29), which is also reflected in the distribution of social duties among the people. The performance of one's duties (*svadharma*) should be understood as an enactment of one's natural condition (*svā prakṛti*).[63] This closes the argument, since one inevitably contributes to 'keeping the world together' by performing one's duties and behaving according to one's nature. However, in doing this knowingly, one makes a difference because one works towards liberation by reducing karmic bondage. The concept of *prakṛti* is used in order to argue that all beings contribute to the *lokasaṃgraha*, to maintaining cosmic order, when they follow their duties naturally. By blending Sāṃkhya notions with concepts of sacrifice and *dharma*, the chapter defends action against its ascetic renunciation and its reduction to a mere instrument for achieving individual desires.[64]

This doctrine could be misunderstood as a call to take the line of least resistance or to be 'in harmony with nature'. However, wiping out attachment is quite a demanding task, since it involves a struggle with the powers of nature. This is expressed in the last section of the chapter, where it is prompted by Arjuna's question about the causes of evil-doing (3.36). Kṛṣṇa's reply again draws on Sāṃkhya terminology in that he spots the enemy in one of the powers of nature, the *guṇa* called *rajas*. This power of nature (*guṇa*) is characterised by desire and anger, as well as other passions that drive people to action;[65] literally it means 'dust', which, among other things, covers knowledge. As a power of nature, *rajas* has the capacity to dominate all elements of the body because they are its field of operation (*adhiṣṭhāna*):[66]

63 Cf. *BhG* 18.41 where *svadharma* is said to result from 'one's way of being' (*svabhāvaja*).

64 This is why I see no need to regard 3.35 as an interpolation; cf. Ježic (1979a: 552).

65 In the *SK*, *rajas* is the *guṇa* that dominates the *tattva*, ego-consciousness, *ahaṃkāra*.

66 This term is again used in *BhG* 4.7 to describe Kṛṣṇa's influence on *prakṛti*. Vallee Poussin notes a similar use of this word in Buddhist texts (quoted in Lamotte 1929: 56f.).

> The senses (*indriya*), the mind (*manas*), and the faculty of discrimination (*buddhi*) are called its operational basis (*adhiṣṭhāna*) . . . Therefore, at first you must control the senses, then kill off[67] that evil which destroys insight and knowledge. The senses, they [the Sāṃkhya teachers] say, are superior to their objects; the mind is higher than the senses; the faculty of discrimination is higher than the mind; and beyond the faculty of discrimination is he (*saḥ*). Thus knowing the one beyond the faculty of discrimination, pull yourself together and kill the indomitable enemy, strong-armed prince. (3.41–43).

This passage gives the typical Sāṃkhya hierarchy of the senses and faculties of cognition (though omitting *ahaṃkāra*) that we also find in *KaṭhU* 3.10–11; 6.7–9 and elsewhere in the epic.

The parallel passage has incited an interesting discussion about the pronoun *saḥ*, 'he', used at the end of 3.42. While in the *KaṭhU* it clearly means 'self', it is not that clear in the *BhG*. Is it the 'enemy' mentioned in the next verse, or the 'self', as one would expect in a Sāṃkhya context? Following the majority of the later Sanskrit commentators, most translations render 'he' as the self,[68] while some, with Rāmānuja, understand it as referring to the enemy. I suggest that this interpretation not only suits the grammatical structure better, but is also consonant with the gist of the whole passage, which is concerned to demonstrate the power of the enemy, who is even capable of using the *buddhi* as its field of operation and is therefore 'higher' than it (cf. 3.40). This is also in accordance with the Sāṃkhya scheme that places *buddhi* below the powers of nature. In consequence, one needs to fight and destroy the enemy at its basis and to start with the senses. Arjuna is asked to fight this enemy first in order to be able to act appropriately. When one manages to equate the activity of (one's) nature (*prakṛti*) with the social and ritual duties that 'keep the world together', the purpose of action is led away from reaping the fruits of action towards an impersonal mechanism, and no karmic bondage is produced. Seen from this perspective, Arjuna has had the wrong idea about the purpose of *dharma*, since it is not about pleasure, family or even the kingdom (as listed in 1.32ff.), but about 'keeping the world together'. Performing one's duty is one's individual contribution to the reciprocal structure of creation. Accordingly, it is regarded as violence and evil when one uses this structure without contributing to it. As the most prominent and resourceful actor, the king is

67 Note the ambiguity of the imperative form used here (perhaps a *śleṣa* is intended), which can be understood as *prajahihi* (root *hā*, to leave behind) or *prajahi hi* (root *han*, to kill). Cf. Emeneau 1968: 277f.

68 Cf. Edgerton 1944: 41; Zaehner 1969: 177; Minor 1982: 142; Schreiner 1991: 71. Zaehner thinks that the *BhG* quotes the *KaṭhU*, though this is not certain. For a discussion of these parallels, see Malinar 1996: 173f. Van Buitenen passes over this difficulty in silence.

made the representative of this ideal, since the people follow his example. This has repercussions for the interpretation of kingship in that this way of acting becomes a criterion for assessing a king.[69] The Sāṃkhya doctrine of *prakṛti* is an important factor in this interpretation because it serves not only to argue that there is no escape from action while living, but also to welcome it as an arena in which to prove one's ascetic achievements. How this should be done is further explained in the second half of *BhG* 4, where ascetic practices are described in terms of ritual activities.

Text-historical considerations

Some verses have been excluded from the analysis because they seem to interrupt the argument:

1. Doctrine of the self: 3.17–18 interrupts the line of argument in that it deals with those who are totally detached because they 'delight in the self' (*ātmarati*; 3.17).[70] These verses present the consequence of traditional ascetic renunciation: there is nothing left to do, there is no purpose that would demand action, no obligation towards the creatures (*sarvabhūta*; 3.18). This sudden propagation of the ascetic ideal has led scholars to regard these verses as an interpolation. According to Ježic (1979a: 553), these verses belong to the '*ātman*-interpolations' that serve 'to reaffirm the *nivṛtti* ideal'.[71] While agreeing with this view, I would add that for the later redactors this interpolation was not necessarily provoking a contradiction. This probably points to a situation in which the performance of one's duties for the sake of the world, and renunciation, were considered two legitimate life-orientations, often addressed as *nivṛtti* and *pravṛtti* respectively (Bailey 1985, Strauss 1911) and mentioned in *BhG* 16.7. In contrast to the passage under discussion, the *nivṛtti* ideal of renunciation is often regarded as 'higher', since it leads to liberation. No such hierarchy is established in this passage, in which the interpolation results in a juxtaposition of alternatives.[72]

2. Theistic teachings: 3.30–32 presents a theistic interpretation of the Sāṃkhya model of detached action in asking Arjuna to renounce (*saṃnyasya*) all action in Kṛṣṇa, the god, to concentrate on what pertains to

69 Cf. the demand for '*indriyajaya*' in *ArthaŚ* 1.6.

70 On 'delight in the self', cf. *MuṇḍU* 3.1.4 (*ātmakrīḍa ātmaratiḥ kriyāvān eṣa brahmavidāṃ variṣṭhaḥ*) and *ChU* 7.25.2.

71 Ježic connects it with the *sthitaprajña* section (*BhG* 2.53–72); see above. Zaehner (1969: 168) raised doubts about these verses too.

72 However, one could argue that the adversative *tu* in 2.17 indicates such superiority.

the self (*adhyātmacetasā*), and to fight without attachment. The idea that renunciation is now directed at Kṛṣṇa and that detachment from desire should be turned into attachment to Kṛṣṇa is not explained here, but is explained in chapters 5 and 6 of the *BhG*. Moreover, the subsequent argument is not affected by this idea, and Arjuna is not asked to fight for the sake of Lord Kṛṣṇa. Another possible instance of a theistic interpolation is 3.23. Here, Kṛṣṇa is made the model of action which all human beings follow. In contrast to 3.30–32, this verse does not really interrupt the argument and could be read as continuing the list of royal models. However, the problematic grammatical construction and a parallel in *BhG* 4.11 have raised doubts and made it plausible to regard this verse as an addition too. As was the case with the theistic verses in *BhG* 2, these interpolations have the function of implementing the later theistic doctrine into a layer that presented a doctrine of 'detached action' without propagating a 'highest Lord'. These passages are based on what is said in later chapters of the *BhG*. They interrupt not only the line of argument in those chapters that deal with concepts of yoga, ritual action and liberation, but also the compositional structure, because in those chapters, in which Kṛṣṇa is revealed as a god, it is stressed that this is something new and unheard of before. A text-historical perspective allows one to cope with these contradictions by treating these passages as later interpolations that were inserted in the earlier textual layers when the theistic doctrine was imposed on to the older text.

BHAGAVADGĪTĀ 4: DIVINE ACTION AND THE 'SACRIFICE OF KNOWLEDGE'

Thematically this chapter can be divided into two parts, which probably belong to different stages in the text's composition. The first part (4.1–14) deals with various aspects of Kṛṣṇa's divinity that connect the god with the yoga teachings of the previous chapters, while the second (4.15–42) describes ascetic practice in terms of ritual action and continues themes in *BhG* 3.

Kṛṣṇa's 'divine appearance'

The chapter starts not with a motivating question, but with a 'genealogical account' of the yoga doctrine in which Kṛṣṇa is turned into the founder of a lineage of yoga teachers beginning with Vivasvat, who is followed by Manu and Ikṣvāku, the famous king of the solar dynasty. It is pointed out that this yoga is handed down in a tradition of 'royal seers' (*rājarṣi*; 4.2), who combine their royal function with a specific form of knowledge usually accorded to Brahmin sages.[73] However, 'in the long course of time this yoga was lost here on earth' (4.2). The argument of a 'lost tradition' serves on the one hand to enhance its authority by vesting it in a pedigree which reaches back to the primordial time of creation. On the other hand, it explains why it needs to be revealed again by its author, Kṛṣṇa. He explains to Arjuna that he will teach 'ancient yoga' because 'you are my loyal follower and comrade' (*bhakto 'asi me sakhā ca*; 4.3). This fact is regarded as the 'highest secret' (*rahasyam uttamam*). By teaching Arjuna this doctrine, Kṛṣṇa not only adopts him into the line of royal seers, he also vests him with the task of following the doctrine due to his personal loyalty and attachment to his teacher. In this passage, Kṛṣṇa appears as the teacher whom Arjuna has asked for in *BhG* 2.7. This is one important step in the reinterpretation of Arjuna's loyalty as a warrior along the lines of a doctrine of *bhakti* that ties Arjuna to Kṛṣṇa's divine cause and culminates in ch. 11. In the present context this is done by referring to their comradeship, their already being *sakhas*, friends and allies in a common cause. For Arjuna all this seems unfamiliar, and he wonders how Kṛṣṇa could have taught Vivasvat, who is much older (4.4).

For the first time, Kṛṣṇa explains his supremacy by initially pointing to his yogic achievements. He claims to have memory of former births and to be in full control of his future appearances.[74] These, as well as his present existence, are not caused by *karman*, as is the case with Arjuna, but he deliberately takes a body. This is possible because he makes the power of creation (*prakṛti*, 4.6) act according to his will and produce an outward form for him: 'Although I am unborn and imperishable and the Lord of the creatures indeed, I transform nature who is mine and take birth through (or as) an appearance of myself.' The creative process described in this verse draws on two concepts: (1) *prakṛti*, nature, the agent of creation according to Sāṃkhya; and (2) *māyā*, the exceptional power and capacity of gods and other beings to produce forms and disguises for themselves. It is taken for granted that *prakṛti* is in charge of all creative activity while being directed by an inactive 'self' who remains untouched by its embodiment. However, while in classical Sāṃkhya the emphasis is on liberation from embodiments, here it lies rather with the capacity to control creative processes. This emphasis is prominent in contexts of yoga in that the *yogin* at one point gains access to the powers of nature and becomes

[73] This genealogy is also used in other texts, e.g. *MBh* 12.236.46–47; see Malinar 1997: 283–285.
[74] Cf. *YS* 2.39; 3.16, 18. *BhG* 15.10 describes how *yogins* see transmigrating selves.

its powerful master (*iśvara*). Since Kṛṣṇa is in control of 'his *prakṛti*',[75] his appearance is in line with the acquisition of power (*aiśvarya*) over nature that is ascribed to successful *yogin*s and other *siddha*s. In contexts of yoga, but also of early Buddhism, the power over the elements and other creative powers is an inevitable but also necessary result of meditative and ascetic practices. Although this acquisition of power is more prominent in yoga than in Sāṃkhya, they share the view that it is the self which, one way or the other, activates the powers of nature. While this is usually done because the self does not know of its distinction from nature, in the case of powerful lords the activation of *prakṛti* is brought about knowingly, being a process of *adhiṣṭhāna*, that is, of using it as a field of operation for a specific purpose. Thus we need to distinguish between two aspects of the position of an *īśvara*: on the one hand, this implies control over nature and thus a certain degree of separation from its realm; on the other hand, one is an *iśvara* only when one can use these powers, and the already detached self deliberately turns to the realm of *prakṛti*, activates it and yet manages to stay in control. When in this position, a god, like a successful *yogin*, is still connected to *prakṛti*, but already 'liberated' from any egoistic appropriation of its manifestations. This 'detached connection' to the powers of nature is characteristic of the *yogin* too. The enactment of his yogic power results in the paradox that Kṛṣṇa appears on earth and yet remains unborn and invisible. This is possible because the activation of *prakṛti* results not in a body that is subject to karmic bondage, but in a temporary appearance or disguise that disappears when it has fulfilled its purpose. This is described in 4.6: 'I transform nature (*prakṛti*) that is mine and take birth with an appearance of myself (*ātmamāyā*).'[76] The somehow puzzling juxtaposition of the words *prakṛti* and *māyā* in this verse has led to various interpretations. While some suggest that *māyā* is the instrument for activating *prakṛti*, others connect it with the somehow magical and artificial character of Kṛṣṇa's appearance.[77] The polyvalence of the word

75 This puts Kṛṣṇa's control in contrast with the 'wise' man described in *BhG* 3.33, since even he follows 'his nature' (*svasyāḥ prakṛter*). The god Nārāyaṇa is also depicted as being in charge of 'his *prakṛti*' (see Malinar 1997).

76 The reflexive pronoun is used to translate *ātman* here because Kṛṣṇa *is* the imperishable self, and therefore an impersonal rendering as 'apparition of the self' makes no sense. This aspect needs to be considered when dealing with the ambiguities and semantic polyvalence of the word *ātman* in the *BhG*.

77 Zaehner (1969: 183f.) states that *māyā* should not be understood as 'illusion' and translates 'by my creative energy (*ātmāmāyā*) I consort with Nature – which is mine – and come to be'. However, this reverses the process described here, since directing *prakṛti* is regarded as the precondition for taking birth as and through *māyā*. This is clearly brought out in van Buitenen's translation of *māyā* as 'wizardry', indicating the apparitional nature of this birth. Cf. also Hacker 1960: 4.

māyā allows for both views. Gonda (1959: 128) notes that '*māyā* . . . refers to a special ability to create forms, or rather to the inexplicable power of a High Being to assume forms, to project itself into externality, to assume an outward appearance'. However, *māyā* can also mean the result of this process, as highlighted by Goudriaan (1978: 3): '*Māyā* can stand for various aspects of the process involved: the power which creates a new appearance, the creation of that appearance as an abstract performance, and the result of the process, i.e. the created form itself. The power, its manifestation and its result are not distinguished by name.' While keeping the blending of these different levels in mind, an emphasis on what appears would suit the context of the verse well and would qualify the character of Kṛṣṇa's birth as the appearance of an 'outward form', an artificial or even apparitional body. What is born is not he himself as the 'self', but an appearance (*māyā*) of himself which allows him to be present in the world while at the same time remaining transcendent and for ever 'unborn'.

By using his *prakṛti*, Kṛṣṇa is born in the world as an appearance of himself, which is created by using *prakṛti*, the elements of nature. When controlled by a powerful god, *prakṛti* turns into *māyā* (and can then delude all creatures; cf. *BhG* 7.14). When Kṛṣṇa uses his *prakṛti* for his own purpose, it results in an outward appearance of an already and forever liberated self, which appears as *māyā*. Kṛṣṇa's appearance is similar to the production of the artificial bodies (*nirmāṇakāya*) that *yogins* and *buddhas* are capable of producing, which in turn recalls the capacity of Vedic gods and demons to appear in various disguises.

This power of controlling *prakṛti* and then activating it in the form of *māyā* is a major characteristic of Kṛṣṇa as the 'highest god' in the monotheistic framework developed in the *BhG*. On the one hand, it serves to deal with the paradox that the god is absent from the world and yet present in it (again addressed in *BhG* 9.4–5). On the other hand, it delineates the god's position with regard to other forms of power, such as the powers of kings and *yogins*, which have both been referred to already in the genealogies of teachers. With regard to the *yogin*, the god is distinguished by his being forever in the position of a liberated self, and therefore he is never in danger of losing his control over the powers of nature that the *yogin* has taken so much effort to gain. In addition, the god uses this power for the sake of others, such as the world or *dharma*, or, as we shall see in *BhG* 11, in order to fulfil Arjuna's quest to see him in his divine form. In the case of *yogins*, it seems that they do not pursue a specific purpose apart from proving the efficacy and reality of their yogic practice or enjoying the display of power and the freedom it allows. The purposefulness of the god's appearance connects it with the task of the other wielder of power, the king.

According to *BhG* 4.7–8, the motif of Kṛṣṇa's appearance is the decay of *dharma* in each world-age (*yuga*),[78] and it serves three purposes: rescuing the good, destroying evil-doers, and re-establishing *dharma*. These programmatic verses delineate the nature of the god's relationship to the world along the lines of the tasks of a king who should equally protect *dharma* through a combination of reward and punishment. However, the fact that a god appears on earth to perform these tasks indicates that kings are either no longer capable of upholding them or that they have turned into 'evil-doers'. This situation points to the limited power of kings with regard to the powers of creation, as their own power is based on the ritual consecration which results in turning the king into a god-like being who unites the powers and qualities of the cosmic in his consecrated body. However, according to Vedic tradition this position must be re-confirmed annually by repeated unction. The king is thus in an intermediate position, which makes him exceptional, but yet vulnerable due to his engagement with the violent tasks of defending and expanding his kingdom. In contrast to *yogins* or a highest god like Kṛṣṇa, a king may very well reach the limits of his power in terms of his physical capacity (*bala*, *tejas*), his moral integrity (*dharma*, *maryādā*) or the resources he relies on, such as the army or his councillors. These resources are significantly called *prakṛtis* in the most influential text on the role and politics of kings, the *Arthaśāstra* of Kauṭilya 6.1. The king himself is among the constitutive factors of his rule (cf. Scharfe 1989: 28–29). The use of the word *prakṛti* in this sense indicates that, while the king controls and uses 'natural' powers, he is not in charge of *prakṛti* as the singular and unique cause of creation, as is claimed in the case of Kṛṣṇa. On the contrary, he is himself regarded as a *prakṛti*, a natural resource and power of the kingdom. The beginning of chapter 4 thus presents Kṛṣṇa as set in the position of a yogic *īśvara* who is clearly recognisable through his yogic powers, but differs, on the one hand, from *yogins* by its purposeful usage and his being the forever liberated self. On the other hand, the god's purpose is similar to the other powerful master the world knows, the king, but he is distinguished from him because he

78 'For whenever the Law languishes, Bhārata, and lawlessness flourishes, I create myself. I take on existence from eon to eon, for the rescue of the good and the destruction of the evil, in order to re-establish the Law' (4.7–8, trans. van Buitenen). Later, more elaborate texts on divine manifestations establish the connection with the *yuga* doctrine only selectively. Cf. *MBh* 12.326.61ff.; 12.337.16–37. These stanzas can be regarded as an expansion of the topic of 'purpose' that is so prominent in *BhG* 3.

rules over *prakṛti* as a whole, yet remains 'unborn', and therefore may come to rescue *dharma* and fight 'evil' kings.

For some scholars, *BhG* 4.6–8 summarises the '*avatāra* doctrine', the notion of the multiple embodiments or 'descents' of gods for specific purposes.[79] While those who originally proposed this view, such as Hacker (1960: 47), presented a rather complex and differentiated picture, this has subsequently resulted in a rather inaccurate use of the word *avatāra* with regard to the *BhG*. Not only are *BhG* 4.6–8 regularly summarised as the Gītā's '*avatāra* doctrine', but Kṛṣṇa is even regarded as an *avatāra* of the god Viṣṇu. However, there is no textual basis for either claim. First, the word *avatāra* is not used in the *BhG*, where instead we find *janma* (birth), *vibhūti* (power manifestation) and *tanu* (body; 9.11). Secondly, nowhere in the *BhG* is Kṛṣṇa called an '*avatāra* of Viṣṇu'. This is not to deny the connection of the *BhG* to concepts and traditions of divine manifestations, but one cannot make this link by applying terms and concepts to the text that are not used in it. In the case of the *BhG*, the unqualified use of the word *avatāra* for what the text describes has led to other possible connections in the teaching, such as between Kṛṣṇa's birth and the creation of 'apparitional bodies' ascribed to *yogins* and *buddhas*, to be overlooked. This also connects the passage to an important aspect of the development of the *avatāra* concept: 'its connection with the world of theatre' (Couture 2001: 313). Couture shows that the word '*avataraṇa*' implies not only 'descent', but also entering a stage in various disguises; it is used as a technical term for 'that movement performed by actors who move from the stage wings onto the stage itself' (2001: 319). A similar idea is implied in the concept of *māyā*, discussed earlier, which may allow *BhG* 4.7 to be seen as foreshadowing fully elaborated *avatāra* doctrines.

In the present context, Kṛṣṇa's appearance is connected with his task as a teacher who is interested in re-establishing his doctrine and with that of a divine king who must uphold *dharma*. The structure of the repeated revelations of a religious doctrine and of equally multiple appearances of its teacher is well-established in Buddhism and Jainism. Like a Buddha or a Jina, Kṛṣṇa is confronted with the decay of his teaching, which necessitates repeated manifestations.[80] The revelation of a doctrine, even if forever true and perfect, is subject to decay, as is the rest of the cosmos. This view differs from the unchanged nature of the Veda as texts handed down in their original form as *śruti*. It mirrors a situation in which new teachers

79 See e.g. Lamotte 1929: 58f.; Kosambi 1962. For a discussion of what Biardeau calls the '*avatāra* model' developed not only in the *BhG* but in the whole epic, see below, pp. 178ff.

80 See e.g. Mahāpadāna Sutta (*DN* 14) and Schubring 1935: 17ff.

claiming to reveal timeless truths had to cope with the presence of an already established, 'primordial' religious truth, the Veda. The doctrine of repeated revelations can be regarded as an answer to the question of why an eternal truth is not eternally present. By claiming that it was there once, but has vanished and needs another proclamation, the fate of truth is assimilated to the conditions of the socio-cosmic order in which it is revealed. If decay is considered a characteristic feature of the created world, the pledge of repeated revelations can be regarded as proving its persistence. In contrast to the Buddhist and Jaina traditions, which separate the task of the spiritual teacher from that of the worldly promoter and protector of order, these two aspects are blended in Kṛṣṇa. He not only teaches, he is also actively engaged in the royal task of establishing order. The god not only reveals a religious doctrine on the basis of his secret alliance with his loyal follower, but also appears on earth to make room for the socio-cosmic implications of his being the creator of the world who will appear time and again as the protector of his creation. While in Buddhism the royal and the soteriological functions are separated in the figure of the *cakravartin* and the *buddha* respectively (cf. Reynolds 1972), the *BhG* and also later texts combine both in the figure of the highest god, who protects the created world, but also guarantees liberation from it. The verses on Kṛṣṇa's birth acquire their full significance when they are connected with the doctrine of repeated revelations and appearances as an important strategy in establishing textual authority. However, this is not the only way in which this issue is addressed, since we will meet a different explanation in *BhG* 11. There the answer to the question of why the imperishable, eternal god Kṛṣṇa has never been heard of before is to declare that it is something that has indeed not been 'seen before'. The important point in *BhG* 4 is that the god's appearance is related to both doctrinal revelation and the rescue of the socio-cosmic order.

This can be corroborated by tracing the interplay of these two aspects in the rest of the chapter. *BhG* 4.9–11 explain the soteriological implications of the doctrine of Kṛṣṇa's divine birth and activity: 'Who thus truthfully understands my birth (*janma*) and my activity (*karma*) as (being) divine (*divyam*), he will not be reborn after death, but he will come to me, Arjuna' (4.9). In order to gain liberation, his followers need to possess the necessary ascetic and cognitive qualifications. Those who come to share the god's 'mode of being' (*madbhāva*) are free from passion, fear and anger, since they are purified by 'the ascetic heat that is knowledge' (*jñānatapasā*). While Zaehner (1969: 185) rightly notes that Kṛṣṇa's mode of being is still 'undefined', he suggests that it 'must surely mean his timeless Being which is in fact Nirvāṇa'. This is not supported by the text, since Kṛṣṇa's 'mode of being' is not explained in detail. Although we obtain some more information in the following chapters, it is by no means a complete picture. One reason for this lack of theological specification could lie in the reciprocal character of the relationship between god and his follower as described in 4.11: 'In the manner in which they approach me, in that very manner I engage with them. Everywhere men follow my path, O Pārtha.' The last part of this verse is identical to 3.23cd and indicates a remarkable shift of meaning. While the statement serves in 3.23 to stress the function of kings and other social elites as models of right conduct, in 4.11cd it suggests that all beings, knowingly or unknowingly, follow Kṛṣṇa, who is the creator of the world, to whom everyone belongs. However, the god shows and engages himself in exactly the way an individual relates to him. Although being the same with regard to all embodied beings, he appears in a form that matches the condition of the individual who approaches him. This explains why this statement obviously includes also those who turn away from him or even against him. The god shows himself accordingly as the force of punishment. Thus, reciprocity is at the centre not only of the ritual transactions (cf. *BhG* 3), but also of the doctrine of *bhakti*. Yet the structure and framework of reciprocity have changed because one party has been removed from the 'wheel of sacrifice'. This is because the transcendent god is not dependent on ritual nourishment, but instead represents a different type of reciprocity in that he is connected to all beings, irrespective of their status. He is accessible to all, but not in the same way or form.

In contrast to the invariance and impersonality implied in the context of Vedic ritual performances, in which correctness and the skilful application of ritual formulas and gestures are the preconditions for success, the personal, intimate character of the *bhakti* relationship between the highest god and his followers is stressed. However, Kṛṣṇa is connected to the wheel of sacrifice in that he also guarantees success to those who are not devoted to him and keep sacrificing. All beings are connected to this god because he is responsible for the way the world functions, which means that people strive for prosperity and engage in ritual performances according to their position in the hierarchy of the four castes (*cāturvarṇyam*). Kṛṣṇa claims that he has created this system (4.12–13), which mirrors different qualities (*guṇa*) and activities (*karma*). In this way, each and every being participates in the divine order through its ritual, social and even mere physical activity. At this point, the concept of 'acting in accordance with *prakṛti*' (cf. 3.27–29; 33) is reinterpreted by vesting Kṛṣṇa with the agency of creation and subsuming the world and all beings under his more or less hidden sovereignty.

Since the Sāṃkhya doctrine of *prakṛti* has been given a theistic interpretation by turning Kṛṣṇa into the overarching inciter of all creative activity, it is necessary to stress that this does not affect his being detached and unchanging: 'Although I am its [the caste hierarchy's] creator, you must understand that I am not an agent, because I am unchanging. Actions do not stick to me, nor do I yearn for their fruits – who knows me thus will not be bound by actions' (4.13–14). Kṛṣṇa is regarded as an inciter of all activity but is not involved in its operation. At first sight, this notion seems to be similar to Aristotle's 'unmoved mover'. However, the god Kṛṣṇa maintains a relationship to the world when it is in danger and can be approached by devotees. Moreover, the reason for his being 'unmoved' is that he has no desire for the fruits of his action. This idea is based on the doctrine of 'disinterested action' (*BhG* 2), as it is used without further explanation.

The whole argument is completed in 4.15 by pointing out that this knowledge has been practised since ancient times by those 'seeking liberation' (*mumukṣu*), and therefore Arjuna must act (*kuru karma*) likewise. The first part of the chapter ends by mentioning an ancient tradition and thus refers back to the beginning, when Kṛṣṇa is declared the teacher of an old tradition of yoga. This yoga consists in the disinterested performance of one's social duties because one knows Kṛṣṇa to be the creator of the world, and the liberated self who guarantees liberation in his 'state of being' to those who consciously follow him out of devotion. When Kṛṣṇa appears to re-establish *dharma*, knowing devotees must also follow him and gain liberation by emulating his mode of action, which means performing one's duty for the sake of the world and redirecting one's desire from personal liberation to the cause of god. Seen in the context of the preceding chapters, one can regard this section as a monotheistic interpretation of the *lokasaṃgraha* concept and the purpose of action advocated in *BhG* 3. Seen from a text-historical perspective, this section seems to have been inserted between *BhG* 3 and *BhG* 4.15–42. The theistic framework plays no role in the rest of the chapter (with the exception of 4.35) and will be more consistently established in chapters 7–11.

The sacrifice of knowledge

The second half of this chapter expands on themes and concepts that were important in *BhG* 3. While *BhG* 3 proposes that the purpose of *karmayoga*, detached activity, is to protect and uphold the ritual-cosmic order (*lokasaṃgraha*) and attend to the 'welfare of all beings', 4.15–42 offers an interpretation of ascetic and yogic practices as forms of Vedic sacrifice (*yajña*). In describing a sequence of purifying rituals that culminates in the 'sacrifice of knowledge' (*jñanayajña*), practices of yogic asceticism are equated with ritual activities. Ritual *karman* is interpreted as ascetic activity, and ascetic practices are turned into rituals.

The section begins by addressing the question of *karman* on a rather fundamental level (4.16–17) which serves to connect the two halves of the chapter. Having declared that even the wise poets are confused when it comes to defining *karman*, Kṛṣṇa notes: 'For one must understand what is action, what is wrong action and what is non-action. Profound is the course of action' (4.17). Three aspects of *karman* are distinguished here: *karman* (action), *akarman* (non-action) and *vikarman* (wrong action). This invites one to consider the conceptual framework in which Arjuna's problem and the question of negative consequences are dealt with in the *BhG*. Much has been said about the ethics of the *BhG*, and comparisons have been made with Western moral discourse (especially Kant). However, an important difference in the basic assumptions worked out in the *BhG* and in much of the Western discourse seems to have been neglected. While Western ethics are often based on the binary opposition between 'right' and 'wrong' behaviour and 'good' and 'bad' deeds, the *BhG* deals with a triadic structure, the fundamental distinction of which is that between 'action' and 'non-action'. Only by clarifying this distinction can 'wrong action' be defined. Without considering this, Arjuna proposes 'non-action' as a way to avoid what he deems 'wrong action' or evil. Moreover, such a clarification is also necessary because of the semantic polyvalence of *karman*. However, while this polyvalence is addressed, it is also played upon, since it is not explained which of the following aspects of *karman* is meant: (1) 'action', 'activity' in general; (2) ritual action; or (3) accumulation of 'deeds' and their fruits, that is, *karman* as the accumulation of retributive activity. Yet these aspects can help us interpret the quite paradoxical definition in 4.18: 'The one who can see the absence of (binding) consequences in activity and (binding) consequences in inactivity is the one who among men possesses the faculty of discrimination (*buddhimān*); he, while being in control (*yukta*), performs all acts.' In translating the verse, one has a choice of assuming either the same or a different meaning for *karman* and its negation *akarman* respectively.[81] Here I follow van Buitenen (1981: 164), who notes that '*karman* is used in the sense of "act" . . . while in *akarman* it

[81] Cf. Garbe 1921: 100: 'Who can see action in non-action and non-action in action' (my trans.).

has the connotation of its binding consequences'. This interpretation allows the verse to be seen not only as a display of the rhetorical figure of chiasm, but also as a conceptual statement serving to identify the renunciation of social duties or any other form of 'non-activity' as a form of self-delusion that does not automatically liberate one from karmic bondage. Rather, one should act without activating the usual retributive mechanism. As pointed out in *BhG* 2.49f., this may be when one possesses the 'faculty of discrimination' (*buddhi*) that ensures detachment. According to 4.19, this means to be 'free from desires and imaginations'; or, according to another possible rendering of the compound, 'free from (ritual) commitments caused by desire' (*kāma-saṃkalpa-varjita*; 4.19). Both translations make sense because *saṃkalpa* means either the ritual declaration of the intention and purpose expressed by the sacrificer at the beginning of the sacrifice, which binds its fruits to him alone, or else the imaginations or volitions that arise in the mind when it is in contact with sense-objects. Both aspects are blended when they are connected with a more generalised understanding of *karman* as a retributive activity in that *saṃkalpa* seems to refer to any activity (cognitive, verbal, etc.) which results in appropriative attachment. This is put in more concrete terms in the following description of the practice of such knowledge as a ritual activity. In this connection, discrimination and knowledge are not regarded as something 'theoretical', but as a practice which consumes, purifies and destroys whatever it comes into contact with. 'Knowing' thus means being capable of burning the consequences of one's doings in the 'fire of knowledge' or in the 'fire that is knowledge' (*jñāna-agni*; 4.19). By drawing on the doctrine of 'disinterested action' (cf. *BhG* 2 and 3), this is explained as follows: 'Because he has given up the attachment to the fruits of his deeds, being always satisfied and independent, he does not do (effect) anything, although he is engaged in activity. Because he hopes nothing, has himself and his mind under control and gives up all possessions, he does not acquire defilement, since he performs the act only physically (*śarīram*)' (4.20–21). The idea of letting only the body act draws on the Sāṃkhyistic notion of *prakṛti*, who is self-active and does not bind the 'embodied self' when it does not appropriate 'natural' activity through desire and egotism. Again this mode of acting is given a purpose, and again, as in *BhG* 3.9, it is sacrifice: 'For the liberated man, whose attachment has vanished, and who has his mind steadied by knowledge, *karman* (the aggregated consequences of deeds) dissolves completely, since he lives for the sake of sacrifice (*yajñāya*)' (4.23).

As has been demonstrated already, sacrifice is redefined in the *BhG* according to the concepts of 'indifference' and the 'relinquishment of fruits', and thus it differs from the Vedic understanding, in which the performance of ritual (*karman*) serves to connect the sacrificer to its fruits (*phala*). In *BhG* 3 this redefinition was introduced with an emphasis on the socio-cosmic necessity of maintaining the ritual world of reciprocal relationships (*lokasaṃgraha*). When acting within and for the sake of the 'wheel' of sacrifice without asking for more than eating 'leftovers', no karmic surplus will stick. This interpretation of sacrificial action is used in the present context to reinterpret sacrifice as an ascetic practice and, conversely, ascetic practices as rituals. In this way, the soteriological dimension of *karmayoga* as a practice of liberating knowledge is explored. The oppositions between 'theory' and 'practice', 'meditation' and 'action', are superseded in the request to practise knowledge by climbing the ladder of ascetic rituals. In the description of these rituals, the term *brahman* is as prominent as was the case in the 'wheel of sacrifice', which serves to establish and activate *brahman* in sacrifice (cf. 3.15). This idea is expanded on in the present context in that the elements of ritual are identified with *brahman* and turned into instruments for reaching *brahman*: 'Offering is *brahman*; the oblation that is poured with *brahman* into the fire of *brahman* is *brahman*. He who [thus] meditates on the ritual acts as *brahman* will certainly reach *brahman*' (4.24). Although the semantic polyvalence of *brahman* again invites different interpretations, it seems that there is one meaning emphasised here that was left more in the background in *BhG* 3: *brahman* as a supreme being and a realm of liberation. Van Buitenen (1981: 164) puts it precisely: 'In this context *brahman* signifies at once the complex of the (sacrificial) act and the supreme being.' The two aspects are not only juxtaposed, they are also connected with each other by equating (ritual) acts with *brahman*. In contrast to notions of the 'immortal self' as an inactive principle, activity is accorded to *brahman*, a qualification that does not contradict its status as a realm of liberation from karmic bondage. This is the implication of the statement that one reaches *brahman* if one meditates on action as *brahman*: if an individual equates his action with the source of all activity, no retribution or fruition will bind him to his acts. This is similar to the idea that one should let *prakṛti*, as the cause of all activity, act, thus avoiding karmic consequences (cf. *BhG* 3.27–29). Detachment or 'indifference' (*samatva*) is not only an attitude, but a process and practice of equating one's agency with that of the true agent, who can be called *brahman*, *prakṛti* or even the god Kṛṣṇa (see below). Equation turns into substitution, since the *yogin* gives up his agency and replaces it with that of *brahman* or *prakṛti*. Personal agency is turned into the agency of the ultimate cause; thus any effect of action is connected with this cause only. This is described in 4.24, where all elements of sacrifice are identified as *brahman*: all effects are poured into *brahman* by *brahman* and are then destroyed in the fire that is *brahman* (*brahma-agni*). The recursive structure of ritual action, which was analysed with regard to the 'wheel of sacrifice', returns on a different level, but it serves the same goal: to explain how to rid oneself of karmic bondage while practising *karman*. Detachment is therefore efficient only when it is based on the knowledge that the substrate, cause and instruments of action are ultimately the same (here: *brahman*) and when it is practised as a process of equation which becomes conducive to gaining liberation. Liberation from *karman* can then be interpreted either as separation from the cause (as is the case with *prakṛti*) or as merger with it (as is the case with *brahman*).

The convergence of all these aspects in the concept of *brahman* is further explored by establishing a taxonomy of rituals according to their proximity to *brahman* as the realm of liberation. The sacrificers are *yogins* and are distinguished by their ritual fires and offerings (4.24–33). *BhG* 4.25 draws a basic distinction between sacrifice to the gods, in which material goods (*dravya*) are offered, and the 'sacrifice of knowledge', in which all the elements are equated with *brahman*. It is concluded that 'the sacrifice of knowledge is better than the sacrifice of material goods' (4.33). This is the case because all sacrifices are based on and processed by *brahman*: 'In this way, various sacrifices are spread out in the mouth of *brahman* (the sacrificial fire). Understand that they all spring from acts – knowing this, you will be liberated' (4.32). While these two types of sacrifice define the spectrum of rituals considered here, various ascetic practices are now described in terms of sacrifice too (4.26–27, 29–30). Some *yogins* offer their senses (*indriya*) in the 'sacrificial fires of restraint' (*saṃyama-agni*); others offer up the sense-objects (*viṣaya*) in the 'sacrificial fire of the senses' (*indriya-agni*); yet others sacrifice the activities of the senses and the breaths (*prāṇa*) 'into the sacrificial fire of yoga practice of self-control', which is 'kindled by knowledge' (*ātma-samyama-yoga-agni*); some offer 'in-breathing in out-breathing' because they practise 'breath control' (*prāṇāyāma*), while others offer 'the breaths into the breaths' by fasting (*niyatāhāra*). All these different sacrifices – and another list is given in 4.28[82] – effect a purification from defilements. Recalling the praise of those who eat the 'leftovers of sacrifice' (*yajñaśiṣṭa*) in *BhG* 3.13, the soteriological nature of these practices

[82] The sacrifices (*yajñas*) are distinguished here by the offerings: material goods (*dravya*), ascetic heat (*tapas*), yoga, self-study of holy texts like the Veda (*svādhyāya*) and knowledge (*jñāna*). For a detailed discussion of this classification (including commentarial interpretations), see Hill 1928: 142, note 2. For a description of Buddhist ascetic practices as an alternative to Vedic sacrifice, cf. *SN* 7.1.9 and Barua 1956.

is explained to Arjuna as follows: 'By enjoying the leftovers of sacrifice[83] as the nectar of immortality (*amṛta*), they reach eternal *brahman*. This world is not for him who does not sacrifice (*ayajña*) – how could the other [world] be his, O best of Kurus?' (4.31).

This passage rejects any attempt to declare asceticism and sacrificial activity mutually exclusive. Rather, it reflects a process that has been analysed by Heesterman (1964) as the 'internalisation of sacrifice' and by Biardeau (1968, 1974) as the expansion of the notion of sacrifice into the realm of asceticism. This culminates in the sacrifice of knowledge because everything culminates in knowledge (4.33), which brings about liberation and ultimate purification (4.34, 36–42).[84] The purifying nature of this fire is emphasised by pointing out that even the worst among all evil-doers can use the 'boat of knowledge' (*jñānaplava*; 4.36). The argument concludes as follows: 'As a kindled fire reduces its fuel to ashes, so does the fire of knowledge reduce all *karman* (the karmic consequences) to ashes' (4.37; trans. Zaehner). Here yogic practices are regarded as the instrument with which to kindle this fire that purifies like nothing else (4.38). The practice of this knowledge is praised by contrasting it with those who lack confidence (*śraddhā*)[85] in the efficacy of the (ritual) action that is necessary for its success. Accordingly, the chapter ends by asking Arjuna not to renounce his duty, but rather to use the 'sword of knowledge' (*jñāna-asi*) to destroy his doubts, which are caused by 'ignorance' (*ajñāna-sambhūta*). The chapter ends by calling Arjuna to action: 'Practise this yoga and stand up!', which can also be rendered, 'Yoke yourself and get up!' (*yogam ātiṣṭhottiṣṭha*; 4.42). By playing on the polyvalence of the word *yoga*, not only is the ascetic character of heroic action indicated, but also the heroic nature of yoga itself. The word *yoga* in the epic is used not only in the sense of traditions of asceticism, of the acquisition of extraordinary powers and liberation, but regularly in the sense of 'yoking', 'harnessing' and preparing for battle.[86] Where the *yogin* fights with his desires and the natural activity of his cognitive-sensual apparatus and needs to harness himself with the right equipment, the warrior needs to do the same in order to defeat his enemies. The internalisation

83 See above, pp. 83ff., and Wezler 1978: 89–93.

84 This praise of knowledge is interrupted in 4.35 when Kṛṣṇa declares that it means seeing all beings in him. Since this statement has no further consequences in this chapter, I regard it as a theistic interpolation.

85 The studies of *śraddhā* by Köhler (1948) and Hacker (1963: 452ff.) stress the relationship between *śraddhā* and sacrifice, which is summarised by Hara (1963–64: 139) as follows: 'The basic idea in *śraddhā* is rather a secular trust in the efficacy of the sacrifice.'

86 Cf. *MBh* 5.160.29; 5.151.17–18; 6.16.21. Often *yoga* means 'yoking the horses', applying the reins, which is echoed when ascetic practices of self-control are compared to driving a chariot (cf. *KaṭhU* 3.3–6; *MBh* 5.34.57). On the use of 'yoga' in this sense in Vedic texts, see Oguibene 1984.

of sacrifice through yoga and, conversely, the ritualisation of yoga are here applied to the equally ritualised duties of the warrior Arjuna. War becomes a yogic sacrifice. He is asked to regard this battle as his ascetic sacrifice of knowledge, which he performs for the sake of the world and to prove his detachment. The 'sacrifice of knowledge' can be regarded as a soteriological counterpart of the *lokasaṃgraha* doctrine in *BhG* 3. Therefore it seems plausible to regard both texts as belonging to the same textual and argumentative layer. This is also corroborated by the fact that both chapters present a doctrine of salvation without referring to the liberation of an immortal self. Liberation is here 'reaching, becoming *brahman*'. This teaching underwent several additions, not only through the theistic teaching of the first half of *BhG* 4 and the theistic interpolation of 4.35 (where, significantly, the word *ātman* is used), but also by introducing notions of 'self' in the subsequent chapters.

BHAGAVADGĪTĀ 5: SUBSTITUTING AGENCY

At the beginning of this chapter, the tension between action and the relinquishing of action is again highlighted in Arjuna's request for clarification: 'You recommend the renunciation (*saṃnyāsa*) of acts, Kṛṣṇa, and then again [their] yogic performance. Explain to me clearly which one is better!' (5.1). Now, the focus is on *saṃnyāsa*, the renunciation[87] of all activities, including ritual and social duties, for the sake of liberation. In Arjuna's opinion, Kṛṣṇa confounds two ideas that are mutually exclusive in that he demands both renunciation and taking action. The question indicates that such a combination seems to have been rather new, since the expectation is to do either one or the other. While van Buitenen (1981: 164) correctly points out that the question shows that 'Arjuna has not yet understood', it also indicates that Kṛṣṇa's teaching is something unfamiliar. As a device to expand on the subject, it invites the following reinterpretation of *saṃnyāsa* in the framework of Sāṃkhya and yoga concepts. First of all, Kṛṣṇa gives the unequivocal answer that *karmayoga*, the yogic performance of acts, is better than *karmasaṃnyāsa*, the renunciation of acts (5.2). However, this assessment is qualified when Kṛṣṇa points out that one can reach the 'highest goal' (*niḥśreyas*) with both (5.2). In 5.4–5 both views are identified as

[87] Although *saṃnyāsa* as the alternative to the performance of social duties is at the centre of Arjuna's refusal to fight, the word has so far occurred only in *BhG* 4.41, when it was claimed that actions do not bind the one 'whose *karman* has been renounced in yoga' (*yogasaṃnyastakarman*). This chapter offers a detailed explanation of this claim. According to Modi (1932: 23f.), Sāṃkhya is generally synonymous with *saṃnyāsa* in the *BhG*. However, this neglects the different reinterpretations of *saṃnyāsa* discernible in the text.

Sāṃkhya and yoga respectively and it is pointed out that both yield the same fruits: 'The position which followers of Sāṃkhya reach is also reached by *yogins*. Sāṃkhya and yoga are one and the same. Who sees this, sees truly' (5.5). While the word *yogin* is usually used for the follower of yoga, in this verse it is *yoga*, which occurs quite frequently in the *MDh*. There we also find similar statements on the unity of both traditions: 'Men satisfied with little insight see them as separate. We, however, know with certainty that they are only one. What is seen by followers of Sāṃkhya is also seen by *yogins*. The one who sees that Sāṃkhya and yoga are one and the same is a knower of truth' (12.304.3–4).[88] Similar statements are not repeated in the *BhG* and may indicate an interest (perhaps of a later redactor) to connect the *BhG* to positions voiced more coherently in the *Mokṣadharmaparvan* (*MDh*). In the present context, the identity of both views does not prevent me from preferring *karmayoga*.

The reason for this preference is given in 5.6: renunciation without expertise in yoga is hard to practise, whereas a *yogin* reaches *brahman* (here, the realm of no return) soon. This refers back to the problem, discussed in *BhG* 3.4–8, that merely 'giving up' may result in a new entanglement in *karman*. Much of chapter 5 argues that yoga is required for true renunciation because it lends the practitioner the necessary self-control when he follows a signposted path of yoga which rests on the cosmological interpretation of activity and knowledge taught in Sāṃkhya. This interpretation allows the practice of yoga to be described as climbing the ladder of the elements of creation by taking control of each of them. It ends in a 'conquest' of the created world, or, as it is put in 5.19, *yogins* have conquered creation (*jita sarga*).

This idea of a conquest of the created world explains how it is possible to act without karmic consequences and why this capability is the precondition for gaining liberation. It echoes the notion of 'equation' dealt with in the previous chapters. While in *BhG* 3 and 4 ascetic detachment was explained along the lines of a sacrificial activity described as 'pouring *brahman* into *brahman*' (4.24) and as the knowledge that 'powers of nature' act in relation to 'powers of nature' (3.28), this chapter deals with the yogic quest actually to 'become *brahman*' and, in consequence, act like it. This is based on self-control, which means gaining control over the different powers of nature that are active in the 'self', that is, the physical-mental apparatus produced

[88] *Pṛthakpṛthak tu paśyanti ye 'lpabuddhiratā narāḥ / vayaṃ tu rājan paśyāma ekam eva tu niścayāt* //12.304.3/. *Yad eva yogāḥ paśyanti tat sāṃkhyair api dṛśyate / ekam sāṃkhyaṃ ca yogaṃ ca yaḥ paśyati sa tattvavit* //12.304.4/. Cf. also 12.293.30. Variant readings in some manuscripts indicate attempts to assimilate the *BhG* and the *MDh* passages (see Malinar 1996: 195, note 3).

for the 'embodied self'. As a product of nature, this 'active self' is hierarchically structured, with the cognitive faculties (*buddhi*, etc.) at the top and the senses at the bottom. As a consequence, self-control means reaching the top position, which allows all the other faculties to be controlled. As we have already seen with regard to chapter 2, *buddhiyoga*, the techniques that allow the 'faculty of discrimination' (*buddhi*) to gain control, rests on this idea of a hierarchy of faculties. However, this process is not merely regarded as 'subjective', but is also given a cosmological dimension. Yoga results not only in transformations of the physical and mental condition of the adept, but also in reaching the corresponding cosmological levels.[89] While a *yogin* gains control over his active self, he also gains access to the powers of nature contained in each faculty and is connected to their cosmological potential too. This is based on the continuum between the cosmological and individual levels of existence that is assumed in Sāṃkhya philosophy. Accordingly, nature (*prakṛti*) creates not only individual beings, but also the cosmos. All created beings are regarded as specific manifestations of a cosmological matrix and hierarchy of basic, ontological constituents (*tattva*). Therefore, yogic self-control is accompanied by empowerment, as well as by gaining access to and uniting with the cosmological powers. This is the basis of the extraordinary powers ascribed to successful *yogin*s which allow them to fly or have 'divine vision', and are called *siddhi*, *vibhūti* or *bala* in different texts. In the *BhG* they are explicitly discussed only in relation to the *yoga aiśvara*, the yoga of supremacy, ascribed to the god Kṛṣṇa (*BhG* 9 and 10). In the present context, the liberating aspect of this process of empowerment and control is highlighted when it is declared that a *yogin* who has reached the highest stage in the cosmic hierarchy of powers is 'free from *karman*'. This highest cosmic stage is called *brahman* (here synonymous with *prakṛti* with respect to its creative powers).[90] Upon reaching this position, the *yogin*'s 'active, physical self' is transformed in that he becomes identical with this stage; he is now *brahman* (*brahmabhūta*; 5.24). As will be seen, this has two consequences. First, since the *yogin* is still alive, activities continue. However, because these are identical with *brahman*, they are now 'cosmic'. Since the *yogin* as a person is no longer involved in them, he is free from karmic bondage. Secondly, should he remain in this detached equation or union with cosmic activity, he will be liberated at the moment

89 This correspondence between the structure of the cosmos and the individual being is not only characteristic of the *BhG* interpretation of yoga, but is also important in the *YS* and in Buddhist traditions; cf. Gethin 1997.

90 The use of *brahman* in the sense of *prakṛti* also occurs elsewhere in the *BhG* (see Schreiner 1991: 150), as well as in commentaries on the *SK*.

of death. The state of 'being *brahman*' is thus one of transition: while the *yogin* is ready for liberation, he is still alive and united with the source of all cosmic activity. Therefore he is also a very powerful being, what is called elsewhere a *siddha* or *īśvara*. Correspondingly, the realm of *brahman* also has two aspects, on the one hand being depicted as the full potential of creation, and on the other as that stage at which all beings are the same because they are not yet individualised as manifest beings. Therefore, this stage is also called *avyakta*, the non-manifest stage of creation; or, when the agency of this creative potential is highlighted, it is called *mahān ātman*, the 'mighty self'. These different levels must be taken into account in order better to understand the description of yogic achievements in this chapter.

'Self of all beings'

The explanation of how this rather complex stage of *brahman* is reached starts with the very end of the process, which is described in 5.7 in quite a dense way and explains why an accomplished *yogin* is not defiled by his activities: 'He is accomplished in yoga who has purified himself, conquered himself and (conquered) his senses. Although he is active, he is not defiled because his self is identical with the self of all beings (*sarvabhūtātmabhūtātmā*).' The explanatory character of this statement is itself in need of explanation, especially with regard to the puzzling compound, *sarva-bhūta-ātma-bhūta-ātman*. Yet as I am going to argue, it provides one of the keys for understanding why 'being *brahman*' means both freedom from *karman* while acting, and fitness for liberation. Let us consider the exegetical problems first, which are indicated by the various translations of the compound. Garbe (1921: 105; cf. Otto 1935a: 49) translates 'whose Self has become the Self of all beings'. This suggests that the immortal Self (usually indicated by the capital letter) of the *yogin* has become identical with the immortal Self of all beings. Others seem to indicate that the *yogin* himself, which perhaps means in his physical self, is identical with the other selves, as suggested by van Buitenen (1981: 91), who translates 'identifying himself with the selves of all creatures',[91] and Schreiner (1991: 152): 'he is at once himself and all creatures'. The basic question is whether we are dealing here with a process of identification of the immortal self with what is present in all beings or with a process of equating one's elemental

[91] Zaehner (1969: 205) gives no interpretation of this self ('be this as it may'), but thinks that 'what the Gītā is describing is . . . the common experience of "nature mystics"'. Cf. also Minor 1982: 191.

self – that is, the 'active self' as the physical-mental complex created by the nature – with that of all beings. This means regarding all creatures as identical with regard to their basic constituents. The difficulty with the first interpretation is that this does not explain why ongoing activity does not defile the *yogin* and that we do not hear of an 'immortal self' elsewhere in this chapter. The second interpretation, however, is in line not only with the overall argument, but also with the immediate context of the verse, which will be considered in what follows.

The verses following 5.7 describe how and what the *yogin* is doing in this state. First of all, he is doing something[92] while he thinks: '"I do nothing at all." This is what the accomplished one, the knower of reality shall think when he sees, hears, feels, smells, eats, walks, dreams, breathes, talks, excretes, grasps, opens the eyes and shuts them, because he bears in mind that "the senses are busy with the sense-objects"' (5.8–9). Obviously, the *yogin* who has reached the position of a *sarvabhūtātmabhūtātman* has detached himself from the activities of his body and senses. He regards himself as no longer acting, since he does not appropriate activities by deeming himself the agent. He knows that 'activity' is nothing more than the senses doing their business. Consequently, it is not the *yogin* who acts, but only natural activity working on and in itself. This point is made in 5.10: 'Having cast all activities on *brahman* and given up attachment, he, who acts, is not defiled by evil (*brahmaṇy ādhāya karmāṇi saṅgaṃ tyaktvā karoti yaḥ / lipyate na sa pāpena*), just as a lotus petal is not [defiled] by water.' Renouncing does not mean stopping acting, but letting the cosmological source of all activity be active. This is achieved by equating one's physical-mental apparatus, one's 'active self', with its ultimate cause, *brahman*. As is said in 5.10, the *yogin* casts (his) acts on *brahman*.

The equation of one's physical self with that entity which is the cause of all physical existence results in detachment and indifference, as well as in a capacity still to be active, since this process connects the *yogin* with the cosmological dimension of his 'active self' in that all his faculties are depersonalised and can therefore expand into their cosmological and thus unspecified form. However, reaching this position also means reaching a decisive stage in the quest for liberation because it opens up the possibility of turning away from activity and leaving the world for good. It should be noted that we are given no further information about this liberation, and nothing is said about an immortal self. This shows that it is not the

92 This description is in striking contrast with what is said about the condition of a *sthitaprajñā* in *BhG* 2.54ff., in which sense perception or thoughts vanish.

immortal self that is in the centre of interest, but the explanation of how a *yogin* can act and still be free from karmic consequences.

In reaching this stage, the *yogin* is described as *sarvabhūtātmabhūtātma*. As already indicated, this state of being demarcates a cosmological interface and soteriological crossroads. Either one can stay in control of one's own corporeal self and the creative powers of the source of creation with which one is connected (*brahman, prakṛti*), or else one leaves this state of being and liberates the immortal self. Seen from the top-down perspective of the upcoming creation, this is the stage of 'unmanifest' creation, that is, of full creative potential, but before the creation of individualised beings begins. Seen from the bottom-up perspective of the *yogin*, it is the final state before liberation, in which he stays until he dies. This intermediate state is important not only in the Sāṃkhya-yoga teachings in the *BhG*, but also elsewhere in the epic and in some Upaniṣads. We also find it in other traditions, like Buddhism, which postulate both a correspondence between the structure of individual beings and that of the cosmos and a hierarchy of cognitive-sensual faculties, levels of consciousness and (cosmological) realms of being(s), and which teach the acquisition of extraordinary powers (*iddhis*) as a component of the path to liberation (Gethin 1997). A brief digression into this context not only helps us to understand the teachings in chapters 5 and 6 more clearly; it also provides the conceptual framework for Kṛṣṇa's position as the liberated yet 'mighty lord of all beings' (*sarvalokamaheśvara*). In addition it will throw some light on the complex compound discussed earlier.

Meanings of ātman

In interpreting this stage, it is helpful first of all to deal with the semantic polyvalence of the word *ātman* (self) implied not only in the compound *sarvabhūtātmabhūtātma*, but also in other passages of the *BhG*.[93] The first and original meaning of *ātman* is as the reflexive pronoun, thus referring to the body or the empirical person (see Divanji 1961–62: 160). In many instances the word is used in this sense of the 'physical-mental complex' created by the cause of creation. This is also the *ātman* which needs to be restrained and checked in yogic and ascetic practice as depicted in *BhG* 5.7. In some texts this self is called *bhūtātman*, the 'elemental self'.[94] It is this

93 For a survey of all the passages in the *BhG* in which *ātman* is used (excluding those referring to Kṛṣṇa as god), see Divanji 1961–62.

94 In *MaitU* 3.2 the body (*śarīra*) is called *bhūtātman* (the passage, according to van Buitenen (1962: 128), is a late addition). *ManuS* 12.12 distinguishes between an 'inner self' (*kṣetrajña*) and the 'elemental

self that needs to be conquered and purified or that can turn into an enemy when not checked (cf. 6.6). Ascetic practices work on this self, which is then, in the course of the practice, transformed into a state of being that shares the qualities of the source of all manifest beings. This use of *ātman* is well attested elsewhere in the *MBh* and also in Buddhist texts,[95] and must be distinguished from *ātman* in the sense of an immortal or higher self that is forever liberated and thus cannot become the object of yogic practices of control.[96] Rather, it appears only as the 'true' self when the 'active, physical self' has been purified, equated with, and dissolved into its cosmic cause. What or who appears as this self and to what extent it demarcates the state of liberation depend on the philosophical or theological doctrine employed for its interpretation. In the present context, the identity between the elemental self, all other elemental selves and the cause of their existence is highlighted. Seen from this perspective, the following interpretation of the compound *sarvabhūtātmabhūtātma* can be suggested: 'his elemental self has become the elemental self of all', 'all' (*sarva*) meaning the cosmos, the whole of creatures. This interpretation makes it clear that the *yogin* connects himself with the cosmological dimensions of his existence by reaching the 'elemental self' of the universe, which is *brahman*, the cause and plenitude of creation.

However, what appears right now as a neat binary structure is in fact a triadic one, since the empirical self consists not only of the elements of nature, but also of an embodied self which lends coherence and purposefulness to the aggregation of elements called the body. The texts use different words for this embodied self: *antar-ātman* (inner self), *antaryāmin* (the inner controller; cf. *BĀU* 3.7), *jīva-ātman* (the living self), *kṣetrajña* (knower of the field) and also *bhūtātman*, which in this connection means 'self of the elements', not 'elemental self'. This self can create the elements in which it abides and is similar to a creator god.[97] The interplay between the two levels

self' (*bhūtātman*): 'the one who makes this body act is called Kṣetrajña, "the knower of the field"; the one who does the actions, on the other hand, the wise call Bhūtātman, "the elemental self"' (*yo 'syātmanaḥ kārayitvā ta kṣetrajñaṃ pracakṣate / ya karoti tu karmāṇi sa bhūtātmotcyate buddhaiḥ* //12.12/ trans. Olivelle). See also Edgerton 1965: 256, note 1.

95 Cf. Zaehner 1969: 205, and below, pp. 122ff.

96 Cf. Zaehner 1969: 205. While accepting this distinction, Minor (1982: 190) notes: 'One must be careful not to build too much metaphysics on what is clearly a play on the meanings of *ātman*.' While this is certainly the case in some passages, this does not excuse the interpreter from dealing with what is going on. Cf. Gonda (1974). In most instances, the authors of the *BhG* were careful to draw these distinctions: too much ambiguity would have been counterproductive.

97 Cf. *MBh* 12.187.6–7: 'As a tortoise stretches out its limbs and draws them in again, the self of the elements (*bhūtātman*) creates the beings and withdraws them again.' I do not agree with Edgerton (1965: 256) that the 'elemental self' is meant here because the passage suggests rather control over the elements.

of 'self' is described in the different texts using various terms, which points to the fluidity of terminologies and concepts before they are systematically elaborated.[98] However, in most texts the relationship between these two selves is described as one in which the 'inner self' controls, directs and even transforms the 'elemental self'. Thus, in *MuṇḍU* 2.1 the cosmic creator, here called *puruṣa*, is described as *sarvabhūtāntarātman*, the 'inner self of every being' (2.1.4) because the 'inner-self abides in beings' (*eṣa bhūtais tiṣṭhate hy antarātmā*; 2.1.9).

From the 'classical' Sāṃkhya perspective, this self is indeed responsible for the design and soteriological status of its material embodiment, since *prakṛti* creates a body in response to the inner self. In the process of creation, an immortal but ignorant self unites with the cause of creation and becomes an embodied self. In this moment, it comes into contact with the cause of creation as a whole and is thus for a moment in charge of its whole creative potential. The availability of this potential is usually restricted due to the karmic impact and defilement. Thus taking a body means making restricted use of the power of creation and one becomes an individual elemental self. In earlier texts and in some texts of 'epic Sāṃkhya', this stage in the process of embodiment and creation is at the same time a state of the 'creator' or 'cause of creation', called *sarvabhūtātman*, the self of all beings (Johnston 1937: 49) or *mahān ātman* (van Buitenen 1964). It is the first stage in the process of creation, in which it is still undifferentiated, and thus a state before the manifestation of individualised bodies. It is unmanifest (*avyakta*), yet 'creation in full potential', and therefore it is sometimes described as 'multiform' or 'universal'. This is also the reason why this entity appears as multiform and is described as possessing 'a thousand arms, heads', etc. Therefore creator gods and other entities regarded as the source of the universe (*puruṣa, brahman, prakṛti*) can be regarded as the *sarvabhūtātman* or *mahān ātman* of 'all beings' and can appear in a *viśvarūpa* form, that is, a form which contains all possible forms. This means that cosmogony is interpreted in terms of embodiment, the creator regarded 'as embodied in creation'. In this connection, cosmogony is also the template for the creation of individual bodies, becoming the 'prototype of somatogony' (van Buitenen 1964: 108).

Creator and creative power converge in this stage of contact between an actually liberated self and the power of creation. Being 'the self of all', the 'large self' means a state of expansion and wholeness, which then becomes

98 This is corroborated by Goudriaan (1992: 171f.): 'The term *antarātman* suggests the primeval state of purity, independence and sovereignty; the *bhūtātman* is not really different, but this term implies an emphasis upon its involvement with material existence.'

manifest in and through creation. All possible beings exist, unmanifest and virtually, in this state before they become manifest in distinct and separate bodies and cosmic realms – so this state also implies 'muchness' (van Buitenen 1964: 104). Therefore it can be called *avyakta* when seen from the perspective of the creative power, as well as *mahān ātman* when the emphasis is on the embodied self.[99] In fact, the characteristic feature of this state is that it implies both, which is why it can be a crossroads for either creation or liberation. In 'classical' Sāṃkhya, the epistemological and soteriological aspects are given greater emphasis, and the first product of the contact between an embodied self and nature is *buddhi*, the faculty of discrimination, the highest and greatest in the hierarchy of creation. However, what is emphasised in *BhG* 5 is the perspective of a *yogin* who reaches this stage and therefore experiences it as a state of 'identity' and 'wholeness' in that all beings are seen to be the same because they are created by the very same cause. As a consequence, it is not the immortal self, but 'being *brahman*' and thus turning into a *sarvabhūtātman* (having become the self of all beings) that is the centre of interest.[100]

Liberation as 'sameness'

Our text describes this state from the perspective, not of a self about to be embodied, but of an embodied self striving for liberation. Seen from this angle, reaching the stage of convergence between the self and the creative powers implies the acquisition of knowledge in that the *yogin* becomes capable of distinguishing the business of *karman* and creation from the position of the self. However, since he is still in contact with the cause of creation, action continues, though it is impersonal and thus similar to what *prakṛti* is doing, without repercussions for the *yogin*. When a *yogin* heads for liberation, this stage becomes the final stop on the path to liberation, or if he fails, a place from where he 'falls down' (*yogabhraṣṭa*; cf. *BhG* 6.38). In the context of *BhG* 5 it is the exit door to liberation, and thus this stage becomes an obstacle, or rather, something that must vanish. At this

99 This distinction may account for the fact that in some texts the *avyakta* is regarded as the stage above *mahat*. Cf. *KaṭhU* 3.10–11; van Buitenen 1964: 106–7.

100 A similar idea is also dealt with in *MBh* 12.231.19–23, where the state of 'those seeing the same' (*samadarśin*) is explained as follows: 'For in all beings, mobile and immobile, lives the one large self, by whom all this was spread out (*eko mahān ātmā yena sarvam idaṃ tatam*). When the self of the elements (*bhūtātmā*) sees itself in all beings and all beings in itself, it reaches *brahman* . . . Even the gods are confused about the path of him who has become the self of all beings (*sarvabhūtātmabhūta*) and is fond of all beings (*sarvabhūtahita*), as they seek for a trace of him who leaves no trace.'

point, the question emerges of who or what may in fact exert control over the active, physical self. The previous discussion offers a possible answer: it must be that faculty which is the highest in the hierarchy of faculties. In most texts this is consciousness (*citta*) or the faculty of discrimination (*buddhi*). In *BhG* 5.8–9 it is pointed out that this control of all activity can be achieved when the *yogin* manages to keep his knowledge and his discriminating insight by thinking that he does nothing. The *yogin* controls his activities because he is now *sarvabhūtātman*, having reached the highest stage of the cosmos and having now become 'the self of all beings'. He has reached this position after long uphill struggles, and not, like a 'highest self' or any other cause of creation, from a top-down position. What is the first stage for them is the last stage for him.

Reaching this position explains why true renunciation is directed not at acts, but at attachment to them, as well as why a *yogin* wins a peace that lasts (*śāntiṃ naiṣṭhikīm*; 5.11).[101] However, the verse no longer describes the *yogin*, but the person as the embodied self (*dehin*) who mentally offers up all acts and therefore remains happy (*sukha*) and in control (*vaśī*). All this happens only if these activities are not claimed by an ego, this being the knowledge that cleanses all defilements and guarantees that the *yogin* escapes rebirth (5.16–17). He now exists as the embodied self (*dehin*) that is called 'sovereign' (*prabhu*, 5.14; *vibhu*, 5.15; cf. Zaehner 1969: 208) because its connection with an individualised body has been cut. This means that it is no longer exposed to the actions of mind, senses or body, but controls and understands them as a natural activity (*svabhāva*;[102] 5.14), an impersonal self-reproducing process. Everything is just the same, which is why those who have 'conquered creation' (*jītasarga*; 5.19) see the same in everything (*samadarśin*). The conquest of the self (*jitātman*) corresponds to the conquest of creation: 'The learned see the same in a knowledgeable, well-mannered Brahman, a cow, an elephant, a dog and an eater of dogs.[103] Here in this world indeed they have conquered creation, since their mind rests in sameness (*sāmya*); for devoid of flaws is the indifferent *brahman*; and therefore they abide in *brahman*' (5.18–19). The state of *brahman* is here primarily characterised by its indifference and equality. Again the yogin is said to find happiness in this state: 'He whose self is controlled through contact

101 According to Zaehner (1969: 207), this passage 'seems to be based on *KaṭhU* 6.10–11'. While it seems difficult to decide on any textual dependence, both texts share a similar view of yoga as a process that connects the adept to processes of creation and dissolution as expressed in the definition of yoga in *KaṭhU* 6.11: 'yoga is creation and destruction' (*yogo hi prabhavāpyayau*). Cf. Biardeau 1965.

102 I follow van Buitenen's interpretation (1981: 165): '*Svabhāva* should here be taken in its technical sense of *prakṛti*.'

103 *Śvapāka*, lit. 'dog-cooker', the name of highly despised outcastes.

with *brahman* (*brahmayogayuktātmā*)[104] finds permanent bliss' (5.21). This is followed by a description of what happens at the moment of death: 'The man who in this very life is able to resist the overflow of desire and anger before he is freed from the body, he is accomplished, he is happy. He whose happiness, bliss and light are within is a *yogin* who, being *brahman*, reaches *brahmanirvāṇa*' (5.23–24).

How can *brahmanirvāṇa* be understood here? We have already met a similar use of *brahman* and *brahmanirvāṇa* in the description of the man of steady insight (*sthitaprajña*) in *BhG* 2.72.[105] The context of both passages is yoga and death, and the *brahman* was interpreted variously as (1) the realm of liberation, 'equal[ling] *ātman/puruṣa*' (van Buitenen 1981: 165); (2) a sphere between liberation and creation (Zaehner 1969: 206f.); and (3) as an equivalent of *prakṛti* (Schreiner 1991: 150), the cause of all creative activity. The description of yogic practice and the state of being that is associated with reaching *brahman* lends support to the last two meanings, that is, to regard *brahman* as primarily signifying the cause of creation and as probably present in the world in the different 'owners of the body' (*dehin*). As a creative force, *brahman* here is indeed the equivalent of *prakṛti*[106] and thus is the sphere ready for creation as well as the sphere that allows all activity to cease if the self is separated from it. Given this structure, the question is whether *brahman* is also regarded as the sphere of liberation and thus also as identical with the 'individual owners of bodies', the selves, or whether there is a difference between the self and *brahman* as the final stage before liberation. The view that *brahman* is the realm of liberation too is mirrored in the translation of *brahmanirvāṇa* as '*nirvāṇa* that is *brahman*' (Zaehner 1969: 212ff.; Edgerton 1944: 57; van Buitenen 1981: 93). This translation supports a monistic doctrine found in some passages in the Upaniṣads. However, it does not mention that the embodied self, the *dehin*, is merged with *brahman*.

The alternative view follows a Sāṃkhyistic interpretation in which a merger of the elements of the body in the realm of *prakṛti/brahman* would imply the separation from the body which is 'vanishing in *brahman*' (Garbe 1921: 107) and liberation of the self as a 'vanishing of *brahman*'. This means that all activity has stopped and the self as the *prabhu*, the ruler of the body, is

104 Van Buitenen (1981: 165), pursuing his monistic interpretation of the chapter, interprets yoga here as 'unifying knowledge of the *ātman/brahman*', while my translation stresses the contact with *brahman* as the reason for being in control (cf. also *brahmabhūta* in 5.24).

105 Parallels to this passage can also be seen in the compounds *sthirabuddhi* (5.20) and *brahmanirvāṇa* (5.24, 25, 26; 2.72).

106 Cf. also the similarities between the activity of *prakṛti* described in 3.27–28 and the activity of the one who has placed all activity in *brahman* in 5.8–10.

separated from its activity. The elements of the body and their activity fade away in *brahman*, meaning for the self that *brahman* as the realm of activity fades away too. Again we have no clear statement about the liberation of the self such as we find in the subsequent chapters. The lack of such statements may be explained by recalling that the main object of the chapter is to explain true renunciation and how to achieve a liberating death. What we are given is the pledge that the *yogin* who dies in this way will not be reborn. Otherwise we may assume that the 'elemental self' vanishes in its sources, while the embodied self is liberated in an undefined manner. Yet Arjuna, the warrior, is thus taught the perfect method of dying, the 'death of a *yogin*'.[107] Not only will this prove his ascetic indifference; it also protects him from being bound by the consequences of his deeds. We will hear more about the *ātman* and what else may happen at the moment of liberation in *BhG* 6. Such a specification has already been inserted at the very end of the chapter, where Kṛṣṇa is declared to be the goal of the *yogin*, since he is the 'mighty lord of all beings' (5.29). When we exclude this theistic interpolation from the interpretation of 'reaching *brahman*', we are left with *brahmanirvāṇa* as the final stage, as we were in *BhG* 2.72. It seems that this term reflects a position that was understood and followed as a goal in its own right.[108] Given the lack of information about the liberation of an immortal self, a monistic interpretation of this state seems more plausible. '*Brahmanirvāṇa*' would then mean that the individual self merges and vanishes in *brahman*, the origin and end of all beings. This is of interest for the larger conceptual framework of the doctrines incorporated in the *BhG*, and the relationship with Buddhist doctrines is one aspect of this framework.

There is a general consensus[109] that use of the word *nirvāṇa* indicates that the authors of the *BhG* were familiar with Buddhism. Accordingly, van Buitenen (1981: 163) comments: 'Nirvāṇa: surely a reply to the Buddhists, declaring that even while taking a brahmanistic stance in a life of social activity, a person can attain the serenity which the Buddhists have arrogated to themselves while not socially active.'[110] A detailed discussion is provided by Zaehner (1969: 213), who thinks that this passage intends 'to adopt the Buddhist ideal' by identifying *nirvāṇa* and *brahman*. He also points

107 On yoga as a method of dying and the death of the *yogin*, see Schreiner (1988), who deals also with the *sthitaprajña* section (1988: 16).

108 Cf. *BhG* 12.1–2 on those who meditate on the unmanifest. This may be similar to what in later texts is called 'merging with *prakṛti*' (*prakṛtilaya*), regarded as a result of 'dispassion' (*vairāgyāt prakṛtilayaḥ*; cf. *SK* 45). See also commentaries on *YS* 1.19 contrasting 'merging with *prakṛti*' with *kaivalya* as the liberation from *prakṛti*, what in *BhG* 13.34 is called *bhūtaprakṛtimokṣa*.

109 Dasgupta (1952: 450, note 1) rejects any connection with Buddhism.

110 See also A. P. Karmarkar 1950: 306; Upadhyaya 1971: 351f.

to the numerous occurrences of the compound *brahmabhūta* in Buddhist texts dealing with the position of an *arahant*. Zaehner is certainly right in refusing to open a rift between Buddhism and Hinduism here. This would also be misleading, since at that time we are probably dealing with communities and doctrines in the making. The authors of the *BhG* seem to be dealing with different traditions of yoga and renunciation and their respective notions of liberation. In doing so, two strategies to deal with this soteriological pluralism can be distinguished: reinterpretation through equation, and subordination through hierarchisation. We will deal with hierarchisation in many of the subsequent chapters, the aim of which is to subordinate all cosmological realms and soteriological goals under Kṛṣṇa. In contrast, chapters 2 and 5 (except 5.29) present a practice of yoga that is primarily concerned with destroying *karman* and winning a liberating death that guarantees the end of rebirth. This tradition is probably also referred to in *BhG* 12, where the followers of Kṛṣṇa are distinguished from those who are devoted to the 'imperishable' and 'unmanifest'. Seen against this background, all traditions that regard liberation as a state of being that is devoid of individuality and attributes (non-manifest), yet marked by stability, peace and happiness, would suggest that reaching the final stage of the path means vanishing, fading away: one reaches *nirvāṇa* of some kind. The message of *BhG* 5 (and 2.53ff.) to Buddhist traditions would then be that their doctrine of liberation is nothing new or special, but can easily be described using Upaniṣadic terminology. A similar adaptation can be observed in Buddhist texts, not only in their use of the word *brahman*, but also in their acceptance of meditative methods from adjacent traditions (cf. Bronkhorst 1993). Seen from the perspective of Sāṃkhya, the easiest way to establish a hierarchy is to separate the creative aspect of *brahman* from the liberating one and postulate that liberation is self-realisation, knowledge of the self, rather than knowledge of what the self is not or of the non-self. This opens the door to various interpretations of the self and even the super-imposition of a highest self as the overlord of all selves, as it is done with regard to Kṛṣṇa.

BHAGAVADGĪTĀ 6: TWO GOALS OF LIBERATION

The chapter follows on from the previous one by further expanding on yoga practice and the process of liberation. While Kṛṣṇa was declared to be the goal of yoga practice only once in 5.29, this is mentioned more often in this chapter. As a consequence, other realms of liberation are subordinated to the god and made stages of a path leading to him alone, while other gods or powerful beings are identified as aspects or limited parts of the 'mighty Lord'. This can be observed in the two descriptions of yogic practice and liberation included in this chapter: (1) yoga results in becoming *brahman* and 'seeing the same in everything'; (2) yoga culminates in a vision of Kṛṣṇa as the one being in which everything unites. Although the theistic interpretation is probably a later interpolation, in the extant text it is inserted before and after the non-theistic yoga. Both accounts can be regarded as continuing the themes of the previous chapters, especially with regard to the issue of 'self-control'.

Recalling Arjuna's opening question in 5.1 about the relationship between *karmayoga* and renunciation, this chapter starts with a concise redefinition of *saṃnyāsa* in terms of yoga: 'He who performs the ordained act without desiring its fruits is the renouncer and the *yogin*, not the one who is without sacrificial fire (*niragni*)[111] and ritual' (6.1). The traditional renouncer, who has given up his social and ritual life, is here downgraded in that 'true' renunciation is now based on the figure of the *yogin* who has given up all attachment (*saṅga*) and intentions or commitments (*saṃkalpa*; 6.2, 4), but still performs his social duties. As has been demonstrated in *BhG* 5, this form of renunciation is brought about by casting all activities on the cosmic cause of all activity (*brahman* or *prakṛti*), thus avoiding karmic bondage. Again it is emphasised that giving up attachment is an integral part of yoga practices aimed at controlling the different levels of the 'active self' and the cosmic realms that are linked to it. The agonistic nature of this quest to control the ever-active self that the *yogin* must turn into a vehicle and instrument for gaining liberation is the topic of the next verses (cf. *BhG* 5.7; 19):

One should raise oneself by oneself and not degrade oneself, for oneself alone is one's relative – oneself alone is one's enemy. To him who has conquered himself by himself, his self is a relative, but to him who has no self [i.e. that is under control], his self will function only as an enemy. For him who has mastered himself and has become peaceful, the higher self[112] is completely stable in cold and heat, in joy and pain, in honour and abuse. (6.5–7)

As a consequence, the *yogin* has reached the 'peak' (*kūṭastha*),[113] he stands at the top of creation, and yoga as a struggle for control has turned into a

111 Renunciation of the sacrificial fire is the characteristic feature of *saṃnyāsa* in the traditional, dharmaśāstric context of life stages (*āśrama*).

112 The higher self (*paramātma*) is here the faculty exercising control, that is, the *buddhi*. This is corroborated in 6.9: the *yogin* excels all others because his '*buddhi* is indifferent' (*samabuddhi*). For a discussion of the different interpretations of 6.7, see Malinar 1996: 214–217.

113 Cf. Zaehner (1969: 222f.), who discusses parallel passages in *MBh* 12.242.18–18 and 12.17.19.

state of being, characterised by tranquillity, knowledge and understanding (*jñāna-vijñāna*; 6.8).[114] His faculty of discrimination allows him to see the 'same' in everything because it is itself 'indifferent', 'same' (*samabuddhi*; 6.9), being now connected with its cosmological dimension. This reference to the *buddhi* points to a situation in which this highest faculty of the manifest, active self has now gained control. This theme of '*buddhi* in control' is one of the threads that run through the first six chapters of the *BhG*.

The passage quoted above again highlights the reflexive and recursive structure of yogic practice as working on and with different levels of the self, this being why the reflexive pronoun is often a good choice in translating the stanzas. As already demonstrated with regard to *BhG* 5.7ff., yoga is practised within a hierarchy of faculties and elements of the manifest, active self. We should recall that this self is at the same time an individual formation of the elements common to all manifest beings as the products of one common cause (*prakṛti* or *brahman*) and an embodiment of an immortal entity (*dehin*, *ātman*). This manifest self is characterised by a self-activity that needs to be controlled in order to gain knowledge of liberation. This control can only be exercised by gaining access to the highest faculty of the individual self, which is usually called *buddhi*. Control cannot be exercised by an already liberated or highest self, since this would not be able to produce anything; rather, this self is the goal of the practice. As pointed out in 6.6, in reaching this goal, the manifest self can be either an obstacle (like an enemy, *śatru*) or an ally or friend (*bandhu*, literally 'kin, relative'). It is an obstacle when the higher faculties are dominated by the activities of the senses and the appropriative intentions (*saṃkalpa*) of the mind; it is an ally when it is subdued and controlled, and allows the realisation of the immortal self in the manifest self. The emphasis here is on making oneself one's own ally when the higher self, that is, the highest cognitive faculty, is gaining control. Yogic practice thus shows a recursive or self-referential structure in that the instrument and object of the practice are of the same kind. This structure, which some regard as paradoxical, is expressed in (paranomatic) formulations such as 'conquering oneself by oneself' (6.6) or 'seeing the self

114 No explanation of the difference between *jñāna* and *vijñāna* is given here or on the other occasions on which they occur (3.41; 7.2; 9.1; 13.18). While some have suggested distinguishing between general and particular or theoretical and practical knowledge respectively (Schlegel 1826a; Edgerton 1933); others suggest that *vijñāna* is 'liberating' or 'metaphysical' knowledge (von Humboldt 1826a). For a discussion of different views, see Lacombe 1968. White (1979) suggests that *jñāna* refers to Vedānta and *vijñāna* to Sāṃkhya. Given this uncertainty, I suggest the more neutral and more unspecified translation, 'knowledge and understanding'.

by oneself in oneself' (6.20).[115] In the case of the word *ātman*, this recursive movement is implied in the very use of the word as a reflexive pronoun. It therefore expresses actions of self-reflection and of relating oneself to oneself that are also in more 'worldly' contexts.[116] We find instances of such a usage in the epic and other texts, for example, in the Śakuntalā story, when King Duḥṣanta gives Śakuntalā – who is hesitant to yield to the king's wooing without the permission of her father – the following advice (*MBh* 1.67.7; trans. van Buitenen): 'Oneself is one's own best friend; oneself is one's only recourse. You yourself can lawfully make the gift of yourself.' Being one's own friend or enemy also occurs as a theme in Buddhist texts where ascetic practices are described, as in *DhP* 379: 'Propel yourself by yourself, control yourself by yourself (*āttanā codayāttanan paṭimāse attam attanā*). In this way, O monk, guarding yourself and being mindful, you will live happily.'[117] As is well known, in the context of Buddhist soteriology this serves to realise not a highest self or other being, not to mention a Lord Kṛṣṇa, but the transience of all being, including selves deemed immortal. Although the goal of meditative practices in Buddhism is different, certain techniques and the basic, relational structure are very similar to what is being described here in the *BhG*. The relationship between the different ascetic and religious movements and aspirations in the period we are probably dealing with is not easy to trace in detail because we often do not have enough evidence. Scholars have tended to stress competition and hostility between these movements, which is certainly one aspect of this relationship. However, this must not make us forget that they also share not only a certain distance from the established forms of religious practice and doctrine (such as Veda), but also certain practices, notions and even technical terms (such as *brahmabhūta*). Distinctions and mutually exclusive interpretations often worked on the basis of shared assumptions (such as *karman*, *ātman*, cosmology, deities, etc.), and lines of demarcation were not necessarily

115 The paradoxical character of this formulation is highlighted by Ingalls (1959: 102), who deals with *ātmānam ātmanā* as a rhetorical figure (*lātānuprāsa*): 'It is an English proverb that you cannot raise yourself by your bootstraps. Does it seem any more possible to raise yourself by yourself?' He suggests that only the transcendent *ātman* can take control, which is also doubtful, because *buddhi* seems to be the faculty that is able to exercise control.

116 Other occurrences in the *BhG* are 3.43; 6.20; 10.15; 13.24; 13.28. Emeneau (1968: 274–276) stresses the formulaic character of *ātmānam ātmanā* and points to numerous parallel passages in the epic (especially *MBh* 5.34.62). Brockington (1998: 146) takes this passage as evidence for 'later epic style'. However, paranomatic formulas are already used in Vedic literature (see Gonda 1959) and seem to occur also in the older parts of the epic.

117 See also *DhP* 165; *SN* 3.1.4–5. Claiming that 'oneself is one's own protector, oneself is one's own recourse', *DhP* 380 recommends controlling oneself 'as a merchant controls his noble horse'. The comparison between the self and the horse echoes the epic and Vedic use of *yoga* in the sense of yoking, and the chariot image in *KaṭhU* 3.3–6.

drawn between what today are regarded as different religions, but between different life-styles and institutions based on the acquisition of patronage and support at local levels. This is why there are similar practices in different communities and parallel passages in their respective texts, while they still retain their distinctive character.

As Bronkhorst has demonstrated (1993), sometimes the distinction is not so much one between Hindus and Buddhists, as between those who practise 'hard-core' asceticism aimed at the extinction of the body at all costs (ascribed to Jainas), and those who use the body as a vehicle and advocate more moderate practices. The conquest of the self aims at making it an ally in achieving a higher goal (called *nirvāṇa*, *ātman*/*puruṣa* or Kṛṣṇa respectively). Similarities with Buddhist notions also appear in the following description of the yoga as a path that avoids extreme or painful practices. This description consists of two different accounts of yoga: while *BhG* 6.16–29 gives a detailed account of how the *yogin* gains self-control and liberation, 6.10–15, 30–31 interpret this within the monotheistic framework by proclaiming Kṛṣṇa the goal of the practice and as that very self that the *yogin* should realise. Thus, in its extant form, the text comprises two different goals of yoga:[118] (1) a state of indifference (*samadarśi*); (2) a vision of the god Kṛṣṇa, who is said to surpass *nirvāṇa* (6.15).

The actual practice that leads to the respective goals includes some standard items such as diet, concentration, etc., which are part and parcel of many, if not all, yoga or other meditative traditions. Thus the *yogin* is advised to practise alone in a secluded, secret place, without any social contact. He must set up a seat in a clean place that is covered with cloth, antelope skin and *kuśa* grass. Hoens points out that the use of antelope skin and *kuśa* grass is met with in numerous texts that describe the consecration of the patron of a sacrifice.[119] Then the *yogin* concentrates his mind (*manas*) on them, controls the activities of his thought and senses, sits down on the seat, and practises yoga in order to purify himself. He should sit up rigidly and fix his gaze on the tip of his nose without paying attention to his surroundings. According to the following two verses, he then concentrates

[118] Emeneau (1968: 27ff.) discusses these two paths of yoga, whose description ends by using the same formula (*yuñjann evaṃ sadātmānaṃ yogī*; 6.15a = 6.28a). *BhG* 6.28 is regarded as a repetition of verse 15 indicating a 'subtle antithesis (*virodha*)'. The second yoga teaching ('becoming *brahman*') is regarded as a later interpolation in what was originally a theistic doctrine. According to the text-historical assumptions I follow, the monotheistic teaching is the new element and therefore it is necessary to present it as surpassing other goals.

[119] Hoens 1968: 532: 'In the texts the combination of the cloth, the antelope skin and kuśagrass did not occur together; the combination of cloth and antelope skin or of antelope skin and kuśagrass, however, did.'

on Kṛṣṇa, to whom he is dedicated, after he has fully constrained his mind (*manaḥ saṃyamya*; 6.14): 'When the *yogin* thus constantly controls himself, having his mind under control, he reaches a peace that is higher than *nirvāṇa*, since it rests in me' (*śāntiṃ nirvāṇaparamāṃ matsaṃsthāṃ adhigacchati*) (6.15). This statement recalls 6.8, where the attainment of the 'peak position' was connected to becoming 'indifferent', and 5.26, where this state means to be close to *brahmanirvāṇa*. Now we learn that there is something beyond *nirvāṇa*, or, to put it more neutrally, that the peace of *nirvāṇa* lies in Kṛṣṇa, and neither in *brahman* nor in Buddhist *nirvāṇa*. The verse is important for Kṛṣṇa's position with regard to the alternative goal of reaching an undefined *nirvāṇa*, since it allows two different translations, depending on how one understands the expression *śāntiṃ nirvāṇaparamām*. Following van Buitenen, my translation suggests that reaching Kṛṣṇa surpasses *nirvāṇa*. Other translators suggest that *nirvāṇa* is equated with reaching Kṛṣṇa: for instance, Zaehner translates 'peace which has Nirvāṇa as its end' (cf. also Garbe 1921: 109). I follow van Buitenen's interpretation because it suits the context of both chapters. Kṛṣṇa is not just like the goal of *nirvāṇa* for those who strive for it: rather, their *nirvāṇa* depends on him and is regarded as a stage in reaching Kṛṣṇa, a personal highest Self that guarantees liberation by acquiring his 'state of being'. Kṛṣṇa surpasses whatever kind of *nirvāṇa* Buddhists or other ascetics and renouncers strive for. This position of the god is again asserted after the other account of yoga that leads to *brahman*. Here, the 'sameness' the *yogin* envisions as the self is identified as the god Kṛṣṇa, who is the one and only being in which all beings abide (6.30–31): 'For him, who sees me everywhere and sees all in me, I am not lost, nor is he lost for me. He who is devoted to me as abiding in all beings, since he maintains the state of unitedness (*ekatvam*), he is the *yogin* who moves in me, in whatever way he moves.'[120] Here the state of sameness is regarded as a state of unity or rather unitedness with Kṛṣṇa. He is the 'all', and thus the one and only being in which all beings abide (cf. 5.29). This view is based on explanations given from chapter 7 onwards.

The description of the path of yoga that leads to *brahman* begins with further characterisations of yoga that obviously serve to distinguish the path from other traditions of asceticism, such as Jaina or extreme *tapas* (cf. Bronkhorst 1993). In contrast to these, yoga is defined as what 'puts an end to suffering' (*yogo bhavati duḥkhahā*; 6.17). This implies a moderate

[120] Following Kṛṣṇa's path is also the characteristic feature of Kṛṣṇa's relationship with his creatures in *BhG* 4.11; see above. Hein (1975: 253f.) discusses this passage as an example of what he calls a 'modifying addendum', which is used in order to adjust an older concept to the new theology.

life-style and diet as detailed in 6.16–17 and is similar to the Buddhist path (cf. Minor 1982: 216). Again the results of the practice are described, the aim this time being to stop all activity of the mind (*cittaṃ niruddhaṃ*; 6.20), a characterisation that is rather close to the famous definition of yoga in *YS* 1.2 ('yoga is stopping all activities of the mind'; *cittavṛttinirodha*).[121] This state of being results in a vision of the self: 'When he has put the mind to rest, stopped by the practice of yoga, then he is satisfied, since he sees the self by himself in himself. He then experiences that exceptional happiness which surpasses the senses because it is to be experienced by the *buddhi*' (6.21). Thus yoga has to be understood as 'unlinking the link with suffering' (trans. Zaehner; *duḥkha-samyoga-viyogam*; 6.23). Echoing the description of *BhG* 5.7ff., the Yogin is now presented as 'being *brahman*' (*brahmabhūta*; 6.27) and enjoys the happiness that lies in 'touching *brahman*' (*brahmasaṃsparśa*; 6.28). Again, the result is the realisation of identity in that the *yogin* 'sees the same' (*samadarśana*; 6.29): 'He sees himself (*ātman*) in all beings and all beings in himself. Having controlled himself through yoga, he sees the same everywhere' (6.29). United with the cause of the manifest world, the *yogin* realises that everything is the same because it is produced by the very same cause.

Yet another interpretation of the verse is possible, because the word *ātman* can also be understood as the 'immortal self' that resides in every body (the 'manifest self'), but is ultimately separate from it. The difficulty here is that no explanation of such an immortal self is given. However, as Zaehner shows (1969: 233), this difficulty can be resolved when one assumes that *brahman* is here in the 'self' of every being: 'he becomes Brahman, he sees "self in self"', which means sharing the qualities of *brahman* (immortal, indifferent, etc.). The *yogin* realises his self's (manifest as well as unmanifest) identity with and as *brahman*. An explicit interpretation of this self is given in the next verse, which presents the theological view that the self of all beings is the god Kṛṣṇa (6.30–31; see discussion in the previous subsection).

If we pass over this theological interpretation, the last comment on 'sameness' is given in 6.32, where this ideal state of existence is described for the very last time. The highest *yogin*, it is declared, is he 'who sees the same (*sama*) everywhere by comparing (equating) it with himself (*ātmaupamyena*), O Arjuna' (6.23). Again, nothing is said about the liberation of the embodied self. At this point, Arjuna is made to intervene by raising doubts about the chances of ever gaining yogic 'indifference'

[121] However, I follow Schreiner's view (1991: 157) that the text uses the Sāṃkhya hierarchy of faculties, and understand *citta* as an equivalent of *manas*, rather than of *buddhi*. This also corresponds to 6.25 on the stability of *buddhi* and the use of *manas* in 6.34.

(*samyena*). He argues with the restlessness of the mind (*manas*), which is strong and as difficult to take hold of as the wind (6.33–34). Kṛṣṇa concedes that this is indeed a difficult task, which can, nevertheless, be tackled by effort (*abhyāsa*) and the relinquishing of desire (*vairāgya*).[122] Still doubtful, Arjuna asks what happens if a *yogin* fails (6.37), and wonders: 'Does he not fail in both ways[123] and perish like a torn-off cloud, without foundation, confused on the path to *brahman*, strong-armed lord?' (6.38). Kṛṣṇa seems to be acquainted with this problem, since he aptly assures him that the 'fallen *yogin*' (*yogabhraṣṭa*; literally 'who failed in self-control'; 6.41) expects no negative results or bad rebirth (*durgati*), since he has performed deeds that are full of merit (*kalyāṇa-kṛt*; 6.40). Thus he will be reborn in a circle (*kula*; literally 'family') of *yogin*s and be equipped or united with that very same discriminative faculty (*buddhisaṃyoga*; 4.43) he possessed in his former birth, and continue with his practice. In this way, he will surpass the *śabdabrahman*, the realm of Vedic knowledge and practice (4.44). The praise of the *yogin* culminates in 6.46: 'Such a *yogin* is better than mere ascetics (*tapasvin*), even better than the learned and wise, and also better than those who act (the performers of ritual and social duties). Therefore be a *yogin*, Arjuna!' This conclusion is followed in the extant text by again declaring Kṛṣṇa to be the ultimate goal: 'For me the most accomplished among all *yogin*s is he who, full of confidence (*śraddhāvān*), is devoted to me by having his inner self (*antarātman*) turn to me' (6.47). Again, the relationship with Kṛṣṇa is said to supersede all others, and thus we again meet hierarchisation as the strategy for establishing Kṛṣṇa as the highest god.

In contrast to the one theistic interpolation in the previous chapter, *BhG* 6 shows a more coherent effort to mediate a path of yoga that culminates in being *brahman* (*brahmabhūta*), in reaching *brahma-nirvāṇa* as the realisation of the sameness (*samatva*) of all beings with the doctrine that Kṛṣṇa is the one who in whom all beings unite. This is sought by establishing a hierarchy with the god at the top. For yoga as a path to liberation, this means that, when a *yogin* returns to the cause of existence through an inversion of the process of creation, he still reaches *brahman*, but that beyond that, Kṛṣṇa appears as the ultimate and highest realm. *Brahman* is made a stage and a state on the path that ends in Kṛṣṇa. This mediation and hierarchisation of different traditions and goals of yoga within the monotheistic

122 Cf. *YS* 1.12, where *abhyāsa* and *vairāgya* are taught as instruments (*upāya*; cf. also *BhG* 6.36) of *nirodha*-yoga.

123 I follow van Buitenen's (1981: 165) interpretation of the 'two ways': 'failing both in gainful acting and in reaching *brahman*'. *Contra*: Zaehner 1969: 240.

framework will continue in the ensuing chapters. *BhG* 12 can be regarded as a commentary on this chapter because it addresses the difference between *yogins* who strive for the 'imperishable unmanifest' and those who long for Kṛṣṇa (see below, pp. 187ff.). Seen in the context of the doctrine of 'disinterested action', *BhG* 5 and 6 offer an explanation of why *karmayoga* is possible. It is shown that 'indifference' is not a 'mood' or an individual attitude, but one of the most important features of the cosmic cause of all activity. When one stops appropriating this activity through egoistical desires, the original cosmic 'indifference' is restored. Drawing on the trope of 'conquest', one can say that indifference becomes the shield that protects the *yogin* from the consequences of his acts – he holds 'the sword of knowledge' forged from the thought 'I do nothing'. This conceptual framework is not only fundamental for the doctrine of *karmayoga*, but is also used in the subsequent exposition of the theology of Kṛṣṇa.

BHAGAVADGĪTĀ 7: KṚṢṆA'S NATURE

This chapter marks the beginning of a more coherent presentation of the theology of Kṛṣṇa. With the exception of the first half of *BhG* 4, the previous chapters sought mediation between the performance of social duties and the quest for liberation in the doctrine of 'disinterested action'. While *BhG* 5 and 6 describe yoga as a practice of self-conquest resulting in an identification with the cause of all activity as the technique to prevent further karmic bondage, this doctrine is now used to declare Kṛṣṇa to be responsible for both creation and liberation. He is made to represent the mediation between these two dimensions: on the one hand, he is in charge of the creative process, the maintenance of cosmic order and the destruction of disorder and evil; on the other, he is the ever-liberated 'highest self' and can act for the sake of the world without being attached to these actions. Therefore he guarantees liberation for those who know and worship him. When inciting creation, he controls and incites *prakṛti*, the cause of all manifestations; when he has to fight disorder (*adharma*) and re-establish order (*dharma*), he appears in an outward form, an apparitional body (*māyā*) that is not connected to his eternal self, which remains forever unborn and detached. Approaching this god implies emulating his mode of activity by controlling desire and other egoistic impulses. This control is now exercised on the basis of the realisation that everything should be dedicated to the god Kṛṣṇa because attachment to him brings about liberation from *karman*. This conceptual framework is established from chapter 7 onwards and can be regarded not only as perhaps the most important feature of the *BhG* but also as one of the most influential in the history of Hindu religious traditions. One reason for the paradigmatic position of the theology of the *BhG* is its acceptance of well-known social and religious practices and philosophical doctrines, which are, however, reinterpreted and reframed. While the new theology is connected to these doctrines by sharing important concepts, terms and practices, they are given a different place in a framework that makes affection and devotion (*bhakti*) to Kṛṣṇa, the 'mighty lord', the highest values. Yet the older doctrines, and especially the *karmayoga* teaching developed in the earlier chapters, also shapes the theology in that they establish certain parameters that theologians had to deal with. This can be seen, for instance, in the way Sāṃkhya and yoga concepts are accepted and transformed, in that the liberating knowledge is no longer represented in the figure of the accomplished *yogin* whose 'self is the self of all beings', but in Kṛṣṇa's relationship to the world and the embodied selves. In *BhG* 9 and 11 this is called his '*yoga aiśvara*' and '*rūpa aiśvara*', his yoga and his form as the supreme lord, both being indicative of his ultimate sovereignty as both the liberated self and the cosmic ruler, the 'All-Form' (*viśvarūpa*). These conceptual links allow the monotheistic framework to be analysed not only as a later addition to an ascetic doctrine, but as an organising principle that provides some conceptual coherence for the different textual and conceptual layers. The insertion of 'theistic verses' in the previous chapters indicates an attempt to weave these levels yet more explicitly together, even though the dramatic impetus implied in the revelatory structure of the text is thereby weakened or even taken away, at least in the perspective of audiences who are used to more linear and 'peripatetic' narratives and arguments.

One important element of this framework is offered right at the beginning of chapter 7, when Kṛṣṇa announces that he will teach Arjuna how to turn yogic detachment into attachment to him alone: 'Hear how you will indubitably know in my entirety when you practise yoga with your mind attached to me, having your shelter in me' (7.1). The importance of the *karmayoga* doctrines as a constitutive feature of the new theology is corroborated here in that they are the first issue addressed. The reinterpretation of ascetic detachment and traditional renunciation (*saṃnyāsa*) is now given another twist by declaring that all attachment (*āsakta*) should be directed towards Kṛṣṇa. In this way, all acts and their fruits are cast on him too. All that is needed is the knowledge of Kṛṣṇa's true being, which the god is about to reveal personally to his dear friend because it is otherwise difficult to gain (7.2–3). The text now turns into the self-revelation of Kṛṣṇa as the one and only god, which, as has been pointed out by van Buitenen (1981:

6–13), differs from older 'revealed texts' in being 'personal, historic, and original'.

First of all, Kṛṣṇa's relationship with creation and the created world is explained by drawing, as in chapter 4, on Sāṃkhya terminology. We must again keep in mind that this terminology differs from its 'classical' formulation in the later *Sāṃkhyakārikā* (*SK*). This becomes obvious in the following description of the realm of *prakṛti*, which not only draws a distinction between a higher (*parā*) and a lower (*aparā*) *prakṛti*, but also presents the latter as 'eightfold' (*aṣṭadhā prakṛti*), that is, as consisting of the five elements (water, earth, etc.) and three cognitive faculties (*buddhi, ahaṃkāra, manas*). This pluriform structure of *prakṛti* is a characteristic feature of early Sāṃkhya in epic, Upaniṣadic, Ayurvedic and some Buddhist texts.[124] As Johnston notes (1937: 28), this pluriform notion of *prakṛti* calls for certain attributes when *prakṛti* is dealt with as an unmanifest (*avyakta*), singular realm: 'In the systems which teach the existence of eight *prakṛtis* it is necessary to use an epithet to distinguish the *avyakta*, if it is called *prakṛti*.' In our text it is stated that there is a 'higher *prakṛti*', which is the *jīva* (*jīvabhūta*), the individual, embodied self 'by whom this world is sustained' (7.5). This seems a rather unexpected statement, since, from a Sāṃkhya perspective, the 'self' is usually not regarded as a form of *prakṛti*. Translators again disagree about the interpretation of the word. Some translate 'the individual soul' or 'order of souls' (van Buitenen); others offer 'developed into life' (Zaehner) or '*Lebenskraft*' ('life force'; Schreiner). The context of the passage may help to clarify the meaning because it focusses on Kṛṣṇa's involvement in creation. Thus we are dealing not just with *prakṛti*, but with Kṛṣṇa's *prakṛti*. Therefore, in both its aspects *prakṛti* belongs to him. Seen from this perspective, the individual self is the 'higher *prakṛti*', residing in a body and related to the god as a part himself, as something he owns. As Olivelle notes (1964: 516f.): 'This *prakriti* [*sic*] is spiritual and personal and is considered as the universal soul upholding all things.' This is also made explicit in *BhG* 15.7, where *jīvabhūta* means the 'individual self' as a part of Kṛṣṇa's highest self. It is still a part of this self which is actually involved in creation and therefore belongs to the *prakṛti* aspect of the god. However, since the passage deals with the creation of the cosmos, *jīva* also has the connotation of the life principle suggested by some translators and made explicit when Kṛṣṇa is called the '*jīvana*' or animating principle (7.9). Since the animated pluriform *prakṛti* creates a cosmos as the unified

124 See *MBh* 12.203.27; 12.294.29; 12.298.10, *Buddhacaritam* 13.18–19; *Cārakasaṃhitā*; *Śārīrasthāna* 1.17. *BhG* 13.5 lists elements of the manifest world (the "field", *kṣetra*) and includes *avyakta*, but not *manas*.

ensemble of a variety of beings, as well as individual bodies, *jīvabhūta* has two aspects too, appearing in individual beings as the embodied self, as well as in the form of planets, the Veda, etc. The following verses describe this activation by drawing on notions of procreation, and not, as is the case in classical, non-theistic Sāṃkhya, on concepts of error and ignorance. It seems that the distinction between the two *prakṛtis* is reformulated in terms of the two factors necessary for conception. The 'lower', pluriform *prakṛti* is regarded as the 'womb' (*yoni*; 7.6)[125] of all beings, while the higher, animating principle (*jīva*) is Kṛṣṇa's 'eternal seed (*bīja*) in all beings' (7.10). As a consequence, and in accordance with the traditional, patriarchal model of procreation as 'planting the higher, male seed' in a 'lower, female womb' as the medium for the male's birth, Kṛṣṇa declares himself to be *jīvana*, the 'principle of life', the 'vitality' (van Buitenen) in all beings, including the cosmic elements: 'In earth I am its fragrance, in the sun its fire, in all creatures their vitality (*jīvana*), in the ascetics their austerity. Know, O Pārtha, that I am the eternal seed (*bīja*) of all beings' (7.9). A similar description of creation as procreation is given in *BhG* 14.3 and thus cannot be regarded as an occasional or archaic deviation from Sāṃkhya, but rather displays the influence of older notions that make procreation the model for creation.

When it is said that the higher *prakṛti* has become or is *jīva*, it thus seems to refer to the first stage of activation of *prakṛti*, which results in the 'lower' *prakṛti*'s impregnation by the animating particle of Kṛṣṇa, his 'eternal seed'. As a consequence, the 'eightfold' *prakṛti* appears as the visible world in the form of planets, ascetics, etc. The cosmic and individualised aspects of the Sāṃkhya *prakṛti* are here connected with and subordinated to Kṛṣṇa in making the 'life principle' the god's 'higher nature'. Thus Kṛṣṇa's influence extends to both dimensions of creation, the cosmic and the individual. In being *jīva* and *jīvana*, Kṛṣṇa is related to the created world not only as its 'origin and end' but also during its existence: he is 'the thread on which the whole world is strung like pearls on a string' (7.7). Kṛṣṇa is depicted not as the unmoved mover, but as the inciter of the activity of nature, who is part of what is created in that he is the 'seed'. He is the string that holds together all beings and imparts 'wholeness' to what would otherwise be just a grouping of particles. On the other hand, in each case it is only a particle of Kṛṣṇa that functions as the seed which incites *prakṛti*'s activation. The cosmos is not regarded as the body or embodiment of Kṛṣṇa, as is the case for *brahman* or *akṣara* in some Upaniṣadic texts, where cosmogony is

[125] Cf. *BhG* 14.3, where *brahman* is also called Kṛṣṇa's 'womb' (*yoni*). See below, pp. 199ff.

described in terms of 'somatogony' (van Buitenen 1964: 108). Otherwise it would be difficult to explain Kṛṣṇa's distance and detachment, his position as the ever-liberated self, or why he is higher than all the 'highest' beings one has already heard of in the Upaniṣads. This distinction is made explicit with regard to the activities of *prakṛti* in 7.12: 'Understand that all states of being (*bhāva*), be they qualified by *sattva*, *rajas* or *tamas*,[126] come from me, but I am not in them: they are in me' (cf. 9.4–5 for a similar statement).

Having thus claimed the realm and the mode of operation of *prakṛti* as belonging to Kṛṣṇa, another distinction is introduced with regard to the individual's knowledge of Kṛṣṇa and the divine nature of *prakṛti*. The manifestations of creative power (in 7.14–15 called *māyā*) attract and confuse most creatures and are therefore difficult to overcome (*duratya*, 7.14). Only those who take refuge in Kṛṣṇa may pass beyond this power: those who fail to do so are evil-doers who live a demonic life (*āsura bhāva*; 7.15). In this passage, *prakṛti* and *māyā* are used as synonyms, both designating the realm of creative power and its manifestations. The delusive potential of this power is indicated by using the term *māyā*, which seems to be the preferred term for stressing the apparitional and delusive effects of creativity (see above, pp. 96ff.). The distinction between those who know or at least turn to Kṛṣṇa as the highest being and those who do not serves as the organising principle for a hierarchisation of beings according to their distance from the god. Although this is based on a binary opposition between followers and non-followers, it results in a variety of distinctions, since following Kṛṣṇa permits different practices and degrees of knowledge. Such variety is possible because it is the relationship between the god and his devotee that counts, not the strictness or correctness of the ritual formula, nor the exclusivity of the priests as mediators.

This internal differentiation of devotees (*bhakta*) according to their degree of knowledge is put forward in the following classification:

Four kinds of good men seek my love, Arjuna: the suffering (*ārta*), the seeker of knowledge (*jijñāsu*), the seeker of wealth (*arthārthi*), and the one who knows (me, *jñāni*), best of Bhāratas. Among them, the one who knows (me) is supreme since his devotion is exclusive and he is always self-controlled; therefore I am exceedingly dear (*priya*) to him and he is dear to me. (7.16–18)[127]

Two of the four motives of *bhakti* are connected with knowledge: that of the seeker of knowledge (*jijñāsu*), and that of the knower (*jñānin*). This

[126] The three powers of *prakṛti* (*guṇa*) are tranquillity, transparency (*sattva*); activity, passion (*rajas*); lethargy, darkness (*tamas*).

[127] For a discussion of a similar classification in the Nārāyaṇīya section, see Malinar 1997: 261–264.

covers both those who already worship Kṛṣṇa and those who are still seeking him, or perhaps even those who are still undecided seekers. However, those whose devotion is more closely connected with worldly life are also regarded as *bhaktas*; as van Buitenen (1981: 165–6) puts it, they are 'those who implore Kṛṣṇa to alleviate their sufferings . . . those who pray to him for material benefits'. In opening up the spectrum of followers also to those who do not primarily seek liberation with Kṛṣṇa and practise forms of worship not by relinquishing fruits, but in order to gain them, standard ritual practices become legitimate forms of devotion. However, these can include even practices addressed to other gods too. Therefore, as is made clear in 7.17–18, the knower is the one who is exclusively dedicated to Kṛṣṇa and therefore closest to the god, even being regarded as the god's self (*ātman*; 7.18). This echoes a key passage describing the relationship of the 'highest' *bhakti* in 7.17 in terms of being *priya*. Drawing on the older, original meaning of this term as 'being one's own' ('*eigen*'; Scheller 1950), as expressing this sense of 'belongingness', being part of each other, is also indicated when Kṛṣṇa regards the *bhakta* as being his self, that is, part of him. This relationship is based on the fact that this follower knows that 'Vāsudeva is (the) all' (*vāsudevaṃ sarvam iti*; 7.19). As a consequence he has become a 'mighty self' (*mahātmā*; 7.19), as he has reached the position in which he has realised that all beings belong to Kṛṣṇa. For the first time, the text offers a formula which summarises and formulates the knowledge that the adept acquires in the end. The name of the god is given as Vāsudeva, this being one of the few passages in which Kṛṣṇa identifies himself by name.

The knowledge that there is only one god who is the 'whole' indicates that one has truly understood the new type of divinity who is revealed here. Kṛṣṇa's power and transcendent state of being must be distinguished from the temporary and limited powers of other gods and powerful beings. Therefore the text deals with the worship of these other gods too (7.20–23), which points to an environment of religious practices characterised by the co-existence not only of different Vedic gods and rituals mostly working by reciting mantras and hymns, but also of forms of worship that include visible forms (*tanu*). Worshippers of other gods are regarded as devotees too, and Kṛṣṇa even claims that he agrees to their worship and ensures that their confidence is not frustrated. However, the fruits of these rituals are temporary, and these *bhaktas* will never reach Kṛṣṇa: 'Finite are the rewards of those who understand little. Worshippers of gods go to the gods, while my followers come to me' (7.23). Similar statements on the relationship with other forms of worship occur in 9.22–25, confirming the pattern of hierarchisation already noticed with regard to the subordination of realms of liberation propagated in other traditions (*brahmanirvāṇa, nirvāṇa*). Other realms of liberation and the existence of other gods and powerful beings are considered as lower levels and elements of a world that is created by Kṛṣṇa's creative power. As a consequence, the worship of these other divinities results in reaching their limited and lower realms only. This also explains why other cults are efficient and why a realm called *brahman* actually exists, since they are part of the *sarvam*, the whole that is created by Kṛṣṇa by means of the agency and power of his *prakṛti*. This knowledge is reserved for Kṛṣṇa only: 'I know the beings of past, present and future, but no one knows me' (7.26).

Kṛṣṇa's manifestation in the world is different from other forms of appearance: 'The ignorant think of me as an unmanifest being (*avyakta*) that has taken a visible form (*vyakti*) because they do not know my higher state of being (*para bhāva*), which is unchanging and incomparable' (7.24). This misconception is caused by his *yogamāyā*, the apparitions and disguises produced by the power of his yoga (7.25). This refers to two types of 'manifestation' that do not apply to Kṛṣṇa: he is neither an ordinary transmigrating self travelling from non-manifestation (*avyakta*) to manifestation (*vyakti*) and back again (as described in *BhG* 2.28), nor some unmanifest entity that becomes manifest or is embodied as the cosmos, such as *brahman* or *prakṛti*, who are regarded as having invisible (*amūrta*; *avyakta*) and visible (*mūrta*; *vyakta*) forms. Kṛṣṇa is also not one of the *deva*s who are worshipped in and as their *tanu*, their corporal form (cf. Falk 1994). All these are possible interpretations of what may be meant by the 'wrong notions' that people entertain with regard to Kṛṣṇa. It points to a context in which the god's divinity either would not be accepted or would be understood inappropriately, since it would be equated with existing notions of divinity. Moreover, it may indicate that the 'human' Kṛṣṇa was still the most popular one. While the question of such possible contexts will be addressed in chapter 5 below, the interpretation suggested earlier has the advantage of reading the verse as an assertion of Kṛṣṇa's distinct supremacy with regard to different competing concepts: he is not a simple human being, or an impersonal cause of creation that knows no higher state than invisibility, the non-manifest, or one of those gods who may be present in visible forms and can be worshipped as rulers over their limited realms of power.[128] Kṛṣṇa

[128] This passage, and a similar one in 9.20–25, has stimulated a discussion of whether this points to an attitude of 'religious tolerance' or is characteristic what Hacker (1983: 12) calls the typical Indian strategy of 'inclusivism'. This means considering the central doctrines of an alien religious group as identical with one's own, though still as subordinate. He also thinks that this strategy is typical for minority groups. Whether this points to a minority situation as Hacker (1983) suggests

is all, and even more than all, since his state of being transcends even the non-manifest realms of other 'highest beings'. Kṛṣṇa's position is unique in that he is in command of the creative powers like a *yogin*, protects the created cosmos like a king, and surpasses all cosmic levels and established realms of liberation in that the 'knowing devotee' reaches not just identity with the elements of creation and liberation of the self, but the eternity in which Kṛṣṇa exists. This state of being can be reached only by those who are devoted to him and think of him at the moment of leaving the body: 'Those who strive for liberation from old age and death resort to me . . . and they also know me at their final hour because their mind is united (with me)' (7.29ab, 30cd). This reference to the hour of death is in line with the description of the death of the *yogin* who has become *brahman* (cf. 5.23). It seems to have inspired the subsequent chapter, which deals almost exclusively with the correct way of dying and the knowledge and self-control that are necessary in order to die successfully. This has led to the insertion of two lines in 7.29cd and 30ab that detail the knowledge that a devoted knower of Kṛṣṇa needs in order to reach his lord at the moment of leaving the body. Accordingly, only those reach Kṛṣṇa who 'know the complete *brahman*, what pertains to the (individual) self and what belongs to all activity and who know me together with what belongs to the elements, the gods and the sacrifice'. This rather cryptic list of aspects serves to give instruction about the best way of dying. It is explained in *BhG* 8 and will be dealt with there.

The chapter under discussion has presented an account of Kṛṣṇa as the one who is the seed in all beings when he activates his *prakṛti* as their womb. This procreative model of creation remains dominant in the *BhG*. Since a part of him is present in the world, he lends cohesion to the multitude of beings. However, he is more than other invisible beings who enter their own creation, since an unchanging realm is ascribed to him that supersedes all others, in which he exists as the 'highest'. Only the striving *yogin* is capable of knowing Kṛṣṇa until the end. These distinctions must be kept in mind in treating *bhakti* as an 'easy' path perfect for women and all those with

is difficult to tell, especially when one considers the question of who represents or is the majority at a time that seems to be characterised by pluralism, diversity and many small kings and kingdoms striving for hegemony. In any case, I agree with Minor (1980: 346) and Oberhammer (1983: 98) that these verses are primarily an explanation of why other cults work and continue to exist, even though Kṛṣṇa has been revealed as the one and only highest being. Yet while it is certainly true that the focus is on Kṛṣṇa, the authors comment implicitly on other cults and thus imply a religious environment in which different cults and groups co-exist and probably compete with one another. The subordination and hierarchisation of these other doctrines and gods are characteristic of the 'cosmological monotheism' presented in the *BhG*, as explained in the Introduction and discussed below, pp. 151ff., 237ff.

allegedly limited resources. This interpretation does not find much support in this chapter because it disregards the distinction between different forms of *bhakti* and the emphasis on ascetic practice in the definition of the 'best' *bhakta*. While the path of yoga ends by realising the sameness of all beings, the path of a yogic *bhakta* ends in reaching Kṛṣṇa's highest state of being.

BHAGAVADGĪTĀ 8: DYING SUCCESSFULLY

Dying successfully means liberating oneself from all karmic connections with the created world. This means that one must be able, at the moment of death, to endure the upheaval caused to the lingering connections (emotional, volitional, mental) with one's life, as was described with regard to the death of the *yogin* in 5.23. In this chapter, death and dying are interpreted within the theological framework by drawing on concepts and themes from the Vedas and Upaniṣads. Again, as in the other chapters, hierarchisation and subordination are the strategies used in order to place Kṛṣṇa in the highest position and make him the one to turn to in one's final hours. In this situation memory and awareness are of vital importance, as they allow one to concentrate on the important aspects of the process of dying and thus to influence its further course after death. Ideally, one should think of Kṛṣṇa in order to ensure that one will indeed reach him. The whole process has strong ritual connotations, which point to the character of dying as a liminal situation and as a 'rite of passage' (*saṃskāra*) dealt with in the *Dharmaśāstras*. Dying is not regarded as the end, but as a 'threshold' which brings about another state of being and therefore has to be attended to as well as possible. The ritual dimension provides the chance to control and to address a situation that may be experienced as beyond one's reach. This is possible when ascetic skills are used to turn the process of dying into a final proof of yogic qualifications and devotional detachment. These are instrumental in the transition to death, which determines the future state of being. This transition works on the following principle: 'Whatever state of being (*bhāva*) a man bears in mind when in the end he gives up his body, to that very state he proceeds, son of Kuntī, because he is constantly absorbed in this state of being' (8.6). Of whom or of what one is thinking at the moment of death determines one's afterlife. This is quite similar to what is said about the different types of sacrifice and their patrons in 7.23 and 9.25: those who worship the gods reach the gods, etc. As is the case in other ritual contexts, intention and commitment (*saṃkalpa*) in consonance with the correct practice establishes that karmic connection which produces the desired fruit, here one's destination after death. While this usually means that one is exposed to the consequences of one's actions, which often do not leave much room for influencing one's passage to another form of existence, ascetic practices try to achieve exactly this. In the ideal way of dying, ascetic detachment must prevail, implying a decisive shift from being attached to one's own life to detachment, which in turn allows one to be intent on or dedicated to another, higher state of being. This cannot be a 'last-minute' booking, since one can be confident of one's ability only when an effort has already been made.

Again it becomes clear that detachment is not just a mental event or an intellectual decision, but a thought-practice that implies a comprehensive restructuring of one's physical, emotional and cognitive connections with the world. This is why, in the present chapter, the process of dying is described with regard to different levels of the individual, which have to be attended to. It results in an identification with the very state of being that one wants to reach, to 'die into'. This is brought about by memorisation, dedication and concentration (*bhāvanā*; 'unfolding', 'meditative realisation') and in 8.6 is called 'being constantly absorbed in this state of being' (*tadbhāva-bhāvita*). This description is applicable to ascetic, meditative and devotional concentration and evocation, a fact that is corroborated by the widespread acceptance of the importance and truth of the 'hour of death' across the different religious traditions (cf. Edgerton 1926–27).

In 8.7 this principle is applied to Arjuna and the battlefield situation, when Kṛṣṇa gives the following advice: 'Therefore think of me at all times and fight with your mind and insight fixed on me and you will come to me; there is no doubt about it.' This teaching is rather distant from Arjuna's worry about the downfall of the ancestors because they lack ritual provision, or about himself as a sinner who has committed the crime of killing his relatives. All *karman* and all efforts have to be united and directed at the very moment of dying in order to influence one's future. As mentioned earlier, what may sound like another 'easy' method is, in fact, a rather difficult one, since the relationship of the embodied self to its actual body is usually strong and hard to control. Therefore, the moment of death is not a chance for an instant change of fate, but a moment in which one's actual condition, the impact of a lifetime, takes it toll. Detachment cannot be postponed to the last breath; it can serve to control the 'surge' (*udvega*) of attachment only if one has already accomplished it.

The actual description of what to do in this situation contains quite a few exegetical and terminological problems, which have resulted in various translations, especially of the first four verses of *BhG* 8. Again we are confronted with the polyvalence of terms like *brahman*, *puruṣa* or *akṣara*, and with different states of being after death that are ultimately all subordinated to the all-encompassing sovereignty and transcendence of Kṛṣṇa. As we may recall, at the end of chapter 7 Kṛṣṇa gives a list of items to reflect on while dying, which is loaded with terms in need of specification (*brahman*, *adhyātman*, etc.). He declares:

Those who seek liberation from old age and death by relying on me, they know *brahman*, the whole and as it pertains to the (individual) self (*adhyātman*), and the entire range of activity (*karman*), as well as what belongs to the elements and to the divine, and they know me together with what belongs to the sacrifice, and they, having their mind under control, will know me also in the hour of death. (7.29–30)

As doubtful about the meaning of the terms listed as perhaps anyone else, in 8.1–2 Arjuna asks for an explanation:

What is that *brahman*? What is it that concerns the self (*adhyātma*)? What is *karman*, O Supreme Person? What is taught as the element aspect (*adhibhūta*) and what is said to be the divinity aspect (*adhidaiva*)? Who and in what way in this body is related to sacrifice (*adhiyajña*), O Madhusūdana? And how are you to be known by the self-controlled in the hour of death?

The problem of these verses is not only how to understand the word *brahman* here, but also how to deal with the terms *adhyātma*, etc. Some interpret them as substantives and translate 'highest self', 'highest deity', etc. (cf. Garbe 1921: 116; Edgerton 1925). Zaehner, referring to parallel usages in the Brāhmaṇas and Upaniṣads,[129] rejects this interpretation and suggests that the terms are attributes of *brahman* and refer to its different manifestations in the cosmos. Although I agree that the terms are probably used as designations of aspects, not all can be connected to *brahman*, since the *adhiyajña* aspect is explicitly linked to Kṛṣṇa.[130] What, then, is the common point of reference? I suggest that it is the process of dying itself, because it demands knowledge of the different aspects and levels the dying person is confronted by or should be aware of. This can be corroborated by the brief definitions given for the terms in 8.3–4: the highest *brahman* is 'imperishable' (*akṣara*); what belongs to the 'individual self' (*adhyātma*)

[129] While the other three aspects are frequently used in the Upaniṣads, *adhiyajña* (what pertains to the sacrifice) is common in the Brāhmaṇas; cf. ŚBr 14.6.5.18 (in the parallel passage *BĀU* 3.7 *adhiyajña* is omitted); 10.2.6.10 ff.; 10.5.2.6; 14.6.7.18–19; *ManuS* 6.82–83. Gonda (1977: 45f.) comments on their function: 'Already at an early date the doctrine found acceptance that the Veda as a whole and consequently a given passage of the Ṛk-Saṃhitā etc. admits a threefold interpretation, viz. from the point of view of the performance of rites (*adhiyajña*), with reference to the deities (*adhidaivata*) and with reference to the "Soul" (*adhyātma*).'

[130] Van Buitenen (1981: 101) ascribes some aspects to *brahman*, others to Kṛṣṇa.

is 'one's state of being' (*svabhāva*), that is, the condition the dying person finds himself in; the *karman* aspect of dying is that it brings about the different states of being or forms of existence; with regard to the elements (*adhibhūta*) that constitute the body, death manifests their perishable nature (*kṣaro bhāva*); and the deity or divine being in that situation is the *puruṣa*, who is praised in what follows as the 'imperishable', the 'light' beyond the darkness of death. Whether or not one regards some of the aspects as belonging to *brahman* as the cause of creation,[131] they all apply to the process of dying. The term *brahman* itself can be understood either as the creative realm or, in the older Vedic sense, as 'truth formulation', as suggested by Schreiner (1991: 91–92). The latter interpretation not only makes sense when it is understood as the recommended *mantra* for the dying, but also is supported by 8.13, which describes the use of the syllable *Oṃ* as the 'imperishable *brahman*' during yogic concentration. Furthermore, the process of dying concerns one's present state of being, the impact of *karman* and an orientation towards the deity who presides over death, the *puruṣa* as the imperishable being who is reached through death. All these aspects are commented upon in the following verses, which offer more information about the way of dying.

This leaves us with the last aspect: that which refers to Kṛṣṇa as the one who 'in this body' pertains to the sacrifice (*adhiyajña*). It is the one aspect of dying that is not explicitly dealt with in what follows and is thus left open to speculation.[132] One possible solution is to regard it as another aspect of the process of dying. Dying should be regarded as a sacrifice dedicated to Kṛṣṇa as its recipient, since successfully dying means being dedicated to Kṛṣṇa, to offer oneself up to him, while all the other aspects of one's former existence are relegated to *brahman* as their cause. In assimilating dying and sacrificial activity, a homology between sacrifice and death is established, as both converge in being directed at Kṛṣṇa. Both are based on the right knowledge of the process and the forces of creation that have to be conquered and controlled in order to transcend them. This makes it necessary that the dying individual is in control, that is, that he has succeeded in yoga and has gained the 'power of yoga' (*yogabala*; 8.10) that is to be combined with *bhakti* as its sibling of choice. The ideal way of dying that leads to Kṛṣṇa is interpreted in what follows as passing through different realms of

[131] Cf. Modi 1932: 17, *passim*, and Zaehner 1969: 258ff.

[132] Zaehner (1969: 261) notes that 'it is not at all clear why Krishna here chooses to identify Himself with the sacrifice'. Modi (1932: 18) suggests that this 'refers to the Yajña-philosophy of the Gītā according to which every act of a man is a yajña and every man is the puruṣa.' This does not exactly clarify Kṛṣṇa's role.

the cosmos. Kṛṣṇa is placed at the top of a triadic structure,[133] with the 'divine *puruṣa*' as the second element on the verge of the perishable realm of creation. How is this framework established in chapter 8?

Having declared that one reaches that state of being that one recalls at the moment of death, the most desirable, yogic way of dying is the centre of interest. It is pointed out that the 'highest *puruṣa*, the divine' (*paramaṃ puruṣaṃ divyam*; 8.8) is reached when thought is controlled by the yogic exercise (*abhyāsa-yoga*). In giving additional emphasis through a change of metre in 8.9–11, the *puruṣa* is praised by drawing on epithets and attributes that are well known from Vedic and Upaniṣadic texts:

> Poet of old,[134] the Ruler, more minute than an atom,[135] the Ordainer of all, of form unthinkable,[136] of the colour of the sun beyond darkness[137] – he who may thus recall him with unmoving mind at the hour of death, being united (with him) through devotion (*bhakti*) and the power of yoga (*yogabala*), having pushed his breath between his eyebrows, he reaches this highest *puruṣa*, the divine. (8.9–10)

This description differs from other passages that deal with the yogic character of the liberating death in that there is an emphasis on the necessary yogic power that results from the successful conquest and control of the self. This conquest is combined with a devotion to a highest, divine being called *puruṣa*. The parallel passages of its description, especially in the two theistic Upaniṣads, indicate that the *BhG* shares their terminology based on Vedic tropes. The author of the passages in the *BhG* uses the same method as in these Upaniṣads, when the attributes and epithets of a divine being called *puruṣa* used in older texts are now ascribed to 'highest gods' like Viṣṇu (*KaṭhU*) and Rudra-Śiva (*ŚvetU*). The *BhG* seems to draw on the same repertoire and is in this regard particularly close to the *KaṭhU*.[138]

This praise of the goal of the practice is followed by an account of yogic concentration directed at Kṛṣṇa at the moment of death. This includes closing all the 'gates of the body' (senses), keeping the mind in the heart – which implies stopping it from moving to the 'gates' – holding the breath in

133 We find a similar structure in *BhG* 15.16, where three different levels of *puruṣa* are distinguished.

134 'Poet', *kavi*, is often used in the Veda as an epithet of Agni, the god of sacrificial fire (e.g. *ṚV* 10.91.3; 3.19.1; 7.4.4; 8.84.2; 10.110.1; see Gonda 1959: 87). *Purāṇa*, 'of old', with Rocher (1977: 6), can be understood here in the Vedic sense of 'in existence from time immemorial . . . at the same time still in existence at the time when the speaker uses the term'.

135 Used in the Upaniṣads as a description of the self (*ātman*). Cf. *KaṭhU* 2.20; *ChU* 3.14.3; *ŚvetU* 3.9; 3.20.

136 Cf. *MuṇḍU* 3.1.7.

137 Cf. *ŚvetU* 3.8 (*vedāham etaṃ puruṣaṃ mahāntam ādityavarṇaṃ tamasaḥ parastāt*). Both texts quote the *Vājasaneyi-Saṃhitā;* cf. Oberlies 1988: 56.

138 Cf. *KaṭhU* 2.15 and *BhG* 8.11.

one's head, and practising fixation of the mind in yoga (*yogadhāraṇa*). This sets the stage for the next and final step, evoking Kṛṣṇa by uttering the holy syllable *Oṃ* as the *brahman*: 'He who leaves the body while he remembers me and utters "*Oṃ*", the one-syllable (*eka-akṣara*) *brahman*, will reach the highest goal' (8.13). The use of the syllable *Oṃ* is close to what in *YS* 1.23 and 1.27–28 is described as *īśvarapraṇidhāna*, the worship of god. *Oṃ* is used to evoke (*vācaka*) the god on which the concentration of the *yogin* is fixed. This evocation is brought about by silent recitation (*japa*), which results in the realisation (*bhāvanā*) of the deity. In the *BhG* this practice is recommended especially for the moment of death in that it ensures that the mind is indeed fixed on that (state of) being that the *yogin* wants to reach. This is confirmed in 8.14, where it is said that Kṛṣṇa can be easily obtained by a *yogin* who is always in control and constantly remembers the god. This *yogin* is a 'mighty self' (*mahātman*) who enters the realm of no return, being liberated from the realm of transmigration, which extends 'up to the region of Brahmā' (8.16). This region is the created world which is subject to temporality and the alternation of the 'days and nights of Brahmā' (8.17–19). Within the space and time of the Brahmā world, creatures appear and disappear, they move from the unmanifest state of being (*avyakta*) to the manifest (*vyakta*) and back again. In this passage, a concept of cosmic time is used that does not occur in the older Upaniṣads but does occur elsewhere in the epic, and is standard in the Purāṇas. This is also confirmed by the shift from neutral *brahman* to the creator god Brahmā, who in these later texts is usually entrusted with this task. These features indicate that the chapter belongs to the younger parts of the *BhG* (see Malinar 1996: 394ff.).

Liberation from this realm of Brahmā is possible because, beyond the unmanifest state of being that still belongs to the realm of Brahmā (which is similar to the unmanifest state of *prakṛti* before creation begins), there is yet another unmanifest state of being:

> However, beyond that state of being there is another one, an eternal unmanifest state of being beyond the unmanifest (*paras tasmāt tu bhāvo 'nyo 'vyakto 'vyaktāt sanātanaḥ*), which does not perish when all created beings (elements) perish. This is called the unmanifest (*avyakta*) that is 'imperishable' (*akṣara*). They declare it to be the highest goal; when they have reached it, they do not return: this is my highest domain (*dhāma paramam*). Higher is this *puruṣa*, Pārtha, who can be reached only by exclusive devotion (*bhakti*), in whom all beings exist, by whom all this is spread. (8.20–22)

According to this translation, the realm of *puruṣa* is higher than the imperishable, unmanifest being (*brahman* as the source of creation) that is Kṛṣṇa's *dhāman*.[139] Accordingly, the unmanifest called 'imperishable' is a realm of liberation that could also be reached without *bhakti*, but it is not to be regarded as the ultimate goal, the 'higher' *puruṣa* to be reached by *bhakti*. Again the strategy of hierarchisation is used in order to deal with alternative realms and paths of liberation.

This hierarchy of cosmic realms is close to passages in *KaṭhU* 3.11 and 6.7–8.[140] Again the author seems to have used this text but introduced a significant change. While the Upaniṣad includes *mahān* (mighty) or *mahān ātman* (mighty self) in its list of cosmic realms, the *BhG* refers to *brahmāloka* and *avyakta* when speaking of the intermediary stage in which an embodied self either departs for liberation or enters the created world. A *yogin* who has reached this realm is in contact with both aspects and is therefore regarded as a *mahātman*. This indicates a substitution of older notions, such as the *mahān ātman* (cf. van Buitenen 1964), with the more recent concept of 'days and nights of Brahmā'. This substitution suits the above-mentioned intention to connect the new monotheistic teachings with Upaniṣadic and Vedic concepts. Kṛṣṇa is here superimposed on the realm of the 'imperishable unmanifest', the source of creation, by declaring it to be his *dhāman*, place of residence. In a next step, this is again superseded by the *paraḥ puruṣa* (higher *puruṣa*), of whom *KaṭhU* 6.8 teaches that there is nothing beyond it. Although in *BhG* 8.21 this realm is not explicitly equated with Kṛṣṇa, the use of *bhakti* as the instrument for reaching the *puruṣa* and the idea that all beings abide in him (cf. *BhG* 9.4) point to the theistic framework. Although this interpretation cannot be proposed with ultimate certainty, it can be corroborated by similar hierarchisations of cosmic realms presented elsewhere in the *BhG*.[141]

The final six verses of this chapter confirm its general aim of reinterpreting Vedic and Upaniṣadic notions related to death in terms of new goals of liberation and alternative 'afterworlds'. Here we encounter a reinterpretation of the well-known Upaniṣadic doctrine of the two paths that the deceased can take after death. According to *BĀU* 6.2.15–16 and *ChU* 5.10.1–2 (cf. *PrU* 1.9–10), the deceased travels either on the path to the gods (*devayāna*), ending in *brahman* and non-return, or on the path to the ancestors (*pitṛyāna*), ending on the moon and followed by rebirth. These

[139] I follow Zaehner's (1969: 270) interpretation. The majority of translators, however, equate the *puruṣa* with the *dhāman*. A clear-cut hierarchisation is offered in *BhG* 15.

[140] *Mahataḥ param avyaktam avyaktāt puruṣaḥ paraḥ / puruṣān na paraṃ kiṃcit sa kāṣṭhā sā parā gatiḥ* (*KaṭhU* 3.11), and *sattvād adhi mahān ātmā mahato 'vyaktam uttamam // avyaktāt tu paraḥ puruṣo* (*KaṭhU* 6.7cd-8a).

[141] See the triadic structure in *BhG* 13 and 15. Cf. also *BhG* 9.4.

two paths are referred to in *BhG* 8.24–25 as *uttarāyaṇa* ('northern course' of the sun after the winter solstice) and *dakṣiṇāyaṇa* ('southern course' of the sun after the summer solstice) respectively.[142] Here these paths are defined as the points of time (solstice, half of the month), while in the Upaniṣads, by contrast, they are associated with different life-styles, that is, asceticism (*tapas*) or ritual respectively. As Edgerton points out (1949: 246), 'the Upaniṣad passage is not dealing with the time at which a man dies, at all. The time units mentioned are mere mystic abstractions into which the departed soul is said to pass. The Gītā, however, in common with classical Brahmins generally, understands them as referring to the time at which a man dies.' However, it is not just a 'man' who dies, but a *yogin*. In this passage, the success and fate of the *yogin* is indicated by the time of his death. The *yogin*'s course is either 'white' or 'black' (*śukla-kṛṣṇa-gati*; 8.26), leading to non-return or rebirth, both 'paths' (*sṛti*) being regarded by the 'people' (*jagat*) as eternal. The realm of non-return is, as in the Upaniṣads, equated with reaching *brahman*. This passage seems to advocate *brahman* as the realm of liberation, a statement that would correspond to the *brahmanirvāṇa* concept of *BhG* 2 and 5 and must thus be read as a reaffirmation of this doctrine. However, it contradicts the rest of chapter 8, in which the desirable state of being after death is called *puruṣa* or Kṛṣṇa. Is it thus another interpolation, or is another interpretation possible? Perhaps, because the following two verses can be read as indicating that the 'knowing' *yogin* should even go a step further and not be confused about these two courses:

> No *yogin* who knows these two courses is confused about them, therefore be at all times an accomplished *yogin*, Arjuna! Whatever reward of merit has been assigned in the Vedas to rituals, asceticism (*tapas*) and gifts, all that (merit) the *yogin* leaves behind. When he knows this, he will attain the supreme primordial state. (8.27–28)

The two courses were presented as the 'people's view', and perhaps the 'black and white' option they live by is not the only one. Indeed, Arjuna is not asked to strive to die in the bright half of the month or to reach *brahman*, but to turn away entirely from the realm of *karman*, which produces 'known fruits and merits' by performing either rituals or ascetic exercises as described in the Upaniṣadic doctrine of the 'two paths'. A *yogin* who regards his fate as depending on the time of death still seems entangled in merit and demerit. Therefore, the last verse may also suggest that all these considerations should be left behind by the *yogin* who truly knows; as a

142 *BhG* 8.27 uses *sṛti*, as is the case in *BĀU* 6.2.2, quoting *ṚV* 10.88.15.

consequence, he will reach the highest realm. Although this interpretation cannot be pushed too far, there is a passage in the *Yogasūtra* that corroborates at least the possibility of such a line of thought. In *YS* 4.7, we find the following statement on the *karman* of *yogins*: 'The *karman* of *yogins* is neither black nor white' (*karmāśuklakṣṇayoginas*). This expression means that the *yogin* no longer produces or has *karman*. Therefore, what he does and where he goes no longer depend on external circumstances like time or place. With much of *BhG* 8, one can say that, by concentrating on Kṛṣṇa, a *yogin* can die successfully at any time, once he has managed to gain control of his self and recalls Kṛṣṇa as the one who shines beyond darkness.

BHAGAVADGĪTĀ 9: THE YOGA OF SOVEREIGNTY AND THE KNOWLEDGE OF KINGS

This and the subsequent chapters present the theological basis for Kṛṣṇa's revelation as the highest, the one and only god who not only creates, protects and withdraws from the world, but also transcends it as the ever-liberated highest self. He can therefore guarantee liberation for those who turn to him in love and devotion (*bhakti*), being free from any attachment to egoistical desires. Both aspects are held together in depicting Kṛṣṇa as a powerful *yogin* who is distinguished from other powerful *yogins* in his purposeful, that is, *dharma*-oriented use of this power and his active engagement in the world. In addition, these activities neither threaten nor contradict his being already and forever liberated and 'unborn'. This stands in contrast to the 'human' *yogin*, who starts from being an embodied self loaded with *karman* and sets out to conquer himself and the cosmic realms in a 'bottom-up' movement. Kṛṣṇa, on the other hand, is always connected with the world in 'top-down' relationships, be it to the creative power of *prakṛti* or to the embodied selves. Although his power over *prakṛti* is similar to that of the *yogin*, he does not activate *prakṛti* for his own pleasure (at least not according to the *BhG*).[143] Rather, either Kṛṣṇa activates *prakṛti* for the sake of creation, or else he has it produce bodies for himself in order to appear on earth to protect the cosmic order and punish its enemies. In this regard, the purpose and scope of his holding and using power resembles a king or emperor more than a *yogin*. However, he differs from a human king in that he has the whole of creation and of *prakṛti* at his disposal, while a king is dependent on a multitude of (creative) powers, like his territory, army or

[143] However, the notion of the god's appearances as 'play' or 'sport' is prominent in other texts and traditions.

counsellors. While the king is consecrated by uniting the different powers of the cosmos in his body and assembles a variety of gods (cf. Heesterman 1957, Gonda 1959), Kṛṣṇa as the highest lord commands them all in that he encompasses these powers as a creator, yet transcends them in a still higher 'state of being'.

Since the god is a creator who entertains a relationship with the world by fulfilling royal tasks on the basis of his yogic power, it is mandatory for his followers to do the same, even if they are striving for liberation. The god Kṛṣṇa appears in the world and protects it because he cares for it and, as a consequence, his followers should care as well – they should love the world and take care of it, especially when they find themselves in positions of responsibility, as, for example, is the case with kings. This is one implication of the doctrine of *bhakti*, which is presented in this chapter as something new and unheard of. It changes one's attitude towards the world, one's social duties and one's attachment in that everything is dedicated to the cause of a god who is not to be approached through the correct rituals, but out of affection and a sense of belongingness. *Dharma*, cosmic order and social duties are 'dear' because they are dear (*priya*) to Kṛṣṇa. This too distinguishes Kṛṣṇa, the supreme *yogin*, from other *yogin*s who should not care for 'endearment'. It is more similar to the king, who also ought to love and take care of his people, and not treat them badly. All these aspects show that the theology of the *BhG* is closely related to adjacent figures and positions of power and their related discourses. Most important are the figure of the king and the *yogin*. The strong connection with the debates over the legitimate king and what kingship is all about connect the *BhG* with the epic, especially with the *UdP*. The text does not just deal with theology; it has also socio-political implications, a feature which may account for its incorporation not just somewhere in the epic, but in one of its core books, at one of its dramatic moments. The monotheistic doctrine developed in the *BhG* acquires additional significance when it is seen in the context of the debates on kingship and regarded as a statement about the legitimation of kingship and royal power, which is superseded by divine, yogic power. Right at the beginning of chapter 9, this connection is established by calling the knowledge of Kṛṣṇa's mighty yoga the 'knowledge of kings' (*rājavidyā*; 9.2). This is the only designation given to the doctrine of the *BhG* that occurs in the text itself, and it programmatically summarises the aspects discussed earlier. The god thus not only unites the conflicting values of social responsibility and world renunciation (cf. Biardeau 1981a), it also blends the characteristics of the king and the *yogin*.

Seen against the background of this outline, we may expect many of the themes and concepts dealt with in the previous chapters to be drawn together and reframed in an exposition of the nature of Kṛṣṇa's divinity. This means dealing with Kṛṣṇa's relationship to the world and the 'embodied selves', his transcendence and yogic detachment from all his activities, his divine, yogic capacity to appear in different forms (including a cosmic form), his relationship to other cults, and the method of worshipping him (*bhakti*). The red thread that runs through chapters 9–11 is thus Kṛṣṇa's sovereignty, his being the only *īśvara*, the 'mighty' ruler, lord and god (*maheśvara*), who excels all other 'masters' in being responsible for and fond of the world, as well as of the embodied selves. Chapters 9 and 10 explain Kṛṣṇa's yogic power, his *yoga aiśvara* (9.5), the yoga that is characteristic of him as the supreme Lord and *yogin*, who controls the powers of nature (*prakṛti*), yet remains detached from them. Chapter 11 relates Arjuna's vision of his *rūpa aiśvara*, the appearance of himself as the supreme Lord and thus in the cosmic form that shows his cosmic sovereignty, his encompassing power, which makes all beings a part of him. In his study of the '*īśvara* idea', Gonda (1968) shows that it developed in Vedic texts in contradistinction to the divinity of the Vedic gods (*deva*), as well as the sovereignty or royal function accorded to them (1968: 132). The title *īśvara* revolves around ideas of 'supreme lordship' developed in the older Upaniṣads and expanded upon in the *BhG*. Therefore Gonda renders the expressions *yoga* and *rūpa aiśvara* as 'my yoga as Lord' and 'the form of mine as Lord' respectively (1968: 148–149).

However, the use of an older *īśvara* concept implies a reinterpretation because the god is not completely identical with the powers he unites within himself. Such congruence is characteristic of Vedic gods, as Gonda pointed out (1957: 35; emphasis original): 'A divine being *is* a power-substance, *has* it, and *is to realize* it.' This is different in the case of Vāsudeva-Kṛṣṇa, since he wields power as the supreme *yogin*. Therefore all beings exist in the realm and as parts of his power, while he himself is not part of them. According *BhG* 9.5, this paradox is indicative of Kṛṣṇa's *yoga aiśvara*. As the supreme, most powerful *yogin*, Kṛṣṇa may appear in different forms, including the 'cosmic', which shows the co-presence and consubstantiality of all beings. This form marks the god's presence in the world as being capable of performing the three tasks of creation, protection and destruction, of his being the sovereign of all. This 'All-Form' can be envisioned by *yogin*s and all those who happen to acquire 'divine sight', but is usually invisible to 'human eyes'. However, it is only a 'form' that is a product of the god's yogic power which turns *prakṛti* into *māyā*, appearance and apparition. What is *prakṛti* for the creatures – that is, their physical existence, in which they are entangled – is 'appearance' (*māyā*) for Kṛṣṇa and, as a consequence, any other being who reaches the god, because the god remains 'unborn' and is therefore not co-substantial with the world. This complex structure was already indicated in chapter 4, when Kṛṣṇa's 'birth' was explained, and is now present in more detail in *BhG* 9–11.

The chapter begins with the following statement on the knowledge that Kṛṣṇa is about to reveal:

> I will explain now to you, who knows no envy, the highest secret (*guhyatama*). When you understand this knowledge together with its discriminatory insight, you will be free from defilement. It is knowledge of kings (*rājavidyā*), the highest means of purification to be guarded by kings (*rājaguhya*), which is accessible through perception (*pratyakṣa-avagama*); it is lawful, pleasant to carry out and unchanging. Those men who do not belief in this doctrine (*dharma*), O enemy-burner, fail to reach me and return to the path of recurrent death. (9.1–3)

The stanzas contain some important characteristics of the 'knowledge of kings' (rājavidyā) imparted to Arjuna.[144] First of all, it is directly linked to kings: it is declared to be under their protection and works as a means of purification (*pavitra*). This purifying effect connects this knowledge to the effects of the 'sacrifice of knowledge', which is described in *BhG* 4.38 as the ultimate means of purification. This purification concerns the general karmic defilement that prevents an embodied self from reaching Kṛṣṇa, but it may also point to the more concrete defilement that is caused by the violent duty of kings and warriors. Although this knowledge is somehow secret and needs protection (*guhya*), it is accessible through perception (*pratyakṣa*) and is thus manifest, 'in the open'. This contrasts with the Vedic gods, who prefer to be invisible and hidden: 'for the gods somehow love the hidden while they despise the obvious (or visible)' (*parokṣapriyā iva hi devāḥ pratyakṣadviṣaḥ*; *BĀU* 4.2.2). This juxtaposition of attributes points to the secret, hidden character of that divine power that is behind and beyond the god's presence in and during his appearances. Since *pratyakṣa* can also be understood as 'perception' in the sense of a 'means of knowledge' (*pramāṇa*), this attribute may imply that this knowledge is not proven by inference, as

144 On the basis of commentarial literature, Slaje (1999) suggests 'knowledge for kings only' and criticises my interpretation. While this is an interesting result of the study of commentaries, its validity in the context of the *BhG* is not considered in detail (especially with regard to *bhakti* and the depiction of the god as lord of yoga). However, such a restriction would go against other passages in *BhG* 9 and puts less emphasis on the genealogical dimension implied in the translation 'knowledge of kings'. In his study of parallel passages, Raghavan (1962: 341) notes: 'As this was first taught to the kings, this philosophy, which later spread to others, came to be called *Rājavidyā*.'

in other traditions, but demonstrated by 'direct', sensual evidence. Kṛṣṇa's actual appearance, his visibility, is indicative of his yogic supremacy. This is corroborated elsewhere in the epic, for instance in Kṛṣṇa's appearance in 5.129, and especially at *MBh* 12.289.7, where *pratyakṣa*, perception, is declared to the distinctive means of proof in yoga. The accessibility and somehow public character of the knowledge is also stressed when it is regarded as lawful (*dhārmya*). In this way, the practical and social character of the doctrine is given emphasis, since this is most important for kings as the protectors of order. In 9.3, the word *dharma* seems to be used in the sense of a teaching or even practice (cf. 2.40; see above, pp. 71ff.).

The knowledge that is now disclosed concerns first of all Kṛṣṇa's relationship to the world:

> In my invisible form (*avyaktamūrti*), I have spread out this whole world;[145] in me exist all beings – but I do not exist in them. Yet again, the creatures do not exist in me; behold my yoga of sovereignty (*yoga aiśvara*): while sustaining the creatures and giving them being, my self (*mama ātmā*) does not exist in them. (9.4–5)

Kṛṣṇa's supreme yoga allows for the distinction between an unmanifest form of the god that supports all beings and brings them into being, and Kṛṣṇa's 'self'. This distinction is the basis of the theological doctrine of the god's simultaneous presence in and distance from the world. This distinction demonstrates the specific character of Kṛṣṇa's power, which is referred to as the yoga that is 'majestic', mighty, indicative of his being both the sovereign of all beings and the master of *prakṛti*. While the existence of the world depends on him, his 'self' and thus he himself do not depend on the world. This distinguishes his divinity from the Vedic gods, who are dependent on ritual transactions, and also from godlike ascetics, whose power is accompanied by a disregard for the world.[146] While he shares the power of creative forces with *yogins*, and in certain respects also with kings, his power is not called *aiśvarya*, as is the case in descriptions of yogic power. *Aiśvarya* is a power acquired by an individual's control over himself, which connects him to corresponding elements or regions of the cosmos (cf. *BhG* 5). A *yogin* becomes an *iśvara* in certain respects, and this corresponds to the general understanding of an *īśvara* as a powerful being that rules over specific areas, but is generally not regarded as the overlord of all or the one and only sovereign and god (cf. Gonda 1964: 131–163).

145 This expression is also used in *BhG* 2.17; 8.22; 11.38 and 18.46, and is standard in Vedic and Upaniṣadic texts.

146 They either move away from the world, as described in detail in the story of Śuka, who flies through the cosmic regions and leaves them for good, or else they enter different bodies, as described in *MBh* 12.189.

Kṛṣṇa's relationship to the world is the result of yoga, that is, a control over *prakṛti* that results from his being connected to it as a whole, while yet maintaining his transcendent character. It is *yoga aiśvara*, connection and exertion of power from a position of lordship, that implies a transcendent, liberated state of being. It is not Kṛṣṇa himself who appears as or in the world, but only his 'unmanifest form', his creative nature, while his identity as Kṛṣṇa – indicated by the first-person pronoun 'I' (*aham*) – remains hidden. In one of his forms, he 'spreads out' the universe, but he himself is not co-extensive with creation. This is intended by the statements that the creatures do not exist in him, nor he in them. It seems appropriate to call this the 'highest secret' (9.1), since it is indeed 'mysterious' that the god is not only at once absent and present, revealed and hidden, but also revealed as being hidden.

In explaining this distinction, the author draws on the concept of an unmanifest (*avyakta*) form. Elsewhere in the *BhG*, this term refers to the unmanifest state of being of the creative force (*brahman* or *prakṛti*) or to the inciting presence of the self that causes the activity of *prakṛti*. It seems, however, that again it is the contact of these two spheres that is being described here, as is done using slightly different terminology in *BhG* 7. The creative power, the source of creation, in 9.7–8, called '*prakṛti*', is subordinated to Kṛṣṇa and turned into his 'unmanifest form', which acts as the creator of the cosmos. This is one aspect of his yoga, namely that the whole cosmos is regarded as belonging to him, as expressed in the comparison between 'ether' (*ākāśa*), as the 'unmanifest' encompassing entity, and 'wind', as the actual element moving within it (9.6). When seen against the background of the hierarchical relationship between the two, it can be said that wind depends on ether as its higher and larger causal realm, but that ether does not depend on wind. The comparison suits the theological doctrine, not only in this regard, but also in that it exemplifies the possibility of an invisible entity supporting and encompassing visible elements. While the distinction between visibility and invisibility as two aspects of a highest being is a well-established one, the *BhG* introduces a triadic structure by introducing a 'third', highest state. Kṛṣṇa is more than an unmanifest cause becoming active and manifest, since he is also 'the self' beyond it. It is only Kṛṣṇa's creative appearance, his unmanifest, *prakṛti* form, that sustains all beings: his 'self' or he himself is not present in the beings or embodied in the cosmos.

This triadic structure is further explained in 9.7–10. Creation begins when, from aeon to aeon (*kalpa*), Kṛṣṇa takes control over *prakṛti*, and the 'conglomerate of beings' (*bhūtagrāma*) is emanated. Yet he remains the 'liberated' sovereign because these acts do not cause any karmic bondage:

'These activities do not bind me,[147] Dhanaṃjaya. Like a non-involved party (*udāsīnavad*), I sit detached among these acts. Under my supervision (*adhyakṣa*), nature produces moving and unmoving (beings). This is why the world revolves' (9.9). Here the relationship between Kṛṣṇa and *prakṛti* is described according to Sāṃkhya notions: the inactive *puruṣa* is connected to *prakṛti* by supervising and thus activating her creative powers for his purpose. In Sāṃkhya philosophy, the purpose of a *puruṣa* who is in contact (*saṃyoga*) with *prakṛti* is twofold: experience of the world (*bhoga*), and then separation from it (*kaivalya*). While an embodied self usually acts according to its nature (*svā prakṛti*; cf. *BhG* 3.5, 27–29, 33), Kṛṣṇa the supreme *yogin* does not follow but commands nature. In this position the god does not pursue any personal interest, since he is already separated from *prakṛti*. Therefore, he is present 'like a non-involved party', like an *udāsīna*. This attribute can be understood as again pointing to the royal character of Kṛṣṇa's relationship with his creatures. Emeneau has noted the use of *udāsīna* as a technical term for a 'neutral king' elsewhere in the epic and in the *ArthaŚ*, but he did not apply it to the *BhG* passage. The political treatises distinguish between different types of neutrality, according to the different degrees of involvement in a conflict. Emeneau (1968: 276, note 3) distinguishes the *udāsīna* king from the king who 'stands in the middle' (*madhya-stha*) as follows: 'The *madhyastha* is another kind of neutral, who is sometimes said to hold sentiments that are equal towards both parties; he is involved, whereas the *udāsīna* is not involved, but indifferent.' This classification helps us to understand not only Kṛṣṇa's position, but also Arjuna's dilemma as the warrior who finds himself 'between two armies' (*senayor ubhayor madhye*; cf. 1.21, 24; 2.10). This kind of neutrality is a neutrality of weakness, as indicated in Ajuna's incapacity to act, whereas the *udāsīna* stands for a neutrality of strength. This is corroborated in *ArthaŚ* 6.2.22, where the *udāsīna* is called to be 'stronger' (*balavattara*) than the other kings: 'One outside (the sphere) of the enemy, the conqueror and the middle king, stronger than (their) constituents, capable of helping the enemy, the conqueror and the middle king when they are united or disunited, and suppressing them when they are disunited, is the neutral king (*udāsīna*)' (trans. Kangle). Law (1933: 770) points out that the *udāsīna* is the strongest force in the conflict, since he is free to intervene as a possibly decisive force. All these aspects suggest rendering *udāsīnavat* in a more technical sense as 'like a non-involved party' or 'like a (powerful) neutral king'. Thus, the knowledge of kings (*rājavidyā*) includes realising

147 Cf. *BhG* 4.14.

that Kṛṣṇa is present in the world like a neutral king. He is not subject to any kinship laws or driven by imperialist interests, but is regarded as becoming active when the time is ripe (that is, from aeon to aeon, as in 9.7, or when it is time to rescue *dharma* and crush the enemies of order; see 4.7–8).

Within this structure of power, control and non-involvement, Kṛṣṇa's appearance in a human form is a special, exceptional case, which is, however, highly important as a demonstration of his overlordship and belongs to his *yoga aiśvara* as demonstrated by direct evidence (*pratyakṣa*). It is a potential that can be displayed and withdrawn whenever Kṛṣṇa is called on to act. The idea of a god appearing in a human form does not seem to have been generally accepted, since it is necessary to comment on possible or actual misconceptions: 'The deluded disregard me, the one who has assumed a human form (*mānuṣī tanu*), because they do not know my higher state of being (*para bhāva*) as the mighty lord of beings (*bhūta-mahēśvara*)' (9.11). It seems that an *avatāra* doctrine was not at issue here, either in the form of *avatāras* of Kṛṣṇa or as his being an *avatāra* of another god. This shows that the figure of Kṛṣṇa and the claim that the epic hero is not only a god, but the highest god, who has taken a human body, was not easy to accept for those who had never before heard of anything like this or who would regard 'invisibility' as the yardstick of divinity. Apart from these conceptual implications, the comments on the cults and beliefs of those who are not devoted to Kṛṣṇa also point to the social and historical environment that makes such statements necessary. As Minor notes (1982: 294), 'There seemed to be a competition with other deities reflected in verses such as this in the Gītā as well as an indication that there was opposition to Kṛṣṇa-worship at this time, or possibly the belief that Kṛṣṇa is merely the appearance of another deity who is better worshipped.'[148]

In a next step, the creatures are divided into those who know and follow Kṛṣṇa and those who do not (see 7.14–15; 16.18–20). While those whose self is mighty (*mahātman*) resort to divine *prakṛti* (*daivī prakṛti*), since they know that Kṛṣṇa is the inciter of creation and are attached to him, the

148 This is regarded as a problem not only here. Cf. Brahmā's declaration that only fools mistake Lord Vāsudeva for a man (*nāvajñeyo vāsudevo manuṣyo 'yam iti*; *MBh* 6.62.18), while he is in fact the 'lord of the lord(s) of the worlds' (*lokānām īśvareśvara*; 6.62.23). The passage corroborates my argument about the difference between Vāsudeva's appearance and that of *yogins* when it is declared that 'People of the *tamas* kind (of an ignorant, deluded nature) confuse Vāsudeva with a *yogin*, who, being a mighty self, has entered a human body' (*yoginaṃ taṃ mahātmānaṃ praviṣṭaṃ mānuṣīṃ tanum / avamanyed vāsudevaṃ tam āhus tāṃasaṃ janāḥ*; 6.62.20). The question whether such statements point to a situation of weakness indicative of the follower's minority position (see Hacker 1983 and Schopen 2005, with regard to Mahāyāna Buddhism) needs to be explored further.

others cling to a delusive, demonic nature (*prakṛti mohinī*) that works against them, since all their efforts will be in vain. This also explains why evil-doers move in the realm of *prakṛti* and gain power by using the powers of nature. However, since they disregard the ultimate power that rules over everything, they ultimately fail and receive punishment. This passage applies the well-known theme of the struggle between 'gods' and 'demons' to the workings of *prakṛti*. Deluded, the 'demonic' people misunderstand actual power relations in the world, which results in a counterproductive activation and punishable abuse of *prakṛti*. In contrast to this, acknowledging Kṛṣṇa as the 'overlord' brings success. The world seems to be divided into two sections, and there is no neutral position when it comes to defining and establishing one's relationship with Kṛṣṇa. This exclusiveness is typical of monotheistic theologies in that it demands decisions. In the end, either one reaches Kṛṣṇa or one does not. Yet since we are dealing here with 'cosmological monotheism', the demonic forces are regarded as part of the god-created cosmos and are not excluded from it as 'fallen' angels or as representing 'evil' as the ultimate 'other' of the divine, as is the case, for instance, in Manichaean thought. The classification of demons is similar to the acceptance of the other gods (*deva*) as the rulers of restricted domains: they are all placed on lower levels of creation and made part of the transient world.

Since Kṛṣṇa is responsible for the created world, whether they know it or not, all beings are also connected to him within the socially defined networks of relationship. When they turn to him, they are not rejected by the god, since they can all become 'dear' to him as parts of himself. This is implied in the doctrine of *bhakti*, which is accorded a prominent role in *BhG* 9.[149] In this chapter, *bhakti* is explained within a theological framework, while it treated as something already familiar in the other chapters (cf. *BhG* 4 and 7). The description includes some characteristic practices, such as praising (*kīrtana*), worshipping (*namas*) and keeping observances (*vrata*). These practices (cf. 9.14) are distinguished from performing the 'sacrifice of knowledge' (*jñānayajña*),[150] which is regarded as an equally valid practice. The required knowledge is defined as understanding and worshipping Kṛṣṇa 'in his oneness (as well as his) separateness (*pṛthaktva*) (and as) being manifold in appearing everywhere' (9.15). This verse summarises the important aspect of Kṛṣṇa's relationship to the world in that he

[149] Forms of the verbal root *bhaj* occur twelve times in this chapter, more than in any other chapter of the *BhG* (9.13, 14, 23, 26 (twice), 29 (twice), 30, 31, 33 (twice), 34).

[150] Cf. *BhG* 4.27, 33. This indicates that the theistic framework employs notions dealt with in other parts of the text, since this practice is mentioned here without any explanation.

provides unity in diversity, being present in the world in different forms, yet separated from it (*pṛthaktva*), since he remains the transcendent 'self'. This statement may have motivated the subsequent hymnic praise of Kṛṣṇa's divinity in 9.16–19, which can be read as an exemplification of both a *kīrtana* and the contents of the knowledge that is used for sacrificing to the god. The ritual domain is addressed first when Kṛṣṇa is identified with its essential elements: he is the ritual, the sacrifice, the sacrificial fire, etc. (9.16). He is then declared to be the father, mother, ordainer and grandfather of the world, and is identified with the three Vedas and the syllable *Oṃ*. By ascribing to him parenthood and other relationships of kinship as well as the Vedic tradition, the whole social and ritual order is subordinated to Kṛṣṇa as its creator. His cosmological function and his relationship to the individual beings are further detailed in 9.18. He is praised as the way and goal (*gati*), sustainer and Lord, witness and home, refuge and friend. Then his three activities with regard to the world are grouped together: creation (*prabhava*), destruction (*pralaya*) and stability (*sthāna*). These three functions[151] constitute his overlordship not only because they are united in him alone (and not distributed among different gods), but also because he does not depend on any ritual nourishment in performing these tasks. As a consequence, he is called the 'eternal seed' (*bīja*), since he activates all creative powers.[152] Therefore he controls the natural order (in 9.19, rain and heat) and its rhythm of life and death. This passage can be regarded as an abbreviated 'hymn' of self-praise (*ātmastuti*) or a praise of mightiness (*māhātmya*), of which a more elaborate version has been included, with praise of Kṛṣṇa's 'power manifestations' (*vibhūti*), in *BhG* 10.

In this passage Kṛṣṇa is identified with the older Vedic religious institutions, and this seems to have motivated another comment on the god's relationship to other cults. In doing this, his worship is not established within the framework of Vedic rituals, for instance, by revealing a specific Vedic rite dedicated to the god. Rather, Kṛṣṇa is regarded as the patron and addressee, whether known or not, of all sacrifices, since he guarantees the efficacy of the ritual order as a whole (*BhG* 9.20–23). However, Vedic sacrifice is connected with fruits, and aims to reach a heavenly world based on one's ritual acts. Therefore, the sacrificer will reach the world and gods he desires, not Kṛṣṇa. In this way, Kṛṣṇa is connected to Vedic sacrifice, but at the same time he is distanced from it, because only exclusive devotion (9.22) and correct ritual procedure (9.23) lead to Kṛṣṇa. Although Kṛṣṇa

151 This has been called the '*trimūrti*' function. Cf. also *BhG* 7.6.

152 Cf. *BhG* 7.10 on Kṛṣṇa's seed as the life principle and *prakṛti* as the womb.

guarantees the fruits of all rituals, they do not all lead to him, since Vedic sacrificers are those 'whose desire is desire' (*kāmakāma*; 9.21), not desireless devotion. As already pointed out with regard to similar statements in *BhG* 7.20–23, Vedic sacrifice is accepted as a religious practice that produces temporary sojourns in heaven, but not liberation in Kṛṣṇa – therefore it must be regarded as an inferior practice. As a consequence, only exclusive worship of Kṛṣṇa brings the devotee to his god, who grants devotees prosperity: 'I bring goods (*yogakṣema-vaha*)[153] to those who worship me while they think of no other and are always aligned (to me). Even those devoted to other gods worship me, since they believe in the efficacy (of ritual), O son of Kuntī, (but) without following the correct ritual procedure (*avidhipūrvaka*)' (9.22–23). This statement may concern not the Vedic rituals, but other cults based on devotion, because they combine belief in the efficacy of the rite (*śraddhayā 'nvitāḥ*; 9.23) with inappropriate procedures. According to van Buitenen (1981: 166), this means that the ritual reaches Kṛṣṇa, 'though no such provision is made in the injunction'. However, such a situation is rather unlikely in the case of Vedic ritual performances and seems to have motivated the comments on correct ritual action in *BhG* 17 (see below, pp. 210ff.), stressing that correct ritual provision is mandatory.

The final statement on worshipping Kṛṣṇa excludes a rather large spectrum of practices and religious affiliations: 'Those whose observances are dedicated to the gods come to the gods, those whose observances are to the ancestors go to the ancestors, those whose offerings go to the spirits (*bhūta*) come to the spirits, while those who worship me come to me' (9.25). Although many forms of worship do not result in reaching Kṛṣṇa, their abolition is not called for: being responsible for the cosmos as a whole, Kṛṣṇa guarantees and at the same time downgrades the efficacy of other cults. Like a king who is responsible not only for his family-clan alone, but for 'all the people', the god allows the fulfilment of desires and aspirations that are not directed to him. In this regard, he is indifferent or the same for all beings (cf. 9.29). Nevertheless, he has a special relationship with those who love and know him dearly (9.29) because devotion (*bhakti*) is placed at the centre of the relationship between Kṛṣṇa and his followers. This is made explicit in the depiction of the proper form of worship, which makes one's attitude the crucial element, not a specific ritual substance or priestly mediation. *Bhakti* can be expressed by simple gestures and small

[153] This attribute corroborates the royal character of Kṛṣṇa's role with regard to his devotees, since, according to *ArthaŚ* 1.5.1, providing good things and the happiness that it entails is a characteristic feature of the king.

offerings: 'The leaf, flower, fruit or water[154] that one offers me with love is what I enjoy, since it is proffered with love by him whose self is controlled. Whatever you do, whatever you eat, whatever you sacrifice, whatever you give away, whatever austerity you may perform, son of Kuntī, make it an offering to me' (9.26–27). Dedication, self-control and detachment are the prerequisites of worship: not giving up ritual action (*saṃnyāsa*), but renouncing everything in Kṛṣṇa. With this request, we have reached the final step in the reinterpretation of the *saṃnyāsa* analysed in the previous chapters. True *saṃnyāsa* means neither giving up all social and ritual obligations, nor giving up one's attachment to action (*karmayoga*), but offering it up in Kṛṣṇa as the only agent and lord. Therefore, the devotee whose self is controlled by the 'yoga of renunciation' (*saṃnyāsa-yoga*) will be liberated and reach the god. Since this implies detachment and knowledge of the divine nature of Kṛṣṇa, it is not a simple thing, although the ritual procedure appears simple. The ascetic emphasis is retained, since devotion implies giving up egoistical behaviour and changing bad behaviour. In 9.32 it is even requested that an evil-doer be regarded as a good person when he is a devotee of Kṛṣṇa, because he has made the right decision. Minor (1982: 301) notes that this could be misunderstood as an acceptance of immoral behaviour. However, the expiatory character of *bhakti* must be measured here against the presence of *prāyaścitta* rites that also promise absolution and purity, the difference postulated here being that the attitude of a 'sinner' changes, and thus exculpation is not based exclusively on ritualistic means and prescriptions. This does not protect *bhakti* from bigotry, which is a structural problem of religious doctrines based on 'intention' and 'motive', as in *bhakti*. It has a counterpart in a problem occurring in ritual contexts. Rituals can be manipulated because they do not depend on the 'inner' attitude or the 'good intentions' of either patrons or priests, as the instances of deliberate ritual manipulation in Vedic texts show (see Sahoo 1988–89, B. K. Smith 1996).

While the price of worshipping Kṛṣṇa is the exclusion of any other god or powerful being from the 'highest' realm, it has the advantage of allowing everyone to choose and approach the god. Neither ritual purity nor economic and educational resources regulate access to its practice. Rarely considered social sectors like women, traders and servants are invited to practise *bhakti* and gain liberation (9.32). Regardless of status and achievements, this god cares for everyone. However, this does not mean that one

154 Although the word *pūjā* as the designation for this type of worship is not mentioned here, flowers, water, etc., are its typical elements.

has to strive less, since devotion has to be enacted in a practice demanding a high degree of self-control and detachment. This applies in particular to kings as 'guardians' of the knowledge of Kṛṣṇa. Here, the attribute 'accessible by perception' gains additional significance, since not only the knowledge of god but also devotion to him must be open to perception and observation. Thus, in the context of *bhakti*, a king must prove the legitimacy and efficacy of his rule not only by embodying royal powers and virtues, but also by bringing prosperity and crushing enemies for the sake of Kṛṣṇa. Like any other follower of the god, he must live up to the standards of *bhakti*, which connect a person to the god's cause. Yet since he is the king, he must represent the ideal and the norm that his people should follow.

BHAGAVADGĪTĀ 10: KṚṢṆA'S PRESENCE IN THE WORLD

This chapter continues the theme of *yoga aiśvara*, of Kṛṣṇa's yoga as the overlord of all beings, by praising his presence in different groups and as the most eminent qualities of being. The cosmological character of the god's relationship to the world is highlighted by yet another perspective. While in *BhG* 9 we learned that creation is brought about by the god's unmanifest form, the present chapter explains the ubiquity of the god's power (*vibhūti*) through an enumeration of individual 'power manifestations' in the different realms of the cosmos, such as elements, social groups, gods, sages, animals and abstract principles. In this way, the relationship between the 'unseen' dimension of Kṛṣṇa's being and his manifest, perceptible (*pratyakṣa*; 9.2) presences is put into more concrete terms.[155] At *BhG* 11.2, Arjuna will call this teaching the god's *māhātmya*, a reference to both the mightiness detailed in the chapter and the style of praise, the literary genre of a *māhātmya*, a text that is by definition praise of a powerful being, sacred text or place. In contrast to later *māhātmyas*, the powerful being speaks in the first person and therefore is 'self-praise' (*ātmastuti*). Similar praise is voiced by Duryodhana in *MBh* 5.60, which serves equally to claim his sovereignty and supremacy (see above, pp. 45ff.).

However, the purpose of enumerating Kṛṣṇa's manifestation of power is to impart this knowledge because Arjuna is dear to him and he desires Arjuna's well-being (*hitakāmya*).[156] The god's superiority over the gods and sages is asserted not only when they are depicted as being ignorant of Kṛṣṇa's supremacy, but also when he declares himself their creator and cause (*ādi*; 10.2), while he has none (*anādi*; 10.3). As the 'mighty lord of the world'

[155] An abbreviated version of this concept is presented at *BhG* 7.4–11.

[156] This was also the reason Kṛṣṇa taught Arjuna the ancient yoga in *BhG* 4.3.

(*lokamaheśvara*; 10.3), he is unborn and does not depend on anything. In order to establish this supremacy, it has to be asserted in the face of others who wield power. This explains why all kinds of power positions and places of sovereignty are now turned into primary 'seats' and aspects of the god's power. A characteristic feature of this cosmology, one that is in accordance with Sāṃkhya philosophy, is that cosmic realms and individual beings are regarded as a continuum. The intrinsic connection between these two levels may explain why, first of all, Kṛṣṇa is declared to be the origin of the different 'modes of existence' (*bhāva*; 10.4–5), and then the 'seven sages and four Manus' (10.6). While the 'modes of existence' comprise the different dispositions of an individual being, such as knowledge (*jñāna*), endurance (*kṣamā*), fear (*bhaya*) or suffering (*duḥkha*),[157] the seven sages and four Manus point to the cosmic framework because they are commonly held to be the protectors of the ritual (Vedic) and socio-cosmic order (*dharma*) in each world period. The juxtaposition of the well-known group of seven sages and the four Manus has generated some discussion because this combination has no parallel in other texts that refer to either the group of seven *ṛṣis* or the Manus. According to Garbe (1921: 125, note 2) and Zaehner (1969: 293), the Manus are connected to the four world ages (*yuga*): 'Manu is the founder of the human race. There are four corresponding to the four world ages (*yuga*).'[158] Mitchiner (1982: 22) argues that the 'seven *ṛṣis*' are most probably the seven sons of Brahmā, begotten by his own mental powers, who 'by the time of composition of this passage . . . had come to be identified with the Seven Ṛṣis'. This is corroborated by the statement that Kṛṣṇa has created these sages mentally (*manasā*), as is the case with the 'sons of Brahmā'.

Kṛṣṇa declares that his ubiquitous might (*vibhūti*) is understood when one is 'yoked by unshakeable yoga' (10.7). This yoga is characterised by exclusive concentration and devotion to Kṛṣṇa (10.8–11), which includes the telling of stories about the god. As is pointed out, the adept may be supported by the god in acts of grace, such as granting him *buddhiyoga*, yoking through the faculty of discrimination,[159] or dispelling the darkness of ignorance. The motive for such acts is 'compassion' (*anukampa*; 10.11), an attitude cherished in Buddhism. Arjuna reacts enthusiastically to Kṛṣṇa's revelations and shows himself convinced that Kṛṣṇa is indeed the highest being. He calls him 'highest *brahman*, highest domain, highest means of purification (*pavitra*), the eternal, divine *puruṣa*, the god of

157 Some of the 'positive' *bhāvas* are also listed in *BhG* 16.1–2.

158 For different, less convincing interpretations see Kibe 1941 and Apte 1972: 202, who connects the group with the four *vyūha* of later Pāñcarātra theology. See also Minor 1982: 308.

159 Here too, another concept explained in earlier chapters (cf. *BhG* 2, 5–6) is employed.

beginning, unborn and all-pervading' (10.12). While in chapters 9 and 11 Kṛṣṇa's revelation is regarded as something new and as a truth of which the gods and sages have been oblivious, here Arjuna declares: 'All sages have proclaimed you (as being the god) as did the divine seer Nārada, Asita Devala, Vyāsa and you yourself' (10.13). Minor (1982: 313) comments: 'Arjuna thus confesses who Kṛṣṇa is in terms of names by which the Absolute is designated by the ancient seers.' However, in doing so, the author of this chapter refers not only to the *BhG* itself, but also to other instances in the epic in which Kṛṣṇa is praised or disclosed as being the 'highest'. It seems that this passage already interprets the new theology presented in *BhG* 9 and 11 by placing it in certain lines of transmission. This was also the case in *BhG* 4.1–3, where Kṛṣṇa's yoga doctrine is said to have been handed down in a line of 'royal seers'. Now Kṛṣṇa himself becomes the subject of the teaching. It is not just a matter of chance that the four sages have been singled out as singing the god's praises. Nārada and Vyāsa appear again as Kṛṣṇa's *vibhūti*s (10.26: Nārada is Kṛṣṇa's *vibhūti* among the divine sages, *devarṣi*; 10.37: Vyāsa among the ascetics, *muni*). Other instances can be cited, such as the Nārāyaṇīya section (12.327.91–92), in which Nārada figures prominently. One of the most interesting parallels is the revelation of Kṛṣṇa in *MBh* 6.61–64. Here we are given more information not only about the *ṛṣi*s, but also about their style of praising.

The text deals with the appearance of Vāsudeva-Kṛṣṇa on Gandhamādana Mountain. Only Brahmā recognises and praises the god. The other gods do not understand what Brahmā is doing. He admonishes them that they should not mistake the god because he appears in a human body (cf. 9.11 and above, pp. 151ff.). When asked for the source of his knowledge, Brahmā declares that he has learnt it from Rāma Jāmadagni, Mārkaṇḍeya, Vyāsa and Nārada. *BhG* 6.64.2–6 gives examples of how Kṛṣṇa was praised by different *ṛṣi*s:

> 'He is the lord of the lord of the gods (Indra) and the *sādhya*-gods.[160] You are the knower of the creatures and of the origination of the worlds!' – this is how Nārada praised you. 'What has been, what is to be and what will be' – thus said Mārkaṇḍeya about you. 'You are the sacrifice in the sacrifices, you are the heat in those who practice austerities, you are the god of the gods' – this is how Bhṛgu praised you . . . 'After you had established Indra in his position, you are the Lord of the gods among the gods' [Kṛṣṇa], Dvaipāyana [Vyāsa] said about you. 'You are the unmanifest that rises from the body as the one. You became manifest in the mind. The gods were born from your speech' – thus said Devala Asita.

160 A group of twelve gods; cf. *Nirukta* 12.40.

While the statements ascribed to Nārada and Markaṇḍeya can be corroborated, if not by exact parallel passages, at least by their respective contents, the style of praise ascribed to Bhṛgu matches some of the verses of *BhG* 10 (as at 7.10–11). The importance of Bhṛgu is also made explicit in *BhG* 10.25, when Kṛṣṇa declares himself to be 'Bhṛgu among the great sages'. All this points to a possible text-historical context of *BhG* 10 as an interpolation from Bhṛgu redactors, who are regarded as having played an important role in the final redaction of the epic.[161] The late interpolation of this chapter is also indicated because it interrupts the thematic and dramatic connection between *BhG* 9 and 11 and by features such as the notion of the god's grace and compassion.

After listing the names of those seers who had praised Kṛṣṇa earlier, Arjuna declares that he believes in Kṛṣṇa's words. He is convinced that neither gods nor sages know of his earthly sojourn in a manifest form (*vyakti*): 'You alone know yourself as yourself, supreme *puruṣa*, unfolder of beings, lord of creatures, gods of gods, lord of the world' (10.15). Again the tension between the unseen and unmanifest existence of the highest god and his actual presence as a 'god on earth' in a human body is being addressed. It is indicative of the ignorance of the gods that they cannot cope with the double character of Vāsudeva-Kṛṣṇa as both the visible and accessible ruler of the world and the unseen, detached highest self whose true identity remains hidden. Yet it is the god's presence that interests Arjuna the most:

> Leaving nothing out, will you please tell me of those power manifestations of yourself (*ātmavibhūti*) by means of which you pervade the world and abide. How may I know you, the *yogin*, when I constantly think of you? In what various modes of being shall I think of you, my lord? (10.16–17)

Here, the purpose of knowing the god's power manifestations is that they help one think of or meditate on the yogic god. The manifest forms of the lord are like signposts on the way to his higher, unmanifest state of being. Like his other appearances, these are indicative of the god, whose 'self' remains detached from them.

The word *vibhūti* (sg.), encompassing power, used in 10.7 and 18, sets the main theme for the following enumeration and praise of individual *vibhūti*s (pl.), 'power manifestations' that are the visible evidence of *vibhūti*, the encompassing might and sovereignty of the god as the *yogin*. The distinction between a singular, encompassing power and its being accessible in manifold manifestations is expressed by using the term *vibhūti* in the

161 See Sukthankar 1936. This is also corroborated in making Uśanas, the Bhṛgu poet and sage, the *vibhūti* of Kṛṣṇa amongst the poets in 10.37.

singular and the plural respectively.[162] The term is also connected to the powers of yoga in other texts, as, for example, the *YS*, whose third chapter, which deals with the supernatural capacities acquired in yoga, is called '*vibhūti-pāda*'. While in the Vedic and epic texts a god's power to appear in multiple forms is usually called *māyā*,[163] the supernatural powers of a successful *yogin* that result from his 'conquest of nature' are called *vibhūti* or *siddhi*. Most Western interpreters of yoga concentrate on the spiritual goal of liberation and pay less attention to these powers. They are often regarded as remnants of a 'magical understanding' of the world.[164] However, they play an important role in the epic (see Hopkins 1911) and in later traditions of yoga (see Pensa 1969). There are also texts in which this power is emphasised as a result of yoga, if not as a goal in its own right. One of these texts is *MBh* 12.289, which deals with the characteristic features of yoga in comparison to Sāṃkhya philosophy. While both traditions are regarded as true teachings, yoga differs from Sāṃkhya, first in its emphasis on gaining power, and secondly in regarding *pratyakṣa*, perception, as a means of proving its efficacy and truthfulness. The exposition begins with the following rhetorical question: 'How can one who is not a powerful lord (*anīśvara*)[165] gain liberation?' (*anīśvaraḥ kathaṃ mucyed*; 12.189.3ab). The 'power of yoga' (*yogabala*) and the *yogin*'s reaching the position of an *īśvara*, a lord over the powers of creation, is thus exemplified in the text with regard to the capacity to create or enter different bodies (12.189.24–26):

> Those *yogins* who are independent and full of the power of yoga (*yogabala*), Pārtha, enter into the Prajāpatis, seers, gods and the elements as (their) lords (*īśvara*). Neither Yama nor fierce Antaka, nor Mṛtyu of terrible might, rules over a *yogin* of immeasurable fiery energy (*tejas*). A *yogin* multiplies himself into thousands, Bull of Bhāratas, and when he has gained them, he moves in all the forms on earth.[166]

[162] The discussion of the meaning of *vibhūti* is summarised by Minor (1982: 309) as follows: 'All of these senses are possible with the word *vibhūti*: "lordship, power, immanence, pervasion", and even "manifestation of power or might". All of these could be meant here.' Gupta (1978: 131) emphasises, I think correctly, the connection between *vibhūti* and *aiśvarya*: 'those objects where this superordinary 'aiśvārya' [*sic*] is manifested are also called divine vibhūti-s'. *Contra*: van Buitenen 1981: 167.

[163] See Gonda 1959: 218ff. and the discussion of *māyā* above, pp. 96ff.

[164] E.g. Oberhammer (1977: 197ff.) and Eliade (1970: 94ff.); the latter who feels these powers to be irrelevant in the *BhG*.

[165] My translation differs from Edgerton's (1965: 291) and Deussen and Strauss's (1922: 592) in that it connects this statement to the dominant theme of the chapter, the 'power of yoga' (*yogabala*). However, I do not mean to suggest that the *yogin*'s practice may not be directed towards a god. This is indicated at the end of 12.189, where the *yogin* is said to become Nārāyaṇa.

[166] Cf. also *MBh* 12.326.51 and *SK* 45 on *aiśvarya*.

This combination of a position of power and the capacity to demonstrate it to the senses is also the distinctive feature of the *BhG*'s treatment of Kṛṣṇa's overlordship. However, the terminology and interpretation are different in the *BhG*. Although in *BhG* 10.19 Kṛṣṇa is addressed by Arjuna as a *yogin*, Kṛṣṇa's specific form of yogic power is called '*aiśvara yoga*' and '*vibhūti*' (sg.), both of which refer to the encompassing power of the highest lord, who is in this position because he is a *yogin* too. The god differs from the *yogin* in that he indeed pervades the whole world and is simultaneously present in all that is powerful. He does not take the body of a Prajāpati; rather, each Prajāpati is a *vibhūti*, a manifestation of the power of Kṛṣṇa. As a consequence, a *yogin* taking the body of a Prajāpati would gain its power, but the *yogin* would not be regarded as its ultimate source. This is why the god who is taking a body is explicitly distinguished from the *yogin* who does this too (cf. *MBh* 6.62.21 and above, pp. 151ff.).

In the present context, it can be regarded as an expansion on the theme of the paradoxical, 'most secret' character of Kṛṣṇa's unity/uniqueness-*cum*-manifoldness, his being the one in but also beyond the many, the highest, unseen being, that is, visible and accessible in fragments, in manifold and particular manifestations. In this way, the god is related to the world vertically as well as horizontally, the latter because his 'encompassing power' (*vibhūti*) is behind all manifestations as the co-present and co-extant source of its visibility. The relationship between 'the one' and 'the many' works in both ways: while the unseen power is accessible and present in its various manifestations, the latter point to the unseen as that power which sustains their existence. However, it is not Kṛṣṇa himself who appears here in the world, for he remains the liberated 'self'. This dimension of the god is only partially present in the world as the 'embodied self' in all beings, a self they must ultimately strive to realise and liberate. Kṛṣṇa confirms this relationship in 10.20 as follows: 'I am the self, Guḍākeśa, who exists as the ground of all beings. I am the beginning, middle and end of all beings.'

This is followed by an *ātmastuti*, a type of hymnic praise of oneself going back to Vedic hymns and also occurring elsewhere in the epic. Thus this self-praise not only is expressive of the god's 'inclination to bragging' (Winternitz 1907: 198), but belongs in the context of the rhetoric of the assertion of power known already in Vedic texts. Mainkar (1965: 74) regards *ṚV* 6.47.18, which deals with the many forms of Indra and the 'Vāmadeva song' (*ṚV* 4.2.6), as possible sources of *BhG* 10. Another parallel with regard to style is *ṚV* 10.125, in which the goddess asserts her supremacy over gods and poets (see Thompson 1997). Other parallels are the instances of heroic self-praise contained in the epic, for instance Duryodhana's in

5.60 (cf. above, pp. 47ff.). More frequently, however, epic heroes are praised by others on specific occasions, such as their death (for instance, Dhṛtarāṣṭra's praise of Bhīṣma when he has been mortally wounded; *MBh* 6.15), or their election as the leader of the army or before a battle (cf. *MBh* 5.153.11–14; 3.79.2; 6.14.2). These eulogies can be regarded as additional sources for this chapter. They differ, however, from the self-praise of the gods or of those who claim divine status in that they do not usually identify themselves with the power of other beings, but only compare themselves with them. Of particular interest with regard to the present chapter is Duryodhana's praise of Bhīṣma when he is proclaimed 'leader of the army' in 5.153:

> Be you our leader, like the sun among luminaries, like the moon among the plants, like Kubera among the Yakṣas, like Indra among the Maruts, like Meru among the mountains, like Suparṇa among the birds . . . For when we are guarded by you as the gods are by Indra, we shall surely become invincible. (5.153.11–14)

The style of praise here is similar to that of the present chapter. However, Kṛṣṇa's sovereign position of power is not compared with that of other leaders or sovereigns, but they are identified as a part of him. *BhG* 10 seems to have become influential in this regard, since the praise of divine manifestations of power has developed into a textual genre in the Purāṇa literature. As Gupta points out (1978: 133): 'The description of the various principal divine vibhūti-s as given in the *BhG* has been the model of mentioning the vibhūti-s of Viṣṇu and also of Śiva in the various Gītā-s and the stuti-s contained in the Purāṇas.' In the epic itself, *BhG* 10 seems to have become the model of a certain type of praise hymns, as in a Śaiva text in *MBh* 13.14.155–62 that combines elements of *BhG* 11 and 10, or in the Anugītā (*MBh* 14.43.1–13).

This type of hymn is structured by first-person-pronoun statements in which the speaker ('I', *aham*) identifies himself as the power in other beings, thus claiming supremacy over them. The principle of these identifications is described in *BhG* 10.41: 'Whatever being shows encompassing power (*vibhūtimat*), prosperity (*śrī*), and might (*ūrjita*), consider it as having its origin in a fragment of my splendour (*tejas*).' This turns the 'fragments' into manifestations of the unseen power, which explains why they have become rulers in their domain. Therefore, many of the *vibhūtis* listed are such 'parochial' powers; they are the leaders, kings or simply 'the best' among a group of people or other beings (animals, demons, gods, mountains) or in a certain region of the cosmos (mountains, planets). Such *vibhūtis* are, for instance, Viṣṇu among the Āditya gods (10.21), Indra among the gods (10.22), Śaṅkara (Śiva) among the Rudras (19.22), Kapila, the teacher of Sāṃkhya, among the 'accomplished *yogins*' (*siddha*; 10.26), the Aśvattha among the trees (10.26), the sun among the lights (10.21) and Vāsuki among the serpents (10.28). Apart from some of the gods, the Vedic tradition is also included when we find the following *vibhūti*s: Sāmaveda among the Vedas (10.22), Bṛhaspati among the household priest (*purodhasa*; 10.24), silent recitation (*japa*) among the sacrifices (10.25), the *bṛhat-sāman* (melody) among the melodies (*sāman*; 10.35) and the *gāyatrī* among the metres (*chandas*; 10.35).

Other *vibhūti*s are directly connected to aspects of sovereignty and kingship, being that office that has the socio-cosmic order as its domain. Correspondingly, the king is regarded as Kṛṣṇa's *vibhūti* among men (10.27); leadership positions in Kṣatriya contexts are ascribed to Vāsudeva (of the Vṛṣṇi clan), Arjuna (among the Pāṇḍavas) and Rāma (among the 'sword-carriers'; probably Rāma Jamadagni). Other *vibhūti*s are kings, such as Indra, the king of the gods, Vāsuki and Ananta, kings of snakes, Kubera, king of the Yakṣas, Citraratha, king of the divine musicians (Gāndharvas), Varuṇa (king of aquatic animals) and Prahrada (king of demons).

Thus, chapter 10 deals with a specific form of Kṛṣṇa's yogic presence in the world, to be distinguished from the god's other appearances. As has been pointed out in *BhG* 4, Kṛṣṇa may also 'take divine birth' (*divya janma*) here on earth in order to accomplish the defined purpose of re-establishing *dharma*, which calls for a 'human-like' body. The present chapter considers the visible or accessible fragments of his might in the world (*vibhūti*), while chapter 11 reports Arjuna's vision and praise of the god's *rūpa aiśvara*, the form of the god as the cosmic sovereign, which identifies him as the lord of all beings. Yet other forms of Kṛṣṇa are revealed in this process too, such as his appearance as 'time' and in a four-armed form. All these forms and appearances belong to Kṛṣṇa the 'highest' and must not be reduced to just one, as is done when, for instance, the so-called '*avatāra*' form is singled out as the most characteristic (see Biardeau 1997 and the discussion in the next section).

BHAGAVADGĪTĀ 11: THE COSMIC GOD AND SOVEREIGN

This chapter continues the discourse on Kṛṣṇa's yoga as supreme lord in *BhG* 9 with a vision of his form as supreme lord (*rūpa aiśvara*). The vision confirms the statement in 9.2 that knowledge of Kṛṣṇa's divinity can be obtained through perception (*pratyakṣa*). One dimension of this accessibility has been detailed in chapter 10 in listing the various beings that should be considered manifestations of Kṛṣṇa's divine power. Another form of access is the direct vision that the god grants to his devotees. This is called *darśana* and becomes (or in fact already is at this time: see Laine 1989) one of the most important and desirable events in the relationship between the god and his followers, one that each and every devotee strives for as the culmination of religious practice. In the context of the *BhG*, it serves to lend Kṛṣṇa's teachings ultimate authority and proof. The revelation turns from 'listening' to 'seeing'. This implies a significant change in the speaker's position from Kṛṣṇa to Arjuna, who is given the role of a poet expressing his vision in a way that recalls certain characteristics of Vedic poets or priests, who were originally supposed to compose their hymns during a 'vision' of the god(s) they praise (see Thieme 1952, Gonda 1963). Thus, although the new monotheistic doctrines place an unprecedented emphasis on the physical presence and visibility of the god, so that 'seeing' becomes a prominent practice in institutionalised temple worship and image rituals, it is not the only or even the original context in which the topic and practice of seeing and vision are unfolded. It plays a prominent role not only in Vedic and some Upaniṣadic texts, but also in the context of yoga, when the visualisation of the gods is regarded as part of its practice. The following analysis will show that both contexts are drawn on in the depiction of what in the text is described as 'never seen before' (*adṛṣṭapūrvaka*; 11.45). While the yogic context is made explicit when Arjuna is given 'divine sight', the Vedic context is evoked in the literary devices and some of the themes and imagery. In contrast to the interest in arguments and doctrines which are occasionally exemplified in metaphors and comparisons, this chapter has a poetic and literary quality that should be taken into account.

Setting the stage: narrators and perspectives

The chapter begins with a remarkable caesura and even closure, when Arjuna declares that Kṛṣṇa's words have 'cleared' his mind and solved all his problems. The disclosure of Kṛṣṇa's identity as both the highest self and the cosmic sovereign has dispelled his 'confusion':

> Out of favour for me, you have declared the highest secret (*guhya*), called 'the highest self' (*adhyātma*), thereby my delusion has been dispelled. For I have heard from you about the birth and death of beings, lotus-eyed, and about your unchangeable might (*māhātmya*) too. (11.1–2)

By referring back to Arjuna's crisis, which motivated the whole discourse, the ensuing revelation is explicitly embedded in the epic context and will not remain the only reference. However, this allusion to the beginning of the *BhG* also raises text-historical concerns[167] and the question of which parts of the text Arjuna refers to. Since the present chapter is a continuation of chapter 9, it does not seem too far-fetched to read 11.1–2 as its summary (see also Garbe 1921: 130, note 4). First of all, a characteristic feature of Kṛṣṇa's teaching in *BhG* 9.1–2 is recalled when Arjuna speaks of the 'highest secret'. In contrast to *BhG* 9, this secret is named (*saṃjñita*) *adhyātman* because (*hi*; 11.2) it consists in understanding the creation and destruction of beings, as well as Kṛṣṇa's might. All this is indeed dealt with in *BhG* 9, except that the word *adhyātman* is not used. While this word is used in *BhG* 8 as one of the aspects of the process of dying (see above, pp. 138ff.), such an interpretation seem less plausible here. It seems that, in theological contexts, *adhyātman* refers to the god and therefore can be understood as a substantive meaning 'highest self' (see Garbe 1921). This can be corroborated by considering its occurrence in *BhG* 3.30, where those who have placed their acts in Kṛṣṇa are said to have 'their thoughts on the highest self' (*adhyātmacetas*). In 13.11 *adhyātmajñānanityatvam* (steadiness in the knowledge of the highest self) and *tattvajñānārthadarśanam* (insight into the purpose of the knowledge of *tattvas*) are juxtaposed in the course of a presentation of theistic Sāṃkhya. It is this knowledge of the 'highest self' that helped Arjuna to understand the transience of corporeal existence.

On the basis of this understanding, Arjuna now requests an immediate, sensual confirmation of what he has heard; he wants to see Kṛṣṇa's 'form as supreme lord', the *rūpa aiśvara*. The yoga of Kṛṣṇa as the supreme lord (*yoga aiśvara*) is demonstrated in a corresponding appearance. However, Arjuna seems to be aware of the fact that such a vision is possible only if certain requirements are met, because he asks Kṛṣṇa to appear to him if he deems him capable of seeing. What is meant here becomes clear in 11.8, when Kṛṣṇa replies that Arjuna will need the 'divine sight' (*divya cakṣus*) that the god will confer on him. This is significant in two respects. First, 'divine sight' is an achievement of successful *yogins* and is one of their extraordinary powers (*aiśvarya*). It confirms one of the principles of yoga, theistic or not, that in order to acquire power one has to be powerful oneself, and that in order to gain access to a powerful lord one has to become a powerful one oneself. This is similar to the ritual sphere, in which the sacrificer temporarily leaves the human world and acquires a purified, 'divine' body

[167] Otto (1934), for instance, based his reconstruction of the 'Ur-Gītā' on *BhG* 11.2.

in order ritually to approach the gods. Other texts also state that only 'self-controlled' *bhaktas* are capable of withstanding the intense brightness and radiance of the sovereign, cosmic lord who appears not only in *BhG* 11, but also in the Nārāyaṇiya section as radiating like 'a thousand suns' (cf. *MBh* 12.323.35; 12.332.55; and the story of Eka-Dvita-Trita blinded by the god Nārāyaṇa, 12.323.19–53).

Secondly, providing Arjuna with 'divine sight' also has a narrative function, since he now assumes a position similar to that of Saṃjaya, who narrates the *BhG* in the overarching dialogue frame. We may recall here that Saṃjaya too was given 'divine sight' by the epic's composer Vyāsa (*MBh* 6.2.9–11) in order to be able to narrate the events in Kurukṣetra to the blind king (see Mangels 1995, Malinar 2005a). In the present context, Arjuna's function as the narrator is also accompanied by receiving this 'sight', and his narration can be regarded as a 'first-hand' report of something that was actually witnessed. This, in turn, is confirmed by Arjuna's capacity for poetic speech; that actual vision is manifested in the 'truth formulation' (*brahman*) of his hymn. The literary dimension of chapter 11 also becomes manifest in the careful delineation of two narrative perspectives voiced by Arjuna and Saṃjaya respectively. In addition, Kṛṣṇa functions as the interpreter of his own appearances.

Before Kṛṣṇa grants Arjuna's request, he announces (11.5–7) what Arjuna will see:

> Behold my forms, O Pārtha, a hundredfold and a thousandfold, variegated, divine, multicoloured and multi-form. Behold the Ādityas, Vasus, Rudras, Aśvins[168] and Maruts; behold the many wonders that have never been seen before, Bhārata. Behold now the whole world, moving and unmoving, as residing right here in one (place), in my body, Gūḍakeśa, and what else you shall see.

This programmatic anticipation emphasises the paradoxical, 'secretive' relationship between the 'one' and the 'many'. While Kṛṣṇa himself is manifold in his appearances, in relationship to the manifold character of the cosmos he is the one and only. In his cosmic form all beings, including the Vedic gods, reside and find their place. This announcement is important, since much of what Arjuna is going to see corresponds to it. However, Arjuna is not prepared to see the 'fearsome' (*ugra*) form of Kṛṣṇa, which, however, suits the statement that he will see many overwhelming, wondrous things that have not been seen before and therefore need to be explained (11.31).

[168] These four groups of gods are also mentioned at *BhG* 10.21, 22, 23.

Having ensured that Arjuna can function as the seer and narrator of Kṛṣṇa's form as lord by giving him divine sight (11.8), the situation is interrupted by switching back to the overarching dialogue frame. At this point, the audience is reminded that the whole dialogue between Arjuna and Kṛṣṇa is being narrated by Saṃjaya. Even Arjuna's hymnic praise is known only because of Saṃjaya's presence as a narrator. This reference to the dialogue frame establishes a double narrative perspective that allows a distance to be created from Arjuna's vision. What is related in chapter 11 is not a 'live report' of a mystical event, but a vision witnessed by others, like Saṃjaya, but with no participants other than Arjuna and Kṛṣṇa. This spatial and temporal distance between the actual vision and its narration is carefully marked by indexical signs in the text: while Saṃjaya uses imperfect and perfect forms throughout, Arjuna speaks in the present tense; similarly, the bard uses 'there' (11.23) when the vision reported by Arjuna happens 'here' (11.7). In addition, in calling Saṃjaya back on to the stage, it becomes possible to describe Arjuna's reaction and keep him in the position of a narrated figure. Last but not least, Saṃjaya offers his own comments on the situation. The insertion of Saṃjaya's comments between Kṛṣṇa's spoken announcement of what is going to happen and Arjuna's hymn results in an interesting time-frame. While Kṛṣṇa's speech is prospective, Saṃjaya's report is already retrospective and comments on the 'past future' (see its use of past tenses). Only after that does Arjuna's hymn bring us back into the narrative time (the present tense) and the moment of the vision (the 'now'). In its present form, this narrative structure turns Saṃjaya's comments into another programmatic statement of what Arjuna has indeed seen. Paying attention to the literary structure helps us to understand how the vision of an otherwise hidden form of Kṛṣṇa as supreme lord is turned into a text that is handed down as the self-revelation of the highest god, confirmed by the hymn of his devotee.

Saṃjaya first of all informs the audience that Kṛṣṇa, whom he calls Hari,[169] the mighty lord of yoga (*mahayogeśvara*), has indeed shown himself to Arjuna.[170] In 11.10–12, Saṃjaya gives a summary of the vision stressing

169 Kṛṣṇa is here called 'Hari', as is the case elsewhere in the epic. However, two other gods are addressed by this name: Nārāyaṇa and Viṣṇu. This is one of the reasons why some scholars regard Kṛṣṇa as being identical with or even an *avatāra* of Viṣṇu (additional evidence is found in the occurrence of the vocative *viṣṇo* at 11.24 and 11.30). This conclusion stretches the evidence too far, since Viṣṇu is elsewhere regarded as a Vedic god (cf. *BhG* 10.21, where he is regarded as Kṛṣṇa's *vibhūti* among the Ādityas, a statement that has, to my knowledge, not resulted in any claim that Viṣṇu must be regarded as an *avatāra* of Kṛṣṇa). For Viṣṇu as Āditya, see also *MBh* 1.59.14–16; 3.79.2.

170 At the very end of the *BhG*, Saṃjaya repeats this characterisation of Kṛṣṇa (see 18.75, 78) and confirms the author's interest in connecting Kṛṣṇa's position as the mighty ruler with his status as

the multiple body parts, the ornaments and weapons, garlands, robes and divine fragrance of the lord's body. The miraculous aspect of the appearance is highlighted, which culminates in the famous comparison[171] of the god's radiance with that of 'a thousand suns': 'If in the sky should together arise the shining radiance of a thousand suns, then would that perhaps resemble the radiance of that mighty self' (11.12). The 'thousand suns' probably refer here not to the actual number, but to the highest possible number imaginable. The emphasis on the solar character of Kṛṣṇa's appearance connects it with older Vedic concepts that link the power and position of a king to the different forms of fire, primarily the sun and the sacrificial fires (see Gonda 1957, Proferes 2007). After confirming that Arjuna has indeed seen the whole world in the one body of Kṛṣṇa (11.13), as the god had previously announced (11.7), Saṃjaya describes the reaction: 'Filled with amazement (awe) with his hair standing on end, and bowing his head and folding his hands to pay reverence, Arjuna spoke.' Arjuna is depicted here in the typical position of a devotee worshipping and approaching his god, or of a disciple approaching his teacher, that is standardised in iconographic representations. Similar to *BhG* 1.28–29, and at the start of the *BhG*, Arjuna's emotional condition is highlighted. While Arjuna's crisis was characterised by an influx of compassion, its solution is now found in another overwhelming state of being, in amazement and awe. The again overwhelming character of the situation is indicated not only by his 'hair standing on end', but also because at both places Arjuna is regarded as being under the influence (*āveśa*) or possessed by a state of mind or emotion. In the medical and aesthetic traditions this is called *sāttvika-bhāva*, and refers to the uncontrollable aspects of an experience.[172] In both situations, 'seeing' is depicted as a form of knowledge that changes an individual's attitude towards a situation. As a consequence, although Arjuna is shaken by what he sees, he is still capable of expressing what is happening to him in composed speech or, as is the case in *BhG* 11, in hymnic language. The author of this passage thus establishes a strong connection between 'seeing' as an overwhelming insight and the capacity to express this experience. As will be shown in what follows, the author draws on, but also reinterprets, the process of composing *brahman*, 'truth formulations' for Vedic sacrifices and in speech contests (*brahmodaya*) described in Vedic texts.

the mighty lord of yoga. This suggests that, in an earlier version of the text, the final part of chapter 18 followed chapter 12 (cf. Malinar 1996: 394–415).

171 On the use of this comparison in the *Nārāyaṇīya*, see Malinar 1997: 257–258.

172 Cf. 1.28a *kṛpayā parayāviṣṭo* and 11.14a *tataḥ sa vismayāviṣṭo*; 1.29c *romaharṣaś ca jāyate* and 11.14b *hṛṣṭaromā dhanaṃjayaḥ*.

Cosmic Kṛṣṇa, four-armed Kṛṣṇa, fearsome Kṛṣṇa

Following Saṃjaya's comments, Arjuna's hymnic praise begins, and the metre changes from *śloka* to *triṣṭubh*. The initial description of the vision confirms Kṛṣṇa's and Saṃjaya's accounts and stresses the act of seeing as the mode of encounter (cf. *BhG* 1): Kṛṣṇa had asked Arjuna five times that he might behold his form (11.5–8); Arjuna, in turn, declares four times that he sees indeed (11.15–19). At first he describes the gods, including the god Brahmā sitting on a lotus seat, and all the different groups of beings residing in Kṛṣṇa's body (11.15). This fact has by now been pointed out by all three speakers. This repetition indicates the doctrinal relevance of this imagery and even iconography, since it expresses Kṛṣṇa's supremacy as the 'mighty lord of the world'. The cosmological unity of the world in Kṛṣṇa's body is then contrasted with the manifold character and variety of Kṛṣṇa's form as lord: 'I see you with manifold arms, bellies, mouths and eyes, being everywhere in your infinite form. I cannot see your end, middle or your origin, supreme lord of the universe (*viśveśvara*), Form universal (*viśvarūpa*)!' (11.16). Since it is Kṛṣṇa's body in which the whole world resides, he is not only the supreme lord of the universe (*viśva-iśvara*), but also its universal, encompassing form (*viśvarūpa*). The multi-form appearance and the designation '*viśvarūpa*' indicate the use of older traditions in ascribing multiple body parts and bodies to gods and other cosmological powers. While being a favourite theme in poetic discourse and the cosmological speculations of Vedic and Upaniṣadic texts, it had become the template for sculptural representations by the second century BCE. In her comprehensive study of this 'multiplicity convention' as a unique feature of Hindu traditions, Srinivasan (1997: 5, and *passim*) has shown that deities associated with the cosmic creation are already credited with multiple body parts in Vedic texts. In contrast to Gupta and post-Gupta texts and iconographic representations of multiplicity that relate the 'story' or a '*līlā*' (play) of a god or goddess, the earlier depictions make 'theological statements' (1997: 13) on the 'grandeur of the cosmic creator, his extraordinary powers, the unfathomable mystery of creating many from the One, including the unfolding of the One into multifaceted divine aspects that appear on earth'. The aspect stressed most in this depiction of Kṛṣṇa is '*viśva*' (twice in 11.16), which is aligned with older cosmological notions of 'fullness' and 'completeness' ascribed to *brahman* and *mahān ātman* in the Upaniṣads (van Buitenen 1964; Srinivasan 1997: 83–95). As Gonda shows (1955: 54), there are two different ideas regarding 'completeness', indicated by the words *sarva* and *viśva*: '*viśva-* pointing out the inability to proceed after a certain total number has been counted, *sarva-* emphasizing the idea of wholeness and completeness and the inability to discern defectiveness'. *Viśva* points to the highest possible number of enumerable things, as is the case with the number 'a thousand' (*sahasra*), which is highlighted in the hymn as well. Everything needed and available in the cosmos is contained and encompassed in and by '*viśvarūpa*', the 'omniform'. As Srinivasan points out (1997: 134–135): 'The entire Brāhmaṇic tradition – Vedas and epic – unites in designating the form of the creator god as a gigantic Male radiating with the total number of bodily parts on his exterior and containing, in his interior, the material forms to inhabit the worlds.' Yet one has to bear in mind that this form is a product of the god's yogic power and that it expresses sovereignty, but not his highest state of being as the transcendent 'self' beyond the cosmos.

Then another form of the god appears, vested with a similar iconographic potential: 'I see you wearing the royal diadem, mace and discus, and with beams of fiery energy shining all around you, difficult to look at, since on every side there shines the glistening light of the immeasurable solar fire' (11.17). This description of Kṛṣṇa as the lord wearing the insignia of the king (the diadem) and characteristic weapons is repeated at the end of the vision, when Arjuna asks to see the 'four-armed' form again (11.46; other instances of this iconography in the epic occur at 16.9.19–20; 5.129). Although it is not explicitly stated in 11.17 that Kṛṣṇa appears 'four-armed', it may be assumed with some certainty (see Srinivasan 1997: 146–147). The 'royal' character of this imagery is pointed out by Srinivasan in discussing the symbolism of the number 'four' as conveying notions of 'completeness of the world on a horizontal plane' and as the number that completes a 'triad' and thus points to vertical completeness. The 'arms' are the parts of the body that are most closely associated with sovereignty and physical action, as are the weapons. She concludes (1997: 22–23) that the four-armed form of Vāsudeva-Kṛṣṇa 'is composed of mutually supportive ideographs' (four, arms, weapons) which express the 'god's sovereignty over the whole world on the horizontal and vertical planes'. This is also supported by another aspect of the god's appearance: he is surrounded by 'beams of fiery energy' indicating his solar and fiery character as the sovereign. The fiery character of a king is pointed out in *ManuS* 7.4ff., which describes the king as consisting of and uniting different gods and states that he should therefore be regarded as a 'universal form' (*viśvarūpa*; *ManuS* 7.10). This recalls the structure of Vedic kingship expressed in the consecration and other royal rituals (see Heesterman 1957, Gonda 1959). Special emphasis is given to his fiery energy, which allows him to perform his task as the protector and defender of the social order. This 'fire of the king' or the 'fire that is the king' (*rājāgni*) is responsible and necessary for maintaining order and thus procuring the kingdom's prosperity. In combining these aspects and embodying the divine powers of the gods who contribute to his sovereignty, he is called 'a mighty godhead that lives in the form (body) of a man' (*mahatā devatā hy eṣā nararūpeṇa tiṣṭhati*; 7.9; see Hopkins 1931).

While the imagery and notions are old, these are actually displayed much later in the sculptures of Kuṣāna kings (first century CE) and also become a feature in Buddhist iconography (see Verardi 1983, 1985, Scott 1990). The earliest available sculptures of a four-armed Vāsudeva-Kṛṣṇa stem from the second century BCE and will be discussed in chapter 5 below.

Before Arjuna's description of the fiery character of the god's appearance continues, rather abstract epithets and attributes are applied to him in 11.18. The interpretive character of this verse is indicated when Arjuna voices his opinion (*mato me*) that Kṛṣṇa is the 'imperishable, the highest knowledge, the resting place of the universe, the guardian of eternal order (*śāsvatadharmagoptā*), the eternal *puruṣa*'. These epithets reconnect the god to Vedic and Upaniṣadic traditions of the 'highest', but also continue the topic of sovereignty by calling him 'the guardian of eternal *dharma*'.[173] The vision intensifies in the following verses by focussing on the fiery character of the cosmic god:

> Without beginning, middle and end, with infinite strength and infinite arms, with sun and moon as your eyes, I see you with a mouth that is a blazing (sacrificial) fire (*hutāśa*) as you burn up this universe with your own fiery energy. For the space between heaven and earth and all the regions are pervaded by you alone. When I see this marvellous (*adbhuta*), fearsome (*ugra*) form of yours, the three worlds are shaken, O mighty self! (11.19–20)

The god's cosmic power and dominance are here highlighted by focussing on their destructive aspects, the 'fierce' (*ugra*) side of the god's relationship to the world when it comes to punishing evil-doers. Therefore his heroic prowess (*vīrya*) is mentioned and his immeasurable (Kṣatriya) arms. This is combined with allusions to the (sacrificial) fire that is burning as his mouth, allying the god's appearance to the idiom of sacrifice, which here is indicative of the presence of death and the destiny of the battlefield.[174] In depicting

173 Interestingly some manuscripts attempt to connect the passage to the Sātvata tradition. Four Śārada manuscripts (3–6) read *sātvata-dharmagoptā* and create a parallel with *MBh* 12.322.5, where the god Nārāyaṇa is addressed as *sātvatadharmagoptā*. Some manuscripts, in turn, read *śāsvatadharmagoptā* and thus follow the *BhG*. On *gopā* (guardian), see also Gonda 1959: 106. For a survey of names and epithets used in *BhG* 11, see Bhargava 1979.

174 Biardeau (1976: 132) demonstrates that this blending of the sacrificial fire, the fire of war and the deity absorbing the creatures confirms the equation between sacrificial and yogic activity that is typical of the teachings of the *BhG*.

the god as 'burning' the world, the hymn also draws on descriptions of *pralaya* (see Biardeau 1976: 133), the cosmic destruction at the end of an cosmic eon. According to Biardeau (1981: 136–7), the description of *pralaya* is the main purpose of the hymn, though I regard it as part of the depicting of Kṛṣṇa as a supreme cosmic god – the pervading theme and theological message of the text.

The cosmic and royal aspects of Kṛṣṇa's form converge not only at the moment of creation, but also in times of destruction, which serve the double purpose of punishment and purification, as well as re-establishing order and legitimate kings. This implies a fierce and violent display of power, which results in Kṛṣṇa's marvellous (*adbhuta*), terribly powerful (*ugra*) appearance. Since the sovereign's duty includes the capacity to act violently in order to 'keep the world together', this form does not represent a god gone 'wild', nor does it indicate a conceptual contradiction.[175] Rather, it is the complement to Kṛṣṇa's appearance as the friendly and benign ruler and creator of the cosmos, as was described earlier, when Arjuna saw the god adorned with diadem, mace and discus. Since Kṛṣṇa is the one and only encompassing cosmic god, both these aspects are complementary, thus allowing all the cosmic functions that the god claims for himself to be fulfilled. The *ugra* form becomes a well-established aspect of a god with cosmological tasks, and in later iconographical texts is listed as a distinct form of the god suitable for temple worship too (see Pal 2005). In the *BhG*, this form is regarded as 'not seen before', and therefore Arjuna asks for an explanation (11.31).

Up to this point, Kṛṣṇa is depicted in the forms that highlight the following aspects of his presence in the world: (1) as a cosmic god (*viśvarūpa*), (2) as a royal god with a specific four-armed iconography, and (3) as the fearsome, violent protector of the cosmic order (*ugra*), which in what follows is further explained as a manifestation of *kāla*, time and death (11.32–34). In these contexts, the god is twice addressed by Arjuna as 'Viṣṇu' (11.24, 30), which has been taken to support the thesis that Kṛṣṇa is identified with or even as Viṣṇu. While such an identification is certainly made in these two verses, this does not mean that Kṛṣṇa loses his identity as the god Vāsudeva-Kṛṣṇa, for this would make him a mere incarnation of Viṣṇu. In accordance with the way Kṛṣṇa is identified throughout the hymn with

[175] Therefore neither do I agree with Garbe's (1921: 170) view that the 'pantheistic' verses are interpolations, since they contradict the information that the gods see Kṛṣṇa's form; or with Ježic (1979a), who suggests two different textual layers because he sees a contradiction between the *adbhuta* and *ugra* forms. It should also be borne in mind that *ugra* derives from Vedic *ojas*, an indispensable, fiery 'power-substance' of the gods (cf. Gonda 1957: 31).

other gods or entities, the passages can also be regarded as equating Kṛṣṇa's form with Viṣṇu in certain respects. Most important seems to be Viṣṇu's solar and fiery character, as well as the expansion of his body, which is a theme of both verses.[176] These are characteristic features of Viṣṇu in Vedic and Brāhmaṇa texts and have certainly contributed to Viṣṇu's position as the 'highest' god in his own right. However, the later interpretation of Kṛṣṇa as a form of Viṣṇu must not be projected on to the *BhG* (see van Buitenen 1981: 28; Srinivasan 1997: 134, 240–259). Although the text thus presents different images of the god, it presents them not statically, but as a sequence of elements that structure Arjuna's vision. The text thus provides a dynamic account of these forms in that it also includes the reaction of other creatures to Kṛṣṇa's appearance. The vision culminates in identifying the god's manifestation with the battle of Kurukṣetra as the epicentre of cosmic destruction. Therefore the different forms of the god are reported in changing narrative perspectives. Thus, having given a first-person narrative of the vision in 11.15–19, Arjuna reports the reaction of other creatures to Kṛṣṇa's appearance in 11.20. True to his position as the overall narrator, Arjuna's 'divine sight' not only allows Kṛṣṇa's form to be seen, but also relates other views and reactions. He reports the 'shudder' (*pravyathitam*) of the 'three worlds' and that the gods approach the cosmic god praising him fearfully with folded hands. Sages (*ṛṣi*) and successful ascetics (*siddha*) greet him with praise (11.21). They are again shown in 11.22, full of amazement as they behold the 'large form' (*rūpam mahat*). The gods and other beings are in a position to see all this because Kṛṣṇa's form pervades the space between heaven and earth only (11.20, 24), leaving the heavenly regions untouched by the destruction taking place at Kurukṣetra, which is the theme of the following verses.[177] In 11.24 Arjuna again assumes the position of a first-person narrator who is frightened of the god's dreadful mouths, 'spiky with fangs' and resembling 'the fire at the end of time' (*kālanala*). Arjuna once again loses his bearings and asks the god for mercy before he describes what is happening in these blazing mouths: 'And yonder all sons of Dhṛtarāṣṭra, along with the hosts of kings, such as Bhīṣma, Droṇa and Karṇa, along with our own chief warriors too, are rushing into your mouths, spiky with fangs and horrifying; some are dangling between your teeth with their heads

[176] The Vāmana-Trivikrama myth deals with the god's expansion, which is already mentioned in *ṚV* 7.99.1–2. See also Tripathi (1968: 68–70), who points out that, in the oldest epic version of the myth, Viṣṇu is said to have a divine, exceptionally marvellous form. Expansion is also an important aspect of Viṣṇu's connection with sacrifice (for instance, *ŚBr* 14.1.1.6). His royal, solar character is indicated, for instance, at *ṚV* 1.155.5, where he is called 'sun-eyed' (*svardṛśo*).

[177] Biardeau (1981: 136) has pointed out that the change of the narrative perspective indicates the different relationships of the creatures to destruction and salvation.

already crushed to bits' (11.26–27). Arjuna's fears are now proven right, and what he was 'foreseeing' when he looked at his relatives 'between the armies' is confirmed as something that has already happened. The 'future' is envisioned as already past. This vision leaves the agency of the situation with Kṛṣṇa and presents the destruction as something inevitable, almost natural: the warriors who enter the mouth of death are compared with the torrent of rivers that rush into the ocean (11.28) and with moths plunging swiftly into a blazing fire.[178] Similar to what happened at the beginning, when Arjuna imagined the killing of his relations, he is lost and does not understand what he is seeing. Although he has declared at the beginning of *BhG* 11 that his confusion is gone and that all his questions have been answered, he now sees something he is not prepared for. Yet this vision contains the theological answer to his original doubt: 'Tell me who you are in your fearsome form (*ugrarūpa*)! Homage to you, lord of the gods; have mercy. I wish to understand you, who exist since the beginning, because I do not comprehend your course' (11.31).

Kṛṣṇa explains this 'fearsome' form as follows:

> Deadly Time (*kāla*) I am, ready to bring about the end of the world, coming forward to absorb the worlds here. Except for you, all these warriors, who are arrayed against one another, will no longer exist. Therefore stand up, win glory, defeat the enemies and enjoy a prosperous kingdom (*rājya*)! Long ago all these were killed by me; be only the sign (*nimitta*) of this, left-handed archer! Slay Droṇa, Bhīma, Jayadratha and Karṇa and other warrior-heroes who have all already been slain by me. Tarry not! Fight and you will defeat your enemies in battle! (11.32–34)

By interpreting Kṛṣṇa as time-embodied, the imminent battle is turned into a future that has already passed. The warriors will no longer exist, since they have already been killed by the agency of time. This addresses Arjuna's problem by disclosing the inevitability of events. Any attempt to change the course of events is futile because they have already happened and can no longer be prevented. In addition, Arjuna is instructed about how to behave in this situation: his task is to carry out the action and terminate the situation and kill warriors and heroes doomed long ago. Again, yet in a different framework of meaning, the battle is presented as a win-win situation: Arjuna will not only survive and enjoy a kingdom, but will do it deliberately as an act of worship to the god, who guarantees him liberation

[178] Both comparisons occur elsewhere in the epic in order to describe inevitable events, e.g. *MBh* 5.56.27 and 5.52.12. Arjuna's bow Gāṇḍiva is regarded as being as destructive as is fire for moths; e.g. *MBh* 5.56.27; 5.52.12; 5.128.42; 5.40.28–30; 5.50.58–59. The image of rivers flowing into the ocean was also used in *BhG* 2.70 and is already found in Vedic and Upaniṣadic texts.

as well. In becoming the god's instrument and sign (*nimitta*), Arjuna has no negative karmic consequences to fear.

The agency of time

This depiction of the agency of and behind time draws on discourses on time and destiny elsewhere in the epic. In these contexts, time is regarded as a cosmic force defined not only in terms of quantity (units of time), but also of quality (auspicious or inauspicious; 'ripe'[179] or 'unripe'). The agency and course of time are accessible only to those who are expert in interpreting the signs of time, the *nimitta*, which indicate the course of events before they actually happen. These omens appear as anticipation and are based on a suspension of the otherwise chronological sequence of past, present and future. This is demonstrated when Kṛṣṇa, in his appearance as time, shows those whom Arjuna should kill as having been killed already. The future is presented as already past; conversely, the present appears as the moment in which this future is disclosed as an actual fact. Seen in this perspective, the present moment is not a chance to influence or change the course of time according to one's individual preferences, as the doctrine of *karman* would have it (even if the past were to set certain limits to one's aspirations). When drawn into the agency of time, individual agency is confined to corresponding to and enacting what has already taken its course – in brief, to be sign and executor, a *nimitta* – which is what Kṛṣṇa asks Arjuna to be. This structure has often been regarded as 'determinism' or 'fatalism' (Otto 1934; Radhakrishnan 1948: 322), without sufficiently considering the specific time-structure implied in the notion of fate. This structure is dealt with elsewhere in the epic and provides yet another link between the theology of the *BhG* and its epic context. Scheftelowitz (1929) has shown that notions of 'destiny' in the epic are part of the discourse on heroism and are often connected to astrological knowledge (*kālavāda*) and the presence of astrologers (*kālavādin*).[180] Astrology works on the assumption that time is not only a quantity measured in units of time (such as the dark and bright halves of the month) but also a quality and even a cosmic power disclosed in *nimitta*, signs that can be interpreted by experts. These signs lend visibility

179 Instead of 'matured' (*pravṛddha* in 11.32), we also find 'cooked' or 'ripe' (*kālapakka*; e.g. *MBh* 5.130.3; 5.126.31).

180 Astronomical and astrological knowledge converges in this context. Elsewhere in the epic, Kṛṣṇa is also called *kālavid* (knower of time) and *kālavādin* (e.g. *MBh* 16.5.17, where he understands that 'his time' has come and he prepares for death; cf. Schneider 1982 on Vyāsa as *kālavid*; see also Vassilkow 1999.

to the otherwise hidden course of time. This notion is used in Kṛṣṇa's speech, when Arjuna is asked to reinterpret what he himself has regarded as frightening *nimitta* at the beginning of the *BhG* (see 1.31) and become himself a 'sign' and enactor of time. This implies reconsidering once again the place of one's own agency and responsibility for events, this time in the light of larger time-frames in which individual acts are embedded and which they depend on.

The Sanskrit language offers quite a spectrum of words for 'destiny' as the interface between human aspirations and the agency of time (see Schrader 1902), and the epic includes several discourses on the relationship between them.[181] One of them is particularly relevant to the present analysis because it deals with the distinct features of cosmic time mentioned earlier and also contains some textual parallels to the *BhG*: the dialogue between Indra and Bali in *MBh* 12.116–117. According to Schrader (1902: 33), this dialogue is relatively old and can be considered a paradigmatic presentation of 'epic *kāla-vāda*'. Indra, the king of the gods, meets Bali, the former king of the demons, who presently finds himself reborn in the body of a donkey. Like Arjuna at the beginning of the *BhG*, Indra feels that one should bemoan one's losses, and asks Bali why he does not feel grief for the loss of his kingdom.[182] Bali replies that bodies are finite (*antavanta ime dehe*; 12.217.60 = *BhG* 2.18a) and subject to the course of time, which causes the aggregation (birth) and separation (death) of the elements of the body. Since he is not responsible for this, he cannot lament. All change is subject to the course of time, as is also true for a king's fortune, *śrī*, whose presence or absence does not depend on the king alone. Bali then turns to one characteristic feature of the relationship between human efforts and the workings of time already noticed with regard to the *BhG*:

> One (already) dead kills another dead person. A man kills another. Neither know who kills and who is killed. The one who is killed, having lived before, is not an agent – the agent is another. The one who brings about the creation and destruction of the people brings about only what has already been brought about. Its agent is another . . . Someone may be learned or ignorant, strong or weak, handsome or plain, happy or unhappy – all of this, time, the profound one, creates with its own energy. I am subject to time – why should I, who understand this perfectly, worry? Man burns down what has already been burned down; he kills what has already

[181] Cf. *MBh* 5.75, a conversation between Arjuna, Bhīma and Kṛṣṇa on the relationship between human (*pauruṣa*) and 'divine' (*daivam*) agency.

[182] 'You do not complain about something that is deplorable indeed' (*śocasyāho na śocasi*; 12.117.4). Conversely, Kṛṣṇa criticises Arjuna for complaining about something which is not deplorable (*aśocyān anvaśocas tvam*; *BhG* 2.11).

been killed; he destroys what has already been destroyed from its very beginning – he gains what he must gain.[183] (12.217.14–20)

This passage stresses that humans are not capable of achieving anything outside the activity of time; to a large extent, their efforts depend on the right moment. Human activity is embedded in larger temporal frameworks that restrict chances and open them up. Rather than being only the 'creator of one's own destiny', a human being can only respond to and enact the potential of a given moment. Not everything is possible at all times. Therefore it is necessary to understand the signs of the time in order to secure the success of one's actions or to refrain from acting when the time to do so has not come. Time is regarded not as a sequence of neutral units of time, but as vested with its own agency and quality, which determine the scope of human activities. This agency of time is referred to in notions of 'destiny', 'fate' and 'auspiciousness'. Therefore time can even drive creatures to action, even against their will. This, at least, is the experience reported by some members of the Kuru family when they find themselves entrapped in a course of events that inevitably results in war and destruction. It is not possible to escape this agency, which turns the future into something that has already happened, and the present into the moment of disclosure. When Arjuna thinks he can prevent war, or Bali laments his loss of power, thinking it could be otherwise, it is like wishing to reverse the course of a river and make it flow back to its mountain spring. The agency of time is the condition of the possibility of human action; conversely, human beings disclose and enact this very agency through their activities. This dialectic is at the centre of the discourse on the relationship between human capacities and the agency of time, called destiny. Destiny works only when there is an agent who is involved in its enactment. This is also why, in some debates on time, it is pointed out not only that one must surrender to fate, but also that one must calculate one's chances and try to protect oneself from whatever appears to be inevitable and incontrollable.

Seen against the epic discussions on time and human agency, it is significant that Kṛṣṇa appears as time (*kāla*), since this allows the limitations and constraints to which even powerful beings and mighty kings are subject to be explained. On the other hand – and this is also made very clear in Kṛṣṇa's speech as well as in Bali's – what is fatality and loss for some is victory and gain for others. While confirming the death of his relatives, Arjuna is promised kingship. Thus, not only with regard to the explicit reference to the epic battle, but also in drawing on an important conceptual framework

183 *MBh* 217.14cd is parallel to *BhG* 2.19 and *KaṭhU* 2.19.

of the epic, Arjuna's vision is intimately connected to the *MBh*. However, in presenting Kṛṣṇa as time, the author creates a theistic version of the epic discourse on time (*kālavāda*). Time here is regarded as a form of the cosmic god as sovereign who brings about a necessary and purifying destruction in order to re-establish order. This theological reinterpretation also touches on the term *nimitta*, usually used for the visible signs, the omens, indicating the otherwise hidden course and agency of time. Arjuna is asked to become Kṛṣṇa's *nimitta*, the sign and instrument of the god. In rendering *nimitta* by two words, 'sign' and 'instrument', the other meaning of the word, 'instrument' or 'cause', is also taken into account.[184] While Arjuna's fighting is indicative of the inevitable destruction that has come, it is also instrumental in bringing this about. He is fulfilling and concluding a course of events that has driven all the participants into war. Although Arjuna himself is subject to this inevitability, he is yet required to accept it and even actively enact it. Rather than complain about what will happen anyway, he should take his bearings by looking at the chances that the destruction offers, that is, winning a 'prosperous kingdom' (*rājya samṛddha*; 11.33). This he should enjoy, because Arjuna is not the cause of the destruction – the blood of his relatives will not be on his hands, because it has already been swallowed up and burned in the mouth, the fire of time.

The destruction lays the basis for establishing a prosperous and legitimate kingdom sanctioned and demanded by the overlord of all kings and of all worlds, that is, by Kṛṣṇa himself. While the cosmos and the earth are faced with the coming and going of 'thousands of Indras', as Bali puts it (12.217), Kṛṣṇa guarantees the continuity of the institution of kingship, even when this means killing kings. This is also one of the main purposes of later, elaborate *avatāra* doctrines that guarantee this continuity in the future, a doctrine which is already articulated in *BhG* 4.7, though without referring to *avatāras*. Arjuna's task is thus to fight for the continuity of kingship and not of the family as a whole. His loyality must be transferred from the *kula*, the family, and even from the warrior's duty, to Kṛṣṇa alone, since Kṛṣṇa encompasses and transcends all these particular loyalties and obligations. Biardeau points out that Arjuna is depicted here as the 'ideal king' who is the devotee of the *avatāra* god who grants victory and protection. The *bhakti* doctrine offers the king a chance to be liberated, even if he performs his violent, social duties. Accordingly, he is liberated because he does not fight for his kingdom, but for *dharma*: 'he imitates the Supreme God who becomes incarnate on earth in order to save the *dharma*' (1981a: 94). In

184 Johnston (1930: 861) suggests rendering *nimitta* in 11.33 as 'outward appearance'.

accordance with her emphasis on the *avatāra* myth, Biardeau finds Kṛṣṇa's promising Arjuna a kingdom irrelevant: 'Even though the war should result in kingship being restored to the Pāṇḍavas, kingship is not the aim, but *dharma* and the welfare of the world' (1981a: 93). However, there is neither *dharma* nor welfare without a 'real' kingdom, as Biardeau (1997: 79) seems to acknowledge when she describes *bhakti* as 'an intimate relationship . . . between the king and the supreme god in his *avatāra* form. The *avatāra* is not only the model for the king, but his necessary companion, the true protector of his kingdom.'

Just as god and devotee cannot be separated from each other, politics and religion, kingship and liberation, are not separate realms either, since they belong to a discourse which has them interact in the same socio-cosmic order. This is one of the reasons why the problem raised by Arjuna is so complex and has provoked a multi-layered argument that cannot be reduced to one doctrine only, although the *bhakti* doctrine and the monotheistic framework are its most innovative and paradigmatic features. Although I agree with Biardeau that the *BhG* plays a central role in the epic discourse on *dharma*, her emphasis on the *avatāra* myth as the model of the whole epic and the *BhG* (see 1976: 173) certainly highlights an important aspect of the new theological framework, there are terminological and conceptual differences within the text that are worth exploring in detail. For instance, the description of his 'divine birth' in chapter 4 deals with a different aspect of Kṛṣṇa's divinity from the enumeration of his 'manifestations of power' (*vibhūti*) in chapter 10, which is, in turn, complemented by the forms of the god described in the present chapter. With regard to Kṛṣṇa's appearance as time, the author draws not only on the discourse on yogic and royal power, but also on epic debates on time and destiny. Arjuna's task is to recognise Kṛṣṇa as the agent in the form of time. Conversely, time has been given a form and even an agent. Although this does not result in bringing destiny under control, it is given a 'name, address and face', in the words of Bertolt Brecht (*War Primer* 21). In response to Kṛṣṇa's explanation, Arjuna now turns from the narration of his vision to praising of Kṛṣṇa as the highest god.

Praising the god

The change of style and intention from 'vision' to 'praise' is marked by a comment by Saṃjaya (11.35): 'Upon hearing these words of Keśava, (Arjuna) the trembling (*vepamāṇa*) wearer of the royal diadem (*kirīṭin*) folded his hands, again bowed his head and spoke to Kṛṣṇa, stammering, paying homage, while struck by awe.' Saṃjaya depicts Arjuna as overwhelmed and shaken by Kṛṣṇa's appearance, as he himself had pointed out before (11.25, 31). Faced with Kṛṣṇa's blazing mouth and the revelation of his identity, Arjuna praises Kṛṣṇa stammering and trembling (*vepamāna*). He is described, like Kṛṣṇa (11.17), as wearing the royal diadem (*kirīṭin*). The contrast between the royal status ascribed to Arjuna with the royal diadem[185] and his 'trembling' underscores the amazement and awe caused by the vision. However, it seems that this 'trembling' is also indicative of Arjuna's position as the composer of hymnic praise. Verbal forms of the root '*vip*' (to tremble) are frequently used in Ṛgvedic texts dealing with poetic creativity. According to Oldenberg (1909: 299, my trans.) '*vip* is vibrant excitement (of the poet, worshipper, priest) and the utterances born of such excitement'. Accordingly, priests are addressed as *vipra*, 'the trembling one', referring to the 'excitement in which the poet creates' (Thieme 1952: 104f.; also Gonda 1963: 39). Seen from this perspective, Arjuna is now put in a position similar to a Vedic seer or poet, as he is now shown praising the god of the vision in a poetic-ecstatic state that makes him tremble. However, Arjuna is not a priest, but a warrior and an 'ideal' king. Therefore the god is revealed by a 'royal' actor, perhaps a *rājarṣi*, a royal seer in the position of priest. Using poetic language, the 'trembling king' (*vepamāna kirīṭin*) praises and addresses the god who appears as a blazing fire and thus in a form alluding to the sacrificial fire. In this way, hymn and revelation are authorised, which seems necessary because something that 'has not been seen before' (*adṛṣṭapūrva*) is proclaimed the ultimate truth. In this respect, *BhG* 11 differs from other forms of revelation, such as the Mīmāṃsā views of Vedic texts as authorless, self-validating and exempt from time (see van Buitenen 1981: 9).

As already indicated, the text also draws heavily on the Vedic tradition. Whillier (1987: 157) suggests that Arjuna's vision is achieved in a way that is similar to poetic visions in the Veda: 'In RV 10.71 an instrument of the vision-experience and that which provides the link between the mortal and the immortal is māyā. In the BG. the term "yoga" is used to the same end in the account of Arjuna's vision. Buddhiyogam (10.10) sets the stage for the vision, and the divine yoga is that which is envisioned.' However, Whillier neglects the fact that Kṛṣṇa gives Arjuna 'divine sight', indicating a convergence of poetic and yogic faculties (see above). For him the 'divine eye' points to the changing social contexts of poetic vision by turning

[185] On Arjuna as the 'ideal king' and wearing the diadem, see Biardeau 1978: 87–111; 1997: 99. These aspects are ignored when the *BhG* is regarded as a text for the 'masses', in which Arjuna represents 'the common man', as suggested, for instance, by Hill (1928: 44).

it into something 'private', and is basically an expression of 'solipsism'. In contrast to this, the vision of Vedic poets was embedded in a priestly brotherhood and subject to evaluation in poetic competition. While there is certainly a difference between these two contexts, it seems doubtful whether a Vedic poet's vision was less 'private' than Arjuna's, since other poets and priests know of his vision only through his poetic formulations and perhaps from seeing him 'trembling'.[186] We may recall that there are three participants relating the vision: Kṛṣṇa announcing and explaining his appearances, Saṃjaya's comments and Arjuna's own words. This narrative structure points to a rather intense concern for authorising the vision by establishing an appropriate, but also familiar, referential framework. An important dimension of this framework, not considered by Whillier, is the relationship between Kṛṣṇa and Arjuna, which is the basis not only of the vision, but also of Arjuna's temporary capacity to praise. The fact that this does not result in Arjuna becoming a 'professional' poet corroborates the situational and interpersonal character of hymnic praise in the context of *bhakti* theology. After losing his 'divine sight', Arjuna ceases composing stanzas.

However, in our text the personal relationship is also a social one, as has been made clear in characterising both Arjuna and Kṛṣṇa as kings who wear the diadem (11.6, 35, 46). Neither Brahman priests nor Vedic rituals are required for the 'sacrifice of war' that is presided over and brought about by the god in the form of time. Arjuna is the royal priest-poet who finds the hymnic formulation when facing the sacrificial fire that is kindled by time. While the god himself is the sacrificial fire, the presiding god and patron of the sacrifice, Arjuna is called on to act as his priest in this imminent sacrifice of destruction as one who sings the praises of the god to whom he is going to sacrifice other warriors and family members. This establishes a direct relationship between the earthly ruler and the divinity which does not need direct brahmanical legitimacy, but uses the idiom and structure of Vedic sacrifice in order to authorise the truth of its revelation. It confirms an important dimension of the Vedic discourse and subsequent brahmanical order, in that the alliance and mutual dependence between 'priest' and 'king' are acknowledged (Heesterman 1985): there is no king without a priest to offer and praise. No god is revealed or envisaged outside poetic and ritual language. Although Arjuna remains a Kṣatriya, in this precise moment he is performing priestly functions.

[186] For a more complex account of the Vedic contexts, see Gonda 1963.

Yet this does not contradict the innovative character of the new theology, which depicts the god as being a powerful *yogin* and supreme ruler, as well as the 'father' and 'beloved' friend who takes care of those who realise that they belong to him. Neither correct ritual nor 'good' birth is required when approaching the god: he is related to all beings as the protector and creator of the cosmos and the procurer of liberation. Similarly, 'his' earthly king is responsible for all beings and the maintenance of social order, not as an absolute ruler, but as subordinated to and protected by the supreme god (Biardeau 1997: 78ff.). This entails the inclusion of all people in his realm and in proximity to the god. The communication between god and devotee by means of a personal vision is one of the bases of *bhakti* that has been retained even when access to images of the god in temples becomes subject to brahmanic priests and the corresponding notions of ritual purity. However, as the case of Arjuna shows, the personal attachment based on *bhakti* is not the only requirement of the vision; the *bhakta* needs to have additional, often yogic, qualities, as is indicated by the 'divine sight'. In order to see the god, Arjuna has to acquire one of the powers of a successful *yogin* first. Once both requirements have been fulfilled, vision becomes possible. This may suggest that the *darśana* concept of *bhakti* theologies was perhaps developed by drawing on notions of visualisations of gods and even conquests of their domains in yogic practices.[187]

The context-sensitivity of a *darśana* can be regarded as one of its characteristic features. Apart from the iconographical standardisation that temple-based image worship entails, the *darśana* accounts found in earlier epic and purāṇic literature show a remarkable variety in that the god's appearance often corresponds to the quest and situation of the devotee. *BhG* 11 is perhaps one of the oldest examples of this structure when the vision brings Arjuna right back to the situation from which he departed: he is shown the very battleground he stands on.[188] Yet the *BhG* is similar to the original poetic situation described in Vedic texts, in which the hymns are said to have been composed in reaction to a vision, and then handed down and used by sacrificial priests as ritual liturgy. A similar development seems to have taken place in *bhakti* contexts. In later *bhakti* traditions, hymns and

[187] A similar yogic concept of *darśana* is referred to in the Nārāyaṇīya section and corroborated by the counter-example of a failed vision given in the Eka-Dvita-Trita story (see Malinar 1997: 247–258).

[188] For instance, in the *Nārāyaṇīya* section we find different visions of Nārāyaṇa (see Malinar 1997: 264–273). Kṛṣṇa too shows different forms to different people, e.g. in *MBh* 5.129, when he proves his alliance with the Pāṇḍavas by showing them in the form of parts of his body. For other visions in the epic, see Laine 1989.

recitations serve to win the *darśana* of the god, a situation that implies an established tradition of knowledge about the god. This is corroborated by the use of *BhG* 11 for ritual recitation in later traditions (Biardeau 1981: 133ff.). Texts are used to invite the god to show himself to the devotee, a practice similar to the use of mantras and so-called *dhyānas* in meditations that aim at invoking the god. However, poetic skill and expression remained part and parcel of the encounter (*darśana*) with the beloved god or goddess in many *bhakti* traditions. The personal and situational dimensions of the actual vision left room for a continuous production of new hymns and songs in praise of the god in *bhakti* contexts.

The originality of the vision and, as a consequence, of its hymnic expression is repeatedly emphasised ('not seen before', *adṛṣṭapūrva*; 11.6, 45, 47). Therefore explanations are called for, and not until Arjuna knows what and whom he sees does he not only report a vision, but also offer his praise, which means that he interprets and comments on his vision too. He starts by declaring that it is indeed justified that the world is 'enthralled and pleased to sing the praise' of the Lord (11.36). This is expanded on in a rhetorical question answered by a list of vocatives, epithets and identifications addressed to Kṛṣṇa: 'Why should they [the hosts of gods] not praise you? You mighty self, first creator even greater than Brahmā, Infinite, Lord of the gods, home of the world, you are imperishable, what is and is not and what surpasses both' (11.37). Kṛṣṇa is identified with Vedic gods like Vāyu or Varuṇa, and the god Brahmā (or *brahman*; Zaehner 1969: 313ff.) is subordinated to the god. This is followed by identifications introduced with the '*namo namaḥ*' formula used in ritual mantras and means 'homage to you': 'I praise you everywhere, You All (*sarvo*), of infinite strength and immeasurable prowess; you have brought together the all (*sarvam*), and therefore you are all (*sarvo*)' (11.40). Addressing Kṛṣṇa as the 'all' (*sarvaḥ*, masculine) is a significant assertion of Kṛṣṇa's lordship over the cosmos, since other cosmic creators and powerful beings are regarded as 'the whole' (*sarvam*, neut.) too. As D'Sa demonstrates (1982), the shift from the neuter *sarvam* to the masculine *sarvaḥ* marks this transition from being powerful as bringing together 'all' as the cosmic ruler to being 'the all' within the monotheistic framework. The two dimensions of universality that mark a cosmic creator and universal ruler, *viśva* and *sarva* (Gonda 1957), are united in Kṛṣṇa, the one and only. This marks the culmination of Arjuna's praise and, as a consequence, at this point his enthusiasm turns into a concern for their relationship, which now appears in a different light, since his friend and ally, his *sakha*, has now disclosed his other, hidden identities.

(Better) be human

Faced with this revelation, Arjuna worries about perhaps having treated Kṛṣṇa disrespectfully on earlier occasions: 'Believing you to be my companion (*sakha*), I have spontaneously called on you (exclaiming), "Hey, Kṛṣṇa, hey, Yādava, hey, comrade" – unaware of your might out of negligence or perhaps out of affection' (11.41).[189] He begs Kṛṣṇa to forgive him (11.42) and praises his superior position as the 'father' (*pītā*) and venerable 'teacher' (*ācārya, guru*) of the world, whose power is incomparable (11.43). Having acknowledged his divine friend's supremacy, Arjuna then asks that their former relationship be maintained as far as its affective dimension is concerned: 'Therefore, I bow to you, prostrate my body and crave your favour, adorable Lord! Please have patience with me, like a father with his son, like a companion with a companion, like a lover with his beloved, O God!' (11.44). While accepting the new hierarchy between Kṛṣṇa, the god, and Arjuna, his devotee, the actual relationships that are considered expressive of *bhakti* confirm its characteristic features: mutual dependence, reciprocity, affection and a sense of belongingness.[190] Well-established social relationships of kinship (father–son), friendship/comradeship (*sakha*) and love (*priya*) are now placed within the religious framework of *bhakti*.[191] While kinship indicates genealogy and continuity of descent and implies an awareness of one's origin, it also implies a temporal dimension that places the son indebted to his father until he himself becomes a father and reaches, after death, the world of the ancestors. The father, in his turn, has to care for the well-being of the son in all respects. This aspect is also emphasised when relationships of power such as that between a king and his people are described (see Hokpins 1911 on *rājabhakti*). Friendship and companionship, as well as love, depend on the co-existence of both parties and imply affection and a certain degree of intimacy. Although it may not be the case that both partners are always equal or of the same rank, mutual dependence and reciprocity are essential for maintaining this relationship. In particular, the *sakha* relationship also has the character of an alliance, especially of affinal relations. In the context of Kṣatriya relationships, it is connected with the achievement of the warrior's goals, such as victory in

189 The familiarity and affection of the two as *sakhas* is described, for instance, in *MBh* 5.58 and hinted at in the *AG*.

190 This is neglected when Minor (1982: 354) notes that 'the emphasis here is on Kṛṣṇa's side of the relationship'.

191 All three types of relationship were kept in later *bhakti* traditions, while other forms were added, such as *dāsa*, 'being a servant'. Other texts allow for a reversal of the roles in the paternal relationship when a devotee may act as a parent towards the child Kṛṣṇa (*vātsalya*).

war. However, it has to be kept in mind that in Vedic contexts too, there is a quest to establish good and advantageous relationships and alliances with the gods of the sacrifice.[192] In these contexts, 'mutual sharing' (*bhaga*) and other derivatives of the verbal root *bhaj* (from which *bhakti* also derives) are mentioned as important aspects of creating such alliances (Coomarasvamy 1942). In the context of *bhakti* theology, this is made to depend on knowledge, mutual affection, and ascetic or yogic qualifications. However, whether in the context of Vedic sacrificial alliances or of *bhakti*, this results in establishing alliances and personal relationships that do not depend on rules of kinship, but may very well result in kinship alliances.

The request basically to keep their former relationship is substantiated when Arjuna next (11.45–46) asks Kṛṣṇa to show him his four-armed form again as supreme sovereign holding mace and discus and wearing the royal diadem, because his other form is too terrible and frightening. This refers back to 11.17, but now includes the information that the god has four arms (*caturbhuja*; see above, pp. 170ff.). Kṛṣṇa's reply includes a confirmation of Arjuna's description and the exclusiveness of the vision:

> Out of favour for you, Arjuna, I have shown you through the yogic power of myself my highest form, which is of fiery nature, universal, infinite, primeval, and which has not been seen by anyone but you. Not by the Vedas, sacrifices or study, or by gift-giving, or by ritual or grim austerities, can I be seen in this form, but only by you, hero of the Kurus. You must not be shaken or confused when you see this fearsome form of mine. With fear dispelled and in good spirits, see now again that very (familiar) form of mine! (11.47–49)

These verses are programmatic in several respects. First, the manifestation of three different forms of Kṛṣṇa, which are all traced back to Kṛṣṇa's use of his yogic power over or of himself, is confirmed. Secondly, these forms are cosmic and have a fiery and solar character; one of them is terrible, but this should not confuse the true devotee, who knows that even the terrible is just another form of god. Thirdly, the theological statement (repeated in 11.53) that Kṛṣṇa cannot not be reached and seen by other, well-known means such as austerities or Vedic sacrifice reflects the exclusivity demanded from the devotee of Kṛṣṇa (cf. *BhG* 7, 9). Fourthly, the uniqueness and originality of the vision are stressed in the repeated statement that only Arjuna is capable of seeing him like this, and no one before him.

Saṃjaya comments that Kṛṣṇa granted Arjuna's wish and 'showed him once more his form of before, and put that terrified man to rest by becoming

[192] E.g. in *ṚV* 8.48.4 the poet asks Soma to be 'friendly like a father to his son' and 'insightful like a companion towards a companion' (*pitṛva soma sūnāve suśrāvaḥ / sākheva sākhya uruśaṃsa dhīraḥ*).

again his gentle old self' (11.50; trans. van Buitenen). The visionary process is reversed in that Kṛṣṇa appears again in the four-armed form and then resumes his 'gentle', *saumya* form, which in 11.51 is described as 'human' (*mānuṣa rūpa*) and is obviously distinguished from the four-armed form.[193] Seeing Kṛṣṇa again in his familiar appearance, Arjuna is relieved and regains his normal condition (*prakṛti*; 11.51). He loses his divine sight and is no longer shaken; Kṛṣṇa and Arjuna continue to be dear friends. However, theirs is a friendship empowered by the alliance between the supreme god and his royal devotee (see also 18.78, where this alliance is given its final confirmation in the very last verse of the *BhG*). Although Arjuna had declared at the beginning of chapter 11 that all his confusion had gone, the vision again makes him lose his bearings. However, he recovers himself because he is now embedded in a personal and cosmic relationship with what will become manifest on the battlefield. Although all his fears about the destruction of his family are justified, he should now understand that it is his part to be the sign (*nimitta*) and executor of the inevitable regime of the god of time, who calls for the 'sacrifice of battle' in order to re-establish a flourishing kingdom.

After Arjuna has resumed his 'usual' condition, Kṛṣṇa turns to him once more and resumes the position of a teacher (also indicated by another change of metre back to *śloka*). He points out that only Arjuna received the vision, the *darśana* (11.52), although the gods, too, desire to gain it. Nothing but *bhakti* can procure this vision, which is also the basis for reaching the god: 'Only through exclusive devotion (*bhakti*) can I be seen like this and known in my true identity and entered into, enemy-tamer.' This is followed by a concluding summary (11.55): 'Only he comes to me, Pāṇḍava, who acts for me, who holds me as the highest (*mat-parama*), who is devoted to me without self-interest (*saṅga-varjita*) and without any animosity against any creature.' Taking all these aspects of the practice of *bhakti* together, devotion amounts to a change of life-style because it means giving up egoistic motives as is demanded in *karmayoga* (cf. *BhG* 2, 3). The request to act for the sake of the god recalls the reinterpretation of *saṃnyāsa* (renunciation of social and ritual duties) as a practice in which all activity is transferred to and laid down in the cause of all activity (*brahman* or *prakṛti*; *BhG* 3, 5, 6) and is continued for the sake of maintaining the world (*lokasaṃgraha*). Now all actions and their karmic results are given up in Kṛṣṇa, and performing acts becomes a permanent ritual for the 'Supreme'. This is based on knowledge

193 Srinivasan (1997: 147) is of the opinion that *saumya* refers to the four-armed form. However, there is not much textual evidence for this assumption, and two-armed representations of Vāsudeva-Kṛṣṇa are also found at an early date.

and devotion, which means that any affection for other gods must be relinquished too. In combining these aspects, on the one hand, the practice of *bhakti* circumvents karmic bondage caused by entanglement in one's social duties. On the other hand, it avoids the difficulties implied in giving up social life and becoming an ascetic renouncer no longer interested in worldly affairs. The feasibility of this programme is guaranteed by its divine propagator, since Kṛṣṇa embodies both his lordship over all creatures for the sake of the creatures, and his transcendent, separate existence as the highest self. Applied to Arjuna's problem, this means that the conflict between the law of the family and that of the warrior is removed by *bhakti*. Arjuna must understand that he owes loyalty only to the Highest Lord, who guarantees that the institution of the kingship survives the destruction of individual kings, royal families and dynasties.

BHAGAVADGĪTĀ 12: *BHAKTI*

BhG 11 is the culmination not only of the depiction of Kṛṣṇa as the highest being and cosmic god and sovereign, but also of the interpretation of social duty as a means of liberation when it is performed for the sake of the god and the world. Together with the core arguments presented in the previous chapters and at the end of *BhG* 18, *BhG* 1–11 can be regarded as a comprehensive and complete text. Chapters 12 to 18 comment and expand on issues and doctrines in the previous chapters and are probably later additions.[194] This may explain the compounded character of the chapters, which are only loosely connected to each and do not follow any specific argument, but seem to have the function of clarifying some of the notions that were only touched on in earlier chapters. In doing so, the monotheistic framework plays a central role, although not always. Chapters 13 and 17 and parts of chapter 18 include very few references to Kṛṣṇa as god. Most of the chapters are concerned to clarify the relationship between different religious practices, such as *bhakti*, *saṃnyāsa* or yoga, and goals of liberation, such as *puruṣa*, *akṣara* or Kṛṣṇa. According to one tradition of scholarship, the *BhG* advocates a synthesis of different doctrines and thus allows different paths of liberation. As a consequence, the *BhG* is regarded as teaching different forms of yoga, such as *karmayoga*, *jñanayoga* and *bhaktiyoga*, as

194 Von Humboldt (1826a: 46) was the first to suggest that the original text had ended with *BhG* 11; see also Minor 1982: 362; Schreiner 1991: 171; Malinar 1996. With regard to the contrast between *BhG* 11 and 12, Zaehner notes (1969: 321): 'The opening of this chapter must be one of the biggest anti-climaxes in literature.' Bhargava (1977) regards *BhG* 12–18 as older than the preceding chapters, because of the small number of theistic interpolations. See also Szczurek 2005.

equivalent religious practices (see e.g. Lamotte 1929: 115). However, while some doctrines are indeed synthesised by means of identification, this is almost always done in order to establish a hierarchy of goals and practices, with one goal being supreme. This is also true of *BhG* 12, a chapter that is often quoted in support of the 'synthetic' interpretation.

The chapter starts with Arjuna's request for an explanation of the relationship between two different goals that ascetics and devotees strive for: 'Who are best among the *yogins*, those who revere you as (your) devotees and are constantly engaged in yoga practice, or those who (revere) the imperishable (*akṣara*) that is unmanifest (*avyakta*)?' (12.1). The two goals were dealt with earlier: while a realm of liberation called *akṣara*, *avyakta* or *brahman* was discussed in *BhG* 2, 5 and 6, these were superseded by Kṛṣṇa as the 'supreme' in *BhG* 6–9 and 11. In line with the latter, chapter 12 aims to establish Kṛṣṇa as the preferable goal: 'Those I deem the best practitioners of yoga who let their mind enter me and serve me while always practising yoga because they having the highest faith (*śraddhā*)' (12.2). The subordination of the other goal is achieved not by rejecting the salvific nature of the unmanifest, but by making it part of the path to the god. Kṛṣṇa points out that those who revere the 'imperishable' that cannot be expressed (*anirdeśya*) also reach him, since they control their senses, are indifferent and are dedicated to the 'welfare of all beings' (*sarvabhūta-hite ratāḥ*; 12.4).[195] However, the path to Kṛṣṇa via the unmanifest is more difficult and the affliction or toil (*kleśa*) greater: 'The affliction is greater for those whose thought are directed at the Unmanifest, for a goal that is invisible (*avyakta*) is hard (*duḥkham*) to attain for the embodied' (12.5). Along with Zaehner (1969: 322–4), I regard the description of the Unmanifest as based on *BhG* 5, 6 and 8. However, while *BhG* 6 ends by depicting the *yogin* who 'sees everywhere the same', *BhG* 12 qualifies this 'sameness' as a state superseded by Kṛṣṇa, the ultimate goal of yoga. Within the monotheistic framework, different goals can be distinguished according to definitions of the absolute as impersonal and personal respectively, as a state with or without qualities. The 'unmanifest' seems to imply the absence of corporeality or any other 'token', which makes concentration difficult for an embodied being. Moreover, *yogins* 'attaching their consciousness to the unmanifest' (*avyakta-āsakta-cetas*; 12.5) lack not only devotion, but also the knowledge that would allow them to reach Kṛṣṇa directly. This defect is also indicated by the use of two words in 12.5, *kleśa* (affliction) and *duḥkha* (pain, suffering; although used here adverbially), which the *yogin* usually tries to extinguish

[195] This formula is also used in *BhG* 5.25; cf. Hein 1986.

(see also *BhG* 6.17, 23). Thus, the path to Kṛṣṇa is attractive, not because it offers the same as paths or goals taught in other religious or philosophical traditions,[196] but because it means less affliction and pain. This connects chapter 12 with the subordination of other cults and gods to the exclusive worship of Kṛṣṇa proposed in chapters 7 and 9.

In contrast to the difficult path to the Unmanifest, the path of devotion appears here as the more desirable form of yoga: 'But for those who renounce (*saṃnyāsya*) all their acts in me, considering me the highest, paying reverence by meditating on me in exclusive yoga practice, I will soon be the saviour from the ocean of recurrent death, since their consciousness has entered into me' (12.6–7). Instead of equating himself with some unmanifest realm or being, the devoted *yogin* is advised to let his mind enter the god and become absorbed in him (12.8). These verses draw on the reinterpretation of renunciation (*saṃnyāsa*) given in *BhG* 9.27–28 (see also 9.34; 11.55). Renunciation is no longer understood as a way of life based on discarding social and ritual duties, or as renouncing the desire for the fruits, or as substituting the agency of the cosmic source of all activity (*brahman*, *prakṛti*, *BhG* 3, 5) for one's own, but as renouncing them in Kṛṣṇa, who is regarded as the sole supervisor, inciter and (indifferent) enjoyer of all activities. Kṛṣṇa is the only place for renunciation and attachment: there is no devotion without *saṃnyāsa* and, conversely, *saṃnyāsa* is successful only when directed at Kṛṣṇa (Lamotte 1929: 97f.; Biardeau 1976; above, pp. 129ff.). The ideal *bhakta* is the true renouncer because he is capable of redirecting his desires by practising yoga focussed on Kṛṣṇa alone. This is the highest and most efficient form of devotion, since liberation will follow suit. Although this method does not necessarily require one to leave the social world, it is no less demanding than other forms of yoga and asceticism, as Minor has emphasised (1982: 368): 'To understand devotion to Kṛṣṇa as the path for the one of weaker temperament is completely out of keeping with the Gītā.' While this is true with regard to the ascetic version of *bhakti*, the statement needs to be qualified when it comes to including simple acts of devotion, such as offering flowers or singing the Lord's praise, as efficient and respectable expressions of *bhakti* (see 9.14, 26f.), although they may result not in liberation, but in gaining merit and heavenly sojourns (cf. 7.17–18). This is why different types of *bhakta* need to be distinguished in 7.16–19, as in 12.9–11.

196 Zaehner (1969: 326) also subscribes to this distinction, though creating ambiguity by twice noting that there is no distinction between the imperishable and Kṛṣṇa (1969: 325). See also Minor 1982: 367.

These verses offer a spectrum of alternative practices for those who are not capable of performing the yogic form of *bhakti*. Arjuna is told that he should train himself in yoga (*abhyāsa-yoga*) when he is not yet able to practise yogic meditation on Kṛṣṇa (12.9). If this does not suit him, he should perform all acts for the sake of Kṛṣṇa and win success. If this does not do either, he should give up the fruits of his actions (*sarva-karma-phala-tyāga*) by being self-controlled and taking refuge in 'my yoga' (*madyogam āśrita*;[197] 12.11). This kaleidoscopic presentation of the different methods of avoiding karmic bondage recalls similar suggestions in previous chapters. The passage suggests that the common denominator of all these practices is the relinquishment of the fruits of action, as initially proposed to Arjuna in *BhG* 2.47. Performing acts for Kṛṣṇa recalls *BhG* 9.1, while the yogic version of *saṃnyāsa* that aims at liberation in Kṛṣṇa puts the adept on a still different level, a point made in *BhG* 6.15, 30–31. However, this quite clear-cut exposition is complicated by verse 12.12, which seems to introduce a different evaluation of practices that have been outlined before: 'For (*hi*) knowledge (*jñāna*) is better than training (*abhyāsa*); meditation (*dhyāna*) is higher than knowledge; relinquishing (*tyāga*) the fruits of acts is better than meditation; and from relinquishing, peace (*śānti*) immediately springs' (12.12). This verse has puzzled quite a few scholars, the problem being that the relinquishing of fruits is here given a higher rank than in the preceding enumeration of practices. While in *BhG* 12.11 it is regarded as the minimum requirement, in 12.12 it is said that it surpasses all other practices.[198] In order to cope with this tension, it is helpful to consider the particle *hi* (for, since), which connects 12.12 with the demand for relinquishment (*tyāga*) in 12.11 by giving a reason. The reason seems to be that, in contrast to other practices, relinquishment has an immediate (*anantaram*) effect: it gives 'peace' (*śānti*). The relinquishing of desires is not only the precondition of all ascetic practices, it is also a permanent requirement, since desire can emerge at all stages of practice, even when meditating (see *BhG* 3.6; 6.38f.). Relinquishment is thus the first and last thing to do, and in this regard it surpasses all other aspects of *bhakti*. Seen from this perspective, the tension between the two verses seems less strong when one regards 12.12 as explaining the efficacy of relinquishment and as a comment on the whole

[197] Zaehner (1969: 328) rejects the reading '*madyoga*' and prefers '*udyoga*'. However, there is no real reason to do so, since in several passages of the *BhG*, Kṛṣṇa has discussed 'his yoga' (cf. 4.1; 9.5).

[198] Von Humboldt, for instance, calls this 'the most unclear passage of the Gītā' (1826b: 251). Hill (1928: 219) distinguished between relinquishment with (12.9–11) and without (12.12) *bhakti*. Minor (1982: 371) accepts this view, while Zaehner (1968: 329) draws attention to the absence of devotion in 12.11. Without dealing with the problem, van Buitenen (1981: 168) states, with regard to 12.12: 'This is perhaps the most unequivocal statement of the superiority of *karmayoga* to *jñānayoga*.'

list of practices. The passage thus advocates other forms of *bhakti*, apart from its ideal form of yogic absorption in the god, by allowing only some of its components to be practised. In this way, the different capacities of devotees are not only taken care of, but are also connected to one another, thus making the relinquishing of egotistical desires a prerequisite of *bhakti* at all levels.

The rest of the chapter deals with different groups or types of ascetics who are all 'dear' (*priya*) to Kṛṣṇa. Again it may be recalled that the word 'dear' has connotations of being one's 'own' or 'favourite' and thus of belongingness as the basis of affection and preference (see Scheller 1950, Bodewitz 2002). In every verse (except 12.15), it is explicitly stated that the ascetic is also a devotee. The list starts with the *yogin* devoted to Kṛṣṇa (12.13–14). He is free from egotism and aversion (*adveṣṭā*) towards living beings. He is friendly (*maitra*) and compassionate (*karuṇa*) because his mind is dedicated to Kṛṣṇa. The terminology used here recalls Buddhist descriptions of ascetic virtues (for instance, the so-called *brahmavihāra*; Zaehner 1969: 329). When someone is free from joy, intolerance (*āmarṣa*), fear and turmoil (*udvega*), he is dear to Kṛṣṇa (12.15). The same is true of a devotee who is indifferent and has relinquished all undertakings that seek to fulfil desires (*ārambha*), as well as the one who has given up both pleasant and unpleasant things (12.16). The ascetic qualifications are again summarised in 12.18–19, which treats of the lonely ascetic who has given up his home (*aniketa*) and all other attachments. Different ascetic life-styles and virtues are turned into elements of devotion to Kṛṣṇa, all of which help to win the god's favour. Yet a distinction is drawn in the very last verse, which treats of those who are 'exceedingly dear' to the god, the 'believers' (*śraddadhāna*), who put all their confidence in Kṛṣṇa's words (*uktam*) and see his revelation as an 'elixir full of *dharma*' (*dharmyāmṛta*; 12.20). This is a first step in making the 'words' of the god the motive and object of devotional practice and vesting them with an authority and efficacy that surpasses other traditions. Confidence in Kṛṣṇa's words implies that devotion is exclusive ('they have me as their highest'). In claiming that Kṛṣṇa's speech is full of *dharma*, the new doctrine claims a status comparable to what is traditionally regarded as *dharma*, in that it not only determines one's personal life, but also places it in the larger context of cosmology and society in providing a comprehensive explanation of the created world and of liberation from it. The idea that this praise by the devotees is what Kṛṣṇa likes best corroborates the previous analysis (see 3.9; Minor 1980) of the relationship to other traditions. While there is certainly an acknowledgement of other gods, cults and highest beings, they are not considered equal or tolerated as viable alternatives.

Rather, the exclusivity and specific requirements of the devotion to Kṛṣṇa distinguish it from other traditions.

BHAGAVADGĪTĀ 13: *PRAKṚTI* AND *PURUṢA*

The transition to this chapter is indicative of the loose arrangement of the last six chapters of the *BhG*. Neither terminologically not conceptually is Kṛṣṇa's definition of important terms of Sāṃkhya philosophy in 13.1[199] connected with the topic of *bhakti* discussed in *BhG* 12. What is almost exclusively dealt with is Sāṃkhya philosophy. Only occasionally (and not consistently, as is the case in *BhG* 14 and 15) is it made 'theistic' by superimposing Kṛṣṇa on the constituents of being (*tattva*) taught in Sāṃkhya (13.10, 18). While in classical Sāṃkhya only two principles are regarded as without beginning and therefore the 'highest' principles, namely consciousness *(puruṣa)* and creative nature *(prakṛti)*, they are superseded by another principle or a 'highest god', not only in the *BhG*, but also elsewhere in the epic (e.g. 12.296). In *BhG* 13, not only is Kṛṣṇa named as the additional element, but so are *brahman* (13.12), the highest self *(paramātman)* and mighty lord (*maheśvara*; 13.22). The relationship between these entities is not explained in detailed and remains rather vague. This fluidity in terminology and in enumeration of the principles is characteristic of so-called 'epic philosophy'. Epic Sāṃkhya differs from the classical Sāṃkhya of the *SK* in other respects too. First, the epic does not mention the *tanmātras*, the subtle matrices of the visible five elements (fire, water, etc.) that are usually listed in the *SK* (Schrader 1955). Secondly, it deals in more detail with the cosmological nature and powers of the first product of the contact between consciousness and nature, what in the epic is often called *mahat*, the mighty or large, *sattva* ('being', often synonymous with *buddhi*; van Buitenen 1957b) or *avyaktam*, the unmanifest about to create the cosmos or an individual body. In the *SK*, this stage is called *buddhi*, emphasising its cognitive character. Thirdly, *prakṛti* is often considered a plurality of seven or eight *prakṛtis* (see above, pp. 130ff., on *BhG* 7.4), and not the singular cause of all creatures as in the *SK*.

With regard to its terminological fluidity, the present chapter resembles Sāṃkhya teaching elsewhere in the epic. While the first part of the chapter deals with the two highest principles using the terms 'field' (*kṣetra*) for nature and 'knower of the field' (*kṣetrajña*) for consciousness, in the second

[199] Zaehner has the chapter start with a question by Arjuna, transmitted in some manuscripts, and comments that this chapter is 'the most confused in the whole of the Gītā' (1969: 332–333).

part (13.19–21) they are called *prakṛti* and *puruṣa* respectively. Here, *prakṛti* is used in the singular, as is the case in classical Sāṃkhya too.

The first part includes a theological interpretation which comes right at the beginning, when Kṛṣṇa is added to these two principles, thus assuming the role and function of the '*kṣetrajña* in all *kṣetras*' (13.2), of 'consciousness in all bodies'. As a consequence, all individual, embodied 'field-knowers' become parts of his superior consciousness and, conversely, all embodied beings are turned into 'fields' of his knowledge. This echoes *BhG* 7.26 in declaring that the god knows all, but no one knows him. Yet this superimposition of Kṛṣṇa has no further consequences for the account of Sāṃkhya that Kṛṣṇa asks Arjuna to learn in 13.3, which deals with not only with 'field' (defined in 13.1 as the 'body', *śarīra*), and 'field-knower', but also with the latter's 'power' (*prabhāva*; 13.3). This shows that, in the epic, Sāṃkhya-embodied consciousness not only is subject to error or the attractions of nature, but also holds a certain power over it (cf. *BhG* 15.8; see below, pp. 203ff.). Kṛṣṇa declares that his teaching is based on an extant tradition of teachers, since this knowledge has been 'sung' (*gīta*) about by different sages in hymns and in the 'reasoning words in the Brahmasūtras' (van Buitenen 1981: 168). Kṛṣṇa is here presented as a typical teacher seeking to establish his authority on the reputation of the sources he relies on. The occurrence of the compound *brahmasūtra* made scholars speculate whether or not this refers to the Brahmasūtras of Bādārāyaṇa (c. second century CE).[200] I agree with Zaehner (1969: 335) and van Buitenen (1981: 168), who both point out that there are no convincing arguments for either opinion and suggest that the question is better left undecided.

The account begins in 7.5 with an enumeration of the constituents of the body (*kṣetra*) comprising the five gross elements (*mahābhūta*): ego-consciousness (*ahaṃkāra*), the faculty of discrimination (*buddhi*), the unmanifest (*avyakta*), the eleven senses (including *manas*) and the five sense-objects. Although some elements are identical to those of the 'eightfold *prakṛti*' in *BhG* 7.4 (five elements, *manas*, *buddhi*, *ahaṃkāra*), the term *prakṛti* is not mentioned in 13.5, and the mind (*manas*) is not considered a '*prakṛti*' but belongs to the senses, as it does in classical Sāṃkhya. The unmanifest refers to the powers of *prakṛti* in their unmanifest state, before the body actually evolves (Zaehner 1969: 336; van Buitenen 181: 168). As is typical of epic Sāṃkhya, it is not the *tanmātra*, the subtle elements, but

200 Garbe (1921: 140) follows Böhtlingk (1897), who thinks that Bādārāyaṇa is meant here, as does Mainkar (1978: 751–753). Others suggest that the Upaniṣads are being referred to: cf. Edgerton 1946: 127; Modi 1957: 139.

the sense-objects that are regarded as constituents of the body. The conditions or states of being, such as desire, hatred, happiness and suffering, are dealt with next. Other constituents are *saṃghāta*, the aggregation of the constituents of the body that makes a functioning body,[201] and *cetanā*, sensitivity or 'body consciousness' (van Buitenen 1981: 168), that is, the capacity to experience the world in terms of desire, suffering, etc. The list ends with *dhṛti*, stability of the body. Remarkably, the body is considered to possess sensitivity, *cetanā*, rendered by van Buitenen as 'body consciousness'. While *cetanā* certainly does not mean any capacity for reflection, it indicates the receptivity of the body towards experiences.

Next, the role of the 'field-knower' is dealt with as it appears in its knowledge (*jñāna*) of and influence (*prabhāva*) over its body.[202] This influence is based on the relationship that the embodied consciousness entertains towards the activities of the body on the one hand, and to the liberating knowledge on the other. The desirable relationship, allowing the 'field-knower' the greatest influence, consists in moral and physical purity and detachment from the sense-objects and family because one has realised the flaws of physical existence. This is liberating knowledge (*jñāna*), which is further defined as a firm understanding of what pertains to the self (*adhyātmajñānanityatva*)[203] and insight in the purpose of knowing the *tattvas*, the constituents of being (*tattvajñānārthadarśana*). What is described here is no mere 'theoretical' knowledge, but a 'thought-practice' pursued not only intellectually, but also with corresponding demeanour and life-style. Rather out of context, and without further consequences for the main argument of the chapter, ascetic devotion to Kṛṣṇa is mentioned in 13.10 as a practice indicative of true knowledge. This line of thought is not pursued further here as it is not the god Kṛṣṇa but *brahman* that is considered the object (*jñeya*) of knowledge in 13.12: 'I will now tell you what must be known; who knows this will reach immortality: it is called the beginningless, highest[204] *brahman*, which is neither existing nor not

201 Cf. van Buitenen (1981: 168). In the *SK*, *saṃghāta* is one of the causal activities of the three 'powers' (*guṇa*) of *prakṛti*; cf. Malinar 2003.

202 This is in line with topics mentioned in 13.3, and I see no reason to regard 13.7–25 as an interpolation, as Zaehner (1969: 336) suggests: 'It is . . . quite possible that verses 7–25 are an interpolation . . . This seems all the more probable in that the definition of "knowledge" in 7–11 is totally different from that in verses 2 and 34.' However, according to 13.2, the topic being dealt with is not the 'field-knower', but its power. Minor (1982: 382) also sees no reason to assume an interpolation.

203 According to *KaṭhU* 2.12, the god can be reached by *adhyātma-yoga*, yoga with regard to 'the self' or 'what belongs to the self' (*adhyātmayogādhigamena*).

204 The Sanskrit text runs '*anādimatparaṃ brahman*', which can be split up as either *anādimat paraṃ brahman* as suggested (cf. Garbe 1921: 141; Zaehner 1969: 338–339; van Buitenen 1981: 168) or *anādi matparam brahman*, a reading chosen by the philosopher Rāmānuja (twelfth century CE)

existing.' This differs from both the doctrine of the separation of consciousness and nature by realising their difference as proposed in classical Sāṃkhya, and theistic Sāṃkhya, with Kṛṣṇa as the goal of practice. This is quite similar to what we learned in *BhG* 2, 5 and 6 about *brahman* being the highest goal, as well as close to passages in the Upaniṣads and *MBh* 12. This becomes obvious in the subsequent description of *brahman*, which in its cosmic form not only encompasses the whole world but is also embodied in it. The description echoes the appearance of Kṛṣṇa as '*viśvarūpa*' in *BhG* 11. *Brahman* has arms and feet everywhere (cf. *ṚV* 10.90), is devoid of senses but reflects all their qualities, and is free from the powers of nature (*guṇa*), but still enjoys them. It is inside and outside creatures, but cannot be known because of its subtlety (*sūkṣmatva*); it is undivided, yet exists partially in creatures; it sustains, devours and creates. It is 'the light of lights beyond darkness' (*jyotiṣām api taj jyotis, tamasaḥ param ucyate*; 13.17), the knowledge residing in everyone's heart that must be acquired through knowledge. The parallels to this description in the Veda and Upaniṣads help us to understand the concept of *brahman* presented here. One of the closest parallels is the description of the *mahān puruṣa* in *ŚvetU* 3.16–17:

> With hands and feet everywhere, with eyes, heads, and faces everywhere, and with ears everywhere, that remains encompassing everything in the world [3.16 = *BhG* 13.13] – that which appears to possess the powers of all senses but is devoid of every sense, which is the lord, the ruler of the whole world, the vast refuge of the whole world.

Both passages are based on *ṚV* 10.81.3. While *BhG* 13.13[205] is an exact parallel of 3.16, there is a difference between *ŚvetU* 3.17cd and *BhG* 13.14cd.[206] Most scholars are of the opinion that here the *BhG* is quoting the Upaniṣad (Zaehner 1969: 340; Minor 1982: 388). However, Oberlies (1988: 58) considers this unlikely, since the passage in the *BhG* is more coherent and therefore the author of the *ŚvetU* must draw on the *BhG*. Still another possibility is that both texts share a similar discursive and textual environment, which, however, each text uses for its specific purpose. This seems to be the case in other passages where we encounter conceptual rather than exact literal

and accepted by Edgerton (1946: 129), which means 'the beginningless *brahman*, depending on me'. Hein (1975: 256) argues emphatically for this interpretation, regarding it as an example of a 'modifying addendum', a 'stylistic clue' the author of the *BhG* uses to turn non-theistic notions into monotheistic ones (cf. the critique by Minor 1982: 385). While this is certainly true of many other cases studied by Hein, it seems doubtful here; at least, it has not been done here unequivocally.

205 *BhG* 13.13 = *MBh* 12.213.29; 12.291.16; 12.300.14; etc.

206 Cf. *ŚvetU* 3.17: sarvendriyaguṇābhāsaṃ sarvendriyavivarjitam / *sarvasya prabhum īśānaṃ sarvasya śaraṇaṃ suhṛt* // *BhG* 3.14: sarvendriyaguṇābhāsaṃ sarvendriyavivarjitam / *asaktaṃ sarvabhṛc caiva nirguṇaṃ guṇabhoktṛ ca* //.

parallels. For instance, when *brahman* is said to be far away and yet near, within and without creatures, this echoes the description of the 'self' at *ĪśaU* 5 (cf. Zaehner 1969: 341) and *MuṇḍU* 3.1.7. Another example is 13.17, where the reference to another source is made explicit ('so it is said'; *ucyate*): '"The light of lights, beyond darkness" – this is how it is called'. While the 'light of lights' describes the *ātman* in *BĀU* 4.4.16ff., it is used for *brahman* in *MuṇḍU* 2.2.10. The place 'beyond darkness' is ascribed to *brahman* in *MuṇḍU* 2.2.6 and *MaitU* 6.24, and to *puruṣa* in *BhG* 8.9 and *ŚvetU* 3.8. Thus, well-known attributes are used to bring about the convergence of a cosmologically active *brahman* with the concept of the 'mighty self' (*mahān ātman*) that is taught elsewhere in the Upaniṣads and the epic.

As van Buitenen shows (1964), in both texts the *mahān ātman* is still a cosmological stage in its own right (see also *BhG* 5, and above, pp. 113ff.), while in classical Sāṃkhya it becomes absorbed by the stages of *buddhi* and *avyakta* respectively. The 'mighty self' represents 'the conception of a creator existing as *somebody*, and as embodied in creation' (van Buitenen 1964: 109). Cosmogony is 'somatogony'. In the *BhG* too, the impersonal character of *brahman* converges with the more personal of the *ātman*, a convergence that is the distinct feature of this entity in the context of epic Sāṃkhya cosmology. In this way, the individualised nature of *ātman-puruṣa* is linked to the impersonal dimension of the *avyakta-prakṛti* realm. It signifies the full potential of the powers of *prakṛti* and its susceptibility to the presence of *ātman-puruṣa* before the actual process of embodiment starts, which becomes the plenitude and vastness of all the possible forms that nature is capable of creating, and that the 'self' may take as its body as an individual, condensed creature. The entity that has, at first and as the 'first', 'arms' and 'feet' everywhere, appears next as two-armed, a biped or quadruped, etc. (cf. *MBh* 12.231.20ff.). The next step is the descent into an individual body. *MBh* 12.291.15–18 deals with the different terms used for that mighty and large (*mahantaṃ bhūtam*) visible (*mūrtimantam*) being, which is again described as possessing hands and feet everywhere: 'This golden embryo is called *buddhi* or *mahān*, and among *yogins* it is called "*viriñca*" and "imperishable" (*akṣara*). Yet in the manuals of Sāṃkhya, it is addressed by many different names, being called the "Multiform", "Self of the all" or "whose self is the all" (*viśvātmā*), "the only imperishable one" (*ekākṣara*).' In *MBh* 12.300.15 it is called the 'All' (*viśvam*) and the 'Lord' (*īśvara*).

All these parallels show the authors of these texts as especially concerned with this interface between the impersonal and personal, the manifest and unmanifest, that arises as the first product of creative activity. According to Sāṃkhya, it is the first and original union (*sam-yoga*) of nature and consciousness that produces a 'large' and 'mighty' being, a powerful, still cosmic entity that encompasses, sustains and produces the plenitude of creatures and possible embodiments before actual birth.[207] Vedic-Upaniṣadic and Sāṃkhya-Yoga cosmology seems to agree that whoever or whatever is called *mahān ātman*, *brahman*, *viriñca*, *viśva*, *viśvātmā* or *īśvara* is the very first stage of creation – in Sāṃkhya-yoga terminology, the union *(sam-yoga)* of consciousness and nature that the *yogin* and the 'seeker of knowledge' seek to dissolve (*vi-yoga*), as expressed in *BhG* 6.23.

BhG 13 presents the top-down account of this realm, described in *BhG* 5 and 6 from the perspective of a *yogin* 'conquering creation' and therefore becoming '*sarvabhutātman*', the self of all beings (cf. *BhG* 5, and see above, pp. 113ff.), and '*brahman*' (*brahmabhūta*; 5.24; 6.27; etc.). For the *yogin*, the stage is an interface and a crossroads because he becomes a powerful being (an *īśvara*) when he is linked to the powers and the plenitude of creation by exercising his yoga, and as the stage of liberation when he turns away from the manifest world, when yoga is no longer a powerful connection to the potential of nature, but means 'cutting the connection' (*saṃyoga-viyoga*; cf. 6.23). Seen in this context, the presentation of Sāṃkhya in *BhG* 13 becomes less 'confused' (Zaehner 1969: 332): on the contrary, it provides a welcome supplement to the teachings of previous chapters and confirms the Gītā's connection with Upaniṣadic and epic Sāṃkhya cosmology, rather than with classical Sāṃkhya. According to 13.18, a devotee of Kṛṣṇa who understands the difference between *puruṣa* and *prakṛti* will reach the god. This verse indicates that practising Sāṃkhya as a devotee is conducive to reaching the god, but it does not imply any hierarchisation. This is followed by another account of Sāṃkhya (13.19–26), in which the terms 'nature' (*prakṛti*) and 'consciousness' (*puruṣa*), not 'field' and 'field-knower', are used. The focus is on the *puruṣa*, who, on the one hand, is entangled in the realm of nature, experiencing the different qualities of objects. On the other hand, the principle of consciousness is also present on another level, on which it functions as an observer and a mighty lord of nature and is therefore called 'higher (*para*) *puruṣa*' (13.22). As before, the text deals with the two levels on which the principle of *puruṣa* is conceptualised: while in the previous section the stage of the first contact between consciousness

207 As explained in *AG* (*MBh* 14.40.1ff.): 'First, the mighty self (*mahān ātma*), whose thoughts are huge, arises from the unmanifest – it is the beginning and called the first creation of all powers of nature. It has hands and feet everywhere, eyes, heads and mouths on every side, and ears everywhere – it abides, pervading the universe . . . This *puruṣa*, whose radiance is shining brilliantly (*mahāprabhārci*) abides in the heart of every being.' See also 14.19.44–45; 12.298.16.

and nature is conceived in cosmological terms, indicating the vastness and plenitude of creation without the restrictions, the 'self' is still mighty and 'high'. When embodiment starts, the *puruṣa* becomes an embodied self, the 'knower of a (particular) field'. From the 'connection' between 'field' and 'field-knower', everything is created (13.26). This is called either *brahman* or *īśvara*, when the presence of a 'higher' self needs to be emphasised. The two levels implied in the product of the first contact between consciousness and nature form an essential aspect of Sāṃkhya philosophy and remain so in its theistic version, as we shall see in the analysis of *BhG* 15. The task of the embodied *puruṣa* is to return to that 'higher' level which is further described in 13.27–30, which does not deal with 'God immanent in His Creatures', as Zaehner (1969: 347) suggests. As a consequence, it restores its original vastness, plenitude and power as a mighty self and lord (13.22, 28), the 'vast *brahman*' (*vistāraṃ brahma*, 13.30). This is brought about by realising the true identity of the *puruṣa* as untouched by *prakṛti*'s actions (13.29, 31) and as forever separated from the manifest world. The liberating effect of this realisation is stressed in (13.23): 'The one who in this way understands consciousness and nature together with its powers (*guṇa*) will not be born again, irrespective of the state he finds himself in.' Different ways to access this 'highest' being are mentioned in 13.24–25: while some see it through meditation (*dhyāna*), others achieve it through yoga in the context of Sāṃkhya or through *karmayoga*, while still others worship it. It is an imperishable entity, a paramount sovereign (*parama-īśvara*; 13.27; cf. 13.28), who is the same in all beings and in whom all beings reside. Although it resides in the body, it has no qualities and is not affected by what happens to it. It is as subtle and ubiquitous as ether (*ākāśa*) and illuminates the body just as the sun lights up the universe (13.33), which confirms earlier statements such as that it is within and without creatures, distant and yet nearby (13.15). The chapter ends with the following declaration: 'Those who thus understand through the "eyesight of knowledge" (*jñānacakṣus*) the difference between the field and the knower of the field and liberation from material nature (*bhūtaprakṛti*)[208] reach the other side.'

This chapter presents the cosmology and soteriology of Sāṃkhya in the fluctuating terminology that is typical of the epic. The connection with

[208] The compound *bhūtaprakṛti* also occurs in *Cārakasaṃhitā*, *Śārīrasthāna* 1.63 and is defined as follows: 'The five elements, ether, etc., the faculty of discrimination, the unmanifest and ego-consciousness as the eight – this is known as material nature' (*khādīni buddhir avyaktam ahaṅkāras tathāṣṭamaḥ / bhūtaprakṛtir uddiṣṭā*). The list of the eight elements is similar to the first elements of the 'field' listed in *BhG* 13.5, which also include *avyakta*.

the epic and the Upaniṣads is also corroborated in the many parallel passages referred to before. Again, as in *BhG* 5 and, within the monotheistic framework, in *BhG* 11, particular emphasis is placed on the stage of the first, cosmic association between *puruṣa* and *prakṛti*, in which we see the *puruṣa* in command of the powers of nature before it is embodied as 'name and form'. In this stage, both the 'self' and 'nature' are truly cosmic entities in that the self assumes an 'all-form', while nature manifests its fullness and manifold character in showing a self embodied with many arms, eyes, etc. The theological comments inserted in 13.2, 10 and 18 suggest a superimposition of Kṛṣṇa on this scheme, which is, however, not pursued further in the present chapter.

BHAGAVADGĪTĀ 14: KṚṢṆA AND *BRAHMAN*

In this chapter, Kṛṣṇa's superiority with regard to the sphere of *brahman* as the realm of cosmological plenitude is explained. The use of Sāṃkhya terminology connects it to chapter 13 (see Minor 1982: 404; *contra*: Zaehner 1969: 351). The 'highest knowledge' taught in this chapter starts by declaring the 'large *brahman*' (*mahat brahman*) to be the womb (*yoni*) of Kṛṣṇa: 'The large *brahman* is my womb, in which I place the embryo, whence all beings are born, O Bhārata. Of the forms that are born in all wombs, O son of Kuntī, large *brahman* is the womb, I am the seed-giving father' (14.4). This procreative model of creation recalls the description of Kṛṣṇa's relationship to his *prakṛti* in *BhG* 7.5–6 and 10, where he is also regarded as providing the seed that activates the powers of *prakṛti*. Again the realms of *brahman* and *prakṛti* converge in their both being connected with Kṛṣṇa, who assumes the role of *puruṣa* because he is not equated with the 'womb' but regarded as the life-giving power that incites *brahman* (*prakṛti*) to create the universe. In contrast to the Sāṃkhya terminology used in much of this chapter, the first two stanzas allude to the Upaniṣadic concept of *brahman* as the womb of beings containing the 'golden embryo' (*garbha*), who then unfolds in the plenitude and multitude of beings. *MuṇḍU* 3.1.3, for instance, praises the 'person golden-hued, whose womb is *brahman*': 'When the seer sees that Person, the golden-coloured, the creator, the Lord, as the womb of brahman, then . . . the wise man becomes spotless . . .' (trans. Olivelle).

As in *BhG* 7, the procreative model introduces a distinction between the god as the inciter of creation and creation itself, because it results in a partial embodiment only, and the god can still remain unrelated and transcendent to creation. However, he is present in the world as the life-giving principle and as the 'embryo' (*garbha*). Yet after impregnation, the task of creating different bodies for the 'embodied self' is left to *prakṛti* and its three powers (*guṇa*). This process is dealt with in the ensuing description of the relationship between the different *guṇa*s and the embodied self (called *dehin*) (14.5–18), in which the effects of each of the three *guṇa*s on the self are listed. We find such lists, which may be called '*guṇa* texts', in *BhG* 17.7–13, 17–22 and 18.7–10, as well as in 18.19–44. Interpreters sometimes consider them tiresome (e.g. Deussen 1911: xxi), yet these lists are more often than not connected to the central theme of a text, as is the case in chapter 14, which focusses on the different forms of bondage and attachment (*saṅga*) of the embodied self, which can be overcome only by leaving the realm of the *guṇa*s for good. Although *sattva*, the highest, most luminous power of nature, brings the embodied self close to realising its true identity, it is still characterised by attachment to happiness (*sukha-saṅga*) and to knowledge (*jñānasaṅga*; 14.6). The *rajas* form of attachment is to *karman* (14.7), and *tamas*, dullness, ties the self down by negligence.

As a consequence, those who overcome the *guṇa*s acquire Kṛṣṇa's state of being and do not return (14.19). In a style similar to his question about the man 'whose insight is firm' (*sthitaprajña*) in 2.54, Arjuna asks about the characteristics of the one 'who has left the *guṇa*s behind' (14.21). In close similarity to descriptions of the *yogin* in *BhG* 2 and 6, these characteristics are detachment and indifference towards all activities and conditions of the powers of nature.[209] In drawing on the description of Kṛṣṇa's yogic detachment as similar to the 'neutral king' (*udāsīnavad āsīnam*; 9.9), the accomplished adept is said be unmoved by the *guṇa*s 'like a neutral party' (*udāsīnavad āsīno*; 14.23). This attitude results not only in reaching *brahman*, as is the case in *BhG* 6, but also in realising that *brahman* has its basis in Kṛṣṇa (14.27). This is achieved by serving the god with undeviating *bhaktiyoga*, self-control through devotion (14.26): 'The one who worships me with the imperturbable yogic practice of devotion (*bhaktiyogena*) passes beyond these powers of nature and is ready to become *brahman*. For I am the foundation of the immortal, unchanging *brahman*, of eternal *dharma* and unsurpassable happiness.'

This passage suggests that yoga based on *bhakti* not only yields rewards similar to those of other forms of yoga (which result in reaching and becoming *brahman*; 14.26), but also leads to knowing Kṛṣṇa as the beginning of that very *brahman* that others regard and strive for as without

[209] See also the parallels in the description of the indifferent *yogin*:
14.24a *samaduḥkhasukhaḥ* = 2.25c *samaduḥkhasukha*; cf. 6.7c *sītoṣṇasukhaduḥkheṣu*
14.24b *samaloṣṭāśmakāñcanaḥ* = 6.8d *samaloṣṭāśmakāñcanaḥ*
14.25a *mānāvamānayos tulyas* = 6.7d *tathā mānāvamānayoḥ*

beginning. Therefore, by practising *bhaktiyoga*, not only is *brahman* reached, but also a still higher being, Kṛṣṇa. The chapter ends by declaring Kṛṣṇa the 'foundation' (*pratiṣṭhā*)[210] of *brahman*, 'eternal *dharma*' (*śāśvata dharma*) and 'incomparable happiness' (*sukha-aikāntika*). In contrast to the description of yoga in *BhG* 6, which includes an equation between reaching the god and *brahmanirvāṇa*, chapter 14 establishes Kṛṣṇa's superiority by claiming that liberation in the god yields a happiness not to be found anywhere else. The latter claim is important, since 'happiness' is regarded as an element of liberation in other ascetic traditions too.[211] *BhG* 14.26 is the only occurrence of the term *bhaktiyoga* in the entire work. Some interpreters have suggested that the *BhG* teaches three different forms of yoga – *bhaktiyoga*, *karmayoga* and *jñānayoga* – and three different paths of liberation (e.g. Belvalkar 1929). According to some, these paths are synthesised in the *BhG* by placing *bhaktiyoga* at the top, while others think that all three are endorsed, the choice being left to the adept. However, it must be kept in mind that the word *bhaktiyoga* does not seem to be used as a technical term summarising the *bhakti* doctrines taught in the *BhG*, although later traditions would consider it one. It occurs in a context the aim of which is to superimpose Kṛṣṇa on the realms of liberation taught in Sāṃkhya, the Upaniṣads and other yoga traditions. In doing so, the cosmology and constituents of existence (*tattva*) taught in these traditions are retained, but the experience of liberation is modified in being directed towards a god who is both the cause of the cosmos and the highest, ever-liberated self, and who thus represents the ideal attitude towards physical existence: detachment from and therefore supremacy over the powers of nature (*guṇa*). The god not only is the ultimate goal, but also serves as a point of orientation and model of successful practice for those who practise yoga through and with *bhakti*. In *BhG* 14, this type of yoga is regarded as yielding better results than other forms. This is rather a hierarchisation than a synthesis, because the other paths have different goals and therefore cannot be recommended as equally valuable. Yet there is no need to reject them as 'wrong', because they, too, help one ultimately to reach the god, even if it takes longer. Seen from the perspective of the monotheistic framework established in the *BhG*, *bhaktiyoga* is certainly the type of yoga a devoted adept must practise. However, this does not make *bhaktiyoga* the overarching term for the different

210 On the meaning of this term as 'giving support' to another being's manifestation, see above, pp. 86ff.

211 Cf. *BhG* 5.21; 6.27–28 on the happiness of being *brahman*, and 6.21 on the happiness implied in realising the self. Because the adjective *aikāntika* is used, Matsubara (1994) suggests that 14.27 hints at Pāñcarātra doctrines. However, given the parallel passages in the *BhG* and the absence of any other evidence, this is not very convincing.

forms and aspects of *bhakti* taught in the *BhG*, although it is also the ideal form of *bhakti*. The emphasis on asceticism and yoga should not lead one to neglect the other forms of *bhakti* that are mentioned and recommended in the text. Mutual affection, loyalty, worshipping the god with flowers, singing his praises, thinking and talking of him, doing everything for him without looking for personal gain (*karmayoga*) are no less important aspects of *bhakti*. Allowing this large spectrum of *bhakti* is a characteristic feature of the theology of the *BhG*.

BHAGAVADGĪTĀ 15: KṚṢṆA AS 'SUPREME *PURUṢA*'

Without explicitly referring to the last chapter – though perhaps connected to its last verse, which declares Kṛṣṇa to be the 'foundation' of *brahman* and *dharma* – chapter 15 begins with a description of the 'inverted *aśvattha* tree',[212] which symbolises the created world: '"Having its roots above, its branches below and the Vedic hymns as its leaves" – (this is how) they describe the undecaying *aśvattha* tree' (15.1). This refers to the well-known image of the inverted tree that occurs already in ṚV 1.24.7. In her discussion of the Vedic symbolism of the 'mythic world-tree' that provides cosmic stability as the centre of the universe, Viennot (1954: 32) points out that, in contrast to the 'upright tree' as the symbol of cosmic stability, the 'inverted tree', with its leaves and branches filling the world, represents the plenitude of the cosmos. From her analysis of the equation of the inverted *aśvattha* tree with *brahman* in *KaṭhU* 6.1 and *MaitU* 6.3, she concludes that both texts 'invoke the *aśvattha* tree rooted in heaven only in order to describe better the ideal position of the divine principle: *brahman* is present in the whole universe and is, at the same time, solidly rooted in heaven, from which it manifests its power' (1954: 43, my trans.). While the Upaniṣads describe the tree in rather positive terms, the *BhG* offers a different view in the next four (*triṣṭubh*) verses.[213] The origin and proliferation of the tree are traced back to the powers of nature (*guṇa*). Therefore its roots grow downwards, into the world of men, entangling them in *karman*. Its shape, beginning, end and foundation (*sampratiṣṭhā*) cannot be apprehended here on earth.

[212] There has been some discussion of the botanical identification of the *aśvattha*. Emeneau's (1949: 367) identification of it as the 'strangling fig' seems to have become commonly accepted.

[213] Zaehner (1969: 359f.) argues that the author of *BhG* 15 interprets this tree in Buddhist terms as representing the sensual world that needs to be destroyed. He also connects the passage with *ŚvetU* 3.7–9, where the tree is identified with the god Rudra-Śiva, and *AG* (*MBh* 14.47.12–14). While the *ŚvetU* is not a parallel to the *BhG* (see also Arapura 1975: 132), but represents the more positive view of the *ṚV* and the *KaṭhU*, the passage in the *AG* can be read as a variation on *BhG* 15, since it also demands that the tree be chopped down.

So this tree, together with its roots, needs to be cut down with the 'axe of detachment' (*asaṅga-śastreṇa*; 15.3). Only then can the primordial *puruṣa*, the 'imperishable abode', be reached (15.4–5). By interpreting the Vedic symbolism of the tree in terms of Sāṃkhya, the author turns the 'cosmic tree' into a world of bondage and advocates the ascetic pursuit of the realm in which the tree is rooted, its ultimate foundation (*sampratiṣṭhā*). It is the realm of the primeval *puruṣa*, from which one does not return. It is called Kṛṣṇa's 'highest abode' (*dhāman*) and is not illuminated by light, whether sun, moon or fire (15.6). This verse recalls *BhG* 8.21, where the unmanifest, imperishable *puruṣa* was considered to be the god's highest abode, also the realm of no return.

A characteristic feature of this realm is its darkness, a notion found in cosmological accounts that make 'darkness' (*tamas*) the first stage of creation. Other texts speak of a 'light' that is beyond darkness: for instance, *brahman* is called the 'light beyond darkness' in *BhG* 13.17. Similar descriptions of this realm occur in *KaṭhU* 5.15, *MuṇḍU* 2.2.9 and *ŚvetU* 6.14. Zaehner (1969: 363) notes that the *BhG* borrows from the *KaṭhU* 'with a slight modification'. However, the modification is rather significant, since the Upaniṣad explains that sun, moon, etc., do not shine there because all light comes from there: 'The sun does not shine there, nor the moon or stars; there lightning does not shine. Whence is that (yonder) fire? His shining alone does this universe reflect; this whole world radiates his brilliance.'[214] This is omitted in the *BhG*, since this does not suit the author's intention of proclaiming Kṛṣṇa the ultimate light beyond all other realms (see 15.12, 16–19). Again Upaniṣadic notions are reinterpreted according to the *BhG*'s conceptual framework. This allows a connection to be established between the beginning of *BhG* 15 and *BhG* 14.27, where Kṛṣṇa is declared the foundation (*pratiṣṭhā*) of *brahman*. The image of the inverted tree allows the realm of creation and ritual order (*brahman*) to be depicted as being 'rooted' in Kṛṣṇa as its support (*pratiṣṭhā*). The god leaves room for creation to grow while maintaining his separate, transcendent existence.

The hierarchy of cosmic stages and cosmological agents is also the theme of the rest of the chapter, which culminates in the doctrine of the three *puruṣas* in 15.16–20. The account of the different stages starts with the 'individual' or 'embodied self' (*jīva*), which is declared to be a particle (*aṃśa*) of Kṛṣṇa: 'In the world of living beings, a part of me is the embodied self

[214] *KaṭhU* 5.15: *na tatra sūryo bhāti na candratārakaṃ nemā vidyuto bhānti kuto 'yam agniḥ / tam eva bhāntam anubhāti sarvaṃ tasya bhāsā sarvam idaṃ vibhāti //*. Cf. *MuṇḍU* 2.2.10; *ŚvetU* 6.14.

(*jīvabhūta*[215]), the eternal, who takes on the mind and the senses residing in nature (*prakṛti*). Whatever body this sovereign (*īśvara*) takes or leaves, he seizes them [the senses] and moves them around as the wind (takes) the scents away from their abode' (15.7–8). This clarifies certain aspects of the relationship between the god, the embodied self and 'nature' (*prakṛti*). First, the individual self is part of Kṛṣṇa and as eternal as he is: this makes it 'sovereign' (*īśvara*)[216] with regard to its embodiments, since it takes or leaves a body, while carrying the mind and senses as the 'subtle' body that will stay with it until liberation. The emphasis here is not on the powerlessness of the self entangled in the body (cf. *BhG* 3.5), but on the power he yields over the physical realm, a power that is indicated by the term 'sovereign' (*īśvara*). This description perfectly suits its being a 'part' of Kṛṣṇa, the 'highest sovereign'. It is the self that those who possess the 'eye of knowledge' (*jñāna-cakṣus*), the self-controlled *yogins*, see within themselves (15.10–11). The superimposition of a god on the two-part structure of *puruṣa* and *prakṛti* in Sāṃkhya not only results in making the 'embodied self' part of the god, but also has it sharing some divine characteristics, such as immortality and 'power', that is, sovereignty over nature (*prakṛti*). In this way, the god is also vested with a fragmented cosmological immanence, though without denying his transcendence.

The depiction of the 'embodied self' as a sovereign is followed and complemented by an account of Kṛṣṇa's presence in the whole cosmos,[217] since he is the most powerful *īśvara*, and the creative potential of nature is completely at his disposal. He declares himself to be that fiery energy (*tejas*) that illuminates the whole world (15.12). This can be read as a commentary on 15.6, where the realm of the *puruṣa* to be reached after cutting the 'inverted tree' is said to be devoid of light. The god is then identified as the power that makes the plants grow and as the 'internal fire' (*agni vaiśvānara*) that allows food to be digested. The description ends with another, emphatic reference to the Vedic tradition, expressed by a change of metre: 'I dwell in the heart of everyone; from me spring memory, knowledge and reason; I am known through the knowledge of all the Vedas – I make the Vedānta,[218] I know the Veda' (15.15; trans. van Buitenen). The passage discloses an interest in

[215] This compound also occurs in *BhG* 7.5, which describes the god's 'higher *prakṛti*' (see above, pp. 130ff.).

[216] Cf. *BhG* 5.13–15 on the embodied self as the 'ruler' (*prabhu*, *vibhu*).

[217] For similar descriptions, see *BhG* 7.8–11; 9.16–19; and the *vibhūti*-list in *BhG* 10.

[218] Van Buitenen (1981: 169) notes on *vedānta*: 'in this context certainly the Upaniṣads'. The word is used in *MuṇḍU* 3.2.6 in probably the same sense (cf. Olivelle 1998: 400): 'The ascetics who have firmly determined their goal through a full knowledge of Vedānta' (*vedānta-vijñāna-suniścitārthāḥ*).

making Kṛṣṇa part of the Vedic tradition, in contrast to what we learned in chapter 11, when it was declared that the god cannot be known through the Vedas (11.53). This is indicative of the later addition of this chapter, which accords with the tendency in chapters 12–18 to adapt the new theology to Vedic and brahmanic authority (see also chapter 17).

The chapter ends by establishing a triadic order of cosmic and soteriological stages that clarifies and concludes the superimposition of the god Kṛṣṇa on the principles of Sāṃkhya, not only in the present chapter, but also in chapter 14. Both chapters seem to be loosely connected to the predominantly non-theistic presentation of Sāṃkhya teachings in *BhG* 13. This superimposition is accomplished by distinguishing 'three *puruṣas*' (15.16–20): (1) a 'perishable' (*kṣara*) *puruṣa*, the body, the lower self of embodiment; (2) the 'imperishable' (*akṣara*) *puruṣa* as the 'embodied self', immortal when liberated from the body; (3) the 'highest *puruṣa*' (*puruṣottama*), Kṛṣṇa sustaining everything in the world. The first two *puruṣas* exist 'in this world' (*loke*; 15.16); the first is the perishable (*kṣara*) made up of the elements, the second the imperishable (*akṣara*), which 'stands at the top' (*kūṭastha*)[219] of the elements. While these two are also mentioned in *BhG* 8.3–4, 15.17 introduces a still higher *puruṣa*, the *puruṣottama* or the 'highest self' (*paramātman*), 'the unchanging sovereign (*avyaya īśvara*) who, by entering the three-world, sustains it': 'Since I surpass the perishable and am higher than the imperishable, I am praised in this world as *puruṣottama*, the highest *puruṣa*. Whoever knows him as such will partake of the Lord with all his being' (*sarvabhāvena*; 15.19). The chapter ends by calling this doctrine the 'most secret teaching' (*guhyatmam śāstram*). This chapter connects the monotheistic doctrine with the different levels of the self, the ascetic 'conquest of creation' and the course of death given in *BhG* 5, 6 and 8. It also comments on the account of Kṛṣṇa's 'higher' and 'lower' nature (*prakṛti*) in 7.5–7 by presenting these different levels in terms of the *puruṣa* concept: the 'perishable *puruṣa*' corresponds to the 'lower *prakṛti*' made up of the elements, the 'imperishable *puruṣa*' equals the '*jīvabhūta*' as the 'higher *prakṛti*', and the 'highest *puruṣa*' is the god himself. In contrast to non-theistic Sāṃkhya, *prakṛti* is not considered to be independent of the (divine) *puruṣa* principle. This points to a fundamental difference in the construction of creation in both theistic and non-theistic contexts.

219 This term also occurs in *BhG* 6.8 (applied to the successful *yogin*) and 12.3 (applied to the 'imperishable unmanifest'). See Zaehner 1969: 222f., quoting *MBh* 12.242.16–18 on the *yogin* who stands at the top of a mountain and looks down.

According to one model, the world is created as the emanation and formation of different powers of one being or god, while another model suggests that creation results from the association between a god or a 'self' and a creative power that exists independently of him. Frauwallner (1926: 14–20) showed that these different models already occur in the Upaniṣads: according to the so-called 'Kauṣītaki doctrine', the 'self' (*ātman*) as the one source of creation emanates from the manifest world as aspects or embodiments of itself, while the so-called 'Yājñavalkya doctrine' asserts that the *ātman* enters, as the life-giving force, a realm of inert elements existing independently from it. This model is close to later Sāṃkhya. With its doctrine of the 'three *puruṣas*', *BhG* 15 draws on the first model, as did *BhG* 7 with regard to '*prakṛti*' as 'owned' by Kṛṣṇa. With *BhG* 15, the mediation of the monotheistic framework with other cosmologies and soteriologies ends. The sequence of chapters 13–15 contains many important comments, expansions and explanations that help to clarify the notions presented in *BhG* 5–8.

BHAGAVADGĪTĀ 16: 'DEMONIC' CREATURES

This chapter is not directly connected to the previous one and takes up a topic that has been briefly dealt with in 7.13–15 and 9.12–13: the difference between virtuous people and evil-doers. While in the earlier chapters this difference was explained as resulting from either a 'divine' (*daiva*) or a 'demonic' (*asura*) form of attachment to the physical world (*prakṛti*), the present chapter gives a list of characteristics that are respectively indicative of a divine and demonic way of being. This way of being is described by providing a list of attributes called the *daivi* and *āsurī sampad*. According to Wezler (2000: 445), *sampad* means here an 'assemblage of qualities' which in their totality characterise a person's existence. Arjuna is informed that two types of creatures are born in this world (15.6). This dualistic scheme, which is also employed elsewhere in the *BhG*, contrasts with the tripartite classification of beings and behaviour based on the three *guṇas*. It seems that the distinction between 'divine' and 'demonic' is preferred when the relationship to Kṛṣṇa is highlighted, indicating that, when it comes to following or not following the god, there is no 'third way' (see above, p. 132). This distinction draws on the older, Vedic theme of the antagonistic co-existence of gods (*deva*) and demons (*asura*), that is, in *BĀU* 1.3.1, for instance, traced back to Prajāpati as the creator of both. As in 9.12–13, no explanation is given for why Kṛṣṇa as the mighty lord of beings allows demonic creatures to be part of his creation. What in Christian theology is called the problem of theodicy, that is, why God does not prevent suffering and evil, is not addressed and perhaps not considered an issue.[220] However, we are informed elsewhere in the chapter that Kṛṣṇa will personally punish evil-doers.

The list of virtues given in 16.1–3 includes purity, compassion, fearlessness and steadfastness in the yoga of knowledge (*jñānayoga*), the performance of Vedic sacrifice and study of the Veda. Similar virtues are ascribed elsewhere to brahmanical ascetics.[221] In contrast to *BhG* 7 and 9, devotional qualities or belief in Kṛṣṇa are not mentioned. After a brief description of the 'demonic condition' that is indicated by arrogance and ignorance (16.4), the behaviour and world-view of the evil-doers is depicted in lively detail: 'The demonic people do not understand the course of activity and non-activity (*pravṛttinivṛtti*);[222] they are devoid of purity, appropriate behaviour and truthfulness.' They champion the following world-view (*dṛṣṭi*; 16.9): 'They consider this world to be lacking true reality (*asatya*); it has neither a foundation (*apratiṣṭha*) nor a supreme ruler (*anīśvara*) and is not produced by reciprocity (*aparaspara*).[223] What then? It is caused by desire' (16.8). Whose views are being described here? While some scholars suggest a portrayal of Buddhist thought (e.g. R. D. Karmarkar 1950), most see it as a description of a materialistic attitude ascribed to the Cārvaka school of philosophy (e.g. Schreiner 1991: 181). The main point of this world-view is indeed the rejection of the ontological reality or substantiality of the world and of ethical principles. The latter is expressed in the following description of the practical application of this world-view, which amounts to an egotistical pursuit of power and pleasure by means of sacrifice (16.10–17, see below). This makes it rather improbable that Buddhism is meant here (see Minor 1982: 438; Mainkar 1978: 751), although some doctrinal aspects (such as non-substantiality, atheism, etc.) are similar. Rather, it points to 'materialism' in the sense of denying that the world is based on and sustained by

220 Such questions are raised elsewhere in the epic, e.g. by Draupadī in 3.32 or Uttaṅka in 14.53. Later theologies introduce notions of the god's 'play' (*līlā*), or explain suffering as the necessary incentive for the quest of liberation.

221 In the *AG*, some of these characteristics are attributed to the forest hermit and the one who understands liberation (cf. *MBh* 14.46.26ff., 14.46.33–35). Steinmann (1989: 173f.) points to parallels in *ManuS* (*ManuS* 6.92; 10.63; 12.83). Some virtues are mentioned also in *BhG* 13.7–8.

222 The pair *pravṛtti* and *nivṛtti* evokes a wide spectrum of meanings, spanning from 'being active' or 'inactive' to the 'creation' and 'destruction' of the cosmos. For an analysis of these terms, see Strauss 1911: 197–217, 247–300; also Biardeau 1981, Bailey 1985.

223 This compound has been given various interpretations. Garbe (1921: 151) translates it as 'not produced in a regular process', thus implying a rejection of Sāṃkhya cosmology. Edgerton (1944: 149) suggests 'not originated in regular mutual causation' (similarly Zaehner 1969: 371; van Buitenen 1981: 133; Schreiner 1991: 122). R. D. Karmarkar (1950), splitting up the compound differently, translates 'produced from a causal chain', a doctrine typical of Buddhism.

fundamental rules and realities (*satya*), as advocated, for instance, in the Veda and Upaniṣads. The acceptance of a concept and reality of 'cosmic order' results in both traditions requesting individual desire and egotism to be (ascetically) restrained or (ritually) channelled, though for different reasons. All the ideas that express such a concept are rejected by the 'demonic' people, while the 'divine' is inclined to propagate the view that the world has a true reality (*satya*), a foundation (*pratiṣṭhā*) and a supreme lord (*īśvara*) and that it exists through reciprocal relationships (*parasparasambhavam*). This 'positive' list recalls notions dealt with elsewhere in the *BhG*. The term 'foundation' (*pratiṣṭhā*) is prominent in the description of the sacrificial wheel in *BhG* 3.15 (cf. 14.27: Kṛṣṇa as foundation of *brahman*, etc.; 15.3). Mutual dependence or reciprocity (*paraspara*) is also a key concept of a cosmos based on sacrifice, because creatures depend on one another in the 'food-cycle' (*BhG* 3.11; Bailey 1985: 26–32).

Seen against the background of the practical consequences of this 'materialism', the rejection of 'reciprocity' refers not only to a certain concept of causality (as suggested by most interpreters), but also to the reciprocal character of the ritual system that creates and sustains the social and cosmic order. However, in contrast to 'true materialists', who would deny the value of ritual and *karman*, we are dealing here with 'materialists' who are sacrificers and thus quite similar to the demons described in Vedic and later epic and purāṇic literature. While rejecting obligation and responsibility they exploit the resources of ritual and of the world, sacrificing in order to serve their egotistical interest. Since they deny that reciprocity is an essential and 'true' factor of life, they do not reciprocate or care for the 'maintenance of the world' (*lokasaṃgraha*; cf. *BhG* 3.20). They would 'cook only for themselves' (3.13) – theirs are sacrifices in name only (*nāmayajña*; 16.16). They reject anything higher or beyond the pursuit of interests (no foundation, no supreme lord), and they need not fear any repercussions. Since they believe that the world is caused by desire, they live only in order to satisfy their own (16.11). The following passage depicts not only a philosophical school, but also the ideology and life-style of powerful and skilled people who are capable even of destroying the world through their cruel deeds (*ugrakarman*; 16.9):

> Bound by hundreds of fetters of expectation, engrossed in desire and anger, they strive to pile up wealth and disregard any code of conduct while indulging in pleasure. 'This I have gained today, this fancy I am going to entertain; this wealth is mine, and much more there will be in the future. That enemy I have already killed, and others I am going to crush too. I am the Lord (*īśvara*), I take my

pleasure. Successful am I, strong and happy! Rich am I, and of good family. Who could match me? I will sacrifice, give gifts and enjoy myself' – so they speak deluded by their ignorance . . . Puffed up with themselves (*ātmasambhāvita*), they perform sacrifices in name only (*nāmayajña*), as, out of arrogance, they do not follow the prescribed rules. (16.12–15, 17)

This description points to the upper level of society, to those in power, to kings and warriors vested not only with military power, but also with enough resources for sacrifices to increase their prestige. They are also those who call themselves 'lords' (*īśvara*) and see no need to accept any superior.[224] It seems that the *BhG* deals not only with alternative doctrines like Buddhism, but also with the world-view and life-style of those who see no need to accept a 'highest god' and become followers of Kṛṣṇa, as is made explicit in 16.18: 'Because they rely on selfishness, force, arrogance, desire and anger, they hate and envy me, the one who exists in their bodies and in those of others.' They will know better only when they experience Kṛṣṇa punishing them personally and find themselves thrown again and again into lower forms of existence, without any chance to reach the true *īśvara* (16.20). Without further explanation, Kṛṣṇa is presented as the mighty and punishing power, a point that has been taught already in *BhG* 4.6–8 and 11.25ff. This indicates that the chapter is based on the earlier ones.

The combination of disregard for the elementary rules that sustain life and prosperity with the ruthless exploitation of resources and aversion to Kṛṣṇa as the highest god will seal the fate of such people. According to 16.21–22, they have opened wide the 'gate of hell' (*narakasya dvāram*), which consists in 'desire, anger and greed', a triad also found in Buddhist texts dealing with the cause of suffering. As a consequence, it is recommended to give them up and instead follow the authoritative textbooks (*śāstra*; 16.23–24), which prescribe the appropriate code of conduct. The chapter thus demands that Kṛṣṇa be accepted as the highest power and that the traditional, brahmanical teachings be obeyed. Again, this may be taken as indicative of a pragmatic attitude on the part of the followers of Kṛṣṇa towards the brahmanical authority, which is accepted as setting the rules for social life. Arjuna is warned against any form of selfishness and indulgence in power or aversion to his duties. This allegiance to established traditions and authorities can also be detected in *BhG* 17.

[224] Cf. *BhG* 18.43, which ascribes the status of 'ruler' (*īśvarabhāva*) to Kṣatriyas. Compare also Duryodhana's self-praise as surpassing both gods and demons (cf. *MBh* 5.60 and above, pp. 50ff.).

BHAGAVADGĪTĀ 17: THE CORRECT RITUAL METHOD

In contrast to the dualistic scheme used in the last chapter, the tripartite structure of the classification according to the three powers of nature (*guṇa*) is again employed in this chapter. While this connects it to the *guṇa* texts in *BhG* 14 and 18, it differs from them in its general silence about Kṛṣṇa's divinity and the doctrine of *bhakti* (except in 17.6). It presents a clear reassertion of traditional forms of ritual and authority, a tendency that could be observed in *BhG* 16 too, although the theological framework remains prominent. The chapter starts with Arjuna asking Kṛṣṇa to deal with the following problem: what position in the scheme of *guṇas* is accorded to a sacrificer who is full of confidence (*śraddhā*), but disregards the proper injunctions (*avidhipūrvakam*)? The choice of the word *śraddhā* indicates that we are concerned here with traditional Vedic sacrifice, in that confidence in the efficacy of ritual action is one of its basic preconditions (Köhler 1948, Hara 1963–64). Arjuna seeks an explanation for the unusual situation of a sacrificer who has confidence in the sacrifice, but does not follow the rules. This is exceptional because following the prescribed injunctions and rules is one of the main reasons for confidence in the efficacy of the ritual: the success of the sacrifice depends on the correct procedure. Why, then, does this question arise? A textual reference to this problem can be found in 9.23. Kṛṣṇa has already declared that he accepts sacrifices, even if they are not properly addressed to him: 'Even those who offer their sacrifices to other deities, being full of confidence (*śraddhā*), sacrifice only to me, son of Kuntī, without following the proper injunctions (*avidhipūrvakam*).' The claim that Kṛṣṇa is the foundation of all sacrifice is emphasised by extending it to the rituals the god receives, even though he is not properly invoked as the addressee. It is remarkable that such a statement is not repeated here, for instance by pointing out that any sacrifice is welcome to Kṛṣṇa, even when it has not been properly performed. Instead, chapter 17 can be regarded as an implicit correction and rejection of this claim by reasserting the bases of the Vedic ritual system. There is good reason for doing so, because it would fall apart if the performance of rituals were to be left to individual choice. Another implication is that the worship of Kṛṣṇa is considered successful only when the appropriate provisions are made. However, in the present chapter this is commented on only indirectly (the god is not mentioned) and on a general level. Interestingly, the problem raised is never addressed directly, but only implicitly, and Arjuna, for once, is left without having received a clear answer. This may point to the aim of the chapter, which is to offer a critique of an over-liberal interpretation of ritual methods, without openly rejecting the idea of Kṛṣṇa's sovereignty over all sacrifices. Vedic ritual procedure and the Brahmans' stewardship are declared to be the authority in these matters.

In its emphasis on confidence (*śraddhā*), Arjuna's question is not only about whether the combination of confidence and incorrect method is acceptable, but also whether procedural mistakes can be counterbalanced by confidence (*śraddhā*). In an indirect way, both ideas are rejected in what follows. First of all, an evaluation of confidence according to the *guṇa* classification is given. It is said that a person's confidence reflects his way of being (*sattvānurūpa*):[225] 'Man consists of confidence. He is defined by what he has confidence in' (17.3). Therefore, those who are full of *sattva* (the highest *guṇa*, power of nature) worship the gods, people of the *rajas* type offer to the Yakṣas and Rākṣasas, and those dominated by *tamas* offer to spirits and ghosts. The *guṇa* classification is then interrupted by two verses dealing with ascetics who practise austerities (*tapas*) without observing the rules given in the *śāstras*. Since they torment the body and the god Kṛṣṇa who resides in it, their convictions are demonic (*āsura niścaya*; 17.6). These two stanzas deviate from the rest of the chapter because the *asura* terminology is used, as is the case in *BhG* 16. This corroborates what I pointed out earlier, namely that the *guṇa* scheme is not used when the relationship with Kṛṣṇa is being dealt with. The description of this form of *tapas* contrasts with another classification of *tapas* in this chapter (17.14–18). Therefore the two verses might be interpolations, perhaps intending to connect the passage directly with *BhG* 16.[226]

The *guṇa* text is then continued with a classification of different forms of food (*ahāra*), sacrifice (*yajña*), asceticism (*tapas*) and gift-giving (*dāna*). In employing the doctrine of the 'detached' performance of ritual and social duties, the *sattva* type of sacrifice and asceticism is characterised as being devoid of desire for fruits (*aphalakānkṣī*). The (*sattva*) sacrificer's diet is healthy and balanced. When dominated by *rajas*, on the other hand, sacrifice and asceticism are performed in order to obtain fruits and enhance one's pride. Accordingly, the diet of the sacrificer is spicy, thus inciting passions, and unhealthy. Sacrifice performed without confidence (*śraddhāvirahita*) and proper injunctions (*vidhihīna*) belongs to the *tamas* type. Although the characterisation of the *tamas* type seems to address Arjuna's question, it provides only a partial answer because it confirms, *ex negativo*, that confidence and observing the rules are intrinsically connected, and that the

225 *Sattva* does not mean the *guṇa* here, but 'essence', 'way of being' (van Buitenen 1981: 135), similar to *svabhāva* in 17.2.

226 This is indicated in Mālayālam manuscript 4, which places the two stanzas after *BhG* 16.17.

combination of confidence and wrong method is not permitted. This is again emphasised at the very end of the chapter (17.28), where a lack of confidence is said to annul any sacrifice and asceticism; they become non-existent (*asat*). Similarly, there is no place for a person who sacrifices confidently but disregards the rules. Rather, the traditional brahmanical framework of ritual activity is confirmed, as is the case with ascetic practices. Neither yoga nor meditation is mentioned, only the veneration of gods and seniors, non-violence, purity, etc. The brahmanical orientation also becomes obvious at the end of the chapter, when the prescribed forms of invocation are presented as the standard to be followed by every sacrificer: '*Oṃ tat sat* is the traditional triple designation of *brahman*, with it were of yore ordained the brahmins, the Vedas and the sacrifices' (17.2; trans. van Buitenen). The meaning and use of the three elements of this designation is to formulate the intention and declaration of sacrifice,[227] asceticism and gift-giving: *Oṃ* is that evocation of *brahman*, the foundation and plenitude of the ritually structured cosmos (see 8.13; Zaehner 1969: 379–381), which marks the beginning of all rituals. It establishes their connection to the ritual order as a whole. *Tad*, literally 'this', and serves to spell out the intention and purpose of the ritual. They should be performed for the sake not of fruits, but of liberation. '*Sat*', literally 'being', is ascribed a double meaning of 'being' and 'something good' (*sādhu*). This part of the invocation assures the reality and truth of rituals and justifies the confidence (*śraddhā*) in their efficacy. It declares the ritual to be something good, and when, as is pointed out in 17.27, this purpose (to bring about something good) is kept in mind, the acts turn out to be true and real (*sat*). Correct injunction and ritual procedure are intrinsically connected to confidence and vice versa. It seems that the situation suggested in Arjuna's question is ruled out by not even mentioning it. The final statement on the pivotal role of confidence concerns rituals that are performed correctly only: when they are performed without *śraddhā*, they are *a-sat*, neither existing nor good (17.28).

With its emphasis on the correct ritual procedure of traditional sacrifice, the chapter contrasts with the opening of the spectrum of accepted ritual activities and agents in the context of *bhakti* (cf. *BhG* 7 and 9). The interpersonal basis of devotion allows for different forms of worship attracting new clients and ritual actors who were not admitted to Vedic sacrificial arenas. The doctrine of a single highest god allows him to be claimed as the addressee of all rituals, even when he has not been named as their receiver

[227] In later texts, the formula '*oṃ tat sat*' is used for dedicating the fruits of *pūjā* worship to *brahman*, confirming that the purpose of worship is to please the god only (cf. Bühnemann 1988: 180–181).

(cf. 9.23). The author of *BhG* 17 takes exception to this doctrine and the liberties that may result from it. The only way to perform rituals, asceticism and gift-giving successfully is to follow the ordained rules that are handed down in traditional manuals and teachings (*śāstra*). The function of the chapter is to interpret the new doctrine and new forms of ritual within the brahmanical traditional and thus set boundaries to individual choice.

BHAGAVADGĪTĀ 18: SOCIAL DUTIES AND LOYALTY TO KṚṢṆA

According to Zaehner (1969: 384), this chapter falls into two parts: In the first part (18.1–40), we find another '*guṇa* text' classifying certain phenomena according to the three powers of nature. This is followed by some stanzas on the duties of the four castes (41–55) and a summary of the *BhG*'s doctrine of liberation (56–78). This reflects the structure of the chapter well. The first part offers some terminological clarifications on issues raised in *BhG* 2–11. It begins with Arjuna's question about the difference between *tyāga* (relinquishment) and *saṃnyāsa* (renunciation), two of the key words of the doctrine of *karmayoga*. Kṛṣṇa's answer is basically a repetition of the doctrine of 'disinterested action' in *BhG* 2.47, namely that only the fruits of action, not action itself, must be relinquished: 'Giving up actions motivated by desire, the wise call "renunciation" (*saṃnyāsa*). Giving up the fruits of all actions is what insightful men call "relinquishment" (*tyāga*)' (18.2). In line with the use of these two terms elsewhere in the *BhG* (cf. A. Sharma 1975, 1980), 'renunciation' applies only to actions that are motivated by desire, while 'relinquishment' should be practised with regard to the fruits that accrue from the performance of the remaining duties. Both terms refer to two different aspects of actions, especially of social and ritual duties. Seen against the background of the usual tripartite classification of rituals, *saṃnyāsa* would mean giving up all *kāmya* (optional, 'desired') rites, while *tyāga* applies to the occasional (*naimittika*) and permanent, ordained rites (*nitya*) (see also van Buitenen 1981: 170).

Although this distinction echoes core teachings at *BhG* 2.47; 3.7–9 and 6.1–2, they are referred to here as scholarly opinions ('the wise say') that are contrasted with yet other opinions in 18.3: 'Some wise men declare that action must be abandoned (*tyājyam*) because it is full of flaws (*doṣavad*), while other say that sacrifice, gift-giving and asceticism are work that must not be abandoned.' According to Bronkhorst (1993), the first opinion reflects the Jaina view that the only way to prevent karmic bondage is to give up action completely. This view matches that of 'traditional' renouncers (*saṃnyāsin*) in discarding all social and ritual duties for the sake of liberation. The second opinion represents the traditional brahmanical view that sacrifice, gift-giving and ascetic practices must never be given up. True to his role as a teacher, Kṛṣṇa then presents his view in the form of a 'decision' (*niścaya*). While he sides with the definitions offered in 18.2, the traditional view that sacrifice, gift-giving and asceticism must not be given up (18.5) and that renunciation (*saṃnyāsa*) must not extend to prescribed actions (18.7) is strongly endorsed: only attachment to the fruits of these activities must be given up (*tyāga*). What may seem a terminological exercise is in fact an important clarification of the doctrine of 'detachment in action' (*karmayoga*). Since renunciation concerns only a specific type of action ('with desire'), *tyāga* is an activity that in the traditional context is intrinsically connected to (ritual) action because it is that moment of a ritual when the sacrificer 'gives away' his offering. Thus *tyāga* is a part of every sacrifice, and the idea that the 'fruit' of action should be the object of this act of *tyāga* can be reconciled with the sacrificial protocol without difficulty,[228] although doing so goes against the function of sacrifice, which is to fulfil a desire. However, this problem is also removed, because all rituals and activity motivated by desire must be given up in the first place.

In drawing again on the *guṇa* classification, 'detached action' is declared to be the *sattva* type of relinquishment (*tyāga*; 18.9), while the *rajas* form means giving up ordained actions because of the pain and danger they may cause. Relinquishment motivated by delusion and confusion is indicative of a 'dark' (*tamas*) condition. The last two aspects apply to Arjuna's refusal to fight, since he had argued about the painful consequences that his actions may have had and expressed his confusion about *dharma*. The *sattva* form of 'relinquishment' summarises the *karmayoga* doctrine of 'detached action' by drawing on the *guṇa* classification on the one hand and traditional views on the other, and not by relying on the authority of Kṛṣṇa. This indicates that we meet here with yet another reassertion of traditional positions, as was also the case in *BhG* 16 and 17. The theological framework that would allow both terms to be defined in relation to *bhakti* is not mentioned.

The discussion then turns to the wholesome effect of relinquishment: the ending of karmic bondage. No fruits affect those who have truly renounced attachment (18.12). A similar point is made in the following brief discussion of the factors that determine action (18.13–17): 'According to Sāṃkhya', five causes (*kāraṇa*) work together in order to accomplish an

[228] This is also corroborated in later *pūjā* texts, in which *tyāga* means that worship is not performed for the sake of the worshipper, but is 'given away' in order to please the god (cf. Bühnemann 1988: 180f.).

act: (1) an 'operational basis' (*adhiṣṭhāna*),[229] an agent (*kartā*), instruments (*karaṇa*), movements (*ceṣṭā*) and 'fate' (*daivam*), the uncontrollable and 'unpredictable forces influencing actions' (van Buitenen 1981: 170).[230] This notion of causality expands on the previous discussion of renunciation and relinquishment by highlighting the problem of karmic bondage. This list of factors has, to my knowledge, no parallel in any extant Sāṃkhya text. Action is here interpreted as the interplay of different causal factors, and singling out any one factor as the most important is deemed a sign of ignorance. People do this when they think themselves to be the sole cause of their activities: they appropriate the results with their 'ego' and become subject to producing karmic bondage (18.16). In 18.17, this construction of an ego-centred agency is contrasted with those whose existence is not based their egotism (*ahaṃkṛto bhāvo*). They are capable of realising the presence of the other factors and of detaching themselves from any appropriating egotism: 'He whose existence is devoid of egotism and whose insight is not defiled is not bound; even if he kills all these people, he does not kill' (18.17). This 'disturbing doctrine' (Zaehner 1969: 388) echoes teachings about the immortal self in *BhG* 2.39, which served to qualify the importance of the body and to ease the burden of death and violence. The ethical problem implied in this notion consists in the possible legitimation of all kinds of action (including violence) as events in which 'forces of nature' work on 'forces of nature' (*BhG* 3.28): any responsibility would be denied, and individuals could act as they pleased, without facing any consequences, thus opening up the path to moral solipsism and the suspension of all laws and rules of behaviour. However, the stanza must be seen in context. We are dealing here with a description of a successful practice of detachment and of insight into the structure of action, not with 'ethical norms' or 'moral values'. Since this practice implies overcoming egotistic appropriation, it should prevent solipsism, since detachment is intrinsically connected with the acquisition of knowledge about the nature of all beings and a concern for their welfare. This concern must be demonstrated in practice, where it can be assessed. At this point, our discussion returns to issues that have been dealt with in regard to *BhG* 1–3 and certain debates in the *UdP*, as we again encounter the ambiguity of 'indifference' and 'detachment' as a yardstick for correct behaviour and understanding. It cannot serve as a value in itself, since it is indicative of quite different motives, such as ruthlessness,

229 In *BhG* 3.40, *adhiṣṭhāna* is defined as 'the five senses, mind and *buddhi*'.

230 See the discussion of time as fatality and destiny above, pp. 175ff. Minor's (1982: 489) statement that 'fate is the word for Kṛṣṇa' disregards the context of this passage, which is otherwise silent about the god.

so it must be related to specific purposes, such as the 'sacrifice' or 'maintenance of socio-cosmic order' (*lokasaṃgraha*), as in *BhG* 3. It does not call for all norms and laws to be disregarded, but should result in an increased capacity to follow and apply them even more rigorously because all personal interests have been wiped out. Only then does 'detachment' become a path to liberation from *karman*; otherwise it is just an illusion or serves as a pretext for pursuing egotistic goals (see 3.6).

Seen from this perspective, the *guṇa* classification in 18.18–40 can be regarded as commenting on this topic too, since it contains an outline of appropriate and less appropriate behaviour, which helps to put the rather abstract statement about 'non-egotistic agency' in 18.17 into more concrete terms. It corroborates the intimate connection between knowledge and practice that can be regarded as one of the red threads of the *BhG*. Activities are regarded as the results of mental processes, which in turn are indicative of a whole way of being (an individual's disposition or *svabhāva*). Any transformation of the structure of one's agency and involvement in the world touches on one's 'way of being', which is rather difficult to change because it means stopping the 'natural' and thus uncontrolled tendency to follow and enact one's state of being (cf. 3.5) and to replace it with a controlled and purposeful (yoga) practice of (Sāṃkhya) knowledge. This may explain why the following *guṇa* text starts with a classification of subject, form and object of knowledge as inciting action (*karma-codanā*). The prescriptive character of the *guṇa* text, which is often neglected by scholars as tedious description, becomes evident when one puts the different characterisations together. In doing so, the classification provides instructions about desirable and less desirable forms of behaviour. When looking for practical advice and 'rules of behaviour' in the *BhG*, this *guṇa* text is certainly one of the passages to draw upon.

In collecting all the information on the different 'ways of being' that are ascribed to each of the three *guṇa*s, the following typology and taxonomy emerge. The *sattva* person shows the following characteristics. He knows that only one being is present in all creatures; he performs his duties without showing any desire for reward; he acts without egotism and is indifferent to failure and success; and he understands the difference between activity and non-activity, right and wrong, bondage and release. He remains steadfast and self-controlled through the continuous practice of yoga, his happiness resulting from constant self-purification, which results ultimately in liberation from karmic bondage. Although this happiness seems at first like 'drinking poison', it milks the 'nectar of immortality' (18.37). The ideal-typical character of the *sattva* description becomes obvious when it is contrasted with the *rajas* person, who thinks that the each creature lives a separate life and that there is nothing that gives them unity or wholeness. He performs his duties by indulging in being the sole agent, and therefore acts greedily and violently when fulfilling his desires. There is no correct discrimination between law and lawlessness, between what is ordained and what is not: he clings to rules, wealth and pleasure (i.e. the three traditional 'goals of life') because he seeks pleasure. Therefore his happiness at first appears like 'the nectar of immortality', but then turns out to be 'poison' because it further obscures his consciousness (18.38). The person dominated by *tamas* is even further away from liberation and represents the ruthless disregard for the consequences that is characteristic of a 'dark' way of being. His knowledge is unreasonably attached to one task only. When doing his work, he does not care for the consequences and is indifferent to loss and violence. He acts in ways full of arrogance, crookedness and vulgarity, and often feels depressed. He mistakes lawlessness for law and gets it all wrong. His pleasures nourish his delusion, since they result from sleep and laziness. The *guṇa* text concludes with the statement that no embodied being is free from these powers, which stem from nature (*prakṛti*, 18.40), thus repeating similar statements in *BhG* 3.5. The theme that an individual's 'way of being' (*svabhāva*) indicates the dominance of one of the powers of nature (*guṇa*) is continued by turning to the different social groups organised in the caste hierarchy (18.41–48). 'Way of being' here means that the embodied self acquires in each birth a body that corresponds to the quality of its previous lives (*karman*) and, as a consequence, to the soteriological status of the 'embodied self'. Therefore, caste divisions are considered to be indicative of a corresponding 'way of being'. Acceptance of one's social position and obligations is mandatory, since it is not regarded as a 'social rank' superimposed by society, but as expressive of the condition of the embodied self. Therefore social duties suit an individual's 'way of being' (*svabhāva*, 18.41–44), his 'nature' (*svāprakṛti*; *BhG* 3.33–35).[231] Social duty

[231] Hegel (1827: 68, 80–82), like many others after him, voiced the criticism that the *BhG* fails to establish the basic prerequisite for 'true morality', the idea that mankind is 'spirit' and therefore ultimately free from the constraints of nature. Instead it teaches, in a rather primitive way, social duties on the basis of 'natural distinctions'. However, Hegel ignores the soteriological axiom implied in Sāṃkhya's doctrine of the interdependence between the embodied self and its 'natural' body. The question whether the *BhG* teaches 'blind submission' under the law of caste and the hardship this may imply has been discussed repeatedly by scholars and resembles the debate about 'determinism' with regard to Kṛṣṇa's revelation as the 'fatal time' in *BhG* 11. Following the Hegelian tradition that 'freedom of the individual' is the highest value, the discourse revolves around the question of whether the *BhG* allows 'freedom of choice' in terms of social mobility, etc. While Radhakrishnan (1948: 418), for instance, allows this possibility, Minor (1982: 483) denies it. However, it seems doubtful whether 'freedom of choice' is a category that could apply to the conceptual framework

(*svadharma*) and 'one's nature' (*svabhāva*) mirror each other. Therefore it is harmful to practise another's *dharma*, as this goes against 'one's nature' (cf. 3.33, 35). Recalling statements made in *BhG* 3.35, it is again stressed that one must perform one's allotted duties (*svakarma*, 18.45–46; *sahajaṃ karman*, 'innate activity', 18.48) as the path to perfection (*saṃsiddhi*; 18.45). This success is achieved when duties are performed as a homage to the one being that is the cause of the world (18.46): 'That man finds perfection (accomplishes his goal, *siddhi*) who honours with his works that (being) through whom all creatures are active, by whom this all (*sarvam idam*) is spread out.' This recalls *BhG* 3, where one is recommended to perform one's duties for the sake of 'holding together the world' as a ritual-cosmic order (*lokasaṃgraha*, 3.25), thus allowing all creatures to live and prosper on the basis of reciprocal relationships. However, in *BhG* 18.46 the emphasis is on honouring the one who has created 'all this'. Since this can be done irrespective of one's actual social rank, it is better to accept one's allotted duty than to try to do something else (18.47, recalling 3.35).[232] This account of the caste hierarchy offers still another variation on the refrain that pervades this chapter: the rejection of any doctrine calling one to give up one's social duties. Instead they are declared conducive to success and liberation, because they preserve the world and honour its creator. However, the creator has not yet been identified. This is done in the following verses, in which both the realm of *brahman* and then Kṛṣṇa are declared the 'highest' being.

Success is achieved by being indifferent to the fruits of action, and consists in the 'absence of *karman*' (*naiṣkārmya-siddhi*; 18.49), freedom from karmic bondage. This is the fruit of 'renunciation' (*saṃnyāsa*), which is acquired when one has 'conquered oneself' (*jitātman*). It means reaching *brahman* (18.50). This is the culmination of the path to liberation (18.51–56), comprising practices of self-restraint and withdrawal from sense-objects accomplished by secluded ascetics dedicated to the yoga of meditation

of the *BhG*. Other texts, both Buddhist and epic, suggest that the alternative to 'innate *karman*' is not choice, but the actual life-style and demeanour of an individual, which is the true testimony of his social status. A 'true' Brahman, for instance, is one who actually behaves like one, irrespective of whether he is born into a brahmanical family or not. See, for instance, Ambattha Sutta (*DN* 3), Sonadanda Sutta (*DN* 4), *SN* 7.1.9.9 (here the Buddha states: 'Do not ask for the birth; ask for the demeanour', *mā jātiṃ puccha, caraṇañca puccha*). Cf. also *MBh* 5.43.31.

232 Cf. 3.35: *śreyān svadharmo viguṇaḥ paradharmāt svanuṣṭhitā / svadharme nidhanaṃ śreyaḥ paradharmo bhayāvahaḥ* with 18.47: *śreyān svadharmo viguṇaḥ paradharmāt svanuṣṭhitā / svabhāvaniyataṃ karma kurvan nāpnoti kilbiṣam*. In contrast to 3.35, in 18.47 the '*svabhāva*' terminology is used. The ensuing variant reading for 18.47cd (*svadharme nidhanaṃ śreyaḥ paradharmodayād api*) in manuscripts 4.5, Ko6 and D3 confirms the connection between the verses. This reading is adopted in 3.35 in manuscripts 1.3–5, K6 and Cb, k.

(*dhyānayoga*; 18.52), which makes the adept fit to 'become *brahman*' (18.53). This state of dispassion and indifference is described in terms similar to *BhG* 5 and 6. In accordance with the transition between the non-theistic and the monotheistic framework established in parts of *BhG* 6 and then in 7–11, in 18.54 this state is interpreted not as the 'highest' goal, but as a state in which the adept gains 'devotion' (*bhakti*) to the Lord Kṛṣṇa. Only then is he set on the highest path: 'Through devotion, he comes to know me and how great I truly am. Since he has understood me truly, he enters (me) immediately. Even though performing all the acts, he relies on me and reaches by my grace (*prasāda*) the eternal, imperishable abode' (18.55–56). This summarises the theistic interpretation of yoga presented in *BhG* 5 and 6.26–31. As has been pointed out in the analysis of these chapters, 'reaching *brahman*' marks a path of liberation independent of and probably preceding its monotheistic interpretation. The summary in *BhG* 18 corroborates the thesis that the depiction of Kṛṣṇa as the highest goal is based on these older, well-established teachings, which are now reinterpreted as stages on a path leading to Kṛṣṇa. This is one of the clearest statements of a sequence of different yoga practices and of the claim that *dhyānayoga* culminates not in being *brahman* or reaching *nirvāṇa*, but in *bhakti*. This is another instance that does not support the well-established interpretation of the *BhG* as teaching three alternative paths to liberation, each yielding the same result. To reach Kṛṣṇa, *bhakti* is indispensable – only then are other paths efficacious. While there is certainly an acknowledgement of different goals and practices here, much of the *BhG* is concerned with evaluation and hierarchisation, as we have seen, for instance, in the classification of devotees (*BhG* 7, 9) or in the superimposition of Kṛṣṇa on spheres like *brahman*, the Vedic gods or *nirvāṇa*. This emphasis on the monotheistic doctrine is also discernible when Arjuna is given final advice regarding his initial problem (18.57–58):

> Cast in your mind all acts on to me, having me as the highest, and rely on the yogic employment of *buddi* (*buddhiyoga*) while you have me constantly in your mind! Having me in your mind, you will overcome all dangers by my grace. Should you, however, out of self-deceit, not listen, you will perish.

Here the reinterpretation of *saṃnyāsa* as the renunciation of fruits, while casting the actual agency on the god as advocated in 3.30, is repeated and turned into an admonition. Again the distinctive feature of a yoga practice that brings about devotion emerges. In contrast to liberation and non-return, *bhakti* results in an increased capacity to act, since yogic success and devotion are demonstrated in activities that serve the maintenance of cosmic order and the worship of its creator. The passages recall the beginning of the *BhG* in the use of '*buddhiyoga*' (cf. 2.39, 49–50) and the retrospective judgement of Arjuna's refusal to fight as a symptom of self-deceit and egotism (*ahaṃkāra*; 18.58–59):[233] 'Should you, relying on your ego, think "I will not fight", this is idle judgement, since nature will set you on (its) course' (18.59). Should Arjuna stand by his decision, he will be helplessly exposed to the forces of nature that are active and ingrained in one's way of being (*svabhāva*): 'Tied you are, son of Kuntī, to the task belonging to you, since it springs from your way of being (*svabhāva*). What out of delusion you do not want to do, you nevertheless will do, though helplessly (*avaśa*)' (18.60). The only choice is between performing one's duties either with or without accruing karmic consequences. Neither yoga nor *bhakti* changes the actions that must be performed. Not acting is no alternative when one is motivated by fear of death, suffering or confusion. It is not possible just to drop out and rid oneself of one's duties and obligations, since one remains involved in them as long as one does not change one's way of being. This can be brought about only by yoga and *bhakti*, which then, according to the *BhG*, demand the performance of duties as well. As in *BhG* 4.16, when it comes to defining action (*karman*), the discourse on right action again unfolds in relation to non-action as the religious and socio-political alternative. Having diagnosed the dangers implied in the idea of non-action, which are caused by overestimating one's self-control, the desirable relationship to action is delineated. The question of what should be done or not done, or what is 'right', is dealt with not by referring to 'individual freedom' or 'general norms', but in relation to an individual's capacity to cope with inborn, uncontrolled tendencies – in brief, with that very (natural) agency that is ingrained in one's social existence. Therefore, the referential framework of the *Gītā*'s discourse is quite different from modern 'ethics', and this should be kept in mind in comparative studies or when employing categories such as 'freedom' or 'choice'. Correct behaviour is weighed against an individual's capacity for self-control and awareness, which is usually indicated by social existence.

Seen from this perspective, yoga, asceticism and devotion can all be regarded as methods of empowerment whose aim is to overcome ingrained tendencies to act in one way or another by taking control of the consequences of one's agency through detachment and redirecting it at other agents, such as *brahman*, *prakṛti* and Kṛṣṇa. An important aspect of this empowerment is the distancing of the adept from the view that actions are

[233] In doing so, 18.59b quotes *BhG* 2.9c (*na yotsya iti*; 'I will not fight').

at his disposal and may be used to fulfil desires. Although accepting the basic, teleological interpretation of *karman*, namely that it always serves a purpose, the *BhG* teaches one to redirect the purposefulness or intentionality of action away from fulfilling desires towards the 'the well-being of all creatures'. Indifference towards one's own advantage results in an affirmative attitude with regard to the world and, ultimately, towards its creator.

The theme of 'helplessness', of not being in control of one's actions (*avaśa*), is continued in 18.61–62. Both verses show the mediation of the concept of *prakṛti* to be the source of all activity with the monotheistic framework that connects nature to a god that activates and supervises it, as has already been explained in *BhG* 4, 7 and 9. When this relationship is not understood, creatures become inevitably involved and thrown around in the machinery (*yantra*) of actions incited by the creative power (*māyā*)[234] of that sovereign (*īśvara*) who rules over all beings (18.61). Thus it is better to take refuge to him and be liberated (18.62). The author of this passage has Kṛṣṇa talk about himself in the third person. This serves here to stress the distance between the creatures and their lord, thus enhancing the admonishing character of the verses. Since all attributes suit previous descriptions of Kṛṣṇa and since no other lord has been mentioned in this chapter, there is no reason to assume that Kṛṣṇa is being presented here as a merely human teacher (as proposed by Khair 1969). As in *BhG* 9.1, this teaching is called 'the secret of secrets', the highest knowledge. Kṛṣṇa concludes by asking Arjuna to do as he pleases (18.63). What is presented as a conclusion of the whole discourse, marked by summarising the teaching and turning to Arjuna, is opened up again in the next three verses (18.64–66). They not only add to Kṛṣṇa's final words, but supersede them, since now the 'highest of all secrets' is dealt with:

> Once more listen to my highest word, the most secret of all. You are profoundly dear to me and therefore I will tell it for your sake. Keep your mind on me, honour me as my devotee who performs sacrifice for me, (and) you will come to me. This I promise to you truly, you are dear to me. Give up all the laws [or, other teachings] and seek refuge in me alone. I shall free you from all evil – worry not!

This passage stresses the personal, loving relationship between the god and his devotee as an important, if not the most important, dimension of the new theology. The message of these verses is linked to *BhG* 4.3, where the fact that Arjuna is Kṛṣṇa's devotee (*bhakta*) and friend (*sakha*) is considered

234 As in *BhG* 4.6 and 7.14, *prakṛti* becomes *māyā* when it is directed by the lord.

the reason for disclosing the 'ancient yoga doctrine'. Similarly, this relationship is declared to be 'the highest secret' (*rahasya uttama*; 4.3). In *BhG* 11.47–48 too, Arjuna's devotion is regarded as the prerequisite for the god's appearance in his 'form as the cosmic sovereign'. In addition, the passage recalls a core doctrine of *BhG* 9, which culminated in the call to perform all actions for Kṛṣṇa's sake and to renounce all desire and attachment in him. This connection is corroborated by the parallels between 9.34 and 18.65, indicating that 9.34 is being quoted here again at the very end of the *BhG*. However, 18.64–66 established a connection between devotion and liberation from *karman* that, in this form and with this clarity, had not been expressed in the earlier chapters. The fact that Arjuna is said to be Kṛṣṇa's *priya*, his 'dear' and his 'own', is made the basis for the actual efficacy of Arjuna's exclusive devotion with regard to the karmic consequences of his deeds. Since he has given up all other loyalties and obligations, the god will remove all karmic consequences. This means that Arjuna should no longer pay heed to the well-established laws or teachings (*dharmas*) or become confused by their contradictory claims. Neither merit nor demerit will result from his substituting these *dharmas* with Kṛṣṇa. On the contrary, devotion based on the relinquishing of all other desires and obligations is declared to be the key to liberation. While this idea stands in some contrast to the emphasis on abiding with traditional law and customs in *BhG* 17, it makes the consequences of the new doctrine explicit in that it fundamentally changes the devotee's relationship to *dharmas* of all kinds.[235]

Kṛṣṇa's speech ends with some advice about the propagation of the *BhG* (18.67–71), which in 18.70 is called 'the conversation regarding *dharma*' (*dharmya saṃvāda*). Interestingly, the authors are already thinking about the future of their composition and attempting to influence its transmission. First, it is stipulated that the teaching must not be disclosed to those who lack ascetic power (*tapas*) or devotion (*bhakti*). Excluded also are people who do not want to listen to, or do not believe in, the god. In this way, the possible audience of the text is restricted to those who have certain qualifications that permit a proper understanding of the doctrine. This again highlights the context-dependence of the doctrines, in that they are not designed as a 'universal ethics' or to address issues like 'freedom of choice', as has been suggested by some interpreters (see above). The text must also not be used for missionary or educational purposes, or forced upon 'those who

[235] This idea, and with it verse 18.66, gained in importance in later Hindu theologies, such as the doctrine of surrender (*prapatti*) in Pāñcarātra theologies. However, 18.66 should not be confused with this doctrine, since the verse has its own contexts in the *BhG*, to which I did not give enough credit when I suggested that 18.64–66 be regarded as an interpolation (Malinar 1996: 383).

do not want to hear it'. Conversely, by conveying the doctrine to other devotees, a *bhakta* reaches his beloved god (18.68). Kṛṣṇa declares that none is dearer to him than he who propagates this teaching. While propagation is endorsed, conversion or missionising is not. The passage concludes with a pledge to the merits that accrue from memorising and listening to the teaching (18.71): 'He who studies by himself our conversation regarding *dharma* will offer a sacrifice of knowledge to me – this is my view. The man again who shall listen to it, full of confidence (*śraddhā*) and trust, he too is released and reaches the blissful worlds of those who performed good deeds (*puṇyakarma*)'. Such promises of merit are typical of didactic texts and are called '*śruti-phala*' or '*śravaṇa-phala*' (fruits of listening or learning). Not only is the ideal-typical way of dealing with the text rewarded, its recitation by a devotee to devotee, but also the self-study of the text by individuals is acknowledged as a 'sacrifice of knowledge',[236] even though *bhakti* may not be the motivation. Yet it is accepted as being on a par with a sacrificial activity and is accepted by the god, but without promising any particular merit. Listening to the text in turn frees the listener from all negative (but not all) *karman* so that he may reach the 'blissful worlds'. Only that *bhakta* will reach Kṛṣṇa who recites the text not for his own sake, but for that of others, while those who listen reach the heavenly regions. Again the red thread running through the whole text is emphasised, namely acting without egotistical desire. This list of rewards opens up the transmission of the text to audiences other than the already established 'inner circle' of devotees by allowing other forms of study too.

Then, for a last time, Kṛṣṇa turns to Arjuna (18.72), asking whether he has listened with full concentration, and whether his confusion has been dispelled. An enthused Arjuna replies: 'The confusion is gone, and through your grace I have regained clarity of thought. Ready I am and free from doubt. I shall do as you say.' What this means is described at the beginning of the next chapter of the *MBh* (6.41.1), when we see Arjuna taking up his bow and preparing for the battle. The narration of the *BhG* concludes by returning to the overarching dialogue frame between Saṃjaya and King Dhṛtarāṣṭra. Having now reported the whole dialogue to the king, Saṃjaya describes his reaction when he was actually listening to the 'marvellous (*adbhuta*) dialogue'. In doing so, he uses the past tense: 'I was thrilled with delight.' Paying homage to the epic's composer Vyāsa, he points out that he owes him this experience of listening to the conversation (see above 3.1) and highlights the aspects of the text he deems important: 'I have

236 On the 'sacrifice of knowledge', see *BhG* 4.28, 33 and the discussion above, pp. 102ff.

heard this highest secret, the (doctrine of) yoga as told in person by Kṛṣṇa himself, the lord of yoga' (18.75). It is stressed that the teaching is the highest secret, as we have heard several times in the text and again at its very end. According to Saṃjaya, this secret consists of the doctrine of yoga taught by Kṛṣṇa, the lord of yoga, in person. The revelatory character of the text, which has been presented as one of its new and distinctive marks, is made the basis for the authority of the teaching and its 'thrilling' effect on the listener-viewer. This 'thrill' is again stressed by Saṃjaya in 18.76, when he describes how enthused with joy he is each time he recalls the dialogue and the god's appearance: 'Whenever I recall that miraculous form of Hari,[237] I am stunned and I thrill with joy again and again.' Thus, the secrecy and mystery of the doctrines exposed in *BhG* 4, 7 and 9–11 are intrinsically connected with the god's appearance in *BhG* 11, in that his 'marvellous manifestation' proves his divine power and establishes him as the lord of yoga. In the last verse, the yogic character of the god and his teachings is connected to the themes of kingship and royalty that pervade much of the *BhG* and that provide one important link to the epic context of this dialogue: 'Wherever are Kṛṣṇa, the lord of yoga, and Arjuna, the holder of the bow, there is (royal) fortune (*śrī*), victory, success, and a steady course in politics. This is my opinion.' At the very end, the argument put forward in my analysis of the text is corroborated once again: the theology of the *BhG* cannot be separated from its political and socio-cosmic dimensions, and the presence of the revealed highest god allows new alliances to be forged, as between the 'ideal king' and the yogic god in his miraculous appearances. This almost iconographic depiction of their political alliance and personal friendship is based on the revelation of the divinity of Kṛṣṇa and the religious interpretation of *bhakti*. Whenever a future or actual king is allied with the 'lord of yoga', his kingdom will prosper and his reign will succeed. This is stressed in the brief list of virtues that any successful king must have: *śrī*, royal fortune and prosperity, also embodied by the goddess Śrī (see Hiltebeitel 1976), victory in battle, *bhūti* (increase of prosperity and wealth), and a steady political course that ensures the stability of the kingdom and the welfare of all people. This catalogue corroborates the

[237] This verse has certainly contributed to Kṛṣṇa's being regarded as a form of Viṣṇu when one translates 'Hari' by Viṣṇu, as Zaehner, for instance, does. However, Hari is a typical name of Kṛṣṇa elsewhere in the epic, and although there is this strong link between the two gods, I doubt whether Saṃjaya identifies Kṛṣṇa's appearance in *BhG* 11 as the form of any other god, such as Viṣṇu. Rather than identifying both gods at all times, one should be cautious in both respects: they are neither simply identical, nor totally separate. The god of the *BhG* is certainly Vāsudeva-Kṛṣṇa, who is a god in his own right. Nowhere in the *BhG* is he made an *avatāra* of Viṣṇu, but he is identified with Viṣṇu in other, often later, texts and traditions, and vice versa.

claim implied in the teaching called *rājavidyā*, 'knowledge of kings', in that loyalty to a highest god, ascetic qualifications and warrior skills are the basis for a flourishing kingdom and the maintenance of a god-given socio-cosmic order (*dharma*). The lord of yoga and the holder of the bow represent the strongest alliance and the best combination of yogic and military skills, surpassing Duryodhana's claims to power and his self-perception as an absolute king. The model of the alliance between a highest god and a king that is depicted here, at the very end of the text, has become paradigmatic in many later Hindu religions traditions (see Willis 2004 on the Guptas). Seen in the context of the epic, the line 'Where Kṛṣṇa is, there is victory' (Lévy 1917, Katz 1989) receives in the *BhG* its fully fledged theological interpretation.

CHAPTER 4

The doctrines of the Bhagavadgītā: *summary and systematic considerations*

The main features of the arguments and doctrines explored in the analysis of the *BhG* will now be summarised thematically to provide a basis for a consideration of the possible cultural-historical contexts of the text. The text will be treated 'holistically', though departing from the text-historical assumption that the monotheistic framework marks the completion of the argument. In the extant text, the revelation of Kṛṣṇa's divinity and the doctrine of *bhakti* are treated as the solution to Arjuna's dilemma. The previous analysis showed that the *BhG* presents doctrines and ideas, most prominently the concept of disinterested action and the revelation of Kṛṣṇa as the highest god and *yogin*, that are connected intrinsically not only with Vedic and Upaniṣadic traditions or notions of yoga and Sāṃkhya, but also with epic debates on kingship and the use of power. The theology of the *BhG* gains additional layers of meaning when considered in the context of these political debates. It addresses these debates when Arjuna is depicted as the 'ideal king' and turned into a devoted follower of the highest god, who is proclaimed and worshipped as the true sovereign of the cosmos. The religious dimension of *bhakti* is not separated from the political (that is, socio-cosmic) aspects that are indicated when drawing on the symbols and discourse of kingship. Equally important is the interpersonal character of *bhakti* as a relationship based on mutual affection and a sense of belonging. All these aspects acquire shape in the context of the epic in which the authors of the *BhG* have embedded their message. Thus, while the *BhG* may not always have been part of the epic, or the theistic framework may have been built upon other, presumably older ascetic doctrines, this does not preclude the possibility that it has been composed in relation to the epic plot and while giving due consideration to the epic context. The context was regarded as suitable for the text and vice versa, otherwise it would perhaps not have been transmitted in the *BhīṣP*, but rather in the *ŚāntiP*, along with other so-called didactic texts. Even when treated in the commentaries as an independent text, the beginning of the *BhG* has regularly been included, since it provides not only the point of departure, but also the conceptual and personal framework for the doctrines that are revealed in response to Arjuna's dilemma, which acquires full significance and vividness within the epic context, especially because it continues the debates about war and peace contained in the *UdP*.

CONFLICT OF *DHARMA*

The *UdP* showed the epic characters being confronted with contradictory claims and loyalties resulting from a conflict between different dharmic obligations. This creates an irresolvable situation which some actors consider a matter of fate or destiny, as they find themselves forced to act against their better judgement. Arjuna faces a similar dilemma when he stands 'between the two armies' and finds himself torn between the 'kinship law' (*kuladharma*), which demands that he should not kill his relatives, and his duties as a warrior (*kṣatriyadharma*,) which adjure him never to yield to an enemy. While in the past his military pursuits used to serve the interests of his family, Arjuna now realises that fighting will bring about their destruction. In other words, in following one *dharma*, he violates the other. In contrast to Duryodhana, who is shown to have decided a long time ago that his loyalties belong to himself as a king, his kingdom and his people, Arjuna still defines himself in terms of family relationships. Duryodhana has obviously stepped out of this framework and in doing so represents a new perception of himself in his role as king. He regards himself as an absolute king who dominates even the gods, and works miracles when he leads his conquering army, protects his kingdom and brings peace and prosperity to the people. Wielding absolute power, he uses the powers of others and takes advantage of his opponent's weaknesses. He advocates following the 'warrior's law', irrespective of what this may mean for the family. His loyalty is to his kingdom and the institution of kingship alone. This notion of kingship compels others to redefine their loyalties too. What is clear to most of them when they are preparing for battle, namely that kingship, social reputation and personal alliances surpass family interests, seems not to apply to Arjuna as he is depicted at the beginning of the *BhG*. For him the performance of duties and the acquisition of power and kingship are not values in their own right, but are 'smeared with blood' and lack legitimacy. His answer to this situation, which he views as a sign of superior insight, is to decline to fight and give up his social duty in favour of a life 'on alms' (*bhaikṣya*). By choosing renunciation and asceticism as the religious alternative to social life as a whole, he thinks he will escape the conflict between contradictory *dharmas*.

As we have seen, this alternative to the 'bloody work' of war had repeatedly been brought up in the *UdP*, but it was not discussed as a solution to the conflict. Since an ascetic life-style is regarded by Arjuna as being in strict opposition to all the gains and losses that social life has in store, he wants to embrace it as the only way to avoid the negative karmic consequences of killing relatives. In this way, the dilemma of *dharma*, the juridical question of whether killing relatives can ever be justified, is transposed into a problem of personal karmic consequences. Arjuna considers both levels: the social consequences are conjured up when he considers the possible downfall of the ancestors due to the breakdown of proper worship, while the personal level is addressed when Arjuna is shown to dread the pain and suffering that await him because of the destruction of his family. He sees 'negative signs' (*nimitta*) that should be heeded; he sees beloved relatives and friends, but also enemies prepared for the kill, and is overwhelmed with emotions.

At the beginning, Kṛṣṇa's answers move in the familiar territory of speeches of 'encouragement' met with elsewhere in the epic. Arjuna is admonished to think of the disgrace he will bring upon himself and his family over his refusal to fight, because he will be regarded a weakling and eunuch. Then more metaphysical arguments are adduced, using the style of a funeral oration by pointing out the insignificance of earthly life and death when compared to the immortality of the self residing in mortal bodies. However, this does not solve Arjuna's problem: on the contrary, it seems to aggravate it because the discourse provokes the question of why one should be dealing with earthly existence at all when it does not matter. Again, as was the case in the *UdP*, 'indifference' (*samatva*) turns out to be an ambiguous value, since it may indicate both ascetic altruism and egotistic ruthlessness. In order to deal with this problem a new level of discourse is opened up in *BhG* 2.39, introducing the practices and philosophical concepts of Sāṃkhya and yoga.

RENOUNCING AND SUBSTITUTING 'AGENCY': SĀṂKHYA, YOGA AND THE 'WHEEL OF SACRIFICE'

By drawing on the insights and 'faculty of discrimination' (*buddhi*) taught in Sāṃkhya and applying it to yogic practices, Kṛṣṇa refutes Arjuna's opinion that non-action is a sign of insight and a method of ending karmic bondage. Rather than giving up ordained actions, he must give up his attachment to the fruits. Desire and attachment are named as causing Arjuna's problem. He is identified as a 'traditionalist', a stout follower of the teachings of the Veda (*vedavāda*), because those 'fond of Vedic doctrines' assess the value of an action by its outcome only, that is, whether it provides pleasure, power, and ultimately, rebirth in heaven. In accordance with this view, Arjuna wants to act only when he obtains fruits without regrets, happiness without pain. This attitude towards action and duty has to change, and this is the gist of the yoga arguments in *BhG* 2. Only by breaking the attachment to personal involvement can there be any chance to rid oneself of karmic consequences and gain liberation. The yogic path is briefly delineated at the end of the chapter, leading the adept straight to a state of '*brahmanirvāṇa*'. However, this does not solve the problem of action, as Arjuna points out correctly at the beginning of *BhG* 3: if liberation is the goal, why continue acting?

In answering this question, the Sāṃkhya concept of nature (*prakṛti*) as that power that drives all beings to action is introduced to explain that is it impossible to refrain from action as long as one 'travels' in a body. Therefore, inactivity is no solution to the problem of *karman*. Yet again the objection could be raised: why then not follow well-established paths to liberation, such as traditional forms of renunciation or yoga, which seek the end of karmic bondage by avoiding the production of further *karman* in choosing a life of 'social death'? At this stage, the authors apply the doctrine of 'disinterested action' as a criterion for assessing ascetic qualifications. It is argued that the success of yoga needs to be demonstrated in practice, that true detachment and renunciation mean being able to act without egotistical interest. However, this cannot mean just 'acting' because activity is always productive and serves a purpose. Therefore even 'disinterested action' needs a purpose: it must be directed at something and thus connected to a referential framework of meaning that allows discrimination, the application of correct knowledge. This is one of the reasons why 'action' and 'knowledge' are not considered to be two different paths or options, as suggested by Arjuna, but as complementing each other. The purpose suggested at this stage of the argument is Vedic sacrifice (*yajña*), which is interpreted as a cosmogonic activity that recreates and regenerates the reciprocal (*paraspara*) relationships between the creatures and the different cosmic powers which are the basis of life and prosperity in the world. This is explained in the 'wheel of sacrifice', describing the mutual dependence between the elements that are linked in a causality of production and consumption of food (sacrificial offering): rain produces food, food produces creatures, etc. Participating in and contributing to this cycle of exchange is an activity that produces no karmic results for the agent when he does not intend to use the ritual for the fulfilment of desires. The wheel of sacrifice offers an explanation why ritual action for the sake of ritual does not produce karmic bondage: nothing is produced but 'leftovers' of sacrificial food – no other 'surplus' accrues as long as this is not claimed or desired. The sacrificial cycle is one in which each produced element is consumed by the succeeding one: sacrificial production is a process of consumption which is the basis for producing the next element. This is true for *karman* too: while ritual action produces the sacrifice, it is also consumed in the sacrifice, that is, transformed into the sacrificial food that is then consumed again as the 'leftovers' of the sacrifice. Ritual action allows life 'without eating sin', and when it serves no other purpose than to maintain the socio-ritual cosmos based on reciprocal relationships, no karmic bondage arises. The purpose of what from a Sāṃkhya point of view is 'natural' (*prakṛti*) activity is sought in the 'original' idea of sacrifice as the place and the way of acting purposefully for the sake of 'holding the world together' (*lokasaṃgraha*). This concept summarises both the purpose of sacrifice and the purpose of 'disinterested action' or *karmayoga*, defined as ritual activity. The task of 'holding the world together', of maintaining the socio-cosmic order, is a task especially ascribed to kings, that is, a task for which kings provide the role model. Renunciation now means that one must renounce desires and substitute for them an interest in maintaining the cosmic order, the basis of life. The concept and purpose of *lokasaṃgraha* not only allow personal desire and attachment to a higher, impersonal cause to be redirected, but also allow the capacity to act for this purpose to be turned into a characteristic feature of a successful yogic practice.

While this may answer the question of why acting is better than non-acting, it does not address the problem of how to obtain final liberation. The argument then returns in chapters 5 and 6 to Sāṃkhya and yoga concepts, explaining why yogic activity does not result in karmic bondage, but in freedom from *karman*. It teaches that 'self-control' achieved by the *yogin* implies a conquest of cosmological realms and powers that culminates in his reaching *brahman*, the ultimate cosmic cause of creation and all activity (the term used is similar to *prakṛti*). 'Becoming *brahman*' means that the *yogin* acts like *brahman*, like the cosmic cause, and thus substitutes his personal, ego-bound agency for that of *brahman* or *prakṛti*. Since there is no karmic bondage for the cosmic cause of action, but only for a consciousness that is entangled within it, there is no *karman* for a *yogin* who acts as *brahman*. Acting like *prakṛti*, being *brahman*, means that the *yogin* has identified himself with all other beings, that he has become 'the same' and acts like the impersonal, non-attached source of all activity that similarly is not bound by its activity. The *yogin* has reached the position in which he controls and directs the activity of his cognitive and physical powers without identifying with them and becoming attached. A successful *yogin* thus acts like and as *prakṛti*, that is, serving not his own but some other purpose, and therefore not entangled in any karmic consequences. Knowledge of *prakṛti* does not immediately result in a turning away from the world, but in using the powers of nature for the sake of maintaining the cosmic order. This allows the *yogin*, on the one hand, to serve the purpose of 'wishing the well-being of all beings' (*sarvabhūtahitarata*), and on the other, to open the door to liberation at the hour of death, since he has already freed his embodied self from the entanglement with the world of action. This idea is presented by distinguishing it from traditional forms of 'renunciation' (*saṃnyāsa*) that reject ritual and social obligations in order to prevent further karmic bondage, as well as from paths to liberation that demand that all activity cease, up to and including self-extinction, as is the case in Jainism. Using action to fulfil one's desires as proposed in the context of Mīmāṃsā was ruled out earlier, despite the doctrine that sacrifice is an obligation that must not be given up, since the world is based on ritual reciprocity. Instead, liberation is sought through a 'conquest of creation' (5.19) that brings the *yogin* back to the first stage of creation, when the self about to be embodied is in contact with the plenitude of all cosmic powers, the cosmic powers are still an undifferentiated 'whole', and no 'karmic' body is produced that will bring the self into a specific form of existence. This allows the *yogin* to realise ('see') the immortal self in himself, detached from creative activity though potentially capable of using it, and therefore still in danger of becoming attached to it again (as illustrated in the figure of the 'fallen *yogin*' in 6.41). However, when he manages to stay in this position of 'equality' and keeps thinking, 'I do nothing', his agency is replaced by that of the cosmic agent (*brahman* or *prakṛti*,) and no *karman* is produced.

Another aspect of this stage is that the *yogin*, who has become *brahman* (*brahmabhūta*), not only is indifferent, but also experiences bliss (*sukha*). Although the descriptions of what actually happens at the moment of liberation or what liberation is supposed to be are not very elaborate, one can at least say that liberation sets in when the *yogin* turns away from the creative power for ever and remains 'steady' in his detachment (*brahmasthiti*) or gains *brahmanirvāṇa*, which probably means that all (detached) activity stops and that the *yogin*'s physical, active self returns to its cosmic cause and vanishes there. Neither a merger of the self into a higher one is mentioned, recalling Upaniṣadic teachings, nor the ultimate separation of the self from nature and *karman* (*kaivalya*) as taught in 'classical' Sāṃkhya or Jainism, nor the fading away of all notions and intentions as in Buddhism. Instead, the *yogin* is said to be extremely happy never to be born again.

The theological doctrines inserted into these chapters on yoga and then presented in detail in chapters 7–11 make liberation in Kṛṣṇa the final goal that surpasses those other stages called *brahman*, *ātman* or *nirvāṇa*. This is done by superimposing the god as 'the highest' over the other realms and thus solving the problem of alternative and obviously well-established traditions by means of hierarchisation. Becoming *brahman* or reaching *nirvāṇa* is made a stage on the way to Kṛṣṇa, meaning consequently that devotion (*bhakti*) to this god is regarded as a prerequisite for liberation. It is claimed that even a successful *yogin* will need it in order to surpass the stage of *brahman* and reach the highest god. A devotee, on the other hand, makes *bhakti* his point of departure for turning his or her entire life into sacrifice for Kṛṣṇa by offering up all desires and activities to the god, in this way living like a *yogin* or a renouncer, but within the social world. This new framework not only adds another sphere to an already existing cosmos, but also transforms the concepts of liberation and bondage-free activity. Instead of emulating *brahman*'s or *prakṛti*'s indifference and sameness, the devoted adept is now asked to imitate Kṛṣṇa's attitude towards the world by paying attention to the welfare of all creatures as the god himself does. This emulation of the god is interpreted as devotion to him and is therefore directly connected with liberation from *karman* and rebirth. The adept acts for the welfare of all beings because he loves the god who has incited creation. The world is dear to the devotee because it is dear to the god, and the devotee is dear to the god for that very reason. This positive attitude towards the world differs from its depiction as an 'ocean of pain and suffering' stressed in other texts and traditions that endorse the quest for liberation. Turning to the god in devotional attachment is also, in *BhG* 8, recommended as the ideal way of dying. Liberation is now motivated by the desire, not to rid oneself of the world, but to come very close to the god, of which detachment from personal interests and karmic bondage are regarded as welcome byproducts. This is the paradigmatic shift brought about by making 'disinterested action' a medium of *bhakti*.

EMULATING AND WORSHIPPING KṚṢṆA

The foundation for the reinterpretation of renunciation as an act of 'casting all actions on' Kṛṣṇa and redirecting all attachment to the god is set out in chapters 7–11, especially 9 and 11, which 'reveal' Kṛṣṇa as the mighty lord (*maheśvara*) of the universe who has already accomplished the destruction of much of the Bhārata clan as the precondition for re-establishing a righteous and prosperous kingdom. As a consequence, the doctrine taught to Arjuna is called *rājavidyā*, the special knowledge of the king, which establishes a connection to the epic's discussions of the legitimacy of kingship and the different views of the position and power of a king. The *BhG* proposes an interpretation of royal power that stands in contrast to the model of kingship presented in the *UdP* by Duryodhana, who claimed for himself the 'highest' position, the overlordship of all gods and beings. This notion of 'absolute kingship' resembles the concept of the 'god-king' known in other cultural contexts. In Indian texts such 'absolute' kings are usually not regarded as royal role models, but are often depicted as 'evil-doers' or 'demonic' figures (like Duryodhana in the *ArthaŚ* or the Nanda dynasty in later purāṇic accounts). By making the king the devotee of a higher sovereign, his power is delimited by his subordination to a 'highest god'. Yet at the same time the king's special position of power within the socio-cosmic order is reaffirmed by making him the god's ally. Royal knowledge consists in the king's awareness that he is the instrument and sign (*nimitta*) of Lord Kṛṣṇa, who commands power over all creation and can appear on earth whenever the time has come. In order to fulfil his task and serve his god, a king must become a devotee, which means renouncing his personal desire for power or self-indulgence. Ascetic qualifications are demanded of the king, as is done in explicit political texts like the *ArthaŚ* or elsewhere in the epic, but he is not asked to become an ascetic or a *yogin* in terms of adopting the corresponding life-style of renunciation. Rather, he is asked to follow the rules (*dharma* and *śāstra*) and see that his subjects do the same, a task which includes fighting enemies and protecting and extending his kingdom – the traditional tasks of a king.

This loyalty to the highest god, whose interest is in the 'welfare of all beings' and the maintenance of the cosmic order (*dharma*), supersedes both 'warrior's law' and 'family law', making *bhakti* the final answer to Arjuna's initial dilemma. This implies that the performance of the king (or any other devotee) can now be evaluated and judged by drawing on the ideal-typical image and model of the highest god, since the king must now act like a god, that is, as detached, powerful, and exclusively dedicated to the welfare of all beings. Here another paradigmatic shift is implied in the revelation of Kṛṣṇa as the highest god in that his power is now accessible through perception (*pratyakṣa-avagama*). This is demonstrated in an almost iconographical manner in Arjuna's vision of Kṛṣṇa's 'appearance as a sovereign' (*rūpa aiśvara*), which testifies to his 'yoga as a sovereign' (*yoga aiśvara*). Thus Kṛṣṇa appears to Arjuna, his devotee and future restorer of righteous kingship, in 'royal apparel' with four arms, in his cosmic form as '*viśvarūpa*' and in his 'fearsome form' (*ugra*), which stresses the violent task of protecting and defending the socio-cosmic order. This introduces a representational quality that serves as a yardstick and emblem of correct rule and reminds the king of both the sources and the limits of his power. The god becomes the model of sovereignty, and king has to live up to it, in addition being turned into a devotee who must also display his devotion visibly. The king, and any other devotee, must not only be acknowledged, but must also cherish this dependence, because it means that the god regards this devotee as 'dear', as belonging to him. In making visibility a sign of divine presence and the culmination of the loving relationship between the god and his devotees, this doctrine can most probably be used in support of image worship. This is also corroborated by Saṃjaya at the very end of the *BhG*, when he conjures up the alliance between Lord Kṛṣṇa as the 'lord of yoga' and Arjuna as the 'holder of the bow', the wielder of earthly power. Duryodhana's praise of his power (*māhātmya*) is thus rejected by Kṛṣṇa's song (*gītā*) and praise (*māhātmya*).

The ambiguous attitude of 'indifference' towards the results of one's actions is turned into an attachment to the highest god and his divine tasks as the creator and protector of the cosmos. Because Duryodhana's sovereignty is based on taking advantage of the weakness of others (such as gods entangled in ritual reciprocity or ascetics practising non-action and indifference), he will be defeated by those who pursue an allegedly higher purpose and adhere to the highest power. They will prevail because they have accepted their dependence on the god, with whom all creatures are connected, whether they be 'pearls on a string' held by the god, or 'helplessly whirled around in the carrousel of existence' set in motion by the highest lord. In the end, therefore, Arjuna has to deal with Duryodhana's disregard for 'law of the family', although this means that he has to follow him on the road to destruction. Arjuna too must change his loyalty, not to himself or the kingdom, but to the god who appeared to him and who is his secret ally in fighting the 'highest' cause. In doing so, all *dharmas*, all the established rules or regulations, will indeed be given up (as demanded by Kṛṣṇa at the end of *BhG* 18) and defeating Duryodhana means to offend the warrior codex. Although the *BhG* claims that fighting a socio-cosmic crisis calls for 'steadfastness' with regard to one's goal, the moral ambiguity remains when 'unrighteous' acts are committed by 'righteous kings' in the name of a god who is interested in preserving the world and the socio-cosmic order.

THE LORD OF YOGA AND HIS APPEARANCES

The god thus himself represents the mediation of the values of the socio-cosmic order and of liberation when he appears on the one hand as the ally and protector of the 'righteous' or more precisely 'his' kings, and on the other as the highest self, one who is completely detached from the world. Both aspects are bridged in the concept of the god's appearances for specific purposes and his different manifestations as the paramount sovereign, the cosmic ruler, or in human form. This in turn is possible because the 'highest god' is also the 'lord of yoga', not only a sovereign and not only a *yogin*, but a *yogin* who acts and appears as the paramount sovereign. Although in his form as a 'cosmic sovereign' he appears as other rulers and creators of the cosmos before him in the 'All-Form' (*viśvarūpa*), he is neither one of the Vedic gods, nor a cosmic entity taught in the Upaniṣads (*brahman*, the gold-coloured *puruṣa* etc.), nor a human king empowered by rituals conferring cosmic and divine powers on him, but god Vāsudeva-Kṛṣṇa, the 'lord of yoga', 'the highest self' and 'supreme *puruṣa*'. One important implication of interpreting the god's power over the cosmos and over the creative cause of all activities (*brahman*, *prakṛti*) as resulting from yoga is that all his appearances are considered 'appearances' only. Although they reveal his cosmic presence, his overlordship or his being on earth to perform his divine duties as the king of kings, they must not be mistaken for the true identity or 'being' of the god, who remains forever 'unborn'. The god assumes all known and well-established positions and manifestations of power, but as a *yogin*, whether the Vedic-Upaniṣadic '*viśvarūpa*', the All-Form ascribed to creative powers, the overwhelming light and radiation of the sun as the epitome of the cosmic ruler, shining 'as if thousand suns would rise simultaneously' and thus surpassing all imaginable splendour, or the force of time and death when he declares himself to be that all-devouring fire of time whose own agency creates an inevitable course of events that human agents cannot help but follow and enact. He can even take a human body and intervene here on earth in establishing *dharma* and destroying those who abuse and ruin the powers and resources of the cosmos. All this, however, is yogic activity based on the god's control over the cause of creation, over *brahman*, regarded as his 'womb', and over his nature, *prakṛti*, who appears as the material, ever-active visible world when the god becomes the 'seed' (*bīja*) of all beings. He is in the world, but also not in the world, present and absent, hidden and visible. Yoga serves to explain the 'nature' of these appearances, which are the result of the god's power over 'nature' that turns it into '*māyā*', into creating appearances that are devoid of any connection to *karman* and can be withdrawn at any moment. With regard to the god as the 'highest self' these forms are apparitional, but for those who are confronted by them they are dramatically real, lethal and terrifying for the god's enemies, though thrilling and amazing for those who know and want to see the god.

As a god representing both the orderliness and plenitude of the cosmos and liberation from it, he claims to surpass concepts of divinity and power that seem to emphasise only one of these aspects, such as power acquired through ritual procedures necessitating repetition because it vanishes in time or is consumed in its enactment and therefore must be regenerated. This is true not only for Vedic gods who depend on ritual nourishment, but also for human sacrificers empowered through sacrificial procedures. While Kṛṣṇa is presented as a god who receives and reciprocates sacrifice, he does not depend on it. In surpassing other cosmic powers or sovereigns mentioned in Vedic and Upaniṣadic texts, Kṛṣṇa unites them all, making them parts of himself when he appears in his solar cosmic form (*viśvarūpa*), which is brighter than anything ever seen. However, it is not 'himself' appearing but one of his appearances. He is the 'highest' not only because he encompasses all other powers, but also because he transcends them. He is not the sun, nor does he become one; rather, the sun is turned into an appearance of a god whose power is based on yoga. Consequently, although the solar and fiery character of his form as a 'sovereign' (*rūpa aiśvara*) is a characteristic feature of Kṛṣṇa's revelation in *BhG* 11, this appearance is ultimately withdrawn. In fact, he is in this position of ultimate power because of his transcendent position, because he actually does not act, move or perish. However, this concept is combined with the notion that the god is present in the cosmos as the force of procreation ('the seed') and of prosperity (*vibhūti*). In this regard the presence of the god is revealed and perceptible in many different creatures and entities. He can bear many names, since he is the one and only.

This partial pervasion of creation reflects the ideas that there is only one being inciting creation, and, consequently, that the process of creation is brought about by one cause only. In the *BhG* this cause is identified sometimes as *brahman*, but more often as *prakṛti*, the active nature taught in Sāṃkhya philosophy as the source of creation. In turning *prakṛti* into a part of god, supervised and activated by him, the created world becomes the realm in which different realms and creatures enter reciprocal or other forms of purposeful relationships. The world created by the god through *prakṛti* is a whole, not an open cosmos with an open history or a fragile cobweb of gods, humans, animals, demons, plants, etc., forged together by continuous ritual exchanges of food in which all are mutually dependent. Although sacrifice is accorded a central role in 'keeping the world together', it is no longer regarded as the decisive cosmogonic activity. As a consequence, Vedic sacrifice is no longer the only means of approaching the god. In proclaiming Kṛṣṇa the highest god, different ways of connecting with him are permitted (yoga, knowledge, sacrifice, quest for wealth, suffering, etc.), but the one that is privileged is *bhakti*, devotion and loyalty. It is a relationship that is based on and expressed in terms of mutual affection, which is time and again highlighted in the text, for instance when Kṛṣṇa points out that he reveals himself because Arjuna is 'dear' to him or Arjuna asks the god whether they could continue to relate to each other like those who hold each other dear (*priya*) or like friends (*sakha*). Seen against the background of the original meaning of '*priya*', 'own', this implies regarding the 'dear' other as a part of oneself. In its affective dimension it conveys a sense of belonging, while *sakha* emphasises more the advantageousness and stability of a mutual alliance and comradeship. The active interest of the 'highest power' in being connected to his followers and, conversely, being contacted by them is one of the remarkable features of *bhakti*. *Bhakti* is thus a religious practice in which this divine interest is taken as the point of departure. Therefore the god is open to a rather large spectrum of approaches, being the most accessible of all powers, although, and because, he transcends them all while not turning away from the world like a *deus absconditus* or a renouncer. His visible presence in the world proves the promise that 'all' may contact him. As the whole cosmos is his dominion, all creatures are his concern. However, although the god is present and accessible in these different manifestations, ultimately they should help the followers reach the god's true being, which re-confirms the superiority of the value of liberation over any permanent involvement in the world. This brings us, finally, to some more general comments on the theological framework.

COSMOLOGICAL MONOTHEISM

The theology of Kṛṣṇa combines features of a monotheism that make Kṛṣṇa the highest and only god of liberation and creation, and cosmological doctrines presenting the god as partially present in the different aspects of the cosmos. By drawing on older concepts of the special powers of gods, cosmic entities and kings, as well as contemporary doctrines of liberation from *karman* and the realisation of an immortal self, the *BhG* develops a new theological doctrine in that the highest god is regarded as the lord of yoga, the ruler and creator of the cosmos, as well as the ever-detached highest self guaranteeing liberation from rebirth. The theology of the *BhG* thus shows many features that became standard in subsequent Hindu traditions, though they were interpreted differently and enhanced by other concepts. Scholars were hesitant to categorise this doctrine and preferred neutral terms like 'theistic teaching', 'Kṛṣṇaite doctrine', or 'concept of god' (*Gotteslehre*). Rarely, but not as a consequence, the term 'monotheism' was used for the *BhG*. It seems that there is still a certain reluctance to use this term – so cherished in defining the characteristic feature of Christianity, Islam and Judaism – for early Hindu theologies. While this may mirror certain Western preconceptions about 'religion', as well as 'monotheism' as a specific 'achievement' in the history of religion, one should not forget that there are marked differences in the interpretation of the concept of the 'one and only God' that have to be taken into account when speaking of monotheistic theology in the context of Hinduism. These differences explain the hesitation in using the concept for Hindu traditions. The most important is perhaps that, in contrast to other monotheisms that principally deny the existence of other gods, the *BhG*, like many subsequent religious traditions of Hinduism that accept the paradigm of the *BhG*, acknowledges other gods, although on a lower level of existence and thus as having only 'limited divinity'. In contrast to the rejection of other gods in the monotheistic paradigm of Judaism, Christianity and Islam, the *BhG* combines features of a polytheistic and monotheistic understanding of the world and its beyond. While the cosmos is thought of in polytheistic terms as the realm of the many, its cause and transcendence are located only in 'the one'. The *BhG* presents the 'one and only' god in relation to the 'many' and the 'whole'. Monotheism, as thinking of the 'one', and polytheism, as dealing with the relationships between the 'many', are regarded not as being contradictory but as being complementary. The theology of the *BhG* shows characteristic features of what, with J. Assmann (1993: 10), I suggest should be called 'cosmological monotheism'.[1] This allows for acknowledging the existence of other gods as constituents of the created world and partial manifestations of the 'one'. Correspondingly, the one can reveal itself as the 'all', and yet claim to be separate from it. In contrast, the revelation ascribed to Yahweh, for instance, defies such cosmic identifications, since this god reveals himself by referring to nothing but himself. Seen from this perspective, one can say that the characteristic feature of the theology of the *BhG* is its monotheistic core, which, however, is enhanced by the god's cosmic presence, which allows him to appear in different forms and under different names. The *BhG* combines features of a monotheistic theology, making Kṛṣṇa the highest and only god of liberation and creation, with a cosmological doctrine that regards the god as being partially and

[1] Compare Assmann's seminal analysis (1993, 1998) of such a theology in ancient Egypt, which mirrors the development from polytheism via Echnaton's sun cult, the 'monotheistic revolution', to a theology that combined monotheistic and polytheistic features.

secretly present in the different aspects of the cosmos. He is thus accessible in different forms and names, and resides in the form of images in the permanent sacred and ritual space of a temple. However, this accessibility is regarded as merely a partial and temporary revelation of the god in the world, which at the same time disguises his true being and identity as the highest self.

In the *BhG*, this dovetailing of the idea that there is only the one, unique god that is the cause of the world and the promise of liberation, with the concession of the existence of other gods and other 'exceptionally powerful beings' (such as *yogins*), is achieved by moulding the following features into a conceptual framework.

1. The relationship between the 'one' and the 'many' is thought of in terms of the sovereignty of the one over the many as being the creator, protector and maintainer of the world. The one is the lord and the king ruling over the manifold beings and the cosmos as a whole. In this sense he may appear as the 'whole', as is expressed in his appearance as the 'All-Form' (*viśvarūpa*) and when he is called '*sarva*' (masc.), not '*sarvam*' (neut.), as older texts would have it.

2. The 'one' is present in the world, revealing himself, but at the same time remaining 'secret'. Conversely, since he is never totally present in these appearances, the revelation rather paradoxically unveils a 'secret'. The god is not co-substantive with the world, since he ultimately transcends it: all beings reside in him, not he in them. Therefore he surpasses and transcends, like other cosmic entities or realms that were previously regarded as 'whole' (*sarvam*, neut.) or 'highest', such as *brahman*. In revealing the god, the *BhG* thus reveals a new form of wholeness, based not only on completeness and encompassment, but also on separation and transcendence. This mirrors the consequences of the doctrine of an immortal self that exists independently of the mutual dependence of the manifest beings in conceptualising creation and cosmos.

3. The transcendence of the god in the *BhG* is connected to older Upaniṣadic concepts of liberation and traditions of asceticism and yoga, as well as based on central concepts of Sāṃkhya philosophy, most importantly the concepts of *brahman* and *prakṛti*. These concepts are used when the god is presented as the 'mighty lord of yoga' and thus appears for the sake of the world or his followers, but who also guarantees the liberation of 'individual selves' as reaching the 'highest self'. His position as a powerful but detached *yogin* who remains forever liberated, although he repeatedly 'takes birth', explains why he remains unaffected by the disadvantages of power known among the 'many', such as ritual restrictions or ascetic indifference. The

conceptual framework is designed in such a way as to allow the god to be distinguished from other wielders of power, such as gods, successful *yogin*s and ascetics, and kings. He is superior to the Vedic god because he is not dependent on sacrificial nourishment and cannot be 'invoked' and tied to a sacrifice by a patron through the correct ritual invocation. He is more powerful than successful ascetics, since he is forever liberated and commands all the powers of nature without being endangered by any egotistical interest and indulgence in his power. He is not inhibited by the attitude of indifference which demands that ascetics remain impartial and uncommitted, due to their detachment from the world. Finally, the god is superior to any king because he represents and grants the power of kingship. He is the ultimate source of royal power, as is demonstrated by his being regarded as capable of performing royal tasks, however gruesome and devastating they might be.

4. Liberation is conceived as reaching the god by means of devotion and loyalty, that is, based in the realisation and knowledge that one belongs to the god and as a consequence that one is attempting to 'follow his path' and structure one's life as a devotional service performed for the sake of the god's interest in the world and the embodied selves that are part of him. This concept is based in the seminal doctrine of 'disinterested action', which seems to have been regarded as leading to liberation, even in non-theistic traditions. It is not through merely giving up activity that one achieves freedom from the fruits of one's acts, but through detachment from attachment. Within the new theology, this detachment is again redirected in that desire must now be offered up to the god and turned into the devotion and affection that result from understanding the knowledge, concealed and secret, that the god discloses.

5. The god is the principle of living, the 'self' in all beings. The self is the inciter of its embodiment, while at the same time, each embodiment points to the self as its immortal and distant dimension. This relationship between embodiment and embodied self is based on a clear distinction between both realms: while the visible world is a manifestation of its creator, it does not share its most characteristic features – that is, his being immortal, unique, indescribable and hidden – because it is a product of yogic power. This is stressed in the *BhG* in the distinction between the god's 'might' (*vibhūti*) and the different, partial 'manifestations of his might' (*vibhūtaya*), which again introduces a 'polytheistic' feature in that other beings, including other gods, are regarded as 'partial manifestations' of the god's might.

6. The king is no longer the highest representative of the cosmic order – that is, the most complete body in the visible world – but becomes a sign of

the invisible presence of the highest god himself. It is not the king himself but the institution of kingship that is regarded as a manifestation of the interest of the god in protecting and preserving the world. The role and power of the king are thereby stabilised as a permanent, cosmic institution. The actual king embodies the office and its power, but he himself is not the power that sustains it. Rather, he becomes the favourite devotee of the divine sovereign.

7. The simultaneous presence and absence of the god are expressed in terms of a dialectical relationship between secrecy and visibility, appearing and hiding. The god remains ultimately 'invisible' even when he reveals himself, like the knowledge necessary to approach him. The revelation of the god in a visible form and a personally communicated knowledge is also made possible because this does not contradict his transcendence or his being the 'highest secret'. Rather, it opens up a new spectrum of accessibility, which allows the god to reside in a temple, since his forms are disguises that reveal his presence, but at the same time point to a realm and reality beyond it.

8. The god appears in many forms and names and is identified with well-known entities or states of being, such as 'highest *puruṣa*', 'highest self' or 'the all' (*sarva*), and he is identified as approachable under his name of 'Vāsudeva'. However, since the revelation is a personal one, the identity of the god equally rests on his revealing himself as the one who is the first person as such, the ultimate and most comprehensive 'I' (*aham*), for instance when he declares that 'I am the string on which all beings are strung.' In contrast to other monotheistic theologies, which allow no personal name for the god and defy 'translatability', the 'one' within the theological framework of a cosmological monotheism can bear many names.

Thus, the term 'cosmological monotheism' accounts for many features of the theology of the *BhG* and that it is therefore a designation which may invite further comparative studies with traditions not only within India, but also in other cultural contexts. While its emergence and its connections with other texts and contexts need to be explored in more detail (and will be the task of a future study), this should not prevent us from addressing the question of the possible historical and cultural contexts of the composition of the *BhG*.

CHAPTER 5

Historical and cultural contexts

Analysing the *BhG* with regard to its epic context has been a major concern of this study. I hope to have shown that this perspective adds additional aspects of meaning to a text whose interpretation seems to have incited discussion and debate almost since its composition, since it claims to reveal a religious truth or philosophy whose importance is not confined to a concrete historical or cultural context. Yet these contexts need to be taken into account when considering the date of the *BhG*'s composition, the history of its reception and more generally the interplay between 'texts' and 'contexts' in regard to the status of texts and the dissemination of ideas, symbols and myths. While a text like the *BhG* may very well be considered a 'closed universe' in terms of narrative structure, ideological design and characters or voices, it is also connected with other media of social communication, such as images, inscriptions and coins, some of which are still extant. Other media include various forms of textual performance and methods of establishing textual authority, which all contributed to its transmission and kept 'alive' a text which would have otherwise been forgotten. These contexts are no longer available as 'empirical data' – we know of ancient 'textual recitations' only because literary texts narrate them – yet they cannot be regarded as 'fictitious' only. This may illustrate the recursive character of the interplay of the texts and contexts we also meet with in the following discussion of the possible historical and cultural contexts of the *BhG*. For instance, suggestions for the date of the text are usually based on considerations of other sources (texts, inscriptions, etc.) that are regarded as contexts or corroborative evidence for the existence of the teachings of the *BhG*. However, which contexts are taken as evidence depends on the interpretation of the text as being relevant to and in these contexts. The recursive structure or the 'hermeneutical cycle' applies when one attempts to establish an undated text's 'historical context', because this is necessarily based on the assumption that the text is already considered a document of that very historical development that is being used in order to date the text. This situation has to be borne in mind. Therefore any contextualisation is fragmentary: suggestions regarding dates and contexts are based on 'cumulative evidence' and plausibility, because data and materials are used and gathered for detecting and narrating a history that is in many respects not accessible.[1]

CULTURAL CONTEXTS: GENERAL CONSIDERATIONS

In the case of the *BhG*, three fields of contextualisation have received special attention by scholars: the relationship of the *BhG* to the composition of the epic, contexts for individual doctrines of the *BhG*, and the emergence of Kṛṣṇa as god. While the first two fields were addressed in text-historical and text-critical studies, the question of where and when Kṛṣṇa was regarded as a god 'outside' the *BhG* was also addressed by drawing on other materials, inscriptions, etc. However, because there is some overlap between these different contexts, arguments were drawn from each of them. This is mirrored in the connections established between the way in which the text is generally interpreted and the historical context that would suit this interpretation. Some scholars, for instance, interpret the *BhG* as a 'synthesis' of different ideas and groups which mirrors a peaceful, prosperous society in which diversity has been harmonised, as was allegedly achieved under the Gupta dynasty (350–500 CE; cf. Kosambi 1962, 1978). Others, however, regard the text as anti-Buddhist propaganda belonging to an age of conflict that seems to have been especially threatening to the brahmanical establishment, as is claimed to have been the case during the reign of Aśoka. For these scholars, the *BhG* thus belongs to the 'brahmanical revolution' aimed at achieving a 'brahmanical renaissance' under King Puṣyamitra Śuṅga (second century BCE; cf. Lamotte 1958: 433). Still others would regard the presentation of Kṛṣṇa as the highest god as pivotal and would pay attention especially to those sources that deal with Kṛṣṇa (cf. Garbe 1921). Whatever the historical situation and the relative chronology of texts, the *BhG* is usually situated within the historical framework that is generally assumed to apply to the composition of the epic, that is, between 400 BCE and 400 CE. This roughly coincides with historical developments between the reign of the Emperor

[1] As has been pointed out by Bakker (2001: 405), 'the complexity of the historical reality of ancient India is far greater than we can ever hope to recover'. Cf. Koselleck's (1979: 153) discussion of what he calls the 'fictionality of the factual' and the role of 'theoretical anticipation' as part and parcel of historiography. This structure has long been recognised and explored, for instance in Schleiermacher's *Hermeneutik* and Nietzsche's *Unzeitgemäße Betrachtungen*, and has been somewhat revitalised and expanded on recently in so-called 'deconstructive' methods and the 'new historicism'.

Aśoka (268–232 BCE) and the advent of the Guptas (around 350 CE). This temporal framework has been generally accepted for the composition of the *MBh* since Hopkins (1901) and Winternitz (1907). Various suggestions for refining this framework were adduced by van Buitenen (1973–78), Brockington (1998) and Fitzgerald (2006). Others wonder why this framework has been accepted (e.g. Biardeau 1997) and suggest a different setting for the epic's composition (e.g. Hiltebeitel 2001) as the work of one author. Similar suggestions had been made earlier by Kirste (1900) and Pisani (1939), who, however, argued not for unity with regard to authorship, but for unity of 'redaction', and assumed one editorial session, which according to Kirste took place between the third and the second century BCE. Both stressed, with Dahlmann (1895), that there is no need to separate the 'epic' and the 'didactic' parts of the epic too strongly. This discussion introduced still another parameter for dating the text: relative chronology of texts and linguistic or stylistic criteria. Here we have to deal with the place of the *BhG* in the epic's textual history, its relationship to the Upaniṣads (especially the so-called 'middle' or 'theistic' Upaniṣads, *KaṭhU* and *ŚvetU*) and to Buddhist texts. Since most of the dates are uncertain, the relative chronology is too. On linguistic grounds, also, Rajwade (1917) argued for a date close to Pāṇini, which was rejected by Krishnamurti (1930). Brockington (1998: 147–148) analyses the formulas and the style of the *BhG* and concludes that it is rather a 'late epic style' and therefore suggests dating the *BhG* between the first and the third century CE. While the first century seems to match the other parameters, the third century seems rather late, especially when one takes the relationship to the still later *Nārāyaṇīya* section (see studies in Schreiner 1997) and to the slightly later *ŚvetU* (see Oberlies 1988) into account.

While in what follows I accept the general framework in dealing with the historical contexts of the *BhG*, I do not regard it as a time-span of 800 years that needs to be completely covered with layers, interpolations and redactions. In any case, when dealing with the composition of the *BhG*, it certainly must be narrowed down. The following discussion leads me to suggest that the *BhG* does not belong to the oldest epic traditions, nor was it included in the final redaction, but was perhaps completed around the beginning of the Common Era, during the early Kuṣāṇa rule.

While many aspects of this historical period remain uncertain and await further study, some basic parameters with regard to changing ideologies and social formations seem more or less undisputed.

1. Vedic sacrificial religion was transformed by new concepts and practices, such as the immortal self, the idea of liberation as discarding the

physical world and the emphasis on knowledge as surpassing the realm of *karman*, of ritual actions and merits. These new ideas were part and parcel of different ascetic movements, which indicated a breach with Vedic religion and crystallised in Buddhism and Jainism, as well as in emerging philosophical schools such as Sāṃkhya and yoga. Renunciation and distance from the traditional framework of ritual and social duties are characteristic features of all of them, entailing a life-style that may very well have been regarded by some within the brahmanical establishment with hostility and scepticism, even if some of the ideas emerged within their own circle.

2. The emergence of urban centres and more centralised forms of administration became an important feature of society since the Nandas (fourth century BCE) and resulted in changing notions and functions of kingship. This change seems to have caused unease and even rejection, as testified not only in later accounts of Nanda rule, but also in the epic that deals with kings and kingship in a crisis emerging from 'within'.

3. The epic includes not only a lot of material on the various doctrines and intellectual milieus, but also – as can be seen in the final redaction – attempts to mould them into an overarching 'architectural framework' (Bailey) without producing a *grand récite* that would wipe out the multi-layered and multifaceted character of the epic narrative and the discontinuities and ambiguities that testify to the epic's textual history. Parts of the epic are marked by the strong presence of new theologies and gods, the latter now no longer part of a polytheistic, somehow corporate pantheon, but each regarded as 'highest'.

4. This period sees the presence and occasional occupation of parts of northern India by peoples and rulers coming from 'outside', such as the Indo-Greek and Iranian-Greek kings and dynasties, beginning with Alexander the Great's failed invasion, followed by Huns, Scythians and the Kuṣāṇa kings, who managed to establish a considerably more stable rule over a large territory. Some of them introduce new ideas about the roles of the king and the god(s) as the most powerful beings in the cosmos. New symbols, images and methods were sometimes introduced by resident rulers too, as the case of the Maurya dynasty shows (Falk 2006a). The use of a script and the production of images for commemoration and worship seem to have become widely accepted by the third or second century BCE. Inscriptions testify to the self-perceptions of rulers and kings as the patrons of religious cults.

5. The rise of new cults, forms of worship and religious ideas is characteristic of this period. Not only do we meet depictions of gods, kings and sometimes ascetics on coins and in sculptures, but we also have texts

that deal with these ideas and depict ideological debates in narrative form. Monotheistic teachings occur in several texts belonging to this period, and they often show clear traces of the debates on important issues of cults, ways of living and goals of liberation. However, these texts were probably more than mere reflections of debates or solutions achieved elsewhere in society: they seems to have played a rather active part in formulating and authorising ideas and became influential in other social contexts when they were recited and interpreted. Thus, the texts were also contexts themselves, when, for instance, the 'source' for conceptual adjustments was provided for kings who would allow a variety of gods to be worshipped in their kingdom. The relationship between text and historical context is thus not one-way. While texts certainly convey narratives, symbols and reflections of political history or society, the social and political arenas are no less infused and nourished by texts that advocate and articulate certain ideas.[2] This influence of texts on other areas does not always take the form of a conscious 'reception' of the text (such as a quotation, commentary, etc.), but also includes a more fluid, selective and even incomplete picking up of ideas. This dissemination of the epic's texts, ideas and narratives in oral transmission was enhanced by teachers using vernacular languages to spread their ideas, and by the composition of texts for all sorts of people (and not only the initiated 'twice-born', as was the case with Vedic texts). Recent studies show that ascetics played a vital role in this process (see Bailey and Mabbett 2003, Harrison 1995, Cort 2002).

6. In this period, we are witnessing an increasing emphasis on visibility. In this process, the introduction of script in India certainly played an important role (Falk 1993), although it seems to have been used only hesitantly by Hindu or Brahman authorities. This is at least indicated when one looks at the number of inscriptions (see Srinivasan 1997: 313–315). However, this may not be representative of the total situation, as palm-leaf manuscripts from the Kuṣāṇa period show (see Schlingloff 1969). The at least potential visibility of the written word in inscriptions and manuscripts seems to have had similar effects on textual culture in India, as elsewhere. Texts acquired a new form of materiality, which allowed their being treated as solid manifestations not only of thoughts, but also of intentions and political agendas (as was the case with inscriptions). The written form allowed new types of intellectual discourse and debate, as testified, for instance, by the proliferation of voluminous texts and commentarial literature. Yet

[2] As suggested, for instance, by Hein (1989: 231), who credits the *BhG* with a pivotal role in bringing about a synthesis between conflicting ideologies in order to reject Hellenist influence.

orally transmitted and recited text remained significant, if not predominant. However, in combination with the rise of image worship and temple cults and theatrical performances, this period is marked by the emergence of a new visual culture, not only within Hindu traditions, but also in Jaina and Buddhist contexts, which first reached a peak with the Kuṣāṇas and Guptas. With its emphasis on the visual dimensions of the god's revelation, the claim that teaching is 'accessible by perception' and its poetic-mythic imagery, the *BhG* most probably belongs to just such a cultural context. The text works on the basis of the acceptance of such visibility, but it also confirms and endorses it, perhaps even giving it a new conceptual framework by making 'visual appearance' a characteristic feature of a highest god.

Taking these parameters and the extant, complete text of the *BhG* as our point of departure, the question to be addressed is, then, whether it is possible to narrow down the historical contexts that resulted in the composition of the extant *BhG* some time between the Nandas and Guptas. When do we find the most parallels to the most important features of the *BhG*? The latter are: (1) the debate over righteous kingship, which results in making the king subordinate to a highest god as the god's earthly representative and 'instrument'; (2) the mediation of the ascetic values of renunciation of social duties and liberation with the values of 'householders' interested in maintaining the socio-cosmic order through the doctrine of 'disinterested action'; (3) this mediation represented by the one and only 'highest god', who, as the 'lord of yoga', is both turned towards the world as its creator, protector and destroyer while appearing in different forms and names, and detached from the world as the highest, unmanifest self, who guarantees liberation with and in himself; (4) the idea that devotion and loyalty (*bhakti*) to this god will bring about liberation and that approaching the visible manifestations of the god (for instance, sculptural representations) and following his self-revealed teaching will lead to this goal; and (5) the subordination of other gods and goals of liberation, such as the Upaniṣadic *brahman*, the self and the immortal *puruṣa* of Sāṃkhya and Buddhist *nirvāṇa*, under the god Kṛṣṇa as the highest being.

In order to explore the possible contexts of these features, one can draw on iconographical, epigraphic and numismatic data, as well as on other texts, which are again often of uncertain date, such as Upaniṣads and epic and Buddhist texts. This leaves one with the rather complex task of connecting the *BhG* with the history of ideas, the chronology of texts and political events, and the dates of inscriptions, coins and artefacts. Although this may result in statements and opinions less clear-cut than might, strangely enough, seem possible when scholars rely on only a few inscriptions or textual parallels at most, it leaves room for the available evidence and can at least be discussed and criticised because an argument has been put forward. Since the dates of texts and ideas are difficult to establish, the following thematic treatment of the available evidence allows different data to be included and provides some leeway for placing the texts in a certain context by way of establishing a relative chronology. The following analysis is based on the assumption that the importance and innovative character of the *BhG* lie in establishing a 'cosmological monotheism' that mediates between ascetic values and social duties and allows the power of a king to be confined by making him a devotee of a supreme god. However, what is propagated in the text must also be seen against the background of what it rejects, since the text deals with a theoretical or ideological dilemma of contradictory values. For instance, the *BhG* denies that 'renunciation', in the sense of giving up social life, is the best way of living, and insists that participating in the ritual-based reciprocity of the socio-cosmic order leads to liberation for all classes when it is not done for one's personal interest. In addition, the text can be used to deny absolute claims to power by anyone living in this world, especially kings' claims to rule over all beings in the cosmos or to be godlike beings who have nothing and nobody over them. Any concept of kingship that would see the king as god is negated by proclaiming Kṛṣṇa the highest god and the wielder of yogic power over nature.

This doctrine is based on the conflict of values mentioned above and on debates about the desirable form of kingship, which are well attested in the epic, as well as in Upaniṣadic and Buddhist texts that can be dated as belonging to the post-Aśoka period (third to second century BCE). However, corroborative evidence on theistic cults and doctrines can be found from around the beginning of the Common Era, which suggests that the final redaction of the *BhG* should be placed at around this time. We can gather some evidence for reconstructing a milieu in which the concept of a highest god was not developed with regard to one god only, and when several gods were put in this position, as can be seen in texts that are adjacent to the *BhG*, such as the *ŚvetU*, the *KaṭhU* and the *Nārāyaṇīya* section of the epic, as well as in the many images of gods that can be dated to this period. The following analysis will suggest that it is perhaps most plausible to date the final redaction of the *BhG* to the first century CE. Putting forward the argument means considering the evidence from the following fields of inquiry: (1) the emergence of Kṛṣṇa as highest god; (2) the relationship with Buddhism; and (3) the role of kingship and actual dynasties. Before dealing with these aspects, a general outline of the historical period will help to establish the conceptual and temporal framework in which these aspects can be understood.

GENERAL HISTORICAL OUTLINE: FROM THE NANDAS TO THE KUṢĀṆAS

Apart from concrete historical events such as changes of dynasty and the emergence of new religious and philosophical ideas and cultic practices, this period also witnessed major changes in the social and economic structure. The eastern Nanda dynasty (c. 400–320 BCE) seems to have been regarded, at least in later sources, as manifesting and propelling this change in that the Nandas claimed to be rulers of a large kingdom based more on agriculture than on pastoralism and more centralised forms of administration.[3] The *MBh* seems to indicate this change, as Thapar concludes (1977–78: 993) in her analysis of economic data in the epic: 'The epic in origin relates to clan-based tribal society with effective power invested in tribal chiefships and where the term tribal does not preclude social stratification: a society which gradually gave way to monarchies of the more conventional type based on developed agriculture.' As has been pointed out in the analysis of the debates in the *UdP* and Arjuna's dilemma in the *BhG*, this is corroborated by the conflict between the law of the family-clan and the law that applies to the warrior as a member of a social class. However, although this trend towards 'empires' and social stratification became a dominant and persistent feature under subsequent dynasties, other forms of social organisation continued and marked perhaps the limits of imperial expansion, such as the *janapada*s, which remained independent territories with their own structures. This seems to have been the situation at the beginning of Maurya rule, which Bongard-Levin (1985: 60) describes as follows: 'The political life of the period was characterised by two trends: on the one hand, there was the quest for autonomy, independence, even within the framework of a small state formation, and, on the other, the striving for centralisation, for the establishment of a powerful state under one ruler.' However, while the Nandas were based in Magadha (roughly, modern Bihar), the Mauryas started their careers in the north-west. Before them, Persian-Achaemenid kings ruled over Bactria, Punjab and Gāndhāra,[4] before being replaced

[3] Cf. the description of the Nandas in the dynastic accounts (*vaṃśa*) of the Purāṇas. Mahāpadma Nanda is depicted as *ekarāṭ*, the one and only ruler who has conquered all others. See Pargiter 1913: 25; von Stietencron 2005.

[4] The Persian king Cyrus (559–530) conquered Gāndhāra. Greek sources, such as Strabo and Arrian, mention that Indians were in the army of Xerxes when he fought against the Greeks in 480 BCE.

in the aftermath of Alexander the Great's campaign (327–324) to India. After his defeat by the Mauryas, this territory was divided among different satraps and smaller kingdoms struggling for hegemony. However, shortly after Alexander's retreat, the Persian king Seleucus I attempted to reconquer Bactria and defeated King Antigonus in 312 BCE. His advance into Punjab and Sindh was stopped in 305 BCE by Candragupta Maurya. The peace treaty and the exchange of ambassadors did not stop the subsequent expansion of Maurya rule, which reached its peak under Aśoka (268–232 BCE). With him came the public use of script in the form of written commands, and proclamations in the form of edicts and inscriptions installed at important places of worship, often connected to goddess worship (see Falk 2006b). This also marked the advent of regional and local court administrators to supervise the conduct of the people. However, this did not prevent other rulers from fighting or at least striving to keep their territories independent and to maintain a certain degree of autonomy from the central government. The tension between the interests of these smaller units in striving for independence and those of imperial or dynastic authorities in centralising their rule was also a characteristic of Aśoka's reign.[5] This became clear when, after his death, the Maurya empire fell apart into different smaller kingdoms, a process that reached its final stage with Puṣyamitra Śuṅga's coup (c. 187 BCE). The Śuṅgas (187–75 BCE)[6] did not succeed in establishing an empire, since they were in continuous conflict with Indo-Greek kings attempting to conquer the Gangetic plain and gain access to the western sea (now Gujarat). This process had started already under Puṣyamitra Śuṅga, who had to fight against the advance of King Demetrius I (189–167 BCE). Under the leadership of Apollodotus and Menander,[7] Greek armies may have reached Kathiawar and Mathurā (perhaps even Pataliputra, one of the centres of Śuṅga rule; see Tarn 1951: 129–182), but then had to retreat when, in 168 BCE, Eucratides attacked Demetrius I in Bactria. The Śuṅgas are followed by the Kāṇva rulers (75–30). Their reign saw the relatively peaceful co-existence of the Indian and Indo-Greek kings after the latter stopped

[5] Cf. Rapson (1955: 463): 'Over all kingdoms and peoples in these provinces the emperor was supreme. He was the head of a great confederation of states which were united under him for imperial purposes, but which for all purposes of civil government and internal administration retained their independence.' See also Bongard-Levin 1985: 60ff.

[6] In the light of new archaeological evidence pointing to a rather loose connection between kings with names ending with *-mitra*, Härtel (1977: 82) suggests that it is perhaps misleading to speak of a Śuṅga dynasty. See also Bhandare 2006.

[7] Macdonald (1955: 400) is more sceptical with regard to the conquest. Narain (1957: 76ff.) doubts the connection between Menander and Demetrius I and regards the former as being one of the mightiest Indo-Greek kings (1957: 100). He entered Buddhist literature as King Milinda, who is instructed about the teachings of the Buddha in the *Milindapañha*.

advancing on the former. This situation again changed when the Scythians under Maues (90–53 BCE) conquered the whole of north-west India and Madhyadeśa. Mathurā fell under the rule of Scythian satraps, who seem to have respected the local cults.[8] With the beginning of Kuṣāṇa rule, once again a larger empire was established, marked by religious pluralism and the implementation of various symbols of power and sovereignty in the representation of Kuṣāṇa rulers (Verardi 1983, 1985, Falk 2006a).

VĀSUDEVA-KṚṢṆA AS 'HIGHEST GOD'

The history and prehistory of the Kṛṣṇa as hero and god raises perhaps more questions than can be answered with the extant evidence, as the various interpretations of the epic Kṛṣṇa show (see Hiltebeitel 1979). We have to take into account Kṛṣṇa's depiction not only as an epic hero and as the leader of the Vṛṣṇi clan called Vāsudeva, but also as Kṛṣṇa Devakīputra, who is mentioned in the *ChU* 3.17 as a pupil of an Upaniṣadic teacher.[9] How should we understand his different appearances? Do we have to distinguish between different Kṛṣṇas, or are we dealing with different myths, narratives and representations of one character or figure? How should we deal with his identification with Viṣṇu, despite having kept his own mythology, theology and followers in distinct Kṛṣṇaite religious traditions? What history or mythology led to the depiction of Kṛṣṇa as the highest god in the *BhG*? Some scholars distinguish between different Kṛṣṇas or Kṛṣṇa traditions, which were then condensed and combined in one person (e.g. Tadpatrikar 1929). In a structuralist perspective, these different appearances of Kṛṣṇa are regarded as aspects of the one Kṛṣṇa, symbolising the *avatāra* god and the universe of *bhakti* (see Biardeau 1976: 204ff. and Hiltebeitel 1989, tracing the interconnections within the epic). While this perspective offers important insights with regard to the extant epic in which these different aspects are juxtaposed as co-extant and simultaneous, this does not preclude viewing them as belonging to different milieus, traditions, and narrative and historical stages. Seen from a historical perspective, the juxtaposition of 'different Kṛṣṇas' is the 'simultaneity of the non-simultaneous'

[8] On Mathurā, see Härtel 1977 and the essays in Srinivasan 1989a.

[9] In *ChU* 3.17 Ghora Angirasas tells Kṛṣṇa about the similarities between sacrificial activities and daily life. While this teaching vaguely resembles the interpretation of daily life in terms of *bhakti* suggested in *BhG* 9, it belongs to a general trend of thought to be found in other texts too. Although some scholars (Raychaudhuri 1920: 41ff.; Preciado-Solis 1984: 24ff.) suggest a historical connection between the Upaniṣadic and the epic Kṛṣṇa, there is not sufficient historical evidence for such a hypothesis (De 1942). While a direct connection seems difficult to establish, it may have contributed to making Kṛṣṇa a teacher of religious doctrines in the older parts of the *BhG*.

(Koselleck 1979), meaning that history is reflected not only in superimposing the 'new' on the 'old' or simply effacing it, but also in additions, insertions and distributions.

A helpful interpretation of the historical process resulting in the co-existence of these different threads more or less loosely tied to the figure of Kṛṣṇa in the extant epic has been offered by Härtel (1987) and Srinivasan (1997). They put forward the thesis of a 'gradual deification' of Kṛṣṇa from a clan hero (as he is depicted in the epic) to the god and then the 'highest god', provided with a fully fledged theological interpretation in the *BhG*. Three stages can be distinguished in this process of deification, all of which concern not different Kṛṣṇas, but Kṛṣṇa as a single and unique figure. At the beginning, Vāsudeva-Kṛṣṇa and his elder brother Saṃkarṣaṇa-Balarāma were venerated together as heroes of the Vṛṣṇi clan.[10] Then Vāsudeva-Kṛṣṇa came to be worshipped as a quite separate god from Balarāma, as shown in the epic (cf. Bigger 1997). The tradition of worshipping the Vṛṣṇi heroes continued, but it was transformed by turning them into manifestations of Viṣṇu in the context of later Pāñcarātra theology (the *vyūha* doctrine). The identification of Kṛṣṇa and Viṣṇu is the latest development for which evidence can be adduced from the Gupta period onwards. Interestingly, at each new stage the previous tradition was not abandoned completely, but often kept, although adjusted to new contexts. Therefore, these processes of deification resulted on the one hand in the emergence of new cults and theologies, but on the other hand, because certain traditions were kept, in the co-existence of historically different representations and traditions. The co-existence of what, from a historical perspective, may be regarded as different stages also becomes apparent when one looks at the available evidence that may allow us to date these stages.

Epigraphic and numismatic evidence for the worship of the clan heroes Vāsudeva-Kṛṣṇa and his (elder) brother is available from the second century BCE onwards.

1. A coin showing images of both was found in excavations at Ai Khanoum (Afghanistan). It seems to have been minted during the reign of the Indo-Greek king Agathokles (Filliozat 1973), whom Narain (1957: 181) has dated to between 180 and 165 BCE. Both figures are represented with two

[10] Härtel proceeds from the assumption that there is no difference between Vāsudeva and Kṛṣṇa, as suggested by other scholars. According to R. G. Bhandarkar (1913: 11–12) the first step in this development is the identification of Vāsudeva, the god of the Sātvata clan, first with Kṛṣṇa mentioned in *ChU*, and subsequently with the Kṛṣṇa of the epic and the *BhG*. Dandekar (1975–76: 177) accepts this view and places the identification of Vāsudeva with Kṛṣṇa in Pāṇini's time (c. 500 BCE). Contrary to this, Raychaudhuri (1920: 3) argues that Vāsudeva and Kṛṣṇa were always identical.

arms each, Kṛṣṇa holding disc and conch, Saṃkarṣaṇa a mace and plough. This indicates the existence of iconographical conventions at that time and of an independent iconography of each of the figures.

2. Two inscriptions were found in Ghoṣūṇḍī and Hāthibādā, Chitorgah District (Rājasthān). Their almost identical text refers to a place of worship called Nārāyaṇa-Vāṭakā, where Saṃkarṣaṇa and Vāsudeva are jointly worshipped (*pūjā*) as 'invincible lords of the universe' (*anihatabhyām sarveśvarabhyām*; cf. Sircar 1965: 90–91). Since there is some uncertainty regarding the identification of King Bhāgavata Gājāyana Pārāśarīputra as the donor of the inscription, the suggested dates range from the third to the first century BCE, with the later date being more likely.[11]

3. An inscription in the Nānāghaṭ cave (Thānā District, Mahārāṣṭra), ordered by Queen Nāganikā in the second half of the first century BCE (cf. Sircar 1965: 192), mentions Vāsudeva and Saṃkarṣaṇa as gods to be venerated (other gods are Dharma, Indra, Candra, Sūrya and the four guardians of the world).

4. Apart from the appearance of the brothers in the epic, they are mentioned as objects of worship in *Mahāniddesa* 1.4.25, a commentary on the *Khuddaka Nikāya*, a Buddhist canonical text dated by Warder (1970: 347) to the first century BCE.[12] In his *Mahābhāṣya*, the commentary on Pāṇini's grammar, Patañjali mentions a temple for Saṃkarṣaṇa, Vāsudeva and Kubera as members of the Vṛṣṇi clan.[13]

A separate cult of Vāsudeva-Kṛṣṇa alone is indicated by the following sources.

1. The Garuḍa column at Besnagar (Madhya Pradesh), with two inscriptions. The first declares the column to be a gift from Heliodorus,[14] ambassador of the Indo-Greek King Antialkidas, who reigned in north-west India between 130 and 110 BCE.[15] The inscription mentions a King Bhagabhadra,

11 As suggested by J. C. Ghosh 1933; Preciado-Solis 1984: 34–35; Sircar 1965: I: 90, and Filliozat 1973: 121. The connection between the horse sacrifice mentioned in the inscription and the worship of the two brothers corresponds to other sources mentioning *sātvata-vidhi*, a ritual tradition associated with the Sātvata clan; cf. *MBh* 6.62.39; 12.322.5; 12.336.51; 12.330.13. See R. G. Bhandarkar 1913, Dandekar 1975–76, Härtel 1987.

12 Cf. R. G. Bhandarkar 1913: 3; Lamotte 1958: 435; Preciado-Solis 1984: 20, note 7.

13 See *MB* on Pāṇini 2.2.34; 2.2.24 and 4.1.114, where Vāsudeva and Baladeva are mentioned as members of the Vṛṣṇis.

14 Heliodorus is called *bhāgavata*, which has roused speculations whether this should be understood as referring to him as a follower of Kṛṣṇa, who were elsewhere called *bhāgavatas*. Choudhury (1964: 341) concludes: 'The devadeva of the inscription, together with the epithet Bhāgavata of Heliodorus, proves decidedly not only the deification of Kṛṣṇa, but also the existence of the Bhāgavata sect by that time.' This seems to stretch the evidence too far.

15 For the text, see Sircar 1965: 88–89; for a graphic depiction of the Besnagar site, see Irwin 1975–76.

who has not been identified with certainty[16] but is addressed by the title *tratāra*, saviour. Narain (1957: 120) points out that at this time this title referred to the title *sōter*, which some Indo-Greek kings conferred on themselves in order to claim the status of a god-king (cf. Habicht 1970: 172).[17] This indicates the presence of Hellenistic cults of the ruler and their deification in northern India, of which the Indian elites were probably aware. In the context of the epic, Duryodhana's self-perception as king in *MBh* 5.60 comes close to such a concept, and the *BhG*'s doctrine of the subordination of a king under the reign and power of a highest god allows the notion of a god-king to be rejected, as well as any other notion of an absolute king circulating in indigenous contexts, as seems to have been the case with the Nandas.

The column is dedicated to Vāsudeva, who is called 'god of the gods' (*devadeva*). Similar epithets occur in the *BhG* (*devadeva*; 10.2; *deveśa;* 11.37). The second part of the inscription mentions three 'steps leading to heaven', i.e. restraint (*dama*), relinquishment (*tyāga*) and awareness (*apramāda*). Raychaudhuri (1922) and Choudhury (1964) quote parallels from the *MBh* (11.7.19 and 5.34.14) and conclude that Heliodorus knew the epic. *BhG* 16.1–2 is also regarded as a 'closely parallel passage', which, however, is doubtful, since only two of the terms are mentioned, and this not even in sequence (see Preciado-Solis 1984: 34). Rather than proving any knowledge of a concrete text, the inscriptions show that the donor was familiar with a set of values that are also mentioned in the epic, both times in contexts that are didactic and full of references to 'tradition' and established knowledge. However, the inscription testifies to the worship of Vāsudeva in a very high position, although the Besnagar compound seems to have included other gods too (see Härtel 1987: 575ff.).

Some controversy was caused by the presence of Garuḍa at the top of a column (*dhvaja*), since this was regarded as proving the identification of Kṛṣṇa and Viṣṇu, given that Garuḍa became Viṣṇu's vehicle (*vāhana*). However, the epic establishes a connection between Kṛṣṇa and Garuḍa at many points, without implicating Viṣṇu.[18] Härtel (1987: 555) and Srinivasan (1989a: 387) cautiously suggest distinguishing both cults at this early stage, although it must be kept in mind that they seem to have been rather close, which may point to an intended realignment of two gods from different

[16] See the discussions by Tarn 1951: 313–314; Narain 1957: 120; Irwin 1975–76: 168; and Härtel 1977: 81–82.

[17] Indra is already called '*trātā*' in Vedic texts (e.g. *AV* 7.86.1).

[18] E.g. *MBh* 1.29.16 (when Nārāyaṇa and Viṣṇu are mentioned, the *garuḍa-dhvaja* is connected with Kṛṣṇa); 2.2.12; 2.22.22–23; 5.81.20; 7.57.2.

milieus (Vedic in the case of Viṣṇu, epic-heroic in the case of Vāsudeva-Kṛṣṇa). However, on the basis of the extant evidence, it is very difficult to come to any definite conclusion with regard to the relationship between the two.

2. The second Garuḍa column at Besnagar, dated around 100 BCE (D. R. Bhandarkar 1913–14: 190). The inscription reports that the column (*dhvaja*) was given by King Bhāgavata Gotamīputra for a temple of '*bhagavat*'.[19] Scholars agree that Vāsudeva is the god who is here called Bhagavat. Venis (1910) suggests that the king, referred to as a *bhāgavata*, is a follower of Vāsudeva, while D. R. Bhandarkar (1913–14: 190) considers it the proper name of the king. As is the case with Heliodorus mentioned in the first Besnagar inscription, the exact meaning of *bhāgavata* cannot be established with certainty and, as a consequence, cannot be adduced as evidence for the existence of a religious tradition or a group of followers called *bhāgavata*s.

3. The inscription at Koṭhi (near Mathurā), issued by satrap Mahākṣatrapa Śoḍāsa, who reigned between 10 and 25 CE (Sircar 1965: 122; Preciado-Solis 1984: 24). The text as reconstructed and translated by Lüders (1938–39: 208) reports the construction of a part of a temple compound (*mahāsthāna*) for Vāsudeva: 'by Vasu, a gateway of stone (?) and a railing were erected at the . . . of the great temple of *bhagavat* Vāsudeva. May *bhagavat* Vāsudeva, being pleased, promote (the dominion or the life and strength) of *svāmin mahākṣatrapa* Śoḍāsa.' This inscription shows the close connection between the worship of Vāsudeva and the god's role as protector and promoter of a regional king.[20]

4. Several sculptures of a deity with four arms, holding a disc, conch and club, have been ascribed to the Mathurā school of artists, which flourished shortly before and during the Kuṣāṇa dynasty and thus testify to a religious pluralism. The latest date assumed for the extant sculptural remains is the first century CE, by which time the iconography of a four-armed deity had been fully developed. Härtel (1987: 587) has argued against the usual identification of these images as Viṣṇu. Srinivasan (1989b: 383f.; 1997 *passim*) comes to the same conclusion: 'Indeed icons usually identified as Kuṣāṇa Viṣṇu images mainly on the basis of the mace (*gadā*) and discus (*cakra*) held in the extra hands, have herein been considered as

19 D. R. Bhandarkar (1913–14: 190) translates: 'Bhāgavata, son of Gotama, caused a Garuḍa standard to be made in connection with the best temple of Bhagavat (Vāsudeva) when Mahārāja Bhāgavata had been crowned twelve years.'

20 Indicative of the cultural climate at that time, which permitted co-existing cults, is another inscription dated at the time of the satrap's reign. It was found at Mora, near Mathurā, had been dedicated by a lady named Tosā and tells of the establishment of images (*pratimā*) for the five Vṛṣṇi heroes. For text and translation, see Lüders 1938–39: 194ff.

representing the Bhāgavata god Vāsudeva Kṛṣṇa . . . Unquestionably, the main Vaiṣṇava object of worship at Mathurā during the Kuṣāṇa age is four-armed Vāsudeva-Kṛṣṇa, of whom over thirty single representations are known.' The strong presence of the god suits the literary evidence not only in the epic, but also regarding the Kṛṣṇa legend explored in the *Harivaṃśa*, which recounts Kṛṣṇa's conflict with his uncle Kaṃsa in Mathurā. The iconography of the sculptures is identical with that mentioned in *BhG* 11.7 and 11.46 (here Kṛṣṇa is explicitly called 'four-armed'). The relative scarcity of older images does not necessarily point to the non-existence of a Vāsudeva-Kṛṣṇa cult before the Kuṣāṇa kings:[21] the inscriptional sources already adduced suggest the opposite.

Another aspect of the rather fluid transition from hero to god is that, apart from the pairing of Kṛṣṇa with his brother Balarāma, there is a strong association with Arjuna, who came to represent the ideal of *bhakti*, based on a *sakha* (comrade and companion) relationship common between warrior-combatants (Hiltebeitel 1984–85). The epic emphasises this association and even interprets it theologically, while the relationship between the two brothers recedes into the background. This association is already mentioned in Pāṇini's grammar (fifth century BCE). In *sūtra* 4.3.98, Pāṇini addresses the question of what those who possess *bhakti* towards the pair Vāsudeva-Arjuna (joined using the dual case) should be called. The question of whether *bhakti* should be given a religious connotation was debated among scholars without coming to a definite conclusion (cf. Bhattacharjee 1925–26; Subrahmanyam 1926; Dandekar 1975–76: 170–171; Preciado-Solis 1984: 27–28). However, it seems doubtful whether these aspects can be separated from each other (Coomaraswamy 1942). The important difference is introduced when *bhakti* is given a theological interpretation, but it seems likely that the passage points to the epic tradition, which from early times associated Kṛṣṇa with Arjuna, without denying the relationship with Balarāma. Yet although there is no evidence of a cult of the pair Arjuna and Kṛṣṇa that could be compared with that of the two brothers, the epic bards singled them out for further identification, as can be seen in the epic tradition identifying them with the *ṛṣis* Nara and Nārāyaṇa (Biardeau 1991).

Seen against the background of this evidence, the *BhG* can be regarded as lending to the deification of Kṛṣṇa and a contemporary Kṛṣṇa cult a theological explanation that explores the epic partnership between Kṛṣṇa

[21] Cf. Preciado-Solis (1984: 102). See also the admittedly uncertain identification and date of a four-armed image from Malhar (Madhya Pradesh), with an inscription dated to around the first century BCE, studied by Venkataramayya (1959–60). See also Srinivasan 1997.

and Arjuna. Although the divinity of Kṛṣṇa is dealt with elsewhere in the epic, this is not done in a coherent way (see above, chapter 2, the discussion of the *UdP*, pp. 35ff.). Processes of deification also apply to other heroes, as is the case with Rāma in the Rm (cf. Brockington 1984), was accomplished in the idiom of an *avatāra* doctrine, which makes Rāma an embodiment of the god Viṣṇu, the *BhG* proclaims Kṛṣṇa to be the highest god in his own right, and Arjuna is not made his *avatāra*. The 'cosmological monotheism' of the *BhG* is a specific development that marks a shift in the paradigm of divinity and thus bears the stamp of innovation. It is important to note that this development resulted neither in eclipsing Kṛṣṇa as an epic hero, nor in denying other forms of worship of the god, as is attested in the persisting traditions of the worship of the 'Vṛṣṇi heroes', who were later identified in Pāñcarātra theology as the 'four *vyūhas*', the four divine 'formations' of divine qualities (cf. Matsubara 1994). The co-existence of different traditions is a characteristic feature of that period, although there is also a strong tendency towards hierarchisation, as is the case in the *BhG* when devotion to Kṛṣṇa is proclaimed the highest form of religious practice.

THE ROLE OF BUDDHISM

An important aspect of the religious pluralism of the time was the relationship with Buddhism, which attracted many lay followers connected with a strong monastic community. For many scholars this meant a permanent threat to 'brahmanic orthodoxy', resulting in political and cultural upheaval. While competition and conflict cannot be denied, the situation may have been more complex, not only allowing more harmonious interactions, but also varying over the subcontinent. On all points of the religious spectrum we see signs of change. Vedic religion was transformed not only from 'within' (Heesterman 1968) and by ascetic movements of all kinds, but also by the rise of image worship for (new) gods and by the emergence of urban centres and a more centralised administration based on hereditary kingship. However, while older notions were sometimes rejected, we more often than not find them being reinterpreted and implemented within new conceptual frameworks. We see ideas, images and practices not only in conflict, but also travelling and crossing the boundaries between different communities, and even between different cultural realms. This situation and the often uncertain dates of texts and artefacts make it difficult to establish the relationship between religions and the possible exchange of ideas with conclusive proof.[22] Although the different traditions developed their own practice, doctrine, symbolism and imagery, their interaction was influential in creating a shared idiom of terminology, ritual and practice, despite emphatic differences on points of interpretation and with respect to ultimate purpose. Thus, key concepts of this change, such as the 'immortal self' (*ātman*) or *karman*, were shared across the communities and could therefore become points of debate and dissent. This is also true of religious practices, such as 'meditation' or image worship, which were interpreted differently, but yet shared, in Hindu, Jain and Buddhist traditions. All these new groups and communities had to cope with the long-established social and ritual framework formulated by the Brahmans. Not only Buddhists and Jains, but also the authors of the *BhG* confronted well-known Vedic doctrines (*vedavāda*) with their teaching of a path to liberation and social respectability not based on ritual purity. Conversely, Brahmans were themselves active in the formulation of the new ideas and had to adapt to the changing political and cultural context brought about by new social formations, new types of rule and new religious practices such as image and temple worship (von Stietencron 2005). Seen from this perspective, the *BhG* can indeed be regarded as mediating concepts and balancing conflicting values (Biardeau 1981, van Buitenen 1981) by launching a religious alternative to Vedic religion that not only draws on new ascetic and philosophical notions, but also confirms the validity of sacrifice as the epicentre of that reciprocal exchange that 'keeps the worlds together' (*lokasaṃgraha*). In doing this, important features of both ascetic and Vedic-Upaniṣadic traditions are both combined and modified as steps on the path to Kṛṣṇa. Ritual and the traditional (śāstric) rules of social conduct are accorded a central place in this new theology, though concepts and practices not explicitly connected to the Vedic and Upaniṣadic traditions, such as yoga and Sāṃkhya, are also dealt with. In addition, other traditions are considered without naming them. This seems to be the case with Jain and Buddhist notions too, which the authors of the *BhG* do not explicitly identify as such, although they seem to comment or draw on them. This is a feature that the *BhG* shares with both epics, in which similarly only scant traces of the presence or importance of Buddhism are discernible, while terms like *nirvāṇa* point to an implicit acknowledgement of Buddhist influence. The thesis that the *BhG* is a piece of 'anti-Buddhist' propaganda may catch one aspect of the text, but it is

[22] See Scott's (1990) careful study of the relationship between Zoroastrianism and Buddhism, as well as Falk (2006a) on 'tidal waves' of inclusion and exclusion of ideas in 'indigenous' contexts.

only one aspect of a more complex picture (which includes, for instance, a critique of the followers of the Veda too) in which we also find the *BhG* and Buddhism sharing certain ideas, although they interpret them differently (Bronkhorst 1993). Setting 'Buddhism' and 'Hinduism' too strongly in opposition may thus mean overemphasising one aspect of the situation and perhaps inappropriately projecting later notions of religious communalism into the past (see Lamotte 1958, on the interpretation of Aśoka in later Buddhist texts). Recent studies across the different groups show that one must reckon rather with pluralistic, not dualistic, religious environments that were to undergo various transformations and formations with various degrees of exclusion and inclusion under the influence of different rulers, teachers, migrants and invaders. In this situation, interactions range from conflict through competition to coagulation, exchange and even parallel developments independent of any direct influence or 'borrowing'. A good example of such a circulation of concepts, images and practices across the different groups are the Mathurā and Gāndhāra schools of art, which found patrons who were prepared to accept a shared idiom for depicting rather different gods and teachers (Srinivasan 1997: 308–312). Another area of 'floating' concepts and practices is that of the doctrines of yoga, asceticism and meditation, where, too, the authors of the *BhG* seem to share a view also found in early Buddhist texts, namely that asceticism should not mean torturing the mind, body and senses or completely ceasing to act, but a moderate practice of dietetic (e.g. fasting) and social restrictions. According to Bronkhorst's analysis (1993), this shows that both traditions reject the complete suppression of activity practised in Jain circles. Another remarkable feature of this shared attitude is that, in both traditions, the higher stages of meditation are characterised by an experience of 'utmost happiness' (*sukha*). In addition, the Sāṃkhya interpretation of detached action as 'natural activity' (*prakṛti*) used in the *BhG* in order to exempt the acting *yogin* from karmic bondage implies a complete distancing from the 'ego principle' that usually accompanies karmic activity. Both Sāṃkhya and Buddhism agree, though again on quite different philosophical principles, that karmic consequences are produced because one appropriates activities by making them one's own (*mamatva*; *ahaṃkāra*). By withdrawing the word 'I', the adept stops this appropriation and karmic bondage too.

This idea differs from other conceptualisations of action, such as that only non-action extinguishes *karman*. The *BhG* includes an ascetic method that helps to stop 'ego-talk' by propagating a concept of yogic action that emulates *prakṛti* or *brahman* in being indifferent and therefore neither enjoying nor suffering the 'fruits' of their activity. This notion is similar to what happens in Buddhist '*vipassanā*' meditation as described in the Satipaṭṭhāna-sutta of the *DN*, which teaches how to withdraw the pronoun 'I' from all experiences and thus experience the transience and hollowness of ideas such as an 'ego' or a person who suffers, enjoys, etc. In drawing these different features together, it seems likely that the authors of the chapters on *karmayoga*, the 'conquest of creation' and the idea of becoming *brahman* or reaching *brahmanirvāṇa* were familiar with Buddhist ideas, and may even have adopted them in a way similar to the way they used Sāṃkhya and yoga for their own purposes. I do not see enough evidence for postulating that *BhG* 2, 5 and 6 are the product of a serious conflict with Buddhism or an answer to a 'Buddhist threat': it seems more plausible to assume (without forgetting that it *is* an assumption) that not only Sāṃkhya and yoga, but also certain Buddhist notions were adopted. However, it remains significant that, in contrast to Sāṃkhya and yoga, neither Buddhist nor Jain notions are identified as such.

In this regard, the *BhG* is in agreement with the epic authors' attitude in generally passing over these schools in silence – a fact that has not led scholars to believe that Buddhism or Jainism did not exist or were not known to the compilers of the epic. However, this sheds some light on what at this point was regarded as an appropriate philosophical affiliation when launching a reinterpretation or even critique of Vedic notions, and what was not. Although Sāṃkhya retained its scepticism regarding the helpfulness of Vedic, that is, ritual ideas (see *SK* 1–3), it was considered a quotable doctrine, perhaps because it would still advocate the basic principles of Vedic and Upaniṣadic cosmology, the idea of a hierarchy of causes, the importance of reciprocal relationships, the idea of an immortal self and the notion that social duties must be performed in order to sustain the world. Perhaps more than Sāṃkhya, Buddhism presented less a doctrinal 'heresy' than a social alternative, with its new forms of ascetic community supported by lay followers, and even communities that would be open to all and not depend on ritual purity or social rank. Like yoga, the *bhakti* theology presented an alternative to these religious movements by allowing 'open access', but it would still propagate the acknowledgement of a Brahman-interpreted social hierarchy and the performance of prescribed duties. Innovative ideas were thus not necessarily rejected or accepted just because they were associated with a certain group, and mutual influence can be observed in many texts, which also shows that we are dealing with communities and 'religions' still in the making. The degree of competition may have varied considerably from region to region, as well as according to the level on which it was enacted. Yet social competition for patronage, for instance, need not have prevented the exchange of ideas, and the situation 'on the ground' may have necessitated and prompted quite different ideological alliances.

While the uncertain chronology of texts and cults prevents one from coming to definite conclusions about the relationship between the *BhG* and Buddhism, this does not necessarily mean that we should not deal with it at all. However, in doing this, the above-mentioned spectrum of possible relationships should be taken into account. Since the basic obstacle in this task is the uncertain chronology, most scholars have concentrated on establishing textual histories and relative chronologies of texts and ideas. Apart from the above-mentioned parallels with regard to concepts of meditation and probably the priority of Buddhism, two signposts demarcate the relationship of the *BhG* with the development of Buddhism: first, Aśoka and his politics of *dharma*, and second, the emergence of the *bodhisattva* ideal, that is, of a liberated person who decides to postpone liberation and work for the good of the suffering instead. A considerable number of scholars have suggested that the rise of the *bodhisattva* ideal must be regarded as a reaction to the presence and popularity of monotheistic teachings such as the *BhG* (Lamotte 1958: 437; Glasenapp 1954: 471; Basham 1981). Recent studies seem more hesitant and cautious in assessing the impact, presence and even meaning of Mahāyāna in this period (Harrison 1995, Schopen 2005).

More important, perhaps, is the combination of ascetic ideas of liberation with social life offered in the doctrine of 'disinterested action' as a form of 'attending to the welfare of all beings' or of worshipping the highest god in a spirit of *bhakti*. Seen from this perspective, it seems plausible to place the composition of the *BhG* after Aśoka and before the emergence of the *bodhisattva* concept (second to third centuries CE; see Basham 1981, Huntington 1989, R. C. Sharma 1989; but cf. Schopen 2005). This temporal framework matches the evidence of a cult of Vāsudeva-Kṛṣṇa, which suggests that the theological framework may have been composed in the period between the Śuṅgas and the Indo-Greek and Indo-Scythian kings (c. 180 BCE–50 CE).

CONCEPTS OF KINGSHIP: AŚOKA AND BEYOND

Some scholars argue that the authors of the *BhG* have used Aśokan ideas in their concept of 'disinterested action' for the sake of all beings, while others regard the *BhG* as an attempt to counteract the Buddhist rejection of the Vedic ritual and belief in gods.[23] This latter view results in dating the

[23] Upadhyaya (1971: 59) places the *BhG* before Aśoka.

BhG to the time of the Śuṅga kings who usurped the Maurya throne after Aśoka's death. Accordingly, *BhG* is a document of a 'brahmanic renaissance' endorsed by Puṣyamitra Śuṅga (c. 167 BCE), which, according to some, also resulted in a persecution of Buddhists under the Śuṅgas (e.g. N. N. Ghosh 1943). However, this view is often based on later Buddhist texts that depict Aśoka as the great Buddhist emperor whose reign was followed by the 'dark age' under the Śuṅgas (e.g. Lamotte 1958: 431). For other scholars these texts are not reliable historical sources, but tinged by the interests of later Buddhist communities. The fact that important Buddhist monuments, such as the *stūpa* at Barhut, were constructed during the Śuṅga period does not support the view that Buddhists were being persecuted in that period. Thus one has to be cautious when assuming that either a 'revolution' or a 'renaissance' took place.[24] The evidence is too weak to put forward a strong historical argument, as Thapar points out (1961: 201) after her careful analysis of the condition of the Mauryan empire after the death of Aśoka: 'Since the Mauryan empire had shrunk considerably and the kings of the later period were hardly in a position to defend themselves, it did not need a revolution to dispose Bṛhadratha. We are told that he was assassinated by Puṣyamitra whilst reviewing the army. This does not suggest a great revolution. In fact it points very strongly to a palace *coup d'état*.'

In addressing the question of the relationship between the *BhG* and Aśoka, much depends on the interpretation of Aśoka and his idea of *dharma*. Scholars are divided over the question of whether he promoted a Buddhist *dharma* or not. This in turn is connected to the interpretation of what the inscriptions tell us about his understanding of *dharma* and his perception of himself as a ruler. While Aśoka certainly became a patron of Buddhist institutions and even a follower of the movement, scholars are hesitant to regard him as a Buddhist king who promoted Buddhism as part of his task as a ruler. Lamotte (1958: 249) therefore proposed to distinguish between Aśoka's 'personal' *dharma* and Buddhism, noting that it is futile to look for Buddhist notions in his inscriptions. Thapar (1961: 3) in turn points out that Aśoka shows a rather paternalistic attitude: 'The policy of Dhamma was a policy rather of social responsibility than merely of demanding that the entire population should favour Buddhism.'[25] On the

[24] See Banerjee 1953, Prasad 1954, Thapar 1961. Prasad (1954: 38) states that 'the conclusion that Puṣyamitra Śuṅga persecuted the Buddhists is largely based in conjectures and surmises rather than on any sound historical materials which alone can be a basis for the verdict of the historians.' Even Lamotte (1958) does not press the argument in order to advocate the persecution theory.

[25] Cf. Bongard-Levin (1985: 369). Bloch (1950: 31) argues that Aśoka's concept of *dhamma* is quite close to the traditional brahmanical understanding: 'the programme Aśoka gives himself is that of any

other hand, his texts demonstrate that he perceived himself to be a new type of ruler who differed from earlier kings with regard to his relationship towards the people. Moreover, he depicts himself as a ruler who commands not only weapons, but also knowledge.[26] Aśoka's understanding of his rule is thus important with regard to the *BhG*'s and the epic's discourses on kingship and righteousness, and may help to clarify the influence of Buddhist notions too. One point of agreement between the *BhG* and Aśoka is the emphasis on the idea that the king is the model for his people: he can demand obedience to his commands and acceptance of his promotion of *dharma* as the yardstick of moral and social conduct because he himself follows and represents it perfectly. Aśoka declares in the sixth rock edict (Girnar) that he has dispatched his 'officers' to all the regions of his kingdom eager to receive their reports because he is constantly striving for the 'welfare of all people':

For I am never content in exerting myself and in dispatching business. For I consider it my duty (to promote) the welfare of all men (*katavya-mate he me sa[va]-loka-hitam*). But the root of that (is) this, (viz.) exertion and the dispatch of business. For no duty is more important than (promoting) the welfare of all men. And whatever effort I am making, (is made) in order that I may discharge the debt (which I owe) to living beings, (that) I make them happy in this (world), and that they may attain heaven in the other (world). (Hultzsch 1925: 11–13; text and translation)[27]

The formula *savalokahita*, 'welfare of all people', used three times alone in this edict, is similar to the model of acting set out in *BhG* 3, where the king is also regarded as the model of 'altruistic' acting for the sake of 'keeping the world together' (*lokasaṃgraha*) and acknowledging the retributive, ritual character of existence. According to *BhG* 5.25, the successful *yogin* 'wishes the welfare of all creatures' (*sarvabhūtahitarata*).[28] Aśoka points out that he wants to become 'free from debt' with regard to the creatures, which may mean that he wants to perform his allotted duty, which allows him to receive tribute from his subjects. However, there is no sign of his acknowledging a 'superior power' such as a highest god who is also regarded as the creator

Hindu king'. For a more general comparison of *dharma* in the *BhG* and Aśoka's edicts, see Keller 1971.

26 In the fourth rock edict, he is critical of the violence of earlier kings; in the eighth rock edict he talks about his spiritual interest, in contrast to former kings who want only to please themselves; and the seventh rock edict praises the success of his reign and the efficacy of his *dhamma* policy.

27 See also Hultzsch 1925: 34–35, and the first rock edict in Dhauli, stating: 'All men are my children. As on behalf of (my own) children I desire that they may be provided with complete welfare and happiness (*save[na hi]ta-sukhena*) in this world and in the other world, the same I desire also on behalf of [all] men' (1925: 92–97).

28 This attribute is also applied to kings elsewhere in the epic; see Hein 1986; see also *ArthaŚ* 1.5.17.

of *dharma*. Rather, *dharma* seems to be a cosmic-social principle that the king must not only protect, but also promote. On the other hand, Aśoka does not depict himself as a *cakravartin* in the Buddhist sense. Both the subordination of kings under a 'highest god', as taught in the monotheistic framework of the *BhG*, and the self-perception of kings as *cakravartins* are perhaps later developments, probably of the Kuṣāṇa period (Reynolds 1972). The inscriptions of Aśoka seem closer to the passages in the *ArthaŚ*.

What connects Aśoka with the *ArthaŚ*, the epic's criticism of Duryodhana's notion of kingship and the *BhG* is the ascetic qualification that is demanded from the king. While the *ArthaŚ* is as silent about a king's dependence on a higher power as are Aśoka's edicts, and thus differ from any monotheistic reinterpretation of kingship, the text stresses the need for a king to conquer his senses (*indriyajaya*) and to act only for the sake of his kingdom and his subjects. This role of the king as model for correct behaviour and the ideal form of social activity is also acknowledged in the *BhG* (especially in *BhG* 3). It indicates a context in which an interpretation of *kṣatriyadharma* primarily in terms of the welfare of the family-clan (*kula*) as proposed by Arjuna has become obsolete, and Duryodhana's recklessness, and his insistence that his responsibility extends to his kingdom only and entirely, point to this new understanding. At the same time, in the epic it is made the cause of a huge problem in that it shows the destruction that a king placed in a position of unlimited power may cause. The *ArthaŚ*, many texts in the epic and Aśoka himself propagate a restriction of royal power through adherence to *dharma* and successful practices of self-control called 'victory of the senses' (*indriyajaya*):

> Control over the senses, which is motivated by training in the sciences, should be secured by giving up lust, anger, greed, pride, arrogance and foolhardiness. Absence of improper indulgence in (the pleasures of) sound, touch, colour, taste, and smell by the senses of hearing, touch and sight, the tongue and the sense of smell, means control over the senses (*indriyajaya*) . . . For, the whole of this science means control over the senses . . . A king, behaving in a manner contrary to that (and hence) having no control over his senses, quickly perishes, though he be ruler right up to the four ends of the earth'. (*ArthaŚ* 1.6.1–4, trans. Kangle)

Later on (1.7.3), the text points out that this means that the king should adopt not an ascetic life-style, but rather only moderation, as, for instance, is also recommended in *BhG* 6.16–17. According to Heesterman (1985: 131–132), successful *indriyajaya* is the touchstone of the king's legitimacy: 'The ideal Kauṭilyan king has an authority and a legitimation not derived from the community but all his own, for here the king's basic qualification is . . . *indriyajaya*, the victory over the senses.'

The ideal of the king as a representative of *dharma* may have been innovative with regard to older notions of kingship – in particular, the task of promoting *dharma* is something new (Gokhale 1966). However, this notion was retained, though reinterpreted, in later traditions as a paradigm and yardstick of kingship. It is very difficult to be certain about the origin of this idea and thus about the chronological relationship between these texts. The *BhG* and Aśoka's edicts formulate somewhat similar ideas, but whether they were the source for Aśoka or were, in their turn, a reinterpretation of his self-perception and ideas within a ritualistic-ascetic framework is anyone's guess.[29]

In many of these texts, the power of the king is thus determined in relation to other areas and positions of power, most importantly gods and successful ascetics and *yogins* who have conquered both themselves and the circumstances of existence or even creation. In each case, the acquisition of power is rooted in the cosmological dimension of the respective position of power: asceticism also implies empowerment on the cosmological level, but restricts the use of this power to non-egotistic purposes, such as the welfare of all beings, while private enjoyment entails the danger that the ascetic loses his powers because he starts to be attached to them again, and, as a consequence, 'falls' down. This career of ascetic empowerment is regarded as different in principle from the acquisition of royal power, which is based on ritual consecration and the interpretation of the royal body as an aggregation of different qualities and powers lent to the king by Vedic gods. This aggregative character of royal power is also mirrored in the different 'limbs' or 'creative powers' (*prakṛti*) he needs to control in order to rule over a prosperous kingdom (cf. *ArthaŚ* 6.1). His office has a cosmological character and implies a temporary deification, since this royal consecration brings him to the position of representing the wholeness of the cosmos with regard to his people (Gonda 1959, Proferes 2007). However, this position is ritually bestowed and implies, first, that he must return from his ritual deification in order to perform his task, and second, that this acquisition must be repeated and the aggregation of cosmic powers in the persona of the king recreated annually (cf. Heesterman 1957). The power of the gods in their turn is restricted by the domain they rule over and the ritual share of nourishment to which they are entitled. While the power, albeit limited, of each god was an accepted fact, the powers of *yogins* and kings were in need of qualification. With regard to the *yogin*, the question arose whether yogic powers contradict those qualifications of the *yogin* that bring him close to liberation. Different answers were given

[29] *Pace* Shrikantha Shastri 1955, Upadhyaya 1971, Malinar 1996.

to the question, such as in Buddhist texts that taught a strict distinction between a *buddha* and the *dharma*-promoting king or *cakravartin*. In the case of the king, his divine character and godlike status became a point of debate. Is he even the 'mover' of the gods, or does he protect the cosmic order in being the highest and most powerful human being within the social realm? Is he one partner in a 'diarchic' arrangement between himself and his brahmanical priest, which makes him responsible for maintaining the connection between the spheres of god and creatures on the level of *dharma*, while the Brahman priest is responsible for sustaining this ritual knowledge, which, in the end, even brings the king to his position? It seems that any tendency to deify kings was regarded with great scepticism, and in later texts deification was attributed to a deceased king only. Another question is whether the divine character of the office also extends to the office-holder.

These questions have been intensively discussed with regard to the epics (see Hopkins 1931, Pollock 1984, Biardeau 1997, Fitzgerald 2004) and the Kuṣāṇa kings, who may in turn have drawn on Hellenistic concepts of a god-king and the Buddhist notion of a *cakravartin* (Verardi 1983) as part of a general syncretistic attitude (Falk 2006a). It seems that some of them have adopted religious ideas connected to kingship in the iconography of their images, which they used in order to gain legitimacy. Not only were the Kuṣāṇas connected with the production of images of Vāsudeva-Kṛṣṇa, but also they associated themselves with other gods, mainly Śiva, as well as with Buddhism and Jainism (see essays in Srinivasan 1989a). Their images were based on the iconography of these deities and other powerful beings. They seem to have accommodated various cults in the different regions of their empire, rather than propagating one religion alone. Some scholars regard this as indicating a strategy of legitimising and stabilising their position as rulers coming from the outside. Verardi (1985) suggests that some Kuṣāṇa kings adopted the *bodhisattva* images for their own iconographical representation. However, in the *BhG* and in subsequent Hindu religious traditions, it is the god who is able to descend in order to rescue *dharma* or meet his devotees. The king then becomes a representative of this god, as well as his most prominent devotee. This model became the paradigm in many of the subsequent traditions, as Biardeau (1997) shows.

FINAL REMARKS

In drawing together the evidence and historical contexts discussed earlier, the following hypothesis regarding the date and chronology of the main layers and conceptual frameworks of the extant *BhG* is suggested. Generally speaking, three major steps in the textual history of the *BhG* can be assumed.[30] First, the conceptual framework explains a doctrine of disinterested action and of concern for the welfare of a ritually structured cosmos represented by the king without reference to Kṛṣṇa as the highest god; doctrines of Sāṃkhya and yoga were adduced in order to explain why this type of action has no karmic consequences. Secondly, Kṛṣṇa is made the model of ideal royal and yogic activity in that he is declared to be the highest god, partially present in the world, but also transcending it as the ever-liberated and detached self who is intimately related to his followers in a relationship of *bhakti*. Thirdly, passages are added that comment on and sometimes reinterpret the earlier chapters. This third stage, and thus the extant *BhG* as a whole, may have been completed at the beginning of the Common Era and of Kuṣāṇa rulers, an assumption based primarily on the chronology relative to other texts, such as the *ŚvetU*, the *AG*, the *Nārāyaṇīya* and other parts of the *ŚāntiP*. In dating the earlier stages, the evidence with regard to the first layer points to the Maurya period in that the edicts of Aśoka, the *ArthaŚ* and the *BhG* declare the king to be a model of conduct who places the welfare of all beings, and ascetic detachment from personal interest, at the centre of righteousness. All the texts point to negative examples of greedy and cruel kings who abused their power to pursue their own personal interests. This may be a reference to the Nanda dynasty, which managed to establish a centralised kingdom and is infamous for its expansionism and cruelty: the *ArthaŚ* mentions Duryodhana as an example of an 'evil king'. While Aśoka promotes his policy on the basis of *dharma*, the *BhG* establishes an argument extolling ritual reciprocity as the basis of creation and life. In this regard, it affirms the validity of the ritual order while denouncing its abuse, which is prevented by the doctrine of *karmayoga*. Scholars are divided over whether they prefer a pre- or post-Aśokan date of composition, and it is indeed difficult to establish a strong argument. While one could settle for the third to second century BCE and avoid a definite date, it seems that a weak argument could be made for placing the date in the post-Aśokan period on the basis of the reinterpretation of ascetic values in the idiom of Vedic sacrifice, a situation that fits this period better, since there is some evidence that the Śuṅgas had Vedic sacrifices performed. The basic idea, also voiced by Aśoka and in the *ArthaŚ*, is that concern for the welfare of the world and the prominent role

[30] These stages are abstracted from the textual analysis and need to be subdivided and internally distinguished. For further details, see Malinar 1996: 394–415.

of the king as a 'role model' in this respect is retained, as is the case with ascetic values. This would push the date more towards the second or first century BCE. However, rather than simply regarding this as a 'renaissance' of Vedic traditions under the Śuṅgas, one must be aware that the *BhG* does not simply advocate Vedic tradition, but also reinterprets it along the lines of ascetic values and Sāṃkhya cosmology and terminology.

This reinterpretation lays the foundation for adopting a monotheistic framework, which may have occurred with the earliest evidence of a cult of Vāsudeva-Kṛṣṇa in the numismatic, epigraphic and sculptural sources. At this time the presence of Indo-Greek and Hellenistic kings, with their tendency towards royal cults of god-kings called *sōter*, *theos* or *basileos*, must be taken into account as a factor which may have influenced, though not caused, the concept of a highest god who is the ultimate ruler and king of the universe, and to whom all earthly kings are subject as his devotees and representatives. This is also corroborated from a geographical perspective, since the cult of Vāsudeva-Kṛṣṇa seems to have emerged in the region around Mathurā, one of the cultural centres at that time. The combination of brahmanical authority and influence with a cosmopolitan situation of religious pluralism is a characteristic feature of the city at that time, which corresponds well to the mediation of different religious idioms under one of the prominent gods of the region and the acceptance of the principles of the Vedic brahmanic values. Srinivasan emphasises that 'foreign rule' (of Scyths, satraps and then Kuṣāṇas) and the strong presence of followers of non-brahmanical religions like Buddhism and Jainism did not prevent the acceptance and persistence of brahmanical culture. On the contrary, Buddhists and Jains 'would find Mathurā an attractive place to settle. Its trading connections were expanding . . . cultural and ethnic diversity could be found there. These changes did not undermine the elevated status of Brahmanism in Mathurā' (Srinivasan 1997: 311–312).

This makes it probable that the monotheistic doctrine of chapters 7–11 and the first part of chapter 4 were composed between the second and first centuries BCE, when Mathurā became a major political and cultural centre in north India. Most of the inscriptions and sculptures point to this period, which was one of strong cultural and artistic exchange between Gāndhāra and Mathurā.[31] While Srinivasan (1981, 1989b, 1997) has analysed contemporary Kṛṣṇa worship on the basis of iconographical data, Thapar (1989: 15) points to the political context of the presence of the Vāsudeva-Kṛṣṇa cult, which 'had the maximum potential to encourage wider networks of

[31] Cf. von Lohuizen-de-Leeuw 1972; Chattopadhyaya 1989.

kin ties which could perhaps be welded into a politically unifying factor'.[32] In addition, this date for the older theistic chapters also accommodates the emergence of a *bodhisattva* concept – if this can be regarded as responding to theologies like the *BhG* – as well as the date of the *ŚvetU*. The addition of chapters 12–18 can perhaps be dated to the beginning of the Common Era and early Kuṣāṇa period (first century CE).[33] This corresponds to the assumed date of texts included in the *MBh* that can be regarded as reactions to and comments on the *BhG*. Placing the *BhG* in the context of Mathurā also means placing it in the 'heartland' of the epic and the *Harivaṃśa*.

Further study of these intertextual relationships will certainly help to refine our understanding of the historical, religious and literary texture of this period, which ended with the final redaction of the *MBh* and the rise of the Gupta empire. The religious traditions of classical Hinduism used many paradigms formulated in the *BhG* and adjacent texts in establishing and delineating their individual theologies, iconographies, rituals and texts. This co-existence of different monotheistic cults and doctrines seems to be an original feature of Hindu traditions. However, this religious pluralism is based on shared philosophical and theological concepts in cosmology, cosmography, ritual idiom and the acceptance of other gods as being responsible for defined ritual spheres and cosmic domains, which are ultimately transcended by worship of Vāsudeva-Kṛṣṇa as the one and only supreme lord. This lord is present in the world and protects the ritual-cosmic order of *dharma*, but is, at the same time, accessible to all beings, irrespective of social rank, kinship, gender or ritual purity. He behaves like a father, companion or lover to those who hold him dear, while those who turn against him or the order he created will be thrown into the burning mouth of his terrible, deadly face. Alliance with him surpasses all the restrictions that social relations entail, on which the god is not dependent, being the perfect ascetic and 'mighty lord of yoga', who is forever detached, like a neutral, most powerful king. He therefore remains hidden and unknown

[32] Schneider (1982) comes to a similar conclusion in his analysis of the Jarāsandha and Śiśupāla stories in the *MBh*. See also Hein 1989.

[33] Jaiswal (1967: 223–224) points to quotations of passages from *BhG* 10 and 11 in a Chinese version of the Tripiṭika (vol. 32, no. 1640, Taisho: 156–158). In this passage, a heretic called Māṭhara proclaims the doctrine of *iśvara-deva*, praising himself as follows: 'I created all things. I am the supreme among all living beings. I gave birth to all living things and produce all non-living things in all worlds. I am the king of the mountain Mahā Sumeru, among all Mountains. I am the great sea of all rivers. I am the grain of all medicines. I am Kapila Muni of all . . . If a man offers me wholeheartedly water, herbs, flowers and fruits, I will not miss him and he will not miss me.' Jaiswal (1967: 223–224) concludes: 'the *Bhagavadgītā* must have been a well-known scripture of the Bhāgavatas in the second century A.D. when Māṭhara, the minister of Kaniṣka II, is supposed to have lived.'

in spite of all his manifestations, which ultimately serve to indicate that the god's ultimate being remains a well-kept 'highest secret'.

Although the *BhG* and its followers proclaim that there is only 'one god' of the 'many' that must be worshipped in order to gain liberation, there were obviously other groups who thought the same of their god. We see Rudra-Śiva in the *ŚvetU* and Hari-Nārāyaṇa in the *Nārāyaṇīya* section of the epic depicted in a similar position, yet both show distinct features, not resembling the *BhG* conceptually, but apparently being almost contemporaneous. While the *Nārāyaṇīya* section most probably belongs to the period between the Kuṣāṇas and the Guptas (see essays in Schreiner 1997) and seems to have drawn on the theology of the *BhG* (Malinar 1997), the *ŚvetU* appears very close to the *BhG*, though perhaps a little later (Oberlies 1988). Thus, even in its beginning, this type of theology developed its most elaborate form in the *BhG* and is also discernible in other texts dealing with other gods. The co-existence of several such 'highest' gods and corresponding theologies showing the features of a 'cosmological monotheism' is characteristic of the development of early Hindu religious traditions, which branched out and were consolidated as distinct religious traditions in later 'classical' or purāṇic Hinduism. Not only Vāsudeva-Kṛṣṇa, but also Viṣṇu, Nārāyaṇa, Śiva and later goddesses like Durgā were placed in this position and worshipped as the highest being, who granted both protection and prosperity in life on earth, as well as final liberation. The origin(s) and exact circumstances of the rise of this theology are uncertain, and it is difficult to establish the priority of one or other text or cult on the basis of the extant evidence. What one can say is that it obviously emerged with regard to co-existing cults and the imagery and myths of different gods. It seems that the *BhG* became so influential because it formulates a paradigm of this theology that could serve to reject any one-sided emphasis on ascetic renunciation, while at the same time accommodating it together with other Vedic polytheism, Upaniṣadic thoughts in the cosmic 'one' and the values of social-ritual life.

However, the *BhG* is a watershed in this situation, since it provides probably the earliest comprehensive formulation of the new theology in the form of the self-revelation of the highest god. This invited the comments and debates that we encounter earlier in the epic itself. We find, for instance, a text that is presented as a repetition of the *BhG*, the *AG*, though in fact it represents a revised version of the text, including material that may be older than the theological sections of the *BhG*. Other echoes of the *BhG* are the debate between Kṛṣṇa and the sage Uttaṅka, who raises the question of why Kṛṣṇa did not prevent the war if he is the 'mighty god' he claims to be (cf. *MBh* 14.53), and the dialogue between the female mendicant Sulabhā and King Janaka about the latter's claim that he is already liberated, though still in fact performing his royal duties perfectly. This dialogue examines whether 'disinterested action' is indeed practicable (*MBh* 12.308; Fitzgerald 2002).

The relative chronology of these texts cannot always be established with certainty, although it seems likely that most of the epic texts are later than the *BhG*, while the theistic sections of the *BhG* seem to be contemporary with or slightly older than the *ŚvetU*, but perhaps younger than some parts of the *KaṭhU*. However, the chronology of texts must not be equated with a chronology of cults. Indeed, numismatic and iconographic evidence points rather to the contrary, namely that different theistic cults (probably of different origins and affiliations) co-existed before the theological texts were written and before some of the gods were proclaimed the highest and unique gods, worthy of exclusive worship. The cults and images were perhaps not as distinctive as the theology, but they were probably unique with regard to their mythology and provenance. We find evidence not only for gods like Śiva or Kṛṣṇa, but also for Vāyu, Sūrya and goddesses (Srinivasan 1997). Nevertheless, only a few were moved into the centre of a monotheistic theology and have kept their distinct identity, which was enhanced in the subsequent history of Hinduism. Although it is somehow convenient to regard this religious pluralism either as polytheistic or, from a monistic perspective such as the Advaita-Vedanta, as 'manifestations of an impersonal, supreme being', such views tend to misrepresent the doctrinal framework of these traditions, making their religious truth and goal something unique that cannot to be achieved by following any other god or practice. The followers of Vāsudeva-Kṛṣṇa strive for liberation with him, not with Śiva. However, the actual and perhaps original pluralism resulted in the acceptance of other cults and gods on lower levels of the cosmos created by the 'one and only' god. The structures and terminologies used in delineating this framework in the different textual sources resemble one another, although they are interpreted differently, and different concepts are emphasised. A comprehensive, comparative analysis of these early theologies is beyond the scope of this work, but will be taken up in a future study.

Bibliography

Aṅguttara Nikāya 1961. *The Aṅguttara-Nikāya*, ed. A. K. Warder. London: Pali Text Society.

Apte, P. 1972. 'Claim of Pāñcarātra on Bhagavadgītā', *ABORI* 53: 200–203.

Arapura, J. G. 1975. 'The Upside Down Tree of the Bhagavadgītā ch. xv – An Exegesis', *Numen* 22: 131–144.

Assmann, J. 1986. 'Arbeit am Polytheismus. Die Idee der Einheit Gottes und die Entfaltung des theologischen Diskurses in Ägypten', in H. v. Stietencron, ed., *Theologen und Theologien in verschiedenen Kulturkreisen*: 49–69. Düsseldorf: Patmos.

1993. *Monotheismus und Kosmotheismus. Ägyptische Formen eines 'Denkens des Einen' und ihre europäische Rezeptionsgeschichte.* Heidelberg: Winter.

1996. 'Translating Gods: Religion as a Factor of Cultural (Un)Translatability', in S. Budick and W. Iser, eds., *The Translatability of Cultures. Figurations of the Space Between*: 25–36. Stanford: Stanford University Press.

Aṣṭādhyāyī 1839–40. *Pāṇini's acht Bücher grammatischer Regeln. Herausgegeben und erläutert von Otto Böhtlingk.* Bonn: König.

Arthaśāstra 1960–63. *The Kauṭilya Arthaśāstra.* Part 1: *A Critical Edition with a Glossary.* Part 2: *An English Translation with Critical and Explanatory Notes* by R. P. Kangle. Bombay: University of Bombay.

Atharvaveda 1865. *Atharva Veda Sanhita* herausgegeben von R. Roth und W. D. Whitney, 1: *Text.* Berlin.

Bailey, G. M. 1983a. *The Mythology of Brahmā.* Delhi: Motilal Banarsidass.

1983b. 'Suffering in the Mahābhārata. Draupadī and Yudhiṣṭhira', *Puruṣārtha* 7: 109–129.

1984. 'On D. D. Kosambi's Interpretation of the Bhagavadgītā', *IT* 12: 343–353.

1985. *Materials for the Study of Ancient Indian Ideologies: Pravṛtti and Nivṛtti.* Torino: Jollygrafica.

1987. 'Narrative Coherence in the Upāsanākhaṇḍa of the Gaṇeśa Purāṇa: the Interlocutory System', *IT* 14: 29–45.

Bailey, G. M., and I. Mabbett 2003. *The Sociology of Early Buddhism.* Cambridge: Cambridge University Press.

Bakker, H. 1982. 'On the Origin of Sāṃkhya Psychology', *WZKS* 26: 117–148.

2001. 'Sources for Reconstructing Ancient Forms of Śiva Worship', in F. Grimal, ed., *Les sources et le temps. Sources and Time*: 397–412. Pondichéry: Institute Français de Pondichéry.

Banerjee, P. 1953. 'Some Observations on the So-Called Theory of the Brahmanical Revolution under Puṣyamitraśuṅga', *JASBeng, Letters* 29: 145–149.

1954. 'Some Observations on the Interpretation of the Pāṇini Sūtra Vāsudevārjunābhyām-vun and the Antiquity of the Bhāgavatas', *JBRS* 40: 74–79.

Barua, P. R. 1956. 'The Brahmin Doctrine of Sacrifice and Rituals in the Pali Canon', *Journal of the Asiatic Society of Pakistan* 1: 87–106.

Basham, A. L. 1981. 'The Evolution of the Concept of the Boddhisattva', in L. S. Kawamura, ed., *The Bodhisattva Doctrine in Buddhism*: 19–59. Waterloo: Wilfrid Laurier University Press.

Behler, E. 1968. 'Das Indienbild der deutschen Romantik', *Germanisch-Romanische Monatsschrift* NF 28, 1: 21–37.

Belvalkar, S. K. 1929. *Shree Gopal Basu Mallik Fellowship Lectures on Vedānta Philosophy*. Poona: Bhandarkar Oriental Institute.

1937. 'Miscarriage of the Attempted Stratification of the Bhagavadgītā', *JUB* 5: 66–133.

1939. 'The Bhagavadgītā "Riddle" Unriddled', *ABORI* 19: 335–348.

Berg, Richard A. 1987. 'Theories of Action in the Bhagavad-Gītā', in A. Sharma 1987: 36–50.

Bhandare, S. 2006. 'Numismatics and History. The Maurya-Gupta Interlude in the Gangetic Plain', in Olivelle 2006: 67–112.

Bhandarkar, D. R. 1913–14. 'Excavations at Besnagar', *ASIAR* 186–226.

Bhandarkar, R. G. 1874. 'Allusions to Kṛṣṇa in Patañjali's Mahābhāsya', *IA* 3: 14–16.

1910. 'Vāsudeva of Pāṇini 4.3.98', *JRAS*: 168–170.

1913. *Vaiṣṇavism, Shaivism and Minor Religious Systems*. Strassburg: Trübner.

Bhargava, P. L. 1977. 'Additions and Interpolations in the Bhagavadgītā', *EW* 27: 357–361.

1979. 'Names and Epithets of Kṛṣṇa in the Bhagavadgītā', *IT* 7: 93–96.

Bhattacharjee, U. C. 1925–26. 'The Evidence of Pāṇini on Vāsudeva Worship', *IHQ* 1: 483–489; 2: 409–410, 865.

Bhusari, R. M. 1927. 'A Short Note on the Term Bhakti in Pāṇini's Sūtras iv.3.95–100', *ABORI* 8: 198–199.

Biardeau, M. 1965. 'Ahaṃkāra, The Ego Principle in the Upaniṣads', *CIS* 8: 1–18.

1976. 'Etudes de mythologie hindoue IV', *BEFEO* 63: 111–262.

1978. 'Etudes de mythologie hindoue V', *BEFEO* 65: 87–237.

1981. 'The Salvation of the King in the Mahābhārata', *CIS* NS 15: 75–97.

1991. 'Nara et Nārāyaṇa', *WZKS* 35: 75–108.

1997. 'Some Remarks on the Links between the Epics, the Purāṇas, and Their Vedic Sources', in G. Oberhammer, ed., *Studies in Hinduism. Vedism and Hinduism*: 69–177. Vienna: Verlag der Österreichischen Akademie der Wissenschaften.

Biardeau, M., and Ch. Malamoud 1976. *Le sacrifice dans l'Inde ancienne*. Paris: Presses Universitaires de France.

Bigger, A. 1997. *Balarāma im Mahābhārata: seine Darstellung im Rahmen des Textes und seiner Entwicklung*. Wiesbaden: Harrassowitz.

Bloch, J. 1950. *Les inscriptions d'Aśoka, traduites et commentées*. Paris: Les Belles Lettres.

Bodewitz, H. W. 2002. 'Where and What is the *priyām dhāma'* of a Vedic God?', *IIJ* 45: 153–171.

Böhtlingk, O. 1897. 'Bemerkungen zur Bhagavadgītā', *Berichte über die Verhandlungen der Königlich-Sächsischen Gesellschaft der Wissenschaften zu Leipzig, Philologisch-Historische Classe* 49: 1–16.

Bongard-Levin, G. M. 1985. *Mauryan India*. New Delhi: Sterling.

Brockington, J. L. 1984. *Righteous Rāma. The Evolution of an Epic*. Delhi: Oxford University Press.

1998. *The Sanskrit Epics*. Leiden: Brill.

Bronkhorst, J. 1993. *Two Traditions of Meditation in Ancient India*. Delhi: Motilal Banarsidass.

Brückner, H. et al., eds. 2003. *Indien-Forschung im Zeitenwandel. Analysen und Dokumente zur Indologie und Religionswissenschaft in Tübingen*. Tübingen: Attempto.

Buddhacarita 1984. *The Buddhacarita, or, Acts of the Buddha* ed. and trans. E. H. Johnston. 2 parts. Delhi: Motilal Banarsidass.

Buitenen, J. A. B. van 1957a. 'Studies in Sāṃkhya II: Ahaṃkāra', *JAOS* 77: 15–25.

1957b. 'Studies in Sāṃkhya III. Sattva', *JAOS* 77: 88–107.

1959. 'Akṣara', *JAOS* 79: 176–187.

1962. *The Maitrāyaṇīya Upaniṣad. A Critical Essay, with Text, Translation and Commentary*. 'S-Gravenhage: Mouton.

1964. 'The Large Ātman', *HR* 4: 103–114.

1965. 'A Contribution to the Critical Edition of the Bhagavadgītā', *JAOS* 85: 99–109.

ed. and trans. 1973–78. *The Mahābhārata*, Vols. I–III. Chicago: Chicago University Press.

1981. *The Bhagavadgītā in the Mahābhārata. Text and Translation*. Chicago: Chicago University Press.

Bühnemann, G. 1988. *Puja. A Study in Smārta Ritual*. Vienna: de Nobili Research Publications.

Callewaert, W., and S. Hemraj 1983. *Bhagavadgītānuvāda. A Study in Transcultural Translation*. Ranchi: Satya Bharati.

Chanda, R. 1920. *Archaeology and Vaiṣṇava Tradition*. Calcutta: Archaeological Survey of India.

1929. 'Puṣyamitra and the Śuṅga Empire', *IHQ* 5: 393–407, 587–613.

Charpentier, J. 1930. 'Some Remarks on the Bhagavadgītā', *IA* 59: 46–40, 77–80, 101–105, 121–126.

Chattopadhyaya, B. D. 1989. 'Mathurā from the Śuṅga to the Kuṣāṇa Period. A Historical Outline', in Srinivasan 1989a: 19–28.

Choudhury, M. C. 1964. 'Besnagar Garuda Pillar Inscription of Heliodorus. An Assessment', *VIJ* 2: 334–343.
Coomaraswamy, A. K. 1942. *Spiritual Authority and Temporal Power in the Indian Theory of Government*. New Haven: American Oriental Society.
Cort, J. E. 2002. 'Bhakti in the Early Jain Tradition: Understanding Devotional Religion in South Asia', *HR* 42: 59–86.
Couture, A. 2001. 'From Viṣṇu's Deeds to Viṣṇu's Play, or Observations on the Word *Avatāra* as a Designation for the Manifestations of Viṣṇu', *JIP* 29: 313–326.
Dahlmann, J. 1895. *Das Mahābhārata als Epos und Rechtsbuch*. Berlin: Dames.
Dandekar, R. N. 1963. 'Hinduism and the Bhagavadgītā. A Fresh Approach', *JOIB* 12: 232–237.
1975–76. 'The Beginnings of Vaiṣṇavism', *IT* 3–4: 169–186.
Dasgupta, S. 1952. 'The Philosophy of the Bhagavad-gītā', in S. Dasgupta, *A History of Indian Philosophy*, II: 437–552. Cambridge: Cambridge University Press.
De, S. K. 1942. 'The Vedic and the Epic Kṛṣṇa', *IHQ* 18: 297–301.
Deshpande, M. M. 1991. 'The Epic Context of the Bhagavadgītā', in A. Sharma, ed., *Essays on the Mahābhārata*: 334–348. Leiden: Brill.
Deussen, P. 1911. *Der Gesang des Heiligen*. Leipzig: Brockhaus.
Deussen, P., and O. Strauss. 1922. *Vier philosophische Texte aus dem Mahābhārata*. Leipzig: Brockhaus.
Devasthali, G. V. 1954. 'Bhagavad-gītā and Upaniṣads', in J. N. Agrawal and B. D. Shastri, eds., *Sarūpa-bhāratī or the Homage of Indology*: 132–142. Hoshiarpur: Vishveshvarananda Indological Institute.
Dhadpale, M. G. 1978. 'Two Notes on the *Bhagavadgītā*', in M. G. Dhadpale, ed., *Principle V. A. Apte Commemoration Volume*: 48–58. Poona: Deccan Education Service.
Dhammapada 1931. *The Minor Anthologies of the Pali Canon*. Part I: *Dhammapada: Verses on Dhamma and Khuddaka-Pāṭha: The Text of the Minor Sayings Re-edited and Translated by Mrs. Rhys Davis*. London: Pali Text Society.
Dīgha Nikāya 1947. *The Dīgha Nikāya*. ed. T. W. Rhys Davids and E. Carpentier. London: Pali Text Society.
Divanji, P. C. 1950. 'Bhagavadgītā and Aṣṭādhyāyī', *ABORI* 30: 263–276.
1958–59. 'Brahman and the Terms Allied to it in the Bhagavadgītā', *JOIB* 8: 369–377.
1961–62. 'Atman and the Terms Allied to it in the Bhagavadgītā', *JOIB* 11: 157–165.
D'Sa, F. X. 1980. 'Dharma as Delight in Cosmic Welfare: A Study of dharma in the Gītā', *Biblebhashyam*: 335–357.
1982. 'Zur Eigenart des Bhagavadgītā-Theismus', in G. Oberhammer, ed., *Offenbarung als Heilserfahrung*: 97–125. Vienna: Verlag der Österreichischen Akademie der Wissenschaften.
Dumont, L. 1960. 'World Renunciation in Indian Religions', *CIS* 4: 33–62.
Edgerton, F. 1924. 'The Meaning of Sāṃkhya and Yoga', *AJP* 45: 1–65.

1925. *The Bhagavad Gītā or Song of the Blessed or India's Favorite Bible*. Chicago: Chicago University Press.

1926–27. 'The Hour of Death', *ABORI* 8: 219–249.

1932. 'Review of F. Otto Schrader, *The Kashmir Recension of the Bhagavadgītā*', *JAOS* 53: 68–75.

1933. 'Jñāna and Vijñāna', in O. Stein and W. Gampert, eds., *Festschrift Moriz Winternitz. 1863 – 23. Dezember – 1933*: 217–220. Leipzig: Harrassowitz.

1940. 'Review of "The Original Gītā: The Song of the Supreme Exalted One" by Rudolf Otto, translated and edited by J. E. Turner', *Review of Religion* 4: 448.

1944. *The Bhagavad Gītā. Text and Translation*. Cambridge, MA: Harvard University Press.

1965. *The Beginnings of Indian Philosophy*. Cambridge, MA.: Harvard University Press.

Eliade, M. 1970. *Yoga: Immortality and Freedom*. Princeton: Princeton University Press.

Emeneau, M. B. 1949. 'The Strangling Fig Trees in Sanskrit Literature', *University of California Publications in Classical Philology* 10: 345–370.

1968. 'Bhagavadgītā Notes', in *Mélanges d'Indianism à la mémoire de Louis Renou*: 269–278. Paris: Institute de la Civilisation Indienne.

Falk, H. 2003. *Schrift im alten Indien. Ein Forschungsbriecht mit Anmerkungen*. Tübingen: Narr.

1994. 'Von Götterfiguren und menschlichen Göttern', in N. Balbir and K. K. Bautze, eds., *Festschrift Klaus Bruhn*: 313–333. Reinbek: Wezler.

2006a. 'The Tidal Waves of Indian History. Between Empires and Beyond', in Olivelle 2006: 145–166.

2006b. *Aśokan Sites and Artefacts. A Source-Book with Bibliography*. Mainz: von Zabern.

Filliozat, J. 1973. 'Représentations de Vāsudeva et Saṃkarṣaṇa au siècle IIe avant J. C.', *Arts Asiatiques* 26: 113–123.

Fitzgerald, J. L. 2002. 'Nun Befuddles King, Shows Karmayoga Does Not Work. Sulabhā's Refutation of King Janaka at MBh 12.308', *JIP* 30: 641–677.

trans. and ed. 2004. *The Mahābhārata*. VII: *Book 11: The Book of the Women, Book 12: The Book of Peace, Part 1*. Chicago: Chicago University Press.

2006. 'Negotiating the Shape of "Scripture". New Perspectives on the Development and Growth of the Mahābhārata between the Empires', in Olivelle 2006: 257–286.

Folkert, K. W. 1989. 'Jaina Religious Life at Ancient Mathurā: The Heritage of Late Victorian Interpretation', in Srinivasan 1989a: 103–112.

Frauwallner, E. 1926. 'Untersuchungen zu den älteren Upaniṣaden', *ZII* 4: 1–45.

Garbe, R. 1921. *Die Bhagavadgītā*. Leipzig: Harrassowitz.

1922. 'Noch einmal das Bhagavadgītā-Problem', *DLZ* 43: 97–104.

Gauchhwal, B. S. 1958. *A Comparative Study of the Ethical Teachings of Kant and the Bhagavadgītā*. Delhi: Motilal Banarsidass.

Gethin, R. 1997. 'Cosmology and Meditation: From the Aggañña-Sutta to the Mahāyāna', *HR* 36: 183–217.
Ghosh, J. C. 1933. 'Notes on the Ghoṣūndī Stone Inscription', *IHQ* 9: 799–801.
Ghosh, N. N. 1943. 'Did Pusyamitra Sunga Persecute the Buddhists?', *PIHC*: 109–116.
Gitomer, D. 1992. 'King Duryodhana: The Mahābhārata Discourse of Sinning and Virtue in the Epic and Drama', *JAOS* 112, 2: 222–232.
Glasenapp, H. von 1954. *Buddhismus und Gottesidee. Die buddhistische Lehre von den überweltlichen Wesen und Mächten und ihre religionsgeschichtlichen Parallelen.* Wiesbaden: Steiner.
Gokhale, B. G. 1966. 'Early Buddhist Kingship', *JASt* 26, 1: 15–22.
Gonda, J. 1954. 'Pratiṣṭhā', in J. Gonda, *Selected Studies*, II: 338–372. Leiden: Brill.
1955. 'Reflections on *Sarva-* in Vedic texts', *Indian Linguistics* 16: 55–71.
1957. *Some Observations on the Relations between 'Gods' and 'Powers' in the Veda à propos of the Phrase Sūnuḥ Sahasaḥ*. 'S-Gravenhage: Mouton.
1958. 'The "Original" Sense and the Etymology of Skt. Māyā', in J. Gonda, *Four Studies in the Language of the Veda*: 119–194. 's-Gravenhage: Mouton.
1959a. *Stylistic Repetition in the Veda*. Amsterdam: Noord-Hollandsche Uitgevers.
1959b. 'The Sacred Character of Ancient Indian Kingship', *Supplement to Numen* 4: 172–180.
1963. *The Vision of the Vedic poets*. The Hague: Mouton.
1965. *Change and Continuity in Indian Religion*. Delhi: Munshiram Manoharlal.
1966. *Ancient Indian Kingship from the Religious Point of View*. Leiden: Brill.
1967. *The Meaning of the Sanskrit Term 'Dhāman-'*. 's-Gravenhage: Mouton.
1968. 'The Concept of a Personal God in Ancient Indian Religious Thought', *Studia Missionalia* 17: 111–136.
1977. *The Ritual Sūtras*. Wiesbaden: Harrassowitz.
Goudriaan, T. 1978. *Māyā Divine and Human. A Study of Magic and Its Religious Foundations in Sanskrit Texts*. Delhi: Motilal Banarsidass.
1992. 'The Pluriform Ātman from the Upaniṣads to Svacchanda Tantra', *WZKS* 36: 163–186.
Gren-Eklund, G. 1984. 'Causality and the Method of Connecting Concepts in the Upaniṣads', *IT* 12: 107–119.
Gupta, S. P. 1978. 'Vibhūti's of Viṣṇu as mentioned in the Epic and the Purāṇas', *Purāna* 20: 131–135.
Haas, G. C. O. 1922. *Recurrent and Parallel Passages in the Principal Upanishads and the Bhagavadgītā with References to Other Sanskrit Texts*. Boston: Harvard University Press.
Habicht, Ch. 1970. *Gottmenschentum und griechische Städte*. Munich: Beck.
Hacker, P. 1960. 'Zur Entwicklung der Avatāralehre', *WZKSO* 4: 47–70.
1963. 'Śraddhā', *WZKSO* 7: 151–189.
1983. 'Inklusivismus', in G. Oberhammer, ed., *Inklusivismus*: 11–28. Vienna: Verlag der Österreichischen Akademie der Wissenschaften.
Hara, M. 1963–64. 'Note on Two Sanskrit Religious Terms: *Bhakti* and *Śraddhā*', *IIJ* 7: 124–143.

1977–78. 'Tapasvinī', *ABORI* 58–59: 151–159.

1979. '*Śraddhāviveśa*', *IT* 7: 261–273.

Harrison, P. 1995. 'Searching for the Origins of Early Mahayana: What Are We Looking For?', *Eastern Buddhist* 22: 48–69.

Härtel, H. 1977. *Some Results of the Excavations at Sonkh. A Preliminary Report.* New Delhi: National Museum.

1987. 'Archaeological Evidence on the Early Vāsudeva Worship', in G. Gnoli, ed., *Orientalia. Iosephi Tucci memoriae dicata.* II: 573–587. Rome: Istituto Italiano per il Medio ed Estremo Oriente.

1993. *Excavations at Sonkh. 2500 Years of a Town in Mathura District.* Berlin: Reimer.

Hauer, J. W. 1934. *Eine indo-arische Metaphysik des Kampfes und der Tat. Die Bhagavadgītā in neuer Sicht.* Stuttgart: Kohlhammer.

Hazra, R. C. 1970. 'Vāsudeva Worship as Known to Pāṇini', *OH* 18: 1–45, 97–123.

Heesterman, J. C. 1957. *The Ancient Indian Royal Consecration. The Rājasūya Described According to the Yajus Texts and annotated.* 's-Gravenhage: Mouton.

1968. 'Brahmin, Ritual and Renouncer', *WZKS* 8: 1–31.

1985. *The Inner Conflict of Tradition: Essays in Indian Ritual, Kingship, and Society.* Chicago: University of Chicago Press.

1993. *The Broken World of Sacrifice.* Chicago: Chicago University Press.

Hegel, G. W. F. 1827. 'Recension von: "Ueber die unter dem Namen Bhagavad-Gītā bekannte Episode des Mahabharata von W. v. Humboldt. Berlin, 1826"', *Jahrbücher für wissenschaftliche Kritik* 7–8: 51–63; 181–182: 1441–1488; 187–188: 1489–1492.

Hein, N. 1975. 'Monotheism in the Bhagavadgītā: A Stylistic Clue', in *Proceedings, 12th Congress, International Association for the History of Religions*: 250–260. Leiden: Brill.

1986. 'Epic Sarvabhūtahite Rataḥ: A Byword of Non-Bhārgava Editors', *ABORI* 67: 17–34.

1989. 'Kālayavana. A Key to Mathurā's Cultural Self-Perception', in Srinivasan 1989a: 223–235.

Hejib, A., and K. Young. 1980. 'Klība on the Battlefield: Towards a Reinterpretation of Arjuna's Despondency', *ABORI* 61: 235–244.

Hill, W. D. P. 1928. *The Bhagavadgītā. Translated from the Sanskrit with an Introduction and Argument and a Commentary.* London: Oxford University Press.

Hillebrandt, A. 1921. *Aus Brahmanas und Upanisaden. Gedanken altindischer Philosophen übertragen und eingeleitet.* Jena: Diederichs.

Hiltebeitel, A. 1976. *The Ritual of Battle. Kṛṣṇa in the Mahābhārata.* Ithaca: Cornell University Press.

1979. 'Kṛṣṇa in the Mahābhārata: A Bibliographical Essay', *ABORI* 60: 65–107.

1984–85. 'The Two Kṛṣṇas on One Chariot: Upaniṣadic Imagery and Epic Mythology', *HR* 24: 1–26.

1989. 'Kṛṣṇa at Mathurā', in Srinivasan 1989a: 93–102.

2001. *Rethinking the Mahābhārata. A Reader's Guide to the Education of the Dharma King.* Chicago: Chicago University Press.

Hoens, D. J. 1968. 'An Excursus on Bhagavadgītā 6,11', in J. C. Heesterman et al., eds., *Pratidānam. Indian, Iranian and Indo-European Studies Presented to Franciscus Bernardus Jacobus Kuiper on His Sixtieth Birthday*: 523–532. The Hague: Mouton.

Hornung, E. 1971. *Der Eine und die Vielen. Altägyptische Gottesvorstellungen.* Darmstadt: Wissenschaftliche Buchgesellschaft.

Holtzmann, A. 1892–95. *Das Mahābhārata und seine Theile*, 4 vols. Kiel: Haeseler.

Hopkins, E. W. 1895. *The Religions of India.* Boston, MA: Ginn.

1901. 'Yoga Technique in the Great Epic', *JAOS* 22: 333–379.

1902. *The Great Epic of India. Its Character and Origin.* New York: Scribner's.

1911. 'The Epic Use of Bhagavat and Bhakti', *JRAS*: 727–738.

1931. 'The Divinity of Kings', *JAOS* 51: 309–319.

Hufnagel, U. 2003. 'Religionswissenschaft und indische Religionsgeschichte in den Arbeiten Jakob Wilhelm Hauers: Wissenschaftskonzept und politische Orientierung', in Brückner et al.: 145–174.

Hultzsch, E. 1925. *Inscriptions of Aśoka.* New edition. Oxford: Clarendon Press.

Humboldt, W. v. 1826a. 'Über die unter dem Namen Bhagavad-Gītā bekannte Episode des Maha-Bharata', *Abhandlungen der historisch-philologischen Klasse der Königlichen Akademie der Wissenschaften zu Berlin. Aus dem Jahre 1825*: 1–64. Berlin: Akademie der Wissenschaften.

1826b. 'Ueber die Bhagavad-Gītā. Mit Bezug auf die Beurteilung der Schlegelschen Ausgabe im Pariser Asiatischen Journal. Aus einem Briefe des Herrn Staatsminister von Humboldt. Nebst einer Vorerinnerung des Herausgebers', *Indische Bibliothek* 2: 218–258; 3: 338–372.

Huntington, J. C. 1989. 'Mathurā Evidence for the Early Teachings of Mahāyāna', in Srinivasan 1989a: 85–92.

Ingalls, D. H. H. 1959. 'Ātmanātmānam', in C. Vogel, ed., *Jñānamuktāvalī: Commemoration Volume in Honour of Johannes Nobel, on the Occasion of His 70th Birthday Offered by Pupils and Colleagues*: 101–110. New Delhi: International Academy of Indian Culture.

Irwin, J. 1975–76. 'The Heliodorus Pillar at Besnagar', *Puratattva* 8: 166–176.

Jacobi, H. 1918. 'Über die Einfügung der Bhagavadgītā im Mahābhārata', *ZDMG* 72: 323–327.

1921. 'Die Bhagavadgītā', *DLZ* 42: 715–724.

1922. 'Weiteres zum Bhagavadgītā-Problem', *DLZ* 43: 265–273.

Jaiswal, S. 1967. *The Origin and Development of Vaiṣṇavism*, Delhi: Munsihram Manoharlal.

Ježic, M. 1979a. 'The First Yoga Layer in the Bhagavadgītā', in J. P. Sinha, ed., *Ludwik Sternbach Felicitation Volume*: II: 545–557. Lucknow: Akhila Bharatiya Parishad.

1979b. 'Textual Layers of the Bhagavadgītā as Traces of Indian Cultural History', in W. Morgenroth, ed., *Sanskrit and World Culture*: 628–638. Weimar: Akademie Verlag.

Johnston, E. H. 1930. 'Some Sāṃkhya and Yoga Conceptions of the Śvetāśvatara Upaniṣad', *JRAS*: 855–878.

1937. *Early Sāṃkhya*. London: Royal Asiatic Society.

Kalyanov, V. I. 1979. 'On Kṛṣṇa's Diplomatics in the Mahābhārata', *IT* 7: 299–308.

Kapoor, J. C. 1983. *Bhagavad-gītā: An International Bibliography of 1785–1979 Imprints*. New York: Garland.

Karmarkar, A. P. 1950. 'Brahma-Nirvāṇa in the Bhagavadgītā', *ABORI* 31: 305–306.

Karmarkar, R. D. 1950. 'Bhagavadgītā XVI. 8 Asatyampratiṣṭhaṃ Te', *ABORI* 31: 132–137.

Katz, R. C. 1989. *Arjuna in the Mahābhārata: Where Krishna Is, There Is Victory*. Berkeley: University of California Press.

Keller, C.-A. 1971. 'Violence et dharma, chez Asoka et dans la Bhagavadgita', *AS* 25: 175–201.

Khair, G. S. 1969. *Quest for the Original Gītā*. Bombay: Somaiya.

Kibe, M. V. 1941. 'Two Conundrums in the *Bhagavadgītā* explained', *ABORI* 22: 79–84.

Kirste, J. 1900. 'Zur Mahābhāratafrage', *Wiener Zeitschrift für die Kunde des Morgenlandes* 14: 214–224.

Köhler, H.-W. 1948. 'Śrad-dha in der vedischen und altbuddhistischen Literatur'. Göttingen: Universität Göttingen (dissertation).

Kosambi, D. D. 1962. 'Social and Economic Aspects of the Bhagavad-Gītā', in D. D. Kosambi, *Myth and Reality. Studies in the Formation of Indian Culture*: 12–41. Bombay: Popular Prakashan.

1978. 'The Historical Development of the Bhagavad-Gītā', in D. Chattopadhyaya, ed., *Studies in the History of Indian philosophy*, 1: 242–266. Calcutta: Bagchi.

Koselleck, R. 1979. *Vergangene Zukunft. Zur Semantik geschichtlicher Zeiten*. Frankfurt: Suhrkamp.

Krishnamurti, S. B. N. 1930. 'The Grammar of the Gītā: A Vindication', *ABORI* 11: 284–299.

Krishnan, Y. 1954. 'Was There Any Conflict between the Brahmanas and the Buddhists?', *IHQ* 30: 167–173.

Kunhan Raja, C. 1946. 'Bhagavadgītā and the Mīmāṃsā', *ALB* 10: 9–22.

Lacombe, O. 1968. 'Jñānam Savijñānam', in *Mélanges d'Indianisme à la memoire de Louis Renou*: 493–443. Paris: Institute de la Civilisation Indienne.

Laine, James W. 1989. *Vision of God. Narratives of Theophany in the Mahābhārata*. Vienna: De Nobili Research Publications.

Lamotte, E. 1929. *Notes sur la Bhagavadgītā*. Paris: Les Belles Lettres.

1958. *Histoire du Bouddhisme Indien des origines à l'ère śaka*. Louvain: Publications de L'Institute Orientaliste.

Langlois, A. 1824–25. 'Bhagavad-Gītā, id est thespesion melos, etc. traduit par M. A. G. de Schlegel. Critique Littéraire', *JA* 4: 105–116, 236–252; 5: 240–252.

Larson, G. J. 1979. *Classical Sāṃkhya. An Interpretation of Its History and Meaning*. Delhi: Motilal Banarsidass.

1981. 'The Song Celestial: Two Centuries of the Bhagavad Gītā in English', *PEW* 31: 513–541.

Latacz, J. 1979. *Homer: Tradition und Neuerung*. Darmstadt: Wissenschaftliche Buchgesellschaft.

Law, N. N. 1933. 'The Political Significance of the Madhyama and the Udāsīna', *IHQ* 9: 770–783.

Leitzmann, A., ed. 1908. *Briefwechsel zwischen Wilhelm von Humboldt und August Wilhelm Schlegel*. Halle: Niemeyer.

Lévi, S. 1917. 'Tato Jayam Udīrayet', in *R. G. Bhandarkar Commemoration Volume*: 99–106. Delhi: Bharatiya.

Lohuizen-de Leeuw, J. E. van. 1972. 'Gandhāra and Mathura [*sic*]: Their Cultural Relationship', in P. Pal, ed., *Aspects of Indian Art*: 27–43. Leiden: Brill.

Lüders, H. 1938–39. 'Seven Brahmi Inscriptions from Mathura and Its Vicinity', *EI* 24: 194–210.

1961. *Mathurā Inscriptions. Unpublished Papers Edited by Klaus Janert*. Göttingen: Abhandlungen der Akademie der Wissenschaften in Göttingen. Philologisch-Historische Klasse. Dritte Folge, Nr. 47.

Macdonald, G. 1955. 'The Hellenic Kingdoms of Syria, Bactria and Parthia', in Rapson 1955: 384–419.

Mahābhāṣya, 1880–85. *The Vyākarana-Mahābhāshya of Patanjali*, ed. F. Kielhorn, I–III. Nachdruck der Ausgabe von 1880–1885: Osnabrück, 1970.

Mahābhārata, 1933–59. *The Mahābhārata for the First Time Critically Edited*, I–XVIII. Poona: Bhandarkar Oriental Institute.

Mainkar, T. G. 1965. 'The Early Antecedents of the Vibhūti-yoga in the Bhagavadgītā ch. x', in S. N. Gajendragadkar, ed., *H. D. Velankar Commemoration Volume*: 72–75. Bombay: Velankar Committee.

1978. 'Some Thoughts on the Brahmasūtras and the Bhagavadgītā', *ABORI* 58–59: 745–755.

Malamoud, Ch. 1968. 'Un dieu védique: le Courroux: "manyuḥ svayaṃbhūḥ"', in *Mélanges d'indianisme à la mémoire de Louis Renou*: 493–507. Paris: Institute de la Civilisations Indienne.

1972. 'Observations sur la notion de "reste" dans le brahmanisme', *WZKS* 17: 6–26.

Malinar, A. 1996. *Rājavidyā. Das königliche Wissen um Herrschaft und Verzicht. Studien zur Bhagavadgītā*. Wiesbaden: Harrassowitz.

1997. 'Nārāyaṇa und Kṛṣṇa. Aspekte der Gotteslehre des Nārāyaṇīya im Vergleich zur Bhagavadgītā', in Schreiner 1997: 241–295.

2003. '"Kṣatriya-Glaube" und "Opferwesen": Richard Garbe und die Indischen Religionen', in Brückner et al. 2003: 121–141.

2005a. 'Blindheit und Sehen in der Erzählung des Mahābhārata', in A. Luther, ed., *Odyssee-Rezeptionen*: 98–111. Frankfurt: Verlag Antike.

2005b. 'How Purāṇas Relate to the Mahābhārata: The Case of King Parikṣit', in P. Koskikallio, ed., *Epics, Khilas, and Purāṇas. Proceedings of the Third Dubrovnik International Conference on Sanskrit Epics and Purāṇas, September 2002*: 465–494. Zagreb: Croatian Academy of Science.

2007. 'Arguments of a Queen: Draupadī's Views on Kingship', in S. Brodbeck and B. Black, eds., *Gender and Narrative in the Mahābhārata*: 203–231. London: Routledge.

forthcoming. 'Duryodhana's Truths. Kingship and Divinity in *Mahābhārata* 5.50', in J. L. Brockington and P. Dundas, eds., *Proceedings of the 13th World Sanskrit Conference, Edinburgh 2005*. Delhi: Motilal Banarsidass.

Mangels, A. 1994. *Zur Erzähltechnik im Mahābhārata*. Hamburg: Kovac.

Manusmṛti 1983. *Manusmṛti with the Sanskrit Commentary Manvartha-Muktāvalī of Kullūka Bhaṭṭa*, ed. J. L. Shastri. Delhi: Motilal Banarsidass.

Marcovich, M. 1958. *Bhagavadgītā. El canto del señor. Versión del sanscrito con una interpretación racional.* Mérida: Universidad de los Andes.

Matsubara, M. 1994. *Pāñcarātra Saṃhitās and Early Vaiṣṇava Theology*. Delhi: Motilal Banarsidass.

Mazumdar, B. C. 1910. 'Vāsudeva of Pāṇini', *JRAS*: 171–179.

Minkowski, C. Z. 1989. 'Janemejaya's Sattra and Ritual Structure', *JAOS* 109: 401–420.

Mitchiner, J. E. 1982. *Tradition of the Seven Ṛṣis*. Delhi: Motilal Banarsidass.

Minor, R. N. 1980. 'The Gītā's Way as the Only Way', *PEW* 30: 339–354.

1982. *Bhagavad-Gītā: An Exegetical Commentary*. Delhi: Heritage.

1983. 'The Quest for the Gītākāra: Multiple Authorship Revisited', *ABORI* 63: 29–42.

1987. 'Religious Experience in Bhagavadgītā Eleven and the Text's Interpretation', in A. Sharma 1987: 138–150.

ed. 1988. *Modern Interpreters of the Bhagavadgītā*. Albany: SUNY.

Modi, P. M. 1932. *Akṣara: A Forgotten Chapter in the History of Indian Philosophy*. Baroda: State Press.

1933. 'The Doctrine of the Bhagavadgītā: A Triad of the Three Dyads', *PTAIOC* 7: 377–390.

1957. 'Relation between the Bhagavadgītā and the Brahmasūtrakāra', *PTAIOC* 9: 136–139.

Narain, A. K. 1957. *The Indo-Greeks*. Oxford: Clarendon.

1973. 'Two Hindu Divinities on the Coins of Agathocles from Ai-Kharum', *Journal of the Numismatic Society of India* 35: 73–77.

Nietzsche, F. 1980. *Friedrich Nietzsche. Werke in sechs Bänden*, ed. Karl Schlechta. Munich: Piper.

Nilakantam, R. 1964. 'Prakṛti and Puruṣa in the Bhagavadgītā', *IA* 3rd series 1: 254–264.

Oberhammer, G. 1977. *Strukturen yogischer Meditation*. Vienna: Österreichische Akademie der Wissenschaften.

1983. 'Der Inklusivismus-Begriff P. Hackers. Versuch eines Nachwortes', in G. Oberhammer, ed., *Inklusivismus. Eine indische Denkform*: 93–113. Vienna: Verlag der Österreichischen Akademie der Wissenschaften.

Oberlies, T. 1988. 'Die Śvetāśvatara-Upaniṣad: Eine Studie ihrer Gotteslehre', *WZKS* 23: 35–62.

Oldenberg, H. 1909. 'Vedische Untersuchungen', *ZDMG* 63: 287–302.

1917. *Die Religion des Veda*. Stuttgart: Cotta.
1920. 'Bemerkungen zur Bhagavadgita', *NAWG*, Philologisch-historische Klasse: 321–338.
Oguibene, B. 1984. 'Sur le terme Yoga, le verbe yuj- et quelques-uns de leurs dérivés dans les hymnes védiques', *IIJ* 27: 85–101.
Olivelle, P. 1964. 'The Conception of God in the Bhagavadgītā', *IPhQ* 4: 514–540
1998. *The Early Upaniṣads: Annotated Text and Translation*. New York: Oxford University Press.
2004. *The Law Code of Manu. A New Translation*. Oxford: Oxford University Press.
ed. 2006. *Between the Empires. Society in India 300 BCE to 400 CE*. Oxford: Oxford University Press.
Otto, R. 1934. *Die Urgestalt der Bhagavad-Gītā*. Tübingen: Mohr.
1935a. *Lehrtraktate der Bhagavad-Gītā*. Tübingen: Mohr.
1935b. *Der Sang des Hehr-Erhabenen. Die Bhagavad-Gītā übertragen und erläutert*. Stuttgart: Kohlhammer.
Pal, P. 2005. 'The Sāṃkhya Sage Kapila and Kashmiri Viṣṇu Images', in K. A. Jacobsen, ed., *Theory and Practice of Yoga*: 293–302. Leiden: Brill.
Pargiter, F. E. 1913. *The Purāṇa Text of the Dynasties of the Kali Age*. Oxford: Clarendon Press.
Pensa, C. 1969. 'On the Purification Concept in Indian Tradition, with Special Regard to Yoga', *EW* 19: 194–228.
Pisani, V. 1939. 'The Rise of the Mahābhārata', in S. M. Katre, ed., *A Volume of Eastern and Indian Studies Presented to Professor F. W. Thomas*: 166–176. Bombay: Karnatak Publishing.
Pollock, S. 1984. 'The Divine King of the Indian Epic', *JAOS* 104: 505–528.
Prasad, H. K. 1954. 'Puṣyamitra Śuṅga and the Buddhists', *JBRS* 40: 29–38.
Preciado-Solis, B. 1984. *The Kṛṣṇa Cycle in the Purāṇas*. Delhi: Motilal Banarsidass.
Proferes, T. 2007. *Vedic Ideals of Sovereignty and the Poetics of Power*. Cambridge, MA: American Oriental Society.
Quigley, D. ed. 2005. *The Character of Kingship*. Oxford: Berg.
Radhakrishnan, S. 1948. *The Bhagavadgītā with an Introductory Essay, Sanskrit Text, English Translations and Notes*. London: Allen and Unwin.
Raghavan, V. 1962. 'Rajavidya: Manu and the Bhagavadgita', in *Essays in Philosophy Presented to Dr. T. M. P. Mahadevan on His Fiftieth Birthday*: 340–346. Madras: Ganesh & Co.
Rajwade, V. J. 1917. 'The Bhagavadgītā from Grammatical and Literary Points of View', in *R. G. Bhandarkar Commemoration Volume*: 325–338. Delhi: Bharatiya.
Rapson, E. J. ed. 1955. *Ancient India*. Cambridge: Cambridge University Press.
Raychaudhuri, H. 1920. *Materials for the Study of the Early History of the Vaishnava Sect*. Calcutta: Bhattacharya.
1922. 'The Mahābhārata and the Besnagar Inscription of Heliodorus', *Journal and Proceedings of the Asiatic Society of Bengal, NS* 18: 269–271.

1952. 'India in the Age of the Nandas', in K. N. Nilakanta Sāstri, ed., *The Age of the Nandas and Mauryas*: 9–45. Delhi: Motilal Banarsidass.

Reynolds, F. 1972. 'The Two Wheels of Dharma: A Study of Early Buddhism', in F. Reynolds, ed., *The Two Wheels of Dharma: Essays on Theravāda Tradition in India and Ceylon*: 6–30. Cambersbur: American Academy of Religion.

Ṛgveda 1994. *Rig Veda. A Metrically Restored Text with an Introduction and Notes*, ed. B. van Nooten and G. Holland. Cambridge, MA: Harvard University Press.

Robinson, C. A. 2005. *Interpretations of the Bhagavad-Gītā and Images of Hindu Tradition*. London: Routledge.

Rocher, L. 1963. 'Bhagavadgītā 2.20 and Kaṭhopaniṣad 2.18: A New Interpretation', *ALB* 27: 45–58.

1977. 'The Meaning of Purāṇá in the Rgveda', *WZKS* 21: 5–24.

Roy, S. C. 1941. *The Bhagavadgītā and Modern Scholarship*. London: Luzac.

Ruben, W. 1951. 'Die Lehre vom Handeln in der Bhagavadgītā', in *Beiträge zur indischen Philologie und Altertumskunde. Walter Schubring zum 70. Geburtstag dargebracht von der deutschen Indologie*: 170–179. Hamburg: de Gruyter.

Sahoo, P. C. 1988–89. 'Priestly Abhicāra in the Śrauta Ritual', *JOI* 38: 7–15.

Saṃyutta-Nikāya 1960. *Saṃyutta Nikāya of the Sutta Piṭaka*, ed. L. Feer. London: Pali Text Society.

Śatapatha-Brāhmaṇa 1882–1900. *The Śatapatha-Brāhmaṇa Mādhyandina School*, trans. J. Eggeling. Oxford: Clarendon Press.

Scharfe, H. 1989. *The State in the Indian Tradition*. Leiden: Brill.

Scheftelowitz, J. 1929. *Die Zeit als Schicksalsgottheit in der indischen und iranischen Religion Kala und Zruvan*. Stuttgart: Kohlhammer.

Scheller, M. 1950. *Vedisch priyà und die Wortsippe frei, freien, Freund*. Göttingen: Vandenhoek & Ruprecht.

Scheuer, J. 1982. *Śiva dans le Mahābhārata*. Paris: Presses Universitaires de France.

Schlegel, A. W. 1826a. *Bhagavadgītā id est thespesion melos sive almi crishnae et arjunae colloquium de rebus divinis. Textum recensuit, adnotationes criticas et interpretationen latinam. Editio altera auctior et emendatior cura Christiani Lasseni*. Bonnae.

1826b. 'Observations sur la critique du Bhagavad Gītā insérée dans le *Journal Asiatique* 1', *JA* 9: 3–27.

Schlingloff, D. 1969. 'The Oldest Extant Parvan-List of the *Mahābhārata*', *JAOS* 89: 334–338.

Schneider, U. 1982. 'Kṛṣṇas postumer Aufstieg: zur Frühgeschichte der Bhakti-Bewegung', *Saeculum* 33: 38–49.

Schopen, G. 1997. 'Archaeology and Protestant Presuppositions in the Study of Indian Buddhism', in G. Schopen, *Bones, Stones and Buddhist Monks: Collected Papers on the Archaeology, Epigraphy, and Texts of Monastic Buddhism in India*: 1–22. Honolulu: University of Hawai Press.

2005. 'The Mahāyāna and the Middle Period in Indian Buddhism. Through a Chinese Looking-Glass', in G. Schopen, *Figments and Fragments of Mahāyāna Buddhism in India*: 3–24. Honolulu: University of Hawai Press.

Schrader, F. O. 1902. *Über den Stand der indischen Philosophie zur Zeit Mahāvīras und Buddhas*. Leipzig: Harrassowitz.

1910. 'Über BhG II.46', *ZDMG* 64: 336–340.

1929a. 'The Sacrificial Wheel Taught in the Bhagavadgītā', *IHQ* 5: 173–181.

1929b. 'Concerning Bhagavadgītā III, 15', *IHQ* 5: 790–791.

1930. *The Kashmir Recension of the Bhagavadgītā*. Stuttgart: Kohlhammer.

1936. *Sammelbesprechung R. Otto, OLZ* 39: 107–111.

1955. 'Sāṃkhya, Original and Classical', *ALB* 19: 1–2.

Schreiner, P. 1988. 'Yoga: Lebenshilfe oder Sterbetechnik?', *Umwelt und Gesundheit* 3–4: 12–18.

1991. *Bhagavad-Gita. Wege und Weisungen übersetzt und eingeleitet von Peter Schreiner*. Zürich: Benzing.

ed. 1997. *Studien zum Nārāyaṇīya. Studies in the Nārāyaṇīya*. Wiesbaden: Harrassowitz.

1999. 'What Comes First in the Mahābhārata: Sāṃkhya or Yoga?', *AS* 53: 755–777.

Schubring, W. 1935. *Die Lehre der Jainas. Nach den alten Quellen dargestellt*. Berlin: de Gruyter.

Scott, D. A. 1990. 'The Iranian Face of Buddhism', *EW* 40: 43–77.

Sharma, A. 1978. 'The Role of the Anugītā in the Understanding of the Bhagavadgītā', *RS* 14: 261–267.

1980. 'Are Saṃnyāsa and Tyāga Synonyms in the Bhagavadgītā?', *ZDMG* 130: 62–69.

ed. 1986. *The Hindu Gītā: Ancient and Classical Interpretations of the Bhagavadgītā*. London: Duckworth.

ed. 1987. *New Essays in the Bhagavadgītā. Philosophical, Methodological and Cultural Approaches*. New Delhi: Books & Books.

Sharma, R. C. 1989. 'New Inscriptions from Mathurā', in Srinivasan 1989a: 308–315.

Sharpe, E. J. 1985. *The Universal Gītā. Western Images of the Bhagavadgītā. A Bicentenary Survey*. London: Duckworth.

Shastri, M. D. 1933. 'History of the Word "Īśvara" and Its Idea', *PTAIOC* 7: 487–503.

Shrikantha Shastri, S. 1955. 'The Dharma of Ashoka and the Gita', *Karnataka Darshana*: 327–335.

Simson, G. von 1968–69. 'Die Einschaltung der Bhagavadgītā im Bhīṣmaparvan des Mahābhārata', *IIJ* 11: 59–74.

1974. *Altindische epische Schlachtbeschreibung. Untersuchungen zur Kompositionstechnik und Entstehungsgeschichte der Bücher 6–9 des Mahābhārata*. Göttingen Unveröffentlichte Habilitationsschrift.

1984. 'The Mythic Background of the Mahābhārata', *IT* 12: 191–223.

Sircar, D. C. 1965. *Select Inscriptions Bearing on Indian History and Civilization from the Sixth Century BC to the Sixth Century AD*. Calcutta: University of Calcutta.

Slaje, W. 1999. 'Rājavidyā', *Studien zur Indologie und Iranistik* 22: 131–166.

Smet, Richard de 1977. 'A Copernican Reversal: The Gītākāra's Reformulation of Karma', *PEW* 27: 53–63.

Smith, B. K. 1996. 'Ritual Perfection and Ritual Sabotage in the Veda', *HR* 35: 285–306.

Smith, M. R. 1968. 'Statistics of the Bhagavadgītā', *JGJRI* 24: 39–46.

Srinivasan, D. 1981. 'Early Kṛṣṇa Icons: The Case at Mathurā', in J. Williams, ed., *Kalā-Darśana*: 127–136. New Delhi: American Institute of Indian Studies.

ed. 1989a. *Mathurā: The Cultural Heritage*. New Delhi: American Institute of Indian Studies.

1989b. 'Vaiṣṇava Art and Iconography at Mathurā', in Srinivasan 1989a: 383–392.

1997. *Many Heads, Arms and Eyes. Origin, Meaning and Form of Multiplicity in Indian Art*. Leiden: Brill.

Steinmann, R. M. 1989. 'La notion du dharma selon Manu et dans la Bhagavadgītā', *AS* 43, 2: 164–183.

Stenzler, A. F. 1849. *Yājñavalkyadharmasūtram. Yājñavalkya's Gesetzbuch. Sanskrit und Deutsch*. Berlin: Dümmler.

von Stietencron, H. 1998. 'The Non-Existence of Impurity and the Legitimation of Kings', in S. Lienhard and I. Piovano, eds., *Lex et Litterae. Studies in Honour of Oscar Botto*: 487–508. Turin: Edizioni dell' Orso.

2005. *Hindu Myth, Hindu History. Religion, Art, and Politics*. Delhi: Permanent Black.

von Stietencron, H., K.-P. Gietz, A. Malinar, et al., eds. 1992. *Epic and Purāṇic Bibliography up to 1985 Annotated and with Indexes*, 2 vols. Wiesbaden: Harrassowitz.

Strauss, O. 1911. 'Ethische Probleme aus dem Mahābhārata', *GSAI* 24: 193–335.

1934. 'Rezension von "Hauer, J. W.: *Eine indo-arische Metaphysik des Kampfes und der Tat. Die Bhagavadgītā in neuer Sicht*"', *DLZ* 45: 2413–214.

1936. 'Zur Interpretation der Bhagavadgītā', *Nieuw Theologisch Tijdschrift* 25: 247–262.

Subrahmanyam, K. C. 1926. 'A Note on the Evidence of Pāṇini on Vāsudeva Worship', *IHQ* 2: 186–188, 864–865.

Sukthankar, V. S. 1936. 'The Bhṛgus and the Bhārata: A Text-Historical Study', *ABORI* 18: 1–76.

Sullivan, Bruce M. 1990. *Kṛṣṇa Dvaipāyana Vyāsa and the Mahābhārata. A New Interpretation*. Leiden: Brill.

Szczurek, P. 2005. 'Bhakti Interpolations and Additions in the Bhagavadgītā', in P. Koskikallio, ed., *Epics, Khilas, and Purāṇas. Proceedings of the Third Dubrovnik International Conference on Sanskrit Epics and Purāṇas, September 2002*: 183–220. Zagreb: Croatian Academy of Science.

Tadpatrikar, S. N. 1929. 'The Kṛṣṇa Problem', *ABORI* 10: 269–344.

Taittirīya-Brāhmaṇa 1859–1862. *The Taittirīya Brāhmaṇa of the Black Yajur Veda with the Commentary of Sayanacharya*, ed. Rājendralāla Mitra, I and II. Calcutta: Asiatic Society.

Tarn, W. W. 1951. *The Greeks in Bactria and India*. Cambridge: Cambridge University Press.

Telang, K. T. 1882. *The Bhagavadgītā, with the Sanatsujatīya and the Anugītā.* Oxford: Clarendon Press.

Thakur, V. K. 1982. 'Social Roots of the Bhagavad-Gītā', *IT* 10: 289–300.

Thapar, R. 1961. *Aśoka and the Decline of the Mauryas.* Oxford: Oxford University Press.

1977–78. 'Some Aspects of the Economic Data in the Mahābhārata', *ABORI* 58–59: 993–1007.

1979. 'The Historian and the Epic', *ABORI* 60: 199–213.

1989. 'The Early History of Mathurā. Up to and Including the Maurya Period', in Srinivasan 1989a: 12–18.

Thieme, P. 1952. 'Brahman', *ZDMG* 102, NF 27: 91–129.

Thompson, G. 1997. 'Ahamkāra and Ātmastuti. Self-Assertion and Impersonation in the Ṛgveda', *HR* 37: 141–171.

Tschannerl, V. 1992. *Das Lachen in der altindischen Literatur.* Frankfurt: Lang.

Tripathi, G. Ch. 1968. *Der Ursprung und die Entwicklung der Vāmana-Legende in der indischen Literatur.* Wiesbaden: Harrassowitz.

Upadhyaya, K. N. 1968. 'The Impact of Early Buddhism on Hindu Thought with Special Reference to the Bhagavadgītā', *PEW* 18: 163–173.

1971. *Early Buddhism and the Bhagavadgītā.* Delhi: Motilal Banarsidass.

Vassilkov, Y. 1999. 'Kālāvāda (the Doctrine of Cyclical Time) in the Mahābhārata and the Concept of Heroic Didactics', in *Proceedings of the First Dubrovnik International Conference on the Sanskrit Epics and Puranas*: 17–33. Zagreb: Croatian Academy of Science.

Venis, A. 1910. 'A Note on the Two Besnagar Inscriptions', *JRAS*: 813–815.

Venkataramayya, M. 1959–60. 'An Inscribed Vaishnava Image of 2nd cent. BC from Malhar, Bilaspur Distric, M. P.', *JORM* 29: 35–40.

Verardi, G. 1983. 'The Kuṣāṇa Emperors as Cakravartins. Dynastic Art and Cults in India and Central Asia. History of a Theory, Clarifications and Refutations', *EW* 33: 225–294.

1985. 'Avatāraṇa: A Note on the Boddhisattva Image Dated in the Third Year of Kaniṣka in the Sārnātha Museum', *EW* 35: 67–101.

Vetter, T. 1988. *The Ideas and Meditative Practices of Early Buddhism.* Leiden: Brill.

Viennot, O. 1954. *Culte de l'arbre dans l'Inde ancienne: textes et monuments brahmaniques et bouddhiques.* Paris: Presses Universitaires de France.

Viṣṇusmṛti 1881. *Viṣṇusmṛti. The Institutes of Viṣṇu Together with Extracts from the Sanskrit Commentary of Nanda Paṇḍita Called Vaijayanti*, ed. with critical notes, an *anukramaṇika*, and indexes of words and mantras by Julius Jolly. Calcutta: Asiatc Society.

Warder, A. K. 1970. *Indian Buddhism.* Delhi: Motilal Banarsidass.

Weber-Brosamer, W. 1988. *Annam. Untersuchungen zur Bedeutung des Essens und der Speise im vedischen Ritual.* Rheinfelden: Schäuble.

Weller, F. 1953. *Versuch einer Kritik der Kaṭhopaniṣad.* Berlin: Deutsche Akademie der Wissenschaften zu Berlin.

Wezler, A. 1978. *Die wahren "Speiserestesser" Skt. vighāśin.* Wiesbaden: Harrassowitz.

2000. 'Sampad of *Bhagavadgītā* XVI Reconsidered', in R. Tsuchida and A. Wezler, eds., *Harānandalaharī. Volume in Honour of Prof. M. Hara on His Seventieth Birthday*: 433–455. Reinbek: Wezler.

Whillier, W. K. 1987. 'Vision and Authority', in Sharma 1987: pp. 151–160.

White, D. 1979. 'Proto-Sāṃkhya and Advaita Vedānta in the Bhagavadgītā', *PEW* 29: 501–507.

Wilden, E. 2000. *Der Kreislauf der Opfergaben im Veda*. Stuttgart: Steiner.

Willis, M. 2004. 'Archaeology and the Politics of Time', in H. T. Bakker, ed., *The Vākaṭaka Heritage. Indian Culture at the Crossroads*: 33–58. Groningen: Forsten.

Willson, A. L. 1964. *A Mythical Image: The Ideal of India in German Romanticism*. Durham, NC: Duke University Press.

Wilkins, Ch. 1785. *The Bhāgavat-Geetā, or Dialogues of Kreeshna and Arjoon in Eighteen Lectures with Notes*. London.

Winternitz, M. 1907. 'Rezension von P. Deussen, "Vier philosophische Texte des *Mahābhārata*"', *WZKM* 21: 194–202.

1909. *Geschichte der indischen Literatur*, 1. Leipzig: Brockhaus.

Yardi, M. R. 1978. 'Theories of Multiple Authorship of the Bhagavadgītā', *ABORI* 58–59: 1049–1054.

1987. 'Sāṃkhya and Yoga in the Mokṣadharma and the Bhagavadgītā', *ABORI* 68: 309–319.

Zaehner, R. C. 1969. *The Bhagavad-Gītā with a Commentary Based on the Original Sources*. Oxford: Oxford University Press.

Index

CPSIA information can be obtained
at www.ICGtesting.com
Printed in the USA
LVHW030113051221
705326LV00001B/52

9 780521 122115